SWORD AND SWASTIKA

Telford Taylor was born in Schenectady, New York, and studied at Williams College and the Harvard Law School. He has served the federal government and the United States Army in several high-ranking positions, and from 1946 to 1949 was Chief of Counsel for War Crimes at Nuremberg. His other books include *Grand Inquest, The March of Conquest,* and *The Breaking Wave.* Mr. Taylor is now Professor of Law at Columbia University.

SWORD AND SWASTIKA

Generals and Nazis in the Third Reich

by

TELFORD TAYLOR

QUADRANGLE PAPERBACKS

Quadrangle Books / *Chicago*

TO MARY

PREFACE

THE ALLIANCE of the German military leaders with those of Nazi totalitarianism sealed the fate of Germany, cast the die for war, and turned the course of history. It was the direct cause of the desolation and devitalization of Europe, and a major determinant of the international crisis we face today. And thus, although this is a narrative of events that occurred twelve or more years ago, we are scanning here a past which is part and parcel of the present.

This is the story of the combination and clash of old and new forces in Germany at a recent and critical juncture in history. Old and honoured were the German officer class and the hard military tradition that it embodied. New and irreverent was the revolutionary surge of lethal energy that swept Germany in the early thirties, carrying Hitler and the Nazis to power.

The combination of these forces was the corner-stone of the Third Reich and of its resurgent might. The clash between them was the struggle for supreme power in Germany, and for control of the glittering military machine. The interplay of these two drives—collaboration and conflict—was the warp and woof of the Third Reich's pre-war years, and is the major theme of this book.

The protagonists in this apocalyptic drama were strangely matched, the one archaic and the other atavistic. On one side, the stark, tight-lipped galaxy of professional warriors, most of whom would have been more at home in the entourage of the nineteenth-century German emperors. Von Bock, von Rundstedt, von Kleist, von Reichenau—the names throb in our ears like the beats of a heavy war-drum. On the other side, an incredible aggregation of demagogues, adventurers, misfits and thugs; a veritable witches' brew of genius and villainy. Hitler, Goering, Himmler and Goebbels—we have no trouble recalling their features years after their deaths. Whatever their faults, they were not lacking in individuality.

In this book I have sought to portray this remarkable conjunction of generals and Nazis, and to trace their relationship through its fluid and violent course to tyranny and war. Herein

we will see that Hitler and the officers' corps each found in the other a dangerous but necessary vehicle for the attainment of goals which both shared; that mutual suspicions and irritations were submerged in a common design; that Hitler concealed but never neglected his purpose to bend the military to his will; that the power and traditional prestige of the generals survived Hitler's subjection of all other groups in Germany which might have opposed him; that the officers' corps thus emerged, involuntarily, as the last hope of those who sought to restore liberty and preserve peace; and, finally, that the hope was betrayed, and Germany's nightmare became Europe's fate.

If all this makes a dark tale it is, nevertheless, one of deep and immediate interest to us. The German destiny has had a profound and enduring impact on our own. Its effect far transcends the loss of hundreds of thousands of lives and the diversion of incalculable resources to the uses of war. It is not too much to say that, during this century and until her defeat in 1945, Germany exerted the strongest of all foreign influences on the scope and direction of our national development.

There is no need to unravel the ultimate causes of the two world wars and debate the relative responsibility of individual sovereigns, dictators, and diplomats. It has been the volcanic energy and formidable talents of the German nation that have twice enabled her to wage war against great coalitions almost single-handed, and to approach the establishment of a Teutonic *imperium*. These eruptions have accomplished the enfeeblement of Britain and France, and, by counter-reaction, have enormously stimulated the economic and military growth of the United States and Russia and thus precipitated the current dual polarization of *Weltpolitik*. One need only try to envisage the probable balance of power in the world today had these wars not occurred. Alike in Germany herself, rising Phœnix-like from the ashes of defeat, and in the epochal transformations of America and Russia, one may find striking modern illustration of Toynbee's historical theorem of "challenge and response".

Is the German volcano dead or even dormant? In 1945, like many others, I freely accepted the notion that, for better or worse, German dominance of Europe was a thing of the past. There were devastation and apathy from the Rhine to the Oder. The Russian influx was torrential.

Today there is ample warrant for second thoughts. Perhaps the terrible blows rained on the Ruhr have not splintered, but rather tempered, the steel. Will the German steel flash

again and, if so, where and in what array? Of only one thing am I certain—that no question should be more anxiously weighed by the men who are striving to ride the whirlwind of these times, whether in Washington, Moscow, Rocquencourt, or even Berlin and Bonn.

But the story of the Third Reich points domestic as well as international problems. How did a nation such as Germany, with a history rich in the cultural achievements of the individual man, succumb to the Nazi wave of despotism and murderous superstition? We cannot here search for first causes, but surely it will be written that liberty and decency in Germany were the victims of a collapse of leadership. Jurists, doctors, professors, civil officials, business magnates, and—in Germany most honoured of all—generals, alike proved insensitive to or flinched before the warning signals of approaching tyranny and crime, and sold themselves, their callings, and their country into slavery.

The result was black tragedy not only for Germany but for much of the world. Its full harvest of hate and suffering will not be reaped for many years. The mind reels before the consequences of a comparable crumbling of human standards in any of the major democracies today. How can the leaders within the free nations guard against another such catastrophe?

To such problems this book, of course, gives no answers. But perhaps it will serve as one of many lenses through which to examine and ponder what is written in the shifting sands we walk upon.

TELFORD TAYLOR

CONTENTS

CHAPTER I

THE GERMAN OFFICERS' CORPS

TWICE DURING the first half of this century our country has found itself locked in mortal combat with Germany. On each occasion the German legions have been led in battle by an extraordinary and exotic warrior caste. Archaic in manner and social outlook alike, and nurtured in a land rather deficient than abundant in natural resources, these few thousand men have nevertheless been able to exert a crushing pressure on the course of world events for well over a century. It has been an altogether astounding performance which, all too literally, has brought down the house.

Not the least remarkable quality of this caste is its homogeneity. The uniformity of the impact of tradition and training on its members is unparalleled in modern Europe, and inconceivable to an American. And so, while this book is not a history of German militarism, the events with which it deals could not possibly be understood without some grasp of the origins and spirit—the *Geist*, as Germans would call it—of the German officers' corps.

Historically speaking, the corps may be said to have passed through three principal phases. Originally recruited from the eighteenth-century Junker nobility of Prussia, the corps took shape and rose to fame under Frederick the Great. Discredited by abysmal defeat at the hands of Napoleon, the corps was rehabilitated early in the nineteenth century by a remarkable group of leaders known to history as the "Reformers" (Scharnhorst, Gneisenau, Clausewitz, and others), and won back its prestige with the ultimate downfall of Napoleon, in which the Prussian armies under von Bluecher played a vital part. After another period of stagnation, the corps rose to the zenith of its glory during the second half of the nineteenth century under the leadership of the renowned von Moltke and von Schlieffen. Victorious in three wars against Denmark, Austria and France during less than a decade, the military leaders shared with Bismarck the popular acclaim for bringing the German Empire into existence and raising it to the status of a major world

power. The dominating stature of the officers' corps in Germany after the Franco-Prussian War carried it through the ensuing seventy years and enabled it to survive defeat in the First World War. Even the utter disaster of 1945 has not entirely destroyed the prestige of the corps, and it would be reckless indeed to assume lightly that it has no future.

"FRIDERICUS REX"

The military power of eighteenth-century Prussia, like that of other countries at the time, was embodied in a small, professional standing army. Forces of this type developed all over Europe during the seventeenth century, as the era of knighthood came to an end with the collapse of feudalism. They were, for the most part, commanded by the sovereigns themselves—Gustavus Adolphus, Peter the Great and others—by great nobles such as Prince Eugene and the Duke of Marlborough, or by entrepreneur generals like Wallenstein, who recruited and supplied his own forces and, in effect, contracted to furnish military power to such princes as might require it.

The personnel of these armies was mercenary and polyglot. The military profession was not highly regarded in those times, and the ordinary peasant or burgher felt no sense of duty to rally to his sovereign's standard. Nor was he expected to. Much better that he should plough his fields, ply his trade, market his wares and pay his taxes. War was a business for professionals, and soldiers fought, not for glory or for love of country, but for pay.

Eighteenth-century soldiery was a motley collection of adventurers and outcasts. Little initiative or intelligence was required, as the men not only marched but fought in formation. Military *esprit* was as yet unknown, and armies were held together only by money and a most savage and brutal discipline. It was a common saying in the Prussian Army that the men should fear the enemy less than their own officers.

Officers and men, indeed, came from different worlds. The gulf was so wide and deep that it has lasted through three centuries and survived political and social revolutions. With the decline of feudalism, not only did the revenues of the nobility dwindle but their responsibilities were also much curtailed. Contemptuous of and unfit for commerce, uneducated but skilled in riding and hunting, domineering in manner and bored with life on their impoverished estates, the nobles everywhere slid into the military profession as if by force of gravity.

16

So it was in Europe generally, and so it was above all in Prussia. The forbears of Frederick the Great (the "Great Elector" of Brandenburg and King Frederick William I of Prussia) won the support of the agrarian nobles of Pomerania and Prussia—the so-called Junkers—by raising the social status of the military profession and granting them a virtual monopoly of the officerships. Because of the narrow range of enterprise in eighteenth-century Prussia, the class interests and stereotypes thus formed grew extraordinarily rigid and pervasive. The nobility also took to arms in England, France, Austria and Russia, but these countries offered numerous other outlets for energies and ambitions. Prussia, however, had no colonies, no marine traditions, a primitive agrarian economy, small territory and a backward culture. Short of emigration, the young Prussian noble had little choice other than a military life or a rural one.

To be sure, mercenary and adventurist characteristics marked the officer as well as the soldier. It was quite customary among the European nobility to seek a commission in the army of an alien sovereign, nor was it very unusual in such circumstances for an officer to serve against his own country of origin. Gneisenau was a mercenary officer for the English during the American Revolution and, as late as 1812, both Clausewitz and Yorck von Wartenburg fought with the Russians against Napoleon, with whom the King of Prussia was then allied.

But this military cosmopolitanism died out at the time of the French Revolution, and in 1812 Clausewitz and Yorck were actually seeking to free Prussia from the Napoleonic yoke. So regarded, their action illustrates the growing nationalism and group pride which had developed among the Prussian officers under Frederick the Great. In particular, the feats of Prussian arms during the Seven Years' War (1756–63), when the little kingdom stood off the combined forces of the other European powers, served to develop a real *esprit de corps* among the officers and even, though to a far smaller degree, in the ranks.

Frederick's armies were small, and his command was highly personalized. Even his generals were left but a very narrow range of discretion or initiative, and their names are almost completely forgotten. They had hardly any function other than to receive and try to understand the orders from on high, and drive the troops whither he decreed they should go. Despite their noble origin and pride of caste, Frederick's officers were not much more than foremen. Consequently, they had little

need (and much scorn) for education. "Theirs not to reason why," and no one suggested establishing a war academy.

But if "old Fritz" worried little about the level of learning among his officers, he was adamant in his insistence that they meet the qualifications of their caste. Just as he sought to preserve the Junker landed aristocracy and prevent the rise of a rural bourgeoisie by forbidding the sale of land to peasants or burghers, so he strove to confirm the officers' corps as an exclusive preserve of the nobility. At the time of his death in 1786, all the 100-odd generals and colonels of the Prussian infantry were noblemen (though forty-three were noble foreigners), and there were but three non-nobles among over 200 lieutenant-colonels and majors. Not only was Frederick himself thoroughly caste-ridden, but he also thought the nobles more reliable and self-sacrificing as officers because their occupational alternatives were so limited and the personal consequences of military failure correspondingly disastrous.

Thus the Prussian military caste came into full flower. The eighteenth-century Prussian officer was unenlightened, anti-intellectual even in the military field (and for this reason the artillery and other relatively "technical" branches were always less noble-ridden), scornful of all civilians and especially of the middle classes, and obsessed with a quasi-religious devotion to the concept of military "honour". Already several Prussian noble families were becoming army stud-farms bearing names all too familiar today. Even before the turn of the century there had been fourteen generals von Kleist and ten generals von der Goltz. We will encounter their descendants in due course. Frederick the Great was truly the father of the officers' corps, and it is not for nothing that the traditional Prussian military march is "Fridericus Rex".

THE REFORMERS

Even so indurate an institution as the Prussian Army could not survive unchanged the social and political upheavals at the end of the eighteenth century. The ferment in France deeply influenced military thought well before the Revolution. The Enlightenment gave rise not only to a revulsion against war and militarism but to simultaneous pressure against the nobility's monopoly in the military field. Absolutism had been counting on the support of reactionary royalist standing armies. Liberals now urged that the citizenry be armed as a safeguard against tyranny. The Army, they declared, should belong to the whole

people, and not just to the monarch and his nobles. *Aux armes, citoyens*.

From these ideas sprang the mass national armies of revolutionary France. Since they were so much more numerous than the eighteenth-century professional armies, they had to be organized in larger units. "Divisions" had been developed a few decades earlier by French generals, and in the revolutionary armies several divisions were grouped in a "corps". The "national" Army ceased to be a single mass formation, the corps and divisions were independently manœuvrable, and this opened vast new vistas in military science and greatly increased the scope and responsibility of corps and divisional commanders and of the officers generally. Conscription was introduced to raise the French "people's Army", and even a rudimentary "war economy" took shape.

Unprecedented in size, organization, tactics and *esprit*, the French armies rolled back the professional troops of the allied coalition, and inaugurated a new era of military history. Under Napoleon, the advances in military science proved more enduring than the new liberal and democratic social concepts. The armies of the French Emperor overran most of Europe, and in 1806 Napoleon inflicted a disastrous defeat on the Prussian forces at Jena. Prussia succumbed to the Napoleonic yoke, and was forced by the Treaty of Tilsit to reduce its army to 42,000 men, less than a third of its previous size.

After Jena, the problem confronting the Prussian Army was how to convert from a Frederican to a Napoleonic organization, despite the treaty restrictions. "Old Fritz" was not there to solve the problem; he had been dead for twenty years, and his grand-nephew (Frederick William III) was a military nonentity. For the first time, the officers' corps had to develop leadership from its own ranks. And the first great names in the history of the corps are those of the architects of the new army—von Scharnhorst and von Gneisenau, who headed the group known as the "Reformers".

In 1807 Scharnhorst was made the head of the Militaer-Reorganizations-Kommission, of which Gneisenau and Baron vom Stein, the eminent "reformist" Civil Minister, were also members. Working in close collaboration, these men laid the basis for a far-reaching revision of Prussian military theory and practice. Social revolutionaries they were not; they were conservative noblemen imposing reform from above. The officers were still "officers of the king", but the Army was changed

from a mere royal appurtenance into an embodiment of the whole nation's energies. The treaty limitations on its size were evaded by shortening the period of service; the consequent high rate of turnover produced a large "shadow army" of partially trained men. The upper levels of the officers' corps were purged of traitorous and superannuated members to make room for young blood. Constant pressure for general conscription led to its adoption in 1814, when Prussia was again at war with Napoleon.

Most important for our purposes is the *professional* character which the officers' corps acquired for the first time at the hands of the Reformers. The nobility remained the dominant component, but bourgeois officers were accepted in far greater numbers. Technical branches of the service, such as the artillery and the engineers, came into their own, and junior officer candidates for the reorganized General Staff had to be qualified in mathematics and the military sciences. The War Academy (*Kriegsakademie*) at Berlin, founded by Scharnhorst in 1810, was the wellspring of the "General Staff" tradition which ever since has been a major force in German military history.

The reforms of Scharnhorst, Gneisenau and their colleagues bore immediate fruit in the rejuvenated Prussian Army which, under von Bluecher, joined with Wellington's "thin red line" to achieve Napoleon's final overthrow at Waterloo. The long peace that ensued was also a period of general military stagnation throughout Europe. It was relieved, however, by the posthumous publication of the remarkable writings of Karl von Clausewitz, whose name in the history of the officers' corps is linked in triple diadem with those of Scharnhorst and Gneisenau. Nearly a generation younger, he assisted Scharnhorst in effectuating the pre-Waterloo reforms, and died with Gneisenau of cholera in 1831 while serving as the latter's Chief of Staff. Clausewitz' widow published his works, including the famous classic *On War* (*Vom Kriege*).

Clausewitz wrote extensively on technical questions, but it is as a military philosopher that he has attained world-wide fame. He gave the officers' corps a philosophical basis and a spiritual *raison d'être*. He was a general who had captured the intellectual technique of the Enlightenment, and who sought to explore "the nature of military phenomena" and their place in the universal scheme of things. Writing in an era of rising nationalism and of social and military ferment, his works are studded with apothegms that are, even today, constantly used as tools in

military literature. War, as Clausewitz saw, had ceased to be a sort of tournament for kings and nobles playing with professional soldiers, and was in fact "the continuation of state policy by different means" and therefore "an affair of the whole nation". That being so, war must also be recognized as "an act of violence pushed to its utmost bounds" in order "to compel our opponent to fulfil our will". For Clausewitz, tactics and strategy are not mere technical concepts: "Tactics is the theory of the use of military forces in combat", whereas "strategy is the theory of the use of combats for the object of the war"—the science of when and how to use military force to advance the nation's ends. Elsewhere Clausewitz declared that "to introduce into the philosophy of war a principle of moderation would be an absurdity", and his works abound in other foreshadowings of what, a century later, gave rise to the expression "total war".

THE GOLDEN AGE OF MOLTKE AND SCHLIEFFEN

After the fall of Napoleon, the nineteenth century was one of peace (as centuries go), advancing liberalism and political democracy, and the industrial revolution. All these things threatened the prerogatives and, indeed, the continued existence of a reactionary, militaristic, noble caste such as the Prussian officers' corps. In no other country save Germany did the "military aristocracy" survive the century without at least a radical diminution of its privileged status and political importance. In Germany, however, the twentieth century opened with the officers' corps at the peak of its domestic prestige and still in full enjoyment of its traditional prerogatives.

Their position was not maintained without opposition from the bourgeois and democratic elements in Germany. But these groups failed to achieve by peaceful means the political unification of Germany which the mood and trend of the times demanded. King William I, Bismarck, and the officers' corps were able to accomplish what the Frankfurt Assembly could not. The Liberals and Progressives in the Prussian Landtag vigorously opposed the expansion of the Army, and when that same Army won the victories that made possible national unity and Empire, it reaped an enormous harvest of popular acclaim. Political democracy in Germany was not only pushed back into the wings but suffered a disastrous setback from which it has never fully recovered to this day.

While winning victors' laurels, the officers' corps remained the citadel of social reaction. King William I, his Minister of War (von Roon), and the chief of his military cabinet (Edwin von Manteuffel) were all arch-conservatives. Despite the establishment of ministerial government under the Prussian Constitution of 1850, King William asserted and successfully maintained that the Army was outside the purview of parliamentary control, and remained the creature of the sovereign as "Supreme War Lord". In 1860, the military cabinet carried out a veritable purge of bourgeois, liberal, and other "undesirable" elements of the officers' corps. By the end of 1861 four-fifths of the 1,000-odd general and staff officers, and nearly two-thirds of the 2,900 infantry officers, were noble; in 1869, of forty-six senior generals, twenty-six were princes or dukes.

Roon and Manteuffel thus confirmed the Army's independence of civilian control and tightened the aristocracy's grip on the officers' corps. In the meanwhile, Helmuth von Moltke modernized German tactics and brought the General Staff to full maturity. Moltke was appointed Chief of Staff of the Prussian Army in 1858 when William (later William I) became Regent of Prussia, and remained such until 1888. During the early sixties he was overshadowed by Roon and Manteuffel, who took the leadership in handling the Army's political and administrative problems.

Moltke, in contrast, was busy planning future operations. In particular, he mastered the utilization for military purposes of the great scientific and industrial advances of that era. He created a special railway section within the General Staff, and demonstrated the new strategic possibilities opened up by the railways and telegraphy. It was now practicable to handle far larger armies than theretofore, and to transport them much more rapidly. In the words of Vagts,[1] Moltke "brought supreme command to a focus and enabled the Chief of Staff to direct from a single centre . . . enormous bodies of men and operations covering hundreds of miles". It was Moltke, more than any other one man, who finally forced the German officers' corps to regard soldiering as a profession.

In 1866, just before the outbreak of the "Seven Weeks' War", King William gave Moltke, as Chief of Staff, virtual supreme command of the Army. Within a few weeks the Austrians were routed at Sadowa, and Moltke was a national hero. With the victorious conclusion of the Franco-Prussian War and the rebirth of the German Empire at Versailles in 1871, Moltke

achieved undying fame in military annals and in German history alike, and as his renown rose to the summit, the prestige of the General Staff rose too.

Yet these very years of glory and achievement were also the time when the officers' corps did the most damage to German political and cultural institutions. Innately hostile to representative government, the Army (and a few years later the Navy) was continually forced to beat down liberal opposition to military budgets in the Landtag and Reichstag, and the anti-democratic bent of the officers' corps remained incorrigible. Worse still, the Army's phenomenal success swept the university professors and other savants completely off balance. Great scholars such as Sybel (originator of the phrase "place in the sun"), Mommsen, and above all Treitschke succumbed to panoply and fanfare, and preached the gospel of an "epoch of war, age of iron". Teachers seemed to vie with each other in outbursts of national vanity and the worship of armed might. "We Germans are not modest and don't pretend to be", boasted Mommsen, while Treitschke proclaimed that "each dragoon who knocks a Croat on the head does more for the German cause than the finest political brain that ever wielded a tren-chant pen". Thus the intellectuals came almost to despise themselves in comparison with the men of arms, and the German academic world, instead of acting as a salutary check and mitigating influence, became a powerful stimulus to militarism.

Moltke resigned as Chief of Staff the same year that William I died, and two years later (1890) William II forced Bismarck's retirement. Neither the new sovereign nor the series of chancellors that followed Bismarck were able to fill the shoes of their predecessors. In Graf Alfred von Schlieffen, however, the officers' corps discovered a chief of staff worthy of the mantle of Moltke. Indifferent to the philosophical problems of war which had stirred Clausewitz, and too little concerned with broad political questions, Schlieffen's range of vision was narrower than that of his great predecessors. But he was the staff officer *par excellence*. Schlieffen's genius for operational planning and olympian personality had a profound effect on the officers' corps as a whole and the General Staff corps in particular. Able young officers were allowed to handle large military formations in the frequent manœuvres, and the character and quality of Schlieffen's military thinking thus permeated the corps even to the lower ranks.

Schlieffen died in 1913, and never had an opportunity to

exercise high command in actual combat. But his studies and memoranda were the basis of German military planning for the First World War. In particular he developed the famous "Schlieffen plan"—sketched in 1905 and amplified during his last years—which contemplated that, if faced with a two-front war against Russia and France, the main German blow would be delivered first in the west. The essence of this plan was that a very powerful German right wing would sweep through Belgium and southern Holland (in disregard of their neutrality, and of Germany's own participation in the European guarantee of Belgian neutrality), continue south down the Channel coast, and turn inland south of Paris, thus encircling the French Army and pressing it against its own eastern fortifications, the Rhine, and the Swiss frontier.

In 1914 Schlieffen's plan was badly bungled, and in 1940 it was drastically modified. But Schlieffen's approach to operational planning was the touchstone of German General Staff thinking throughout the first four decades of the present century. And his is the last great name but one (von Seeckt) in the history of the officers' corps.

THE FIRST WORLD WAR

The story of the German Army in World War I is not devoid of famous names—von Hindenburg, Ludendorff—or names that were famous not so long ago—the younger von Moltke (nephew of the great Moltke), von Buelow, von Falkenhayn, von Kluck, von Mackensen, von Eichhorn, and von der Goltz. But it is well-nigh barren of distinguished names. To be sure, the officers' corps was not lacking in able men. Ludendorff himself was a highly gifted tactician, but failed abysmally in the bigger role of military dictator which he essayed during the last two years of the war. Hoffmann, Groener and von Seeckt were all superb generals, but they were younger men who did not then attain the top levels of command.

Indeed, too much of the German military mind was still rooted in the eighteenth century. For this archaism the Army and the nation paid dearly; impressive victories like Tannenberg and Gorlice were not turned to full account, and opportunity after opportunity was bungled or passed over. In particular, the rotten caste-consciousness of the officers' corps proved a fatal obstacle to success in the twentieth century. In 1913 the General Staff had proposed the creation of three new Army corps, which the man-power of the country was fully

adequate to support. But the "old guard", acting through the Prussian War Minister, rejected the proposal because it would have required a large number of new officers, most of whom would have to come from bourgeois sources. The "top drawer" could no longer meet the demand for officers, and rather than draw upon "circles hardly fit" and classes "which only in exceptional cases supply useful material for the officer class", the Army was restricted in size. Two or three additional corps on the German right wing in 1914 might well have carried the initial attack in the west to the point of success.

Even more disastrous was the German military contempt for economic and social matters and ignorance of and ineptitude for political and diplomatic questions. Here the narrowness of the Schlieffen school exacted a terrible price. Economic mobilization was delayed by the younger Moltke's indifference to Rathenau's proposals. Schlieffen's military genius could perceive the immediate advantages of attacking France via Belgium, but he failed to come to grips with the consequences which would follow in the wake of the wanton violation of neutrality. Pursuing the illusion of a Polish Army to strengthen the German forces on the eastern front, Ludendorff kicked away the opportunities for peace with Russia which Bethmann-Hollweg's diplomacy had created. Enforcement of the Treaty of Brest-Litovsk, the greedy terms of which were demanded by Ludendorff over the objections of General Hoffmann and the civilian ministers, required that a million German troops be left in the east at a time when the shortage of man-power on the western front was already desperate. German armies of occupation or military expeditions were sent in 1918 to Finland, to Batum and Baku, and to Odessa. German divisions propped up the reactionary Hetman Skoropadsky in the Ukraine, and Field Marshal von Eichhorn was assassinated in Kiev just ten days before the famous "black day of the German Army" (August 8, 1918) near Amiens, when Ludendorff finally realized that his offensive was a lost cause.

Even the new-born German Navy was the result of unsound judgments. The maritime glories of the Hanseatic League lay buried under two centuries and the Navy had played no part in the rise of Prussia. It had no traditions or names to match the Army great; as late as the eighteen-eighties the Navy was commanded by generals (Stosch and Caprivi) and even its ships have had to be named after Army heroes (*Scharnhorst*, *Gneisenau*, *Bleucher* and *Prinz Eugen*) for lack of names in the naval galaxy.

The Navy's role in the Danish and Austrian wars of the sixties was negligible* and in the Franco-Prussian War almost ignominious.

But late in the nineteenth century the commercial ambitions of the rising industrial magnates and the Kaiser's jealousy of England found a catalytic agent in the administrative and advertising genius of von Tirpitz. Germany embarked upon the building of a high-seas battle fleet for reasons described by Tirpitz in his memoirs: [2] "I had heard from many sides of the difficulties which the English were putting in the way of everything German and of the progress of the 'made in Germany' boycott. . . . German trade, the 'Open Door', could no longer be protected by flying squadrons; we had to increase in general power all around, i.e. to qualify ourselves for an alliance with the great powers. But alliance-value could only be achieved by a battle fleet."

However sound that programme might have been in conjunction with diplomatic policies looking toward alliance with a strong naval power, it was sadly out of place as preparation for a virtually single-handed war against an alliance which included Britannia, the ruler of the waves. Von Spee's victory off Coronel, and the dramatic exploits of single cruisers like the *Emden* and *Karlsruhe* and commerce raiders like the *Wolf* and Count von Luckner's *Seeadler*, gave the German sailor something to be proud of, and the High Seas Fleet under Scheer emerged with credit from Jutland.

But the Navy's only real hope of decisively influencing the course of the war was the submarine. The enormous expenditure of men, money and materials for the High Seas Fleet was a waste of resources sadly needed in other quarters. An equivalent investment in submarines or artillery would have been far more rewarding.

Had Germany produced another Bismarck or half a Bismarck, to steer the unstable Kaiser and keep Ludendorff under control, many of these mistakes might have been avoided. Ludendorff's dictatorial role was an anachronism, like the caste structure of the officers' corps. Moltke's success had been too great; even the aged Bismarck, just before his death, told the Kaiser that "as long as you have this officers' corps, you can do everything you want", and Tirpitz thought these words "revealed the master".[3] But they revealed the master of the

* In 1869 the entire naval officers' corps numbered only about 150. Roon was Minister of Marine as well as of War.

26

nineteenth century, not the twentieth. When war came again, its waging required far more than staff training and the ability to manœuvre armies. These other faculties the officers' corps both lacked and scorned, and nowhere was Germany able to find men who could fill the breach.

The root causes of Germany's military downfall did not pass unnoticed by a few discerning members of the corps. Writing in 1924,[4] the retired General Freiherr von Schoenaich laid his finger on some of the worst flaws in the structure, including especially the irresponsible independence of the Chief of Staff which had led to the High Command's dictatorship. His analysis led General Schoenaich to "the irresistible conclusion that we owe our ruin to the supremacy of our military authorities over civilian authorities; and that is the very essence of militarism. In fact, German militarism simply committed suicide."

THE OFFICERS' CORPS IN RECENT TIMES

Such was the background of the German military leaders, who were called upon in this century to cope with so many grave and difficult situations—the defeat of 1918, the restrictions of the Versailles Treaty, the role of the Army in the new-born Republic, and the advent of Hitler and National Socialism. The men who led the officers' corps during these critical years—von Seeckt, von Blomberg, von Fritsch, Beck, von Brauchitsch, von Rundstedt and Halder, to mention only a few—are the central actors in the drama which this story unfolds. With rare exceptions, they faced these issues of the twentieth century ruled by the same standards, traditions and prejudices as those which governed the officers' corps in the time of Bismarck and Moltke. If the face of the world had changed almost beyond recognition in the intervening half-century, their view of it had not.

Prussia was the cradle and Berlin–Potsdam the capital of the corps, but it had long since ceased to be a purely Prussian institution. Indeed, Scharnhorst and Gneisenau themselves were respectively of Hanoverian and Austrian origin, Clausewitz of Polish ancestry, and Moltke a Mecklenburger. Since 1871, the army establishments of the lesser kingdoms had been integrated with that of Prussia, and though Bavaria (and to a lesser degree Wuerttemberg and Saxony) retained a measure of military individuality, these concessions to regional tradition did not interfere with the unified organization and functioning

of the Imperial German Army. A majority of the officers' corps was Prussian, but many prominent Army names—for example von Falkenhausen, List, von Weichs, Adam, Halder, von Leeb, and von Horn—are Bavarian. The last Bavarian Minister of War, Generaloberst Otto Freiherr Kress von Kressenstein, was the leading exemplar of a noble Bavarian family which rivals any of the Junker nurseries of Mars; the list of German officers in the First World War names not less than eleven Kress von Kressensteins.

The aristocratic tradition of the corps, dating from the days of the Prussian Kings, persisted with almost undiminished vigour. To be sure, as the Army grew in size before and during the First World War, the percentage of nobles among the officers decreased. Ludendorff, Hoffmann, and Groener in the First World War, and Heye, Beck, List, Adam, Halder and others in later years attained high rank despite their lack of the emblematic "von". Hitler, whatever his other faults, was no social snob, and elevated numerous plebeian officers—including Keitel, Jodl, Rommel, Dietl, Guderian, Zeitzler and Schoerner —to high staff positions or important field commands.

But noble names continued to dominate the upper levels of the corps, as well as the socially favoured regiments, especially in the cavalry. As late as 1932, the nobles still comprised between a quarter and a third of the entire corps. Furthermore, they "set the tone" for all its members. Although the corps had grown too large for the genetic resources of the Junker families, it was still in thrall to their traditions. Such generals as Beck, though not of noble origin, were well-born and aristocratic in outlook. The bourgeois officers were, for the most part, sons of officials or landowners, or scions of "old officer families". Jews were rigidly excluded from the corps, as they had always been except during the dire emergency of the First World War. The arrogant assumption of superiority to all other classes, and condescension verging on contempt toward civilians, continued to be the basic social characteristics of the German officer and indeed became one of the major points of friction between the officers' corps and the Nazis.

Politically as well as socially, the Army remained the *rocher de bronze* of authoritarian royalism. As we shall soon see, the Weimar Republic never won the allegiance of the officers. To them, the Republican chancellors and other civilian ministers were never the acknowledged embodiment of German sovereignty, but only the distrusted representatives of the parlia-

mentarianism which was their ancient foe. Hindenburg, to be sure, retained their loyalty, not because of his election as President by the German people, but because he was a field marshal, the senior officer of the corps, a monarchist, and in these aspects a symbol of the *ancien régime* for the restoration of which the corps was waiting.

Culturally, the outlook of the corps remained appallingly narrow. Neither at cadet schools like the *Gross Lichterfelde* * nor at the regimental mess was there much attempt to inculcate love of beauty or a spirit of philosophical inquiry. Thus the mental energies of the officers were canalized in a rigid professionalism. Even this was a bit spotty, but the General Staff heritage had been firmly implanted by the great succession of Scharnhorst, Gneisenau, Clausewitz, Moltke and Schlieffen, and it was no longer good form to turn up one's nose at brilliant attainments in staff duties or at manœuvres.

This authentic professional competence, together with the tremendous momentum gained from over half a century of public adulation and social prestige, was the principal capital with which the officers' corps faced the series of national crises which gripped the German nation after its defeat in the First World War. Richly—indeed, too richly—endowed with traditions and past glories, the corps was woefully deficient in the flexibility and adaptability which the times demanded. Thus Republican Germany was corroded by an anachronistic but most potent militarism, and the corps itself was all too easily corrupted when it ultimately came face to face with the equally ruthless and far more versatile Hitler.

* By far the most famous of the cadet schools, and officially called the *Haupt-Kadetten-Anstalt* (Main Cadet Institute), but familiarly known as *Hat Keine Aussicht* or *Homeopathische Kur Anstalt* ("no way out" and "Homeopathic Sanatorium").

CHAPTER II

THE REICHSWEHR AND THE WEIMAR REPUBLIC

THE DOWNFALL of German arms in 1918, the Kaiser's abdication and the Allied surrender terms of the following year smote the officers' corps hip and thigh. No long period of reverses and retreats, such as the thirty months from Stalingrad–Alamein–North Africa to V-E Day, preceded the armistice of November, 1918. Indeed, the last great Ludendorff offensive had ended but three months earlier; in the west the German armies were still on French and Belgian soil, and in the east the enemy had been crushingly defeated, and German troops were roaming in Finland, the Baltic countries, Poland, and the Ukraine. Exhausted as the nation was, the High Command's confession that the war was lost, and its demand that the government seek a prompt cessation of hostilities, came as an unexpected and bitter shock to the civilian ministers and party leaders of the Reichstag, to whom the desperate state of affairs had not been previously revealed.

With defeat came the abdication and flight of the Kaiser, as well as of the lesser German monarchs. These were the sovereigns who had commissioned the German officers, and to whom they had sworn allegiance. Overwhelmingly monarchistic, the corps was left wallowing aimlessly, like a rudderless ship in heavy seas. Republicanism was anathema to them, and their contempt for the Ebert government was exceeded only by their hatred of the Spartacists and other revolutionary factions and regimes that rose and fell in the post-armistice period. Just as after Jena, the corps was obliged to stand on its own feet and seek political guidance within its own ranks—from Hindenburg, who remained in command until the signature of the Versailles Treaty in June, 1919, from the ranking officers of the post-Treaty Reichswehr, and from the chiefs of the many "volunteer corps" (*Freikorps*) of ex-soldiers and adventurers that sprang up all over Germany to put down the leftist uprisings, "protect" the eastern frontier, and loot and fight for love of the game.

Six months after defeat and the end of the Empire came the announcement (May 7, 1919) of the Allied surrender terms, including the reduction of the Army to a maximum strength of 100,000 men. This third and apparently mortal blow was dealt to an Army that still numbered well over half a million effectives. In February, Hindenburg had moved his headquarters to Pomerania in order to be nearer the Baltic provinces, where a German *Freikorps* under von der Goltz had been engaging Bolshevist forces for several months. The Krupp works were still turning out armaments, and the Army was still very much a going concern, with every intention of remaining such. The military restrictions proposed by the Allies aroused such fierce opposition in the Army and, indeed, throughout the nation, that the Treaty escaped rejection only after Hindenburg and Groener (who had replaced Ludendorff just before the armistice) reluctantly advised the government that a renewal of military resistance was out of the question.

In fact, the German Army in 1919 found itself in straits wellnigh as desperate as those of a century earlier, after Jena. If it had been less decisively defeated in battle on the latter occasion, the military limitations embodied in the Treaty of Versailles were proportionately more severe than those imposed by Napoleon at Tilsit. In 1807, Scharnhorst and Gneisenau had been able to use the revolutionary pressures for the Army's benefit, while the monarchy—the focus of the officers' loyalty—had ridden out the political storm. In 1918, the officers' corps was left with nothing it thought worthy of loyalty except itself.

THE ARMS LIMITATIONS OF THE TREATY OF VERSAILLES

The three great new weapons of the First World War were the airplane, the tank and the submarine. Despite its non-use in the Second World War, one might well add poison gas to the list. In any case, all four of these twentieth-century instruments of war were forbidden to Germany under the Treaty of Versailles, signed June 28, 1919.

These and the other arms limitations were embodied in Part V of the Treaty, containing the "military, naval and air clauses". The two latter categories need not detain us long. The High Seas Fleet had been scuttled at Scapa Flow. For the future, the Navy was restricted to six each of battleships and light cruisers, and twelve each of destroyers and torpedo boats. The displacement of the battleships, however, was not

to exceed 10,000 tons, or little more than that of heavy cruisers, and the total strength of the Navy was limited to 15,000 men.

Far more important, in the light of experience during the war, was the unqualified prohibition of the "construction or acquisition of any submarine, even for commercial purposes". From a military standpoint, the banning of all aircraft from the German armed forces was equally categorical. Civil aviation, however, was not forbidden.

Crippling as were these restrictions to Germany's new "big Navy," and totally destructive of the fledgling air arm, to the average German they were overshadowed by the terms meted out to the Army—"that old National Army on which we all depended", as Stresemann, renowned for his pacific and internationalist utterances, once called it.[1] Not only was it reduced to an overall strength of 100,000 men, but its composition and organization were carefully prescribed in order to forestall use of devices like those by which Scharnhorst, Gneisenau and Baron vom Stein had evaded the Treaty of Tilsit. The men were to be recruited for twelve-year enlistments, and new officers engaged to serve for twenty-five years; these long-service requirements were intended to prevent the accumulation of a large trained reserve. The 100,000 men were to constitute not over seven infantry and three cavalry divisions grouped under not more than two corps headquarters. Precise schedules fixed the number and specified the calibres of guns and small arms which the Army might maintain. Arms manufacture was permitted only at factories approved by the Allies; all other munitions plants were to be closed down. The manufacture and possession of tanks and poison gas were completely forbidden.

It was the purpose of the victorious Allies not only to shrink Germany's military establishment and potential, but also to curb her militaristic traditions and foster republican government. Even before the end of the war, President Wilson had inveighed against the German "military authorities and monarchical autocrats", and had demanded that the people bring about a change of government which would eliminate the "arbitrary power" of the Empire, so that it could no longer, "secretly and of its single choice, disturb the peace of the world".

A number of the Treaty's clauses were in line with this mixed politico-military objective. Thus, it was stipulated that all German territory west of the Rhine, and a strip fifty kilometres deep along the east bank, be "demilitarized". Even more

important was the requirement that the "Great General Staff" (*Grosser Generalstab*) of the Army—the symbol and prime carrier of the proud traditions of the past, and at once the heart and the circulatory system of the High Command—be dissolved and not "reconstituted in any form". Ex-soldiers' associations were forbidden to "occupy themselves with any military matters". Most galling to the officers' corps, no doubt, was the requirement that all "military academies" be abolished. The great *Kriegsakademie* at Berlin, founded by Scharnhorst, had to be closed, and on March 10, 1920, *Gross Lichterfelde* signalized its "death" by a parade across Berlin to the tune of "Fridericus Rex", and ceremonial addresses by Ludendorff and Hoffmann, in which they defiantly predicted that the suppression of the military schools would not long endure.

THE HUNDRED-THOUSAND-MAN ARMY

Taking its popular name from the Treaty limitation on its size, the Reichswehr * of the Weimar Republic came into official existence in the autumn of 1919. Its basic organizational scheme had already been worked out by a group of able young General Staff officers under Groener's supervision. Von Hammerstein, von Schleicher, von Bock—these would soon be names to conjure with. Likewise, and far more important, the general character and "tone" of the new Army and its officers had already been established.

Indeed, the composition and leadership of the new Army were perhaps the most fateful of all the problems that confronted post-war Germany and the struggling young Weimar Republic. Had the Army been brought under the effective control of the cabinet (through the Minister of Defence) and the Reichstag, and had the officers' corps been purged of its monarchist, anti-Republican proclivities and caste organization—then indeed the Republic and democracy might have had a better chance to flourish and take root. But it was not so to be. Just as Hindenburg and Ludendorff had cast the Ministers of War (who were, in fact, subordinate generals) into the shade during the war, so did the Army chiefs dominate the Republic's first Minister of Defence (*Reichswehrminister*), Gustav Noske. There were, to be sure, those (such as the Social

---

* Literally and precisely, "Reichswehr" denoted the armed forces of the Reich, including both Army and Navy, and "Reichsheer" the Army alone. In common parlance, however, "Reichswehr" has been used to denote the "100,000-man Army."

Democratic officials Scheidemann and Grzesinski) who saw the danger of turning the Army back to the generals of the imperial tradition, and who urged Noske to "democratize" the military leadership. But Noske was almost as dominated by militarism as the generals themselves; "the German people today is nationally so dissolute that everything must be done to rebuild its nationalism", he declared, and this could best be done "by reviving the proud soldier memories of the World War". As Grzesinski later wrote,[2] it was not Noske's fault alone. German labour—the main strength of the Social Democrats—had had a bellyful of soldiering, and was quite willing to leave such matters to the professionals. They lent no support to Grzesinski's efforts to gain civilian participation in the task of reorganizing the Reichswehr, and the generals remained firmly in the saddle.

The result was, as we have already seen, that the officers' corps re-emerged under the Republic with its outlook and composition substantially unchanged. The official rank lists of the officers' corps started to reappear in 1920. They are not to be recommended as light reading, but no one can peruse these stiff, beautifully organized volumes—replete with von Vollard Bockelbergs, von dem Bussche-Ippenburgs, Kress von Kressensteins, Ritter von Thises, and Freiherr von Thats, and proudly displaying the imperial eagle on the cover—without a feeling of being transported back to the nineteenth century if not, indeed, the eighteenth. The corps was so utterly anachronistic an institution that it would have been absurd had it not been so implacable, cohesive, and professionally competent. The successful transmigration of soul from the imperial *alte Heer* to the Reichswehr caused a fatal flaw in the foundations of the Republic, and was a most fateful event in world history.

The dominance of the civilian *Reichswehrminister* by the generals was symbolized by the tiny staff at the disposal of the Minister—a mere adjutant's office (*Adjutantur*). The "heavy work" of the Ministry was performed by the staffs of the Army and Navy commanders, who were nominally subordinate to the Minister. These staffs constituted, in actuality, the general headquarters of the Army and Navy and were appropriately designated the *Heeresleitung* and *Marineleitung* (Army Command and Navy Command) respectively.* Within the *Heeres-*

---

* The commanders were not, under the Weimar Republic, given the title of "commander-in-chief" (*Oberbefehlshaber*) but the less impressive designation "chief" (*Chef*). Thus the Army commander was called the *Chef der Heeresleitung* (Chef HL).

leitung by far the most important component was the *Truppe-namt* (Troops Department), which was, as we shall see, the successor to the Versailles-outlawed General Staff. Here were to be found the operations, training, intelligence and other branches customarily embodied in a general staff. In addition to the *Truppenamt*, the *Heeresleitung* included personnel, administrative and ordnance departments as well as several special sections.

In the field, the Army's organization reflected the Versailles limitations. Germany was divided into seven military districts (*Wehrkreise*), corresponding to the seven infantry divisions allowed by the Treaty.* Each *Wehrkreis* was commanded by a senior Army general, who also led the division stationed therein. The *Wehrkreis* headquarters were the regional centres for military administration—recruitment, pensions, training and similar matters. Again following the Treaty, limitation of the Army to two corps headquarters, the *Wehrkreise* and divisions of eastern Germany were subordinated to a "group headquarters" (Gruppenkommando 1) at Berlin, and those in the west to a similar headquarters (Gruppenkommando 2) at Kassel. The two commanders-in-chief at Berlin and Kassel were directly subordinate to the Army *Chef* in the Defence Ministry.

Ever since the day of Moltke, the words "German General Staff" had borne a fearsome connotation to the world at large, and this no doubt underlay the Versailles Treaty's attempt to abolish it. The requirement that it be not "reconstituted in any form" could not, of course, have been literally enforced without abolishing the Army itself, since no modern army can function without a staff of some sort. Perhaps no feature of German military history has been so generally misunderstood, or spread so much confusion, as that of the General Staff, partly because its nature and status have changed radically and several times during the century and a half of its existence.

The General Staff originally was the group of officers who advised and assisted the King of Prussia in military operations. Since the King was not only the sovereign but the Commander-in-Chief of the Army, it was natural that he should need such a

---

* The *Wehrkreise* were numbered, and their headquarters were located at Koenigsberg (I), Stettin (II), Berlin (III), Dresden (IV), Stuttgart (V), Muenster (VI) and Munich (VII). The three cavalry divisions permitted by the Treaty were located at Frankfurt an der Oder, Breslau and Kassel, but had no territorial jurisdiction.

staff, and should come to rely on the Chief of his General Staff as his principal operational assistant. Under Scharnhorst (who filled this position from 1808 to 1812), part of the General Staff was allotted to the corps and divisional commanders and called the *Armee-Generalstab*, while the part retained at the royal headquarters in Berlin was called the *Grosser Generalstab* (Great General Staff).

Until the end of the Napoleonic era, the Prussian General Staff was in no fundamental respect different from those of the other European monarchs. In 1821, however, the then Chief of the Great General Staff (General von Müffling) assumed command over the officers of the *Armee-Generalstab* as well, and took the title "Chief of the General Staff of the Army". The military allegiance of the staff officers at field headquarters was thereafter divided between the field commanders to whom they were attached and the Chief of the Army General Staff, who thereby acquired a status and power unknown in the armies of other countries. These were greatly augmented when, during the war with Austria in 1866, William I gave von Moltke (as Chief of Staff) supreme authority in the field. Since von Moltke and the Minister of War (von Roon) were able to work together, their relative authority never came to an open issue, but after von Roon's retirement in 1872 the Minister of War was far outshadowed (as well as outranked, since the Emperor continued to appoint generals to this position) by the Chief of Staff. The distinctive red trouser stripes of the General Staff officers* became a mark of prestige and an object of envy throughout the Army.

During the First World War, the General Staff reached its apogee. The Kaiser did not undertake personal direction of operations, and Hindenburg, though bearing the title of Chief of Staff, was, like Moltke half a century earlier, virtually Commander-in-Chief. Unlike Moltke, however, he delegated major initiative to Ludendorff who, though designated "First Quartermaster General", actually filled the role of Hindenburg's Chief of Staff. Under the ægis of Hindenburg and Ludendorff, the authority exercised by General Staff officers was enormous. A special communications channel linked the staff officers at the various headquarters to which they were assigned, and enabled them to report directly to Supreme Headquarters outside the purview of the field commanders to whom they were attached.

* The General Staff had constituted a separate "corps" of officers with distinctive insignia since the end of the eighteenth century.

36

Upon occasion it was the view of the General Staff officer rather than the commander that prevailed; during the most critical hours of the first Battle of the Marne it was a mere lieutenant-colonel (Hentsch) on von Moltke's* staff who ordered an untimely retreat of von Kluck's and von Buelow's armies on the German right wing.

There was, perhaps, more than met the eye in the fact that the head of the post-war German Army was no longer called the Chief of Staff. To be sure, the Weimar Constitution declared that the President of the Reich should be Commander-in-Chief of the Armed Forces. But what monarchist general would want to be "Chief of Staff" to a civilian and a former saddler to boot? What German officer would want to serve on such a staff? The real Commander-in-Chief of the Army was the *Chef der Heeresleitung*, and from the birth of the Reichswehr the General Staff was his staff, not the President's.

In deference to the Treaty, it was not called a "general staff", but this was a change in name only. For the functions still had to be discharged, as indeed they were, by the *Truppenamt* of the *Heeresleitung* (which corresponded to the old *Grosser Generalstab*) and by the staff officers attached to the *Gruppenkommando* and *Wehrkreis* headquarters (who corresponded to the old *Armee-Generalstab*). The chief of the *Truppenamt* was regarded as the lineal successor to the former Chief of the General Staff. In the post-war Reichswehr, however, he was no longer the actual commander-in-chief, but rather the "chief of staff" to the general who, as *Chef der Heeresleitung*, commanded the Army. The office was consistently held by generals junior in rank not only to the *Chef der Heeresleitung* but to the principal field commanders as well. These changes, however, were the result of the Kaiser's abdication and the shift from imperial to republican government, rather than of the Treaty.

The Treaty, indeed, had little effect other than to suppress the General Staff's name. The authority of the General Staff within the Army was diminished, but not its prestige. The General Staff corps and traditions persisted. Its members continued to wear the red stripe and were selected, as before, from the cream of the officers' corps. When Hitler openly repudiated the Treaty in 1935, the then Chief of the *Truppenamt*, General Beck, had only to restore the old name of his office and department; everything else had been well preserved.

* Nephew of the great von Moltke, and Chief of Staff from 1906 to September, 1914.

Thus did Groener and his assistants ably cope with the seemingly insurmountable problems of organization with which the defeat and Versailles confronted them. From the *Truppenamt* the General Staff could emerge in more propitious times. The *Wehrkreise* could, all in good time, grow into corps, and the *Gruppenkommandos* into Army group headquarters. The organizational foundations for future expansion had been well laid.

But the Army and the officers' corps were cruelly shrunken—4,000 officers and 96,000 men. Three lieutenant-generals, fourteen major-generals, twenty-five brigadier-generals,* 105 colonels—not much room at the top for the members of the officers' corps! † No tanks, no airplanes, no big guns. No amount of organizational genius could compensate for these deficiencies of personnel and weapons. The situation was more than disheartening, even for the most indefatigable German militarist. But the purpose, intelligence, energy and determination to salvage as much as possible from the wreckage of the *alte Heer* and of Tirpitz' Navy were not lacking. And these qualities and talents found a focus in the brain of General Hans von Seeckt—the last in the succession of great names in the annals of the officers' corps, ranking in terms of national importance with those of Scharnhorst and Gneisenau.

THE POLICIES OF VON SEECKT

Seeckt was well qualified for the role he was about to fill, calling as it did for guile and patience as much as for administrative and professional competence. He had served with great distinction as Mackensen's Chief of Staff, and was the principal architect of the great victory over the Russians at Gorlice in 1915. Thereafter he was entrusted with a succession of missions both military and diplomatic in character, to stimulate and co-ordinate the flagging efforts of Germany's eastern allies. During the latter part of the war he acted as Chief of the Turkish General Staff, and when he returned home at the end of the war was attached to the Peace Delegation as a military expert.

Shortly before the transition to the 100,000-man Reichswehr was made late in 1919, Seeckt was serving as Chief of the General Staff and Generalmajor Walther Reinhardt as Minister

---

* The German rank designations for those ranks are *General, Generalleutnant*, and *Generalmajor*. Hereafter the German designations will be used for all officer ranks. See Appendix I, "A Note on German Ranks", p. 359.

† Reichswehrminister Noske estimated that 32,000 officers fit for service returned from the front in 1918.

of War. Groener (who had just retired from the Army) and others urged President Ebert to appoint Seeckt as *Chef der Heeresleitung*, but Ebert, apparently influenced by the new Minister of Defence, Noske, chose Reinhardt. Seeckt did not want to serve under Reinhardt and considered resigning, but was persuaded to remain in the Army as Chief of the *Truppenamt*.* In March, 1920, however, at the conclusion of the Kapp–Luettwitz *Putsch*, Seeckt replaced Reinhardt as Commander of the Army.

The application and effect of the policies pursued by Seeckt will become apparent as we sketch the major military events of the nearly seven years (March, 1920 to October, 1926) of his leadership.[3] His plan of campaign was flexible, but his various moves revolved around several basic principles. The common denominator of them all was their purpose to enable Germany to re-create a formidable military machine. For Seeckt and the other generals, whatever they might say publicly, looked at the Treaty of Versailles just as Scharnhorst and Gneisenau regarded the Treaty of Tilsit, and all their plans were directed to its overthrow.

Under the Treaty of Versailles, however, Seeckt could not utilize the "shadow army" techniques to which Scharnhorst and Gneisenau had resorted, but which were barred to Seeckt by the Treaty's requirements of twelve-year enlistments and twenty-five-year commissions. For the reconstitution of the Army, therefore, Seeckt sought to make necessity a virtue, and to capitalize on the Treaty limits on its size. With thousands of trained officers and millions of men available from which to select the 100,000-man Army, the watchword was not quantity but quality.[4]

The sharp competition for the small number of posts enabled Seeckt to establish the Reichswehr as a true military elite or, as he himself described it, a *Fuehrerheer* (army of leaders). Every member of the Army was trained so that "he would be capable of the next higher step in case of war". The entire officers' corps was to provide commanders down to battalion level, with the newest officers as company commanders. The pick of the non-commissioned officers would fill out the lowest officerships, and the privates would become non-coms. Thus every officer and man carried his superior's insignia in his pocket.

Nor was the closing of the *Kriegsakademie* allowed to interfere

* Seeckt gave up the Versailles-prohibited title of Chief of the General Staff and assumed his new title of *Chef des Truppenamtes* on November 24, 1919.

with the training of the General Staff officers. In essence, the academy was simply transferred to the several *Wehrkreise*, operating under directions from the *Truppenamt* in Berlin. Each year, beginning in 1920, and in each *Wehrkreis*, examinations were given for officers who aspired to General Staff status. On the basis of these examinations, some seventy officers (about ten to each *Wehrkreis*) were selected annually for a two-year course of General Staff instruction under the direction of the *Wehrkreis* commander. As a general rule, about fifteen officers satisfactorily completed the two-year course, after which they were sent for a third year of training at the *Reichswehrministerium* in Berlin. Following a probationary period in a staff position, the selected officers were taken on the roll of *Fuehrerstabsoffiziere* and donned the red trouser stripes of the General Staff corps.

The Versailles prohibition of all military aviation confronted Seeckt with an especially difficult problem for which only make-shift answers were found. Seeckt was "air-minded" and, unlike many of his colleagues, envisaged an independent air arm. As preparation for the future, Seeckt set up a secret "flying group" for planning purposes within the RWM under an officer named Wilberg. About 180 other experienced flying officers were taken into the Reichswehr and carefully distributed throughout the RWM and the *Wehrkreise*. Furthermore, another wartime flier (Brandenburg) was put in charge of aviation within the government Office of Air Transport, so that civil aviation could develop in accordance with military needs.

Finally, and although the primary emphasis was on quality and technique, Seeckt also took such steps as he could to evade the Treaty restrictions on the Army's size. A number of ir-regular and illegal formations—the so-called "Black Reichs-wehr"—were clandestinely maintained in the *Wehrkreise* bordering on Poland. In the handling and concealment from Allied notice of these units, Oberstleutnant Fedor von Bock (then Chief of Staff of Wehrkreis III) played a leading part.

Less sinister at first glance but of more importance in the long run was Seeckt's use of the civilian police as a reservoir of trained man-power. Many combat-hardened officers who could not be taken into the Reichswehr put on police uniforms, and organized the police forces (*Landespolizei*) and frontier guards (*Grenzpolizei*) along military lines. The ex-officers and thou-sands of police recruits were to swell the officers' corps and the ranks after Hitler's repudiation of the Versailles Treaty in 1935. The significance of the militarized police and the calibre

of the police officers may be gauged from the fact that some of them became corps and divisional generals during the war, and many others were selected for General Staff training, and successfully filled General Staff assignments.

In domestic politics, Seeckt's cardinal rule was that the Reichswehr should not stake its prestige on the fortunes of any political party or coalition, nor should individual officers openly engage in party politics. The Army was to hold itself aloof from and above partisan matters, and constitute itself guardian of the unity and interest of the entire nation. Political adventurism was particularly discouraged; military participation in the Kapp–Luettwitz *Putsch* nearly split the Army, and it reaped little credit from the officers' part in the Hitler–Ludendorff Beer-Hall *Putsch* at Munich in 1923.

But it should not be inferred from the foregoing that the Army had no political attitude. On the contrary, Seeckt sought to dominate politics within the range of issues of special concern to the Army, and to draw in his wake the chancellors and ministers who appeared and disappeared at such short intervals, regardless of their party affiliations. The Army was a political fact of the first magnitude, and Seeckt constantly engaged in political manœuvres, in both the domestic and the foreign spheres. Sedulously and skilfully, Seeckt contrived to inspire, among the leading figures of all parties, a feeling that the Republic's continued existence was dependent upon the Reichswehr's favour or, at least, its toleration.

In foreign affairs, Seeckt's policies were anti-Polish and— superficially incongruous—pro-Russian. That the officers' corps was reactionary, aristocratic and violently anti-Communist in domestic politics did not obstruct this pro-Soviet orientation. Since the Army's principal purpose was to scuttle the Versailles Treaty, Seeckt sought alliance with the one major European power that had no interest in upholding it. The Treaty of Rapallo, signed by Germany and the Soviet Union in April, 1922, set the official seal upon the informal collaboration which already had been embarked on by the military chieftains of the two countries.

Neither Seeckt's domestic political "impartiality" nor his Russophile foreign diplomacy was an end in itself. The former was to give the Reichswehr the desired stability, and the latter to provide the necessary opportunity to commence at once the process of clandestine rearmament. And it was to the furtherance of this process by every means and on every occasion that

Seeckt, cautious in his tactics but bold in his conceptions, dedicated himself unswervingly and devotedly.

Of course, it should not be supposed that these and other elements of the Reichswehr strategy were conceived in the brain of Seeckt alone. Nor, indeed, was his the weightiest personal influence with the public or even in the officers' corps. Always in the background was the shadow of the *alte Herr*, von Hindenburg. When the venerable field-marshal re-emerged on the world stage as President, it became the fashion to regard him as a benevolent, patriarchal symbol of the homely German virtues who, in his old age, had revealed the amazing modernity of outlook to throw his vast prestige behind the Republic. In fact, as has since been amply proven,[5] Hindenburg remained an unreconstructed reactionary, and regarded himself as a trustee of the imperial heritage and the traditions of the officers' corps. And it was Hindenburg, more than any other individual, who rescued the Army from the discredit and even odium which the defeat might otherwise have cast upon it.

Less than ten months after the armistice, in his speech on the anniversary of Tannenberg, Germany's greatest hero of the time exhorted German youth "not to lose the spirit of the great age" of Moltke, for 1919 was a "meek and spineless" time. A few weeks later his memoirs were published, in which the myth that the German Army was not broken but betrayed found expression in the Wagnerian simile: "Like Siegfried, stricken down by the teacherous spear of savage Hagen, our weary front collapsed." And in November, 1919, Hindenburg, openly and insolently flouting the authority and procedures of the parliamentary Committee of Inquiry (into the causes of Germany's defeat), publicly launched the "stab-in-the-back" legend in those very words, and threw behind it the full weight of his name and fame. "The good kernel of the Army bears no guilt," he declared; "its achievement is just as worthy of wonderment as that of the officers' corps." The enemy's numerical superiority had made the struggle a most unequal one but, despite these terrible odds, the Army, if loyally supported, could have brought it to a "favourable conclusion". As for the defeat, "it is plain enough upon whom the blame lies". The selfishness of civilian politicians had betrayed the Army's gallant efforts: "partisan interests came to the fore" and "made themselves felt at the front". This failure on the home front led inevitably to military collapse, and the revolution was the "last straw".

These few phrases must rank among the most politically effective words ever uttered, and their echoes have not yet died away. In a few moments, Hindenburg set a mood which was to endure for decades. By restoring the officers' corps to its former proud estate and pointing the finger of shame, if not of treason, at the civilian politicians and officials, he fostered a climate of opinion, prejudice and legend which greatly facilitated Seeckt's task. And six years later, as a President of the Reich who was also a retired field-marshal and dean of the officers' corps, Hindenburg's presence and authority assured the preservation of a political milieu in which Seeckt's less talented (Heye) and less energetic (Hammerstein) successors could carry forward the reconstruction of the Army.

THE REICHSWEHR AND THE *PUTSCHE*

The isolation of the Army from the political vicissitudes and crises of the Weimar Republic was not effected without some difficulty. Even after Seeckt was firmly in the saddle there remained a fringe of "activist" reactionaries in the officers' corps who were always ready to support a rightist *Putsch*. It was, in fact, military participation in the so-called Kapp–Luettwitz *Putsch* of March, 1920, that demonstrated the danger of such adventurism to the unity and prestige of the Reichswehr, and brought Seeckt to the top as *Chef der Heeresleitung*.

This interesting little revolt was precipitated by the process of reducing the Army to the strength of 100,000 fixed by the Versailles Treaty—a process to be completed by March 31, 1920. Early that month the *Reichswehrministerium* issued orders to General Walther von Luettwitz, in command of Gruppenkommando 1 near Berlin, to disband a marine brigade led by a notorious "*Freikorps*" captain named Ehrhardt. Luettwitz flatly refused to obey this order; he associated himself with a fanatically nationalist civilian official named Kapp, and during the night of March 12–13 the Ehrhardt brigade marched on Berlin. President Ebert and the cabinet had to flee Berlin to avoid arrest, going to Dresden and then to Stuttgart. Ebert at once called for a general strike to combat the revolt, and the resultant paralysis of communications and utilities, together with the disorganization of and lack of preparation for the *Putsch*, caused its prompt collapse on March 17th.

From a military standpoint, the significance of this affair was not merely the participation of a number of high-ranking generals, including both Luettwitz (one of the most senior

generals) and Ludendorff, who emerged from retirement to take part. Far more significant was the behaviour of von Seeckt and a number of others. For even though they did not align themselves with Luettwitz,[6] their support of the government and the Republic was anything but militant. When it was learned that the Ehrhardt brigade was marching on Berlin, the civilian Minister of Defence (Noske) requested General Walther Reinhardt (then the *Chef der Heeresleitung*) and von Seeckt (Chief of the *Truppenamt*) to call out loyal Army troops to defend the government. Reinhardt, it appears, was not unwilling but von Seeckt's opposition carried the day: "Reichswehr will never shoot at Reichswehr." For Seeckt saw the affair not as a revolt against the lawfully constituted authorities but as a threat to the unity of the Army. As long as the success or failure of Luettwitz' *coup* hung in the balance, he stood aside and flatly refused to use Army troops against those of Luettwitz and Ehrhardt. "Would you force a battle at the Brandenburger Tor between troops who, a year and a half ago, were fighting shoulder to shoulder against the enemy?" he asked Noske.

So the soldiers of the *Putsch* entered Berlin unopposed, and occupied the public buildings, including the Ministry of Defence. So far from treating this conduct as rebellion or even insubordination, Seeckt acted as if it were a mere petty annoyance. He and Reinhardt "retired to their homes" because, as Seeckt's deputy (Heye) expressed it, "they were unable to carry out their official duties while there was a revolt in Berlin". They gave no information or instructions to the military district commanders, and no directions to their subordinates at the Ministry of Defence, some of whom (including von Schleicher, then a major) also withdrew to their homes, while others (like Heye) remained to carry on their routine work, shutting their eyes to the somewhat unusual events going on around them.

When the *Putsch* collapsed, one might have supposed that the loyalty of those who had supported the Republic would be recognized, and the rebels suitably castigated for their treasonable conduct. On the contrary, Noske, who had pressed the generals to show the true mettle of their devotion to the Republic, was let out of the Ministry of Defence and replaced by the Bavarian Otto Gessler, who, during the eight years that he held this office, proved a faithful civilian collaborator in the Army's clandestine rearmament. Reinhardt, who had been willing to lend active support to the government, was replaced as *Chef der Heeresleitung* by von Seeckt, who had set a higher

value on the Reichswehr's unity than on the Republic's fate. Seeckt promptly gave orders that Luettwitz, Ehrhardt and the other mutinous officers should be allowed to escape.* Scheidemann's demands for "a thorough cleansing" of the Reichswehr, and the appointment of Grzesinski to succeed Noske, were not fulfilled. On the face of things the *Putsch* had failed and the Republic had prevailed, but in fact it was the Reichswehr that emerged victorious from the fray.

The Ehrhardt brigade, which received the mildest of reprimands from Seeckt, wore the swastika on their helmets. This proved a prophetic touch, for the next rightist uprising was Adolf Hitler's first and unsuccessful bid for power at Munich on November 9, 1923. Compared to the Kapp–Luettwitz affair, Hitler's march on the *Feldherrnhalle* was, at the time, of insignificant proportions. Many prominent Reichswehr officers, however, were involved with Hitler, who had been employed soon after the end of the war as an Army intelligence agent, and who picked up considerable support among the extremists of the officers' corps as the National Socialist movement grew.

Some of these officers, like Ernst Roehm, Konstantin Hierl and Generalmajor Ritter von Epp, became part of Hitler's personal entourage. The ubiquitous Ludendorff turned up again, and marched with (and more courageously than) Hitler on the 9th of November. But the "Beer-Hall *Putsch*" would never have been attempted but for the promised collaboration of the *Wehrkreis* commander,[7] General von Lossow, and the Munich commandant, Colonel von Seisser. At the last moment von Lossow deserted the Hitler cause, and his defection resulted in its prompt collapse. But von Lossow's later explanation[8] of his pro-Nazi connivings goes far to explain why, despite the deep social gulf between Nazism and the officers' corps, they were able to make common cause: "We had realized that there was a healthy kernel in the Hitler movement. We saw the healthy kernel in the fact that the movement possessed the power to make converts among the workers for the cause of nationalism." If the German generals were ever again to lead a mass army, this power of conversion was a *sine qua non.*

* In December, 1926, a German court awarded Luettwitz his arrears of pension payments, even for the period during which he was an active rebel or (subsequently) a fugitive from justice. Reinhardt, who was younger than Seeckt and had been junior in rank before his elevation in 1919, did not retire from the Army. He was appointed Commander in Wehrkreis V (Stuttgart), and later (1924–27) commanded Gruppenkommando 2 at Kassel, after which he retired from active service.

The workaday lives of archivists, librarians and historians in the Soviet Union must indeed be perplexing and disheartening. The past must be constantly moulded to fit the preconceptions of the present; like the famous "vanishing islands" of the South Seas, great historical episodes disappear, or are synthesized into reality or transmuted beyond recognition. Orwell's piercing imagination has caught up the stifling and terrifying milieu of thought control and "doublethink" in his masterly caricature of dictatorship, *Nineteen Eighty-Four*.

So it is far from certain that we shall ever know the full scope of Soviet Russia's contribution to German rearmament during the years of the Weimar Republic. It was an episode of deep historical significance, but carefully hidden from the public view. Some hints of what was going on leaked out at the time, but the pages of this story have remained uncut until very recently, and even now only a few of its chapters have been opened to the historian's gaze by means of the Seeckt papers. Since it was necessary in the interests of secrecy for the German end of the business to be handled with a minimum amount of documentation, it is unlikely that we shall get the full story unless some twist of the political wheel enables us to scan the Soviet state archives, or persuades the masters of the Kremlin that publication of the documents covering military collaboration with the Germans would serve the Soviet Union's political interests.

But from the Seeckt papers and other scattered sources the main elements of the undertaking can be examined.[9] Even before the Kapp *Putsch*, when Seeckt was chief of the *Truppenamt*, he had expressed the view that a "future understanding with Greater Russia" ought to be "the permanent target of Germany's foreign policy", and upon taking office as *Chef der Heeresleitung* he lost no time in setting the wheels in motion. His initial approaches to Moscow were made through the Turkish leader Enver Bey, whom Seeckt had known during his wartime tour of duty in Turkey. The Russians were not unreceptive to these advances, and in the latter part of 1920 a special and secret office for Russian affairs, known as *Sondergruppe R*, was set up in the *Reichswehrministerium*. A military mission was then sent to open direct negotiations in Moscow, comprised of a former German military attaché in Russia (Oberstleutnant Schubert), a trusted agent of Seeckt (Major

Fritz Tschunke, who had served under Seeckt in the Baltic in 1919), and a talented Bavarian staff officer who had specialized in Asiatic studies, Oskar von Niedermayer. This interesting character was (like his fellow Bavarian colleague, the famous Haushofer) a curious combination of soldier and geographer. He had travelled widely in Asia before the war, and in time he was entrusted with virtual management of the German Army's interests in Russia.

At the outset, there were many obstacles to be overcome, and the negotiations which preceded actual military collaboration between the Red Army and the Reichswehr were correspondingly protracted. In September, 1921, Leonid Krassin was in Berlin carrying on discussions with Seeckt and Oberst Otto Hasse (one of Seeckt's chief staff assistants, who succeeded Heye as Chief of the *Truppenamt* in 1923), as well as Niedermayer and Schleicher. Complete secrecy was vital, and many of the meetings with Russian representatives in Berlin were held in von Schleicher's private apartment.

In the meantime, Seeckt set out to win over to his point of view several of the leading politicians of the day and made considerable headway, especially with Dr. Josef Wirth, at various times Chancellor and Minister of Finance. Early in 1922, Karl Radek visited Berlin to solicit German assistance in the expansion of Russian war industries and to promote military talks on a General Staff level. In April, 1922, Tchitcherin (then the Soviet Union's Foreign Minister) came to Berlin to confer with Chancellor Wirth, and out of these talks developed the famous Treaty of Rapallo, concluded April 16, 1922, by Wirth, Rathenau, and Tchitcherin. This manifestation of Russo-German friendship at the diplomatic level was most welcome to Seeckt, and the negotiations looking to military arrangements were pursued with renewed vigour.

The Rapallo Treaty, however, encountered considerable Socialist opposition, including that of President Ebert, and even among the Treaty's supporters were many who wished to proceed more cautiously than Seeckt, and were (or would have been if informed) opposed to military collaboration. Even the newly chosen German Ambassador to Russia, Count Brockdorff-Rantzau, was strongly opposed to Seeckt's programme. In a memorandum to Chancellor Wirth of July 15, 1922, he argued that the time had not yet arrived for making a final choice between east and west, such as a military alliance with the Soviet would involve. "Any hint of our forming military

ties with the east would have the most unfavourable effect upon our relations with the west," he declared, and went on to argue that ultimately England would seek allies on the Continent to balance the power of the French. Not only would a Soviet-German alliance preclude the more desirable possibility of an Anglo-German pact; the socialist parties would reject any such military adventurism, and common prudence ruled out military obligations which "would put us at the mercy of the wholly unscrupulous Soviet government". If Russia should then attack Poland, Germany would be defenceless against France, would be "exposed to an assault by the French vassal states" in the south (Czechoslovakia) and in the north, including, "now that it has swallowed the fat morsel of North Schleswig, that yellow dog, Denmark", and in the end Germany "would provide the battlefield for the conflict between east and west". In conclusion, Brockdorff-Rantzau counselled against " military adventures", even though more "sober" policies were "unlikely to satisfy the optimistic and intemperate daredevils in our ranks".

Even without this final cutting remark, the tenor of the Count's memorandum was well calculated to arouse Seeckt, to whom Wirth showed it early in September, 1922. His reaction was a comprehensive essay entitled "Germany's Position on the Russian Problem" and dated September 11th, which is an historical jewel of the first water. "Germany must practise active politics", was his opening gambit, and he pointed to Talleyrand's successful manœuvrings on behalf of a prostrate France in 1815, and to Russia's and Turkey's aggressive policies hard on the heels of disaster and defeat in 1918. The only solid foundation for diplomacy was a hard-bitten *Realpolitik*: "We must assume that the policies of every state are egotistical and must examine how we may exploit the interests of the others to the advantage of our own people." He agreed with Brockdorff-Rantzau that England's traditional pursuit of the Continental "balance of power" would eventually bring her to a search for allies against France, but Seeckt scoffed at the Count's fears that a Russo-German tie would repel the British. On the contrary, such a tie constituted an "increment of strength" for Germany, and England would prefer "the mercenary whose strength is returning" and would be governed far more by fear of neighbouring France than "the remote danger of a Russia strengthened by Germany's aid". Anyhow, no "unilaterally binding military agreement" with Russia was

contemplated. The aim was to strengthen Russia economically, and "to strengthen ourselves directly by helping to build up a useful armaments industry in Russia" beyond the pale of Versailles "which will serve us in case of need".

Brockdorff-Rantzau's other arguments were all swept aside. There was no real danger that Germany would find herself a battleground; neither France nor Russia could march across Germany to engage the other without German help. Socialist opposition was merely disgusting. To be sure, "the foolish cry 'No more war!' has . . . certainly re-echoed in various pacifistic middle-class circles", but "to practise politics means to lead", and "in spite of all, the German people will follow the leader in the fight for its existence". Brockdorff-Rantzau's jibe about "intemperate daredevils" was dearly repaid. "Anyone who . . . insists that Germany has permanently renounced all imperialistic and military aspirations (which, stripped of the demagogic phraseology, means any active policy whatever) is not fitted to represent German interests in Russia. Perhaps nowhere." And in conclusion: "If war should eventuate—and today it already seems tangibly close—it will not be the task of leading statesmen among us to keep Germany out of the conflict, for that will be either vain or suicidal, but to throw our weight as strongly as possible on the right side."

The momentous issues thus hotly debated were not, until several years later, so much as mentioned in the Reichstag. Under cover of the strictest secrecy, Seeckt went ahead, with the tacit approval of the successive chancellors and the support of secret subsidies from the Reich treasury. Under the auspices of *Sondergruppe R*, a company was established in Berlin and Moscow under the innocent name "Society for the Promotion of Industrial Enterprises", and known (from its German initials) as "GEFU".[10] Schleicher was increasingly prominent in the planning and negotiations with the Russians in Berlin, while Tschunke and Niedermayer promoted in Moscow the projects which the Ambassador, Brockdorff-Rantzau, had viewed with so jaundiced an eye. Ambitious plans for the production of Junkers airplanes at a factory near Moscow, and of poison gas at a plant to be built at Samara, did not fully materialize, but in other respects the "accomplishments" were impressive indeed. Large quantities of artillery ammunition were manufactured, under German technical supervision, at plants in the Urals and near Leningrad (including the famous Putilov works). Schools for the training of airplane pilots and tank crews

were opened, and a stream of German officers went to Russia to learn to use these and other (such as heavy artillery) Versailles-banned weapons. Extensive personal and professional contacts between the upper levels of the Red Army and the Reichswehr were the natural concomitant of these activities, and one may be as sure that the Germans did not overlook the opportunity, emphasized in a later memorandum by Tschunke, "to get direct information about the Red Army, its composition, equipment, training, and so on", as that the Russians were equally alert to answer opportunity's knock.

In a speech to the Reichstag in 1926, the veteran Social Democrat Scheidemann's revelation of the existence and general purposes of GEFU proved, as Tschunke described it, "a heavy blow to my work". The manufacturing activities were soon suspended, but collaboration in the strictly military field continued, and Russian orders for German industrial equipment greatly benefited the economy of the Ruhr and other industrial areas and thus indirectly contributed to the German military potential. Even Hitler's accession to power in 1933 did not put an end to this honeymoon; Hitler was not yet strong enough to override the wishes of the generals, and not until after the repudiation of the Treaty of Versailles had ended the era of clandestine German rearmament did Soviet Russia's great (and too little known) contribution to the resurgence of the Wehrmacht come to an end.

But Seeckt's calculated Russophilism had more specific and sinister aims than the strengthening of the Wehrmacht. In the memorandum quoted above, the future victim of Russo-German collaboration was named and marked down to be murdered. "Poland is the heart of the eastern problem," wrote the "Sphinx", and drove ruthlessly to his terrible conclusion: "Poland's existence is intolerable, incompatible with the essential conditions of Germany's life. Poland must go and will go—as a result of her own internal weakness and of action by Russia—with our aid. For Russia, Poland is even more intolerable than she is for us; no Russian government can abide the existence of Poland. With the disappearance of Poland will fall one of the strongest pillars of the Versailles Peace, the hegemony of France." The obliteration of Poland, declared Seeckt, "must be one of the fundamental drives of German policy", and "is attainable, by means of and with the help of Russia". Poland's extinction, it thus appears, was to be the immediate fruit of the Rapallo policy: "The re-establishment of

the former border between Germany and Russia is essential for the recovery of both countries. Russia and Germany must return to the borders of 1914! This should be the basis of an agreement between the two countries. This attitude of Germany's toward Poland need not be an anxiously guarded secret. An explanation of it to Russia could only have the effect of stimulating Russia's confidence in Germany. Poland's hostility to Germany could not possibly be made more intense that it now is."

These implacable pronouncements were at once echoes and harbingers. One hundred and fifty years earlier "Old Fritz" had joined with Catherine the Great and Maria Theresa in the first "partition" of Poland. Seventeen years later Poland's corpse, still hot and quivering, was torn in two by von Brauchitsch's legions and the Red Army. In this woeful *dénouement* Seeckt's hopes and predictions for the future of Rapallo found their fulfilment. Hitler and Stalin had accomplished in ten days what had taken twenty-three years in the evening of the more leisurely eighteenth century. And once again in 1949, twenty-seven years after Seeckt wrote, as whisperings of German rearmament became increasingly audible, the Polish Army found itself under a new commander-in-chief. His name was Rokossovsky, Marshal of the Soviet Union.

THE REICHSWEHR AND KRUPP

If von Seeckt thus felt obliged to seek new and strange friends abroad, it by no means follows that the Army was deserted by all its old associates at home. Foremost among these, and quite as tenacious and intransigent as the Reichswehr, was the famous steel and munitions enterprise of the Krupp family. And though the Krupp lineage was not as ancient or aristocratic as that of the officers' corps, both institutions derived their modern prestige and perquisites from the same heritage. For Alfred Krupp built his first shop for the manufacture of guns at Essen in 1861, and his fame and fortune came from the same series of wars that raised Moltke to Valhalla. The victorious German armies were extensively armed with Krupp guns, and after the Franco-Prussian War Alfred Krupp was commonly called the "cannon king".

With the expansion of their steel mills, the acquisition of coal and iron-ore mines, and the purchase of the Germania shipyards at Kiel, the Krupps became the foremost tycoons of German heavy industry. When the male line gave out at the

turn of the century, the wedding of the heiress-apparent (Bertha Krupp) to Gustav von Bohlen und Halbach was celebrated under imperial auspices, and the dynastic import of the Krupp name was recognized when the Emperor conferred on the bridegroom the right to add it to his own. During the First World War, Krupp's was Germany's main arsenal, and when Ludendorff called for two outstanding industrial leaders to "join his train" and discuss war production, the two invited were Gustav Krupp von Bohlen und Halbach and Carl Duisberg of the gigantic I.G. Farben chemicals combine.

At the close of the war, the Krupp armament plants were running full blast, and the manufacture and repair of guns continued right up to the arrival of Allied Control Commission representatives at Essen in 1920. But under the Versailles Treaty provisions for the control of arms manufacture, Krupp was restricted (as from July 15, 1921) to the manufacture of a single type of gun (calibre exceeding 17 centimetres). Under the supervision of the Control Commission, thousands of Krupp machines and tools for munitions-making were destroyed. These events raised a crucial question of management policy, thus stated in a subsequent Krupp memorandum: "Our firm had to decide whether it wanted to renounce, for all time, the production of war material. . . . Krupp decided, as trustee of a historical inheritance, to safeguard its valuable experience, irreplaceable for the military potential of our nation, and . . . to keep the shop and personnel in readiness if the occasion should arise for armament orders later on."

The story of how the Krupp directors carried out this fateful decision would require another book. The old joke about the Krupp baby carriages which, if once taken apart, could only be reassembled as machine-guns, is not too far-fetched; as Gustav Krupp later boasted, "To the surprise of many people, Krupp began to manufacture products which really appeared to be far distant from the previous work of an armament plant. Even the Allied snooping commissions were duped. Padlocks, cash registers, track repair machines, dustcarts and similar 'small junk' appeared really unsuspicious. . . ." Krupp's clandestine activities were, as a private letter of former Chancellor Josef Wirth reveals, secretly approved by Hindenburg and subsidized by the Weimar Republic's treasury as early as 1921.

Chancellors and finance ministers blessed these mysterious goings-on, but their direct guidance was the preserve of von

Seeckt and his naval opposite number, Admiral Paul Behnke. The Admiral's chief concern was to keep abreast of the developments in the designing of submarines. To this end, and with Behnke's approval, in 1922 Krupp set up a dummy Dutch company known as the "I.v.S." (Ingenieur-Kantoor voor Scheepsbouw) to continue the submarine developmental work theretofore carried out at its Germania shipyards at Kiel. Under instructions from the German Admiralty (*Marineleitung*) "to keep together an efficient German submarine bureau, and, by practical work for foreign navies, keep in constant practice and on top of technical developments", this Dutch branch of Krupp not only built and sold submarines to foreign governments, but so successfully circumvented the anti-submarine clauses of the Versailles Treaty that the rapid construction of a large and up-to-date submarine arm was readily possible as soon as Hitler openly repudiated the Treaty.

In the case of artillery, too, Krupp's first move was to seek a foreign base for the prohibited experimental work. Arrangements were made in 1921 with the Swedish firm of Bofors whereby Krupp designs were used for the manufacture of guns at the Bofors plants, to which Krupp employees and Reichswehr officers were allowed access. Arms, however, can be developed and tested more secretly than submarines, and Krupp's forbidden activities in the artillery field were domestic as well as foreign. They were conducted pursuant to a secret agreement between Krupp and the *Reichswehrministerium*, which provided for exchange of technical data and envisaged that Krupp would carry on developmental work on guns and tanks for the Army. As a Krupp memorandum states: "These most significant agreements of January 25, 1922, were the first step taken by the *Reichswehrministerium* and Krupp jointly to circumvent . . . the provisions of the Treaty of Versailles which strangled Germany's military freedom."

When the French occupied the Ruhr, Krupp's artillery design department was removed to Berlin, where, in 1925, the *Heeresleitung* established a dummy corporation called Kock & Kienzle to camouflage the true nature of the work. But when the Allied Control Commission departed from Germany early in 1927, the work was soon moved back to Essen; this event was hailed in the Krupp files as "an important step on the road towards freedom". Thereafter Krupp extended its developmental work for the Army to the field of tank design and other types of military vehicles and self-propelled guns.

During the period of clandestine rearmament the arrangements between Krupp and the *Reichswehrministerium* could not constitute an official contract; as a Krupp memorandum explains, "for political reasons" the relation was only "a gentlemen's agreement between General Wurtzbacher and Captain (Naval) Hansen on the one hand, and Directors Bauer and Oesterlein (of Krupp) on the other hand". Informal as it was, however, the alliance was ratified at the highest levels. In November, 1925, Gustav Krupp arranged a four-day tour by von Seeckt through the Krupp plant at Essen and other leading Ruhr industrial establishments. Seeckt brought the steel barons up to date with "timely information" on the Reichswehr's rearmament programme, and an "inner circle" discussed with Seeckt the possibility of producing tanks at the Bofors plant in Sweden, as well as a project for moving a substantial part of the munitions industry from the Ruhr to central Germany.

In addition to Seeckt and the Krupp officials, these and other ideas were carefully examined by leaders such as August Thyssen, Ernst Poensgen, and Albert Voegler, and several senior generals, including Otto Hasse and Wetzell (successive chiefs of the *Truppenamt* from 1923 to 1926), and the Chief of the Army Ordnance Office (*Waffenamt*), Generalleutnant Wurtzbacher. After this excursion, Seeckt remarked on the "obliging" attitude of the Ruhr magnates toward the Army's aims, as well as the "correct" attitude of the workers who observed the visitation of high brass. Small enough these first steps toward rearmament must have seemed at the time, but all in all things were beginning to look up again for the Reichswehr, and Seeckt's energy and determination were well balanced with patience.

THE FALL OF VON SEECKT

So, with consummate skill, Seeckt conducted his covert campaign. Domestic opposition was ruthlessly dealt with. When the eminent German scholar and humanitarian Quidde expressed concern over clandestine rearmament, Seeckt promptly threatened him with action "on the basis of emergency powers, and this regardless of whether or not a proceeding for high treason would be instituted". It is perhaps superfluous to note that rearmament and secret mobilization plans violated not only the Versailles Treaty but the domestic law of Germany as well. As a Reichswehr judge advocate put it, the

Treaty was "a law of the Reich", and therefore "binding on all members of the Reich", and furthermore, its provisions "rank even superior to those of the Reich Constitution". Officers who connived at violations of the Treaty, therefore, "could be indicted . . . for culpable violation of their official duties". Their participation in clandestine rearmament or unlawful preparations for mobilization was intramurally justified as "necessary from the point of view of the Fatherland", although "contrary to law". Therefore "high-ranking officers did not participate openly, so that they did not have to bear the odium of a conscious breach of the law. In important fundamental matters they issued directions *sub rosa* to individual confidential agents".

But rough weather lay ahead for the secret designs of the officers' corps—storms which were to prove fatal to Seeckt's personal career. Little known outside Germany, his first five years of supreme military command had nevertheless brought him immense national prestige, and when Ebert died suddenly in February, 1925, Seeckt, despite his aloof and contemptuous attitude toward the politicians, was even considered as a presidential candidate. But such ambition, if in fact cherished by Seeckt, was not fulfilled. Swayed by the wily coaxings of the almost equally septuagenarian and venerable von Tirpitz, the seventy-eight-year-old Hero of Tannenberg emerged from retirement and embarked upon his "third life". After Hindenburg's accession, the constitutional designation of the President as Commander-in-Chief of the Armed Forces was clothed with reality, and Seeckt (who had not been one of Hindenburg's wartime favourites) was inevitably thrown into the shade. At the same time, the policies of Stresemann (Foreign Minister since September, 1923, and the most prescient of the nationalist politicians) began to bear fruit in the progressive Allied evacuation of the Rhineland and the withdrawal of the Inter-Allied Control Commission. When the British troops departed from Cologne early in 1926, it was Hindenburg, not Seeckt, who made the ceremonial entry, and it was Stresemann, not Seeckt, who was the architect of this triumph. All of this weakened Seeckt's position and his ability to weather political crises.

Seeckt passed from the national scene with startling suddenness in the autumn of 1926, as the result of a stupid blunder. Quite possibly against his own better judgment, Seeckt had been persuaded to allow William, eldest son of the Crown Prince and thus in line of succession to his grandfather the Kaiser, to appear in uniform at exercises of the aristocratic

Ninth (Potsdam) Infantry Regiment. Apart from the strong monarchistic implications of this affair, it was a clear if technical violation of the Treaty of Versailles, which required that all Reichswehr officers serve for twenty-four years. Newspaper rumours aroused criticism and demands for an investigation from the Social Democrats and other liberal elements in the Reichstag. Seeckt submitted his resignation, which Hindenburg formally accepted a few days later, on October 9, 1926.

In this episode there seemed to be more than met the eye, and its true inwardness has never been fully exposed. According to press accounts, Seeckt had not informed Gessler (the Minister of War) about the matter, and Gessler, angry at being thus slighted, insisted that Seeckt be sacrificed to placate the Social Democrats. Seeckt himself thought the cause lay deeper. In a memorandum written a few days after his dismissal [11] he opined: "On reflection, I am convinced that the affair of the Prince was the excuse rather than the reason for my dismissal. . . . What was the reason? The conflict between the democratic parliamentary system and a personality not inwardly dependent upon it, and finally the unbridgeable conflict between the representative of the old Germany (and the superior position of its Army) and the concept of the republican-parliamentary civil power." Seeckt also lent substance to the view that Schleicher had a hand in the affair. But whatever the real story may have been, Seeckt's precipitous tumble from the heights was another striking demonstration that even the most brilliant German generals are too often found wanting in political sagacity.

Within the perfervid milieu of Weimar, Seeckt's mischance was symptomatic as well as sensational. Even the massive living legend of Hindenburg had barely carried him into the presidency over the liberal-centrist coalition behind Marx, the Chancellor at the time of Seeckt's debacle. The Social Democrats remained the largest single party, and tough and courageous Socialists like Scheidemann and Grzesinski were active and vocal. Less than two months after Seeckt's retirement, Scheidemann (the Weimar Republic's first Chancellor) electrified the Reichstag (December 16, 1926) with an attack on Gessler and the Reichswehr, charging that illegal rearmament was going on in collaboration with Russia, and exposing the receipt of Russian-manufactured munitions at Stettin. The nationalist deputies did not attempt to deny Scheidemann's accusations, but left the chamber in a body, crying "Traitor"

and "Why reveal these things to our enemies". Scheidemann's motion of "no confidence" brought down the Marx cabinet, and the Reichswehr found itself so much on the defensive as to require radical contraction of its Russian adventures.

Throughout 1927 the officers' corps hovered on the brink of exposure and discredit. The notorious *Fehme* murder trials revealed the implacable and murderous anti-Republicanism that permeated its ranks; liberal politicians attacked its aristocratic and monarchistic predilections. Scheidemann, his face already seared by acid thrown by would-be assassins at the time of the Rathenau and Erzberger murders, received hundreds of death-threats from nationalistic fanatics.

Towards the end of the year, the Navy came in for its share of criticism from the left, as a result of the so-called "Lohmann exposures". Walter Lohmann, son of a former president of the North German Lloyd, was a German naval officer and extreme nationalist who, since 1920, had headed the transportation division of the *Marineleitung*; in 1922 he attained the rank of *Kapitaen zur See*, and at the time his financial adventures were disclosed was the sixteenth ranking officer in the German Navy.* He was a skilful and aggressive negotiator and manipulator, and in 1920 Admiral Behnke (*Chef der Marineleitung*) entrusted him with the administration of the Navy's "special funds". Through dummy corporations financed with these secret funds, Lohmann conducted extensive experimental work with motor launches, from which the mine-sweepers and famous German "E-boats" of the war developed; later these activities were extended to Spain, under the King's personal sponsorship. E-boats led to oil-tanker construction, and soon Lohmann was branching out with Van Sweringen-like audacity. A large investment of Navy funds in the Phœbus Film Company was made to procure a vehicle for pan-German propaganda and a cover for foreign intelligence agents, and thereafter Lohmann plunged in real estate, iron-ore mines and finally bacon! In August, 1927, misfortune began to overtake this zealot, who apparently reaped no personal profit from these transactions and was governed throughout by a misguided and incredibly intense chauvinism.

The Lohmann disclosures resulted not only in the unfortunate captain's dismissal; far bigger heads soon rolled. In January, 1928, accumulated pressure from the left finally forced the

* Under the Versailles restrictions the German Navy boasted only twelve Admirals of all grades, and Lohmann was the fourth ranking captain.

resignation of Gessler as *Reichswehrminister*, and in September Admiral Zenker, who had succeeded Behnke as *Chef* in 1924 and who had personally approved some of Lohmann's fliers, thought it best to take his departure. Thus, within less than two years, Seeckt, Zenker and Gessler were all obliged to walk the plank. The tenure of two of their successors—Heye and Groener—was destined to be short, while that of Admiral Erich Raeder was to endure for fifteen years, until the ebb of the Nazi tide in 1943.

Within Germany these events loomed large, as does Seeckt's fall in historical perspective. But their immediate impact on world opinion was negligible. The spirit of Locarno was abroad, and Stresemann's astute salesmanship made it unfashionable to maintain a reserved attitude towards the Weimar regime. In the United States the financial boom was getting fairly launched, and these scattered clouds on the international horizon attracted little attention and awakened no alarm. After Scheidemann's sensational exposure of the Reichswehr's Russian connections, the *Baltimore Sun* was moved to murmur comfortably that "all of the information that Scheidemann has blurted out in the Reichstag has, beyond doubt, been in the hands of the statesmen of the Allied nations". In England, the *New Statesman* went much further, and roundly declared that France was a more fit subject for inspection of military activities than Germany; there was "no conceivable reason from the British point of view why Germany should not possess as many airplanes as France".

A few days later, the German press reported the story of two German socialist workmen who had spent the winter and spring of 1926 constructing a factory near Samara in Russia for the manufacture of phosgene and mustard gas. The fabulous Major Tschunke and other German officers had been seen at the building site, and the workmen had been paid off by the Wehrmacht's GEFU. But the interesting news that the Germans were preparing to make poison gas in Russia, while Stresemann was launching Locarno and inducing the Allies to withdraw the Control Commission and evacuate the Rhineland, caused hardly a ripple on the placid, sunny international waters. Thus did the very surge of internationalism and pacifism, which emboldened Scheidemann and his fellow socialists in the Reichstag to speak out, smother their own revelations and warnings under a blanket of indifference and good will.

The resignation of Seeckt* left the officers' corps with no dominant personality to guide its destinies. Seeckt himself took to his pen and produced a series of works (military reflections and histories and a *Life of Moltke*) of no great profundity. In the early thirties he went to China as a military adviser to the Chiang government, but he never resumed an active role in Germany, and remained in retirement until his death at the end of 1936. His successor as *Chef der Heeresleitung*, Wilhelm Heye, though not an incompetent officer, was totally unsuited to wear the mantle of von Seeckt. Junior in rank to half a dozen other generals,† he was also a commoner, and not the type to win leadership within the corps. Pompous but rather benevolent, he was known in the Army, with mingled affection and condescension, as "the good uncle".

Heye had served on Hindenburg's staff during the war, and was probably his personal selection. Hindenburg, indeed, continued to regard the Reichswehr as his personal preserve, and the more important appointments and major policy matters were reserved for his own decision. But the Hero of Tannenberg was old and preoccupied with political problems to which he was unaccustomed. Furthermore, because of his very limited initiative and imagination, he had always been prone to rely on the creative ability of his favourite subordinates.

It was this last-mentioned weakness of the aged *Reichspraesident* that made possible the spectacular rise of Kurt von Schleicher. As a pre-war subaltern in Hindenburg's old regiment (the Third Foot Guards) he had become a close friend of Hindenburg's son Oskar. At the *Kreigsakademie* his brilliance had greatly impressed Groener, and when the latter succeeded Ludendorff as First Quartermaster-General, Schleicher was selected to be Groener's adjutant. This brought Schleicher into contact with the highest military and political figures of the early Weimar period. Oskar von Hindenburg's friendship gave him constant access to the field-marshal's home during the

* On January 1, 1926, Seeckt had taken the rank of *Generaloberst*, at which he was retired. Ironically, he was later given the honorary right to wear the uniform of the Ninth (Potsdam) Infantry Regiment, in the manœuvres of which Prince William had participated.

† Upon taking office as *Chef*, Heye was promoted from *Generalleutnant* to *General der Infanterie*, with seniority as of December 1, 1924, so as to give him precedence over the two senior *Generale* (Reinhardt and von Poseck), whose rank dated from January 1, 1925. On January 1, 1930, following Seeckt's precedent, Heye took the rank of *Generaloberst*.

period of his retirement. There Schleicher became a great favourite, and with the old man's accession to the presidency, Schleicher (by that time an *Oberstleutnant* and deputy chief of a section within the *Truppenamt*) was presented with unparalleled opportunities for intrigue and personal advancement, which he proceeded to exploit to the full.

Manœuvrer and apple-polisher that he was, Schleicher was phenomenally deft and did not make the mistake of antagonizing or alarming his official superiors by these extra-curricular connections. Furthermore, he was an extremely able staff officer, and Seeckt relied on him for a variety of delicate missions, such as negotiations with the Russians and liaison with the Reichstag. In 1926, Schleicher was made the chief of a newly established office of the *Reichswehrministerium*, designated the Armed Forces Section (*Wehrmachtabteilung*). Into this unit were gathered the "political" functions which Schleicher had been fulfilling in the *Truppenamt* of the *Heeresleitung*, together with the old *Adjutantur* of the Minister, a budget expert and specialists in intelligence, law and the press. In effect, Schleicher became a sort of chief of staff to the *Reichswehrminister* (Gessler), and thus was enabled to parade a ministerial, rather than a purely military, status. The *Wehrmachtabteilung* dealt with naval as well as army affairs, and thus was a precursor of the OKW (High Command of the Wehrmacht) created by Hitler twelve years later.

The growing tension between the Social Democrats and the Reichswehr, leading to the fall of Seeckt, Gessler and Zenker, presented Schleicher with new opportunities. Indeed, Wheeler-Bennett [12] accuses Schleicher of deliberately undermining Seeckt and Gessler through his private contacts with the *Reichspraesident* and son Oskar. [13] However that may be, there is no doubt that Schleicher's influence was greatly widened by their elimination from the scene. From the unambitious Heye, Schleicher had nothing to fear, and Gessler's successor proved to be none other than Schleicher's old patron, Wilhelm Groener, who was completely under the spell of Schleicher's charm, and referred to him affectionately as "my son". Soon after his retirement from the Army, Groener had held office as Minister of Transportation (just following the Kapp–Luettwitz *Putsch*) for several years, but since 1923 he had been in retirement. In January, 1928, Hindenburg was prevailed upon to approve his First Quartermaster-General of eight years past as the new *Reichswehrminister*. Despite a certain naïveté and sus-

ceptibility to Schleicher's wiles, Groener was a most steadfast and incorruptible servant of the Reich; had there been two or three more like him in high places during those critical years, Hitler might never have come to power.

Secure in the favour of both Hindenburg and Groener, Schleicher soon raised his sights. In 1929, Groener established the "Ministry Office" (*Ministeramt*) in the *Reichswehrministerium*, and put Schleicher in charge, with the status of Deputy Minister or Under-secretary (*Staatssekretaer*). The *Ministeramt* included, and was actually a glorified edition of, the *Wehrmachtabteilung*; all political, press and legal matters remained in Schleicher's domain, as well as a special intelligence section headed by his close friend, Oberstleutnant von Bredow.*

Within the Reichswehr itself (in which Schleicher attained the rank of *Generalmajor* on October 1, 1929), however, a major problem remained to be solved. Heye's shortcomings were increasingly apparent, and in 1929 the question of his successor became acute, though he did not actually resign until August, 1930. At the same time a new name was gaining prominence in the top ranks of the Reichswehr—that of the future and first *Feldmarschall* of the Third Reich, Werner von Blomberg. An able staff officer, Blomberg had been in charge of training during the last two years of Seeckt's regime, and soon after Heye's elevation Blomberg became Chief of the *Truppenamt*. No match for Schleicher at political in-fighting, and emotionally unstable, Blomberg was nonetheless a very personable and intelligent man, and Heye looked on him kindly as his heir-apparent.

But Schleicher had other plans. Blomberg was by no means devoid of political inclinations and was far too ambitious to play second fiddle to an officer so much his junior as Schleicher.† Nor would the other eligible senior generals— such as Otto Hasse, von Rundstedt, von Leeb, von Bock or the von Stuelpnagels—be any more likely to bend the knee to this young "desk" general who had never held a field command.

But the master of intrigue was equal to the situation. Once again he pulled his old tricks to get rid of Blomberg, by saddling him with responsibility for certain "illegal border security measures", as Blomberg puts it in his memoirs. Through the

---

* The Reichswehr also had its own intelligence unit as a section (*Fremde Heere*, designated T3) of the *Truppenamt*.

† As of May 1, 1930, Blomberg was the ninth ranking *Generalleutnant* of fourteen; Schleicher the fifteenth *Generalmajor* of twenty-five.

intervention of Heye, Blomberg avoided the fate of Seeckt, but was relieved as *Chef des Truppenamtes* and transferred from Berlin to the district command in East Prussia. He was succeeded in the *Truppenamt* by Schleicher's intimate friend and candidate for the supreme command, Generalmajor Curt von Hammerstein-Equord.

This was Schleicher's brew of statecraft at its hottest. Hammerstein's was one of the most brilliant military minds of the Reichswehr. Like Schleicher, he was an old favourite of Groener, and had been a member of Groener's "team" in "organizing for disaster" after 1918. Even more important for Schleicher's purposes, Hammerstein was a fellow-alumnus of the old *Dritte Garde*, and stood high in the affections of Oskar von Hindenburg. Thus, when Heye finally stepped down, Schleicher was able to achieve the appointment of Hammerstein, outranked as the latter was by some fifteen senior generals.* In September, 1930, Hammerstein took office as *Chef der Heeresleitung*, and the circle charmed by Schleicher—Hindenburg, Groener and Hammerstein—was complete.

Thus Schleicher laid the foundations for his Icarus-like rise and fall during the next four years. Less than two years later—in June, 1932—Schleicher was *Reichswehrminister*, having added Groener to the lengthening list of his traduced patrons. At the end of that year he was Chancellor—the seven-weeks Chancellor, the last Chancellor of the Weimar Republic. On June 30, 1934, Schleicher and his wife lay dead on the floor of their Berlin home, their bodies riddled by the trigger-men of Goering and Himmler.

Where Schleicher's talents and bent might have carried him in more normal times is an interesting, if academic, question. In the Army he could hardly have risen much higher. He had long been more politician than soldier, and was essentially an *éminence grise*, more gifted to manipulate than to lead. His rise to the highest positions in 1932 was that of a tossed cork, and he was far more helpless and impotent as Chancellor than as the trusted agent and counsellor of Hindenburg and Groener.

For even as Hammerstein took command in September, 1930, the approaching disintegration of the Republic was manifest. That was the very month of the general election in which

---

* On May 1, 1930, four months prior to his elevation, Hammerstein was only a *Generalmajor*, the third in seniority of that rank and immediately junior to von Bock. As had been done in the case of Heye, Hammerstein's new rank of *General der Infanterie* was dated back to March 1, 1929, so as to give him precedence over Otto Hasse, the senior *General*.

Hitler and the Nazis polled six and a half million votes (as compared with 200,000 two years earlier) and emerged overnight as a major political force (the second largest party, with 108 Reichstag seats) instead of an extremist "splinter". From then on, German political history was dominated by the fact and force of National Socialism. The initiative lay in Hitler's hands; his was the offensive role, and it was to his threats and offers and promises that the "constituted authorities" were obliged to react. In the long run, this proved as true of the Army as of the politicians, the industrialists and other leading elements of the Reich. The officers' corps was about to meet the most deadly challenge of its entire history—a challenge with which it proved incapable of coping and which all but brought about its extinction.

CHAPTER III

THE REICHSWEHR AND THE BIRTH
OF THE THIRD REICH

UPON THE wisdom and stability of these four men—Hinden-burg, Groener, Hammerstein and Schleicher—the future of the officers' corps depended while the Nazi storm gathered. To-ward the end of 1929, as the depression gripped Germany with the freezing fingers of winter and unemployment, the socialist-dominated coalition government of Hermann Mueller tottered, and Hitler's shadow lengthened. Groener for one was by no means blind to the danger, and in January, 1930, in a general order to the Army, he stressed the revolutionary charac-ter of Nazism, warned that "a catastrophe for state and economy" was threatening, and called on the armed services "to serve the state far from all party politics and maintain it against . . . insane strife at home".

Indeed, of the four leaders, Groener alone combined the energy, intelligence and steadfastness which the emergency required. Hindenburg was a phenomenally well-preserved octogenarian, but as he slowed down and lost contact with current realities, he was increasingly victimized by the so-called palace *camarilla*—his son Oskar, Otto Meissner (Chief of the Presidential Chancery), Schleicher himself and, later, von Papen. Hammerstein was a brilliant soldier but no statesman, and fell completely under Schleicher's spell. And Schleicher, much the most sophisticated and politically experienced of the four, despite his very real intellectual ability never developed from the clever schemer and wire-puller into a leader of stature.

Until the summer of 1931, however, Groener and Schleicher teamed well. When they saw that the Mueller cabinet was doomed, they settled on Heinrich Bruening, parliamentary leader of the Catholic Centre, to succeed Mueller as Chancellor. Like Stresemann, who had died in the autumn of 1929, Bruen-ing was a conservative nationalist who sought to restore German power by gradualism rather than open intransigence. A front-line captain of machine-gunners during the First World War and holder of the Iron Cross, his relations with Schleicher and

the Reichswehr were excellent, and he played a key role in winning the Reichstag's approval of the military budget in 1929. His war record and personality ingratiated him with Hindenburg, and in the spring of 1930 he became Chancellor with the full backing of Hindenburg and the Reichswehr leadership, and the close personal collaboration of Groener, Hammerstein and Schleicher.

GROENER AND THE SA

When Bruening assumed the chancellorship, Schleicher and Groener appear to have hoped that he and the Centre would furnish a core of nationalist idealism around which a wide "front" of veterans and other patriots would assemble and restore a measure of stability to the political scene. But this dream was shattered by the elections of September, 1930, in which the extreme right and left gained heavily at the expense of the moderate parties, and the phenomenal advance of the National Socialists revealed that the new nationalism was rallying around the demagogue Hitler rather than the "respectable" exemplars of the "old Right" such as Groener and Bruening. And the course of the struggle which now began between the forces led by Bruening and Groener on the one hand and Hitler and Roehm on the other, now a chess game, now a beer-hall brawl, and later a succession of desperate and violent plots and counterplots, can be traced clear through to the *Putsch* of July 20, 1944.

Symbolic of the coming struggle was the Leipzig trial, in the fall of 1930, of three young Reichswehr subalterns who had been arrested in February for spreading Nazi propaganda in their garrison at Ulm, in violation of the Army rule against political activity. Groener's effort to handle this as a routine disciplinary matter was frustrated by the intransigent behaviour of the three lieutenants, and a formal public trial had to be held. Following hard on the heels of the Nazi gains in the September elections, the trial became a political *cause célèbre*; the regimental commander was none other than Oberst Ludwig Beck, soon to be Chief of the General Staff, and master-mind of the July 20th *Putsch* fourteen years later. Hitler, sensing the explosive possibilities of the occasion, appeared as a defence witness and skilfully swept his fingers over the harpstrings of history by comparing his crusade against Versailles to that of the "Reformers" against the Napoleonic yoke. From the testimony of Beck and other officers it clearly appeared that sympathy with Hitler's aims was widespread in the Reichswehr. Even more alarming

65

was the critical reaction in military circles to the sentence of eighteen months' detention imposed on the defendants. From their retirement, Seeckt and von der Goltz accused Groener of "weakening the spirit of comradeship and solidarity within the officers' corps".[1] Only too clearly, many members of the corps were susceptible to Nazi blandishments.

The Leipzig trial was but a foretaste of the coming struggle. Early in 1931, Ernst Roehm took over the leadership of Hitler's Brown Shirts, formally known as the *Sturmabteilung* (SA) of the Nazi Party. Under Roehm, a former regular officer of the Bavarian Army and the Reichswehr, a measure of discipline and organization was imposed on the Nazi thugs and street-fighters. As a private political "para-military" body, the SA not only was a threat to the constituted civil authorities but loomed as a rival to the Reichswehr itself. Both as Minister of Defence and as Minister of the Interior (an office which he assumed in October, 1931), therefore, Groener had ample reason to suppress and dissolve the SA, as a danger to the security of the Republic and the integrity of the Reichswehr.

Fully alive to the menace of the SA throughout 1931, Groener nevertheless felt unable to recommend direct action for its dissolution by presidential decree. The coexistence of the uniformed *Stahlhelm* (veterans) and *Reichsbanner* (Social Democrats) presented an awkward problem. Hindenburg was benevolently disposed toward the *Stahlhelm*, and on legal grounds it would be difficult to discriminate. Far more important in convincing Groener that he must proceed cautiously, however, was the favour which the Nazis, and especially the SA, were winning within the Reichswehr itself.

For the violent nationalism which had activated generals such as von Luettwitz and von Lossow in the early twenties was still abroad in the Reichswehr. And in 1930 and 1931 the impressive Nazi victories at the polls, and the swelling legions of the SA and the Hitler youth organizations, made a deep impression on the officers' corps. As the great German historian Friedrich Meinecke tells us: [2]

> "An intoxication seized upon German youth at this time. . . . So in the early thirties many young people, worthy but wholly unripe politically, began to organize themselves as the Storm Troops (SA, *Sturmabteilungen*) of the Hitler movement. Hitler, one may say, came to power through a typical but dazzled and blinded youth movement.
>
> " 'It would be a pity to have to fire on these splendid youths,'

was now the saying in the Reichswehr ranks. I repeated this saying to Groener, and he replied scoffingly: 'As if there were not a great many worthy youths in the other camp also!' These youths, however, were not so highly inflamed as those in the Hitler camp.

"So we return to the currents within the Reichswehr and come to the strongest material motive in the Reichswehr's growing friendliness toward the Hitler movement. 'We shall create for you a great army, much larger than you yourselves imagine today,' it was intimated in the ranks of the Hitler youth. What a dazzling prospect of quick promotion and breathing space in life for the Officer Corps of the hundred-thousand-man army! And also for the masses of former officers who had been dismissed and were now having a hard time in life!"

The leadership of the SA, indeed, included many such former officers. In Berlin, Hanover, Kassel and other large cities the local SA commanders were former Army captains, majors and lieutenant-colonels, or naval officers. Roehm himself was a former captain. In other branches of the Nazi Party were to be found many others—Generalmajor Franz Ritter von Epp, Oberst Konstantin Hierl and Major Walther Buch, to say nothing of Hermann Goering, one-time captain in the German air arm.

This military ingredient in the SA matched the Party's increasing sway within the Reichswehr, particularly among the younger officers and recent recruits to the ranks. Many of the older generals were repelled by the brash behaviour of the Nazi leaders, but for the most part they were content to stand apart and await developments. Some few, in fact, sympathized more or less openly with the Hitler movement. In East Prussia, the disgruntled von Blomberg was under the influence of his pro-Nazi Chief of Staff (von Reichenau), and during the presidential election campaign in 1932, von Seeckt, who perhaps had not forgiven Hindenburg for his dismissal in 1926, advised his sister to vote against the field-marshal and for the "Bohemian corporal", as Hitler was known in the higher circles of the Reichswehr: "Youth is right. I am too old," declared the aging Sphinx.

To quiet the spreading discontent in economically stricken Germany and take the wind out of the Nazi sails, Bruening and Groener embarked on a vigorous campaign à la Stresemann to gain some further relaxation of the Versailles restrictions. But events were moving too rapidly for them. Furthermore, Schleicher secretly turned against them, and was losing no opportunity to undermine their standing with Hindenburg. Deeply

impressed by the Leipzig trial and the growing prestige of the SA, Schleicher seems to have concluded that the Republic had grown too weak to "wage war on two fronts"—i.e. against both the Communists and the Nazis. He began secret negotiations with Roehm, and openly urged the addition of Nazi members to the cabinet, a step to which Bruening and Groener were firmly opposed.

Into this bubbling political cauldron fell the presidential election of March, 1932, necessitated by the expiration of Hindenburg's first term. The eighty-four-year-old *Feldmarschall* polled over 18,600,000 to Hitler's 11,340,000 but (because of the 7,500,000-odd votes for the Communist and *Stahlhelm* candidates) fell just short of an absolute majority. The run-off election, in which Hindenburg was successful, took place on April 10th, and during the preceding week Groener's hand was finally forced on the question of suppressing the Brown Shirts. Their behaviour during the campaign grew increasingly violent, and at a meeting of important state officials led by the Prussian and Bavarian delegates, Groener was confronted with representations and threats of "independent action" against the SA which he could no longer oppose. Accordingly, he prepared a presidential decree for its dissolution, which was warmly supported by Bruening, Hammerstein and others. Schleicher's initial approval, however, soon shifted, and Hindenburg's attitude was most uncertain. He was eventually persuaded only after Groener agreed to take full public responsibility, and on April 15th the decree was promulgated.

Now, indeed, Bruening and Groener encountered the full and bitter effect of Schleicher's disloyalty. Swinging the unstable Hammerstein to his view, Schleicher whipped up throughout the Reichswehr a wave of opposition to the decree and of dissatisfaction with Groener, and simultaneously plied Hindenburg with unfavourable reports. For a month Groener courageously fought back, but early in May the Nazi and other nationalist deputies, led by Goering, unleashed on him in the Reichstag a fierce attack which, overwrought and weakened by diabetes, Groener was unable to counter with his usual poise. At the conclusion of the debate, Schleicher and Hammerstein accosted their exhausted chief and demanded that he resign at once, declaring that he no longer enjoyed the support of the Reichswehr. His mind poisoned against Groener by Schleicher, Hindenburg "could do nothing for him", and on May 13, 1932, Groener resigned. A few weeks later Schleicher's intrigues

claimed still another victim when Hindenburg dismissed Bruening.

The fall of Groener was a disaster for the Reichswehr and a mortal blow to the Republic. Despite his physical infirmities and somewhat old-fashioned political outlook, Groener's was by far the steadiest hand and clearest eye in the upper levels of the officer caste, and Schleicher did the Reichswehr a grave disservice when he induced the generals to cast off Groener's guiding hand. Groener was wise enough to resist the allure which Nazism held for so many of the officers, and which was to prove their undoing. Therefore he gave loyal and effective service in the struggle to preserve constitutional government in Germany—a struggle which, for all practical purposes, ended with his fall.

SCHLEICHER AND PAPEN

More than the personal leadership of Bruening and Groener was lost in the fateful month of May, 1932. The tradition of ministerial responsibility was lost too, for while Bruening and his predecessors had been leaders of major parties in the Reichstag, his two successors—Franz von Papen and Schleicher—represented nothing except the personal favour of the aged and failing Hindenburg. And the Reichswehr had lost the first round in its battle against the military aspirations of the Nazi Party, for the decree suppressing the SA was withdrawn a few weeks after the Papen cabinet took office.

It was, indeed, a promise that the *SA-Verbot* would be withdrawn which had induced Hitler to "tolerate" the Papen government. For by June, 1932, the German political scene was one of indescribable confusion, and the kaleidoscopic shifts and manœuvres at the top level reflected little but the personal ambitions of the intriguers around Hindenburg. The presidential election itself had been paradoxical enough, with the great industrialists and other upper-class reactionaries backing the proletarian, pseudo-socialist Hitler, and the social democrats, Catholics, Jews and trade unions backing the Prussian nobleman and field-marshal. Now, barely six weeks after his election by the forces of the left, Hindenburg, steered by Schleicher, veered far to the right. The Papen cabinet was heavily laden with conservative nobility; Papen himself—a noble socialite noted more for personal charm than ability and utterly lacking in political stature—was a one-time General Staff officer who had married into a leading Saar industrialist

family. The selection of this aristocratic lightweight (he was not even a member of the Reichstag) as Chancellor was entirely owing to Schleicher's influence with Hindenburg, but by a fitting irony Papen so completely captivated the old gentleman as to rapidly displace Schleicher in his affections.

Schleicher himself had become a *Generalleutnant* in the fall of 1931, and stood fourteenth on the Army list when Groener retired. His military career, however, was at an end, for now at last Schleicher was obliged to come forward in person; the supply of older men upon whose favour he could count was exhausted, largely as a result of his own incessant intrigues. His was the dominant force behind Hindenburg and Papen, and he had little choice other than to give up his commission * and take the civilian office of Minister of Defence so recently vacated by his erstwhile patron.

The eight months of Papen and Schleicher—early June, 1932, to late January, 1933—were a period of presidial government, two elections and, above all, a plot and counter-plot. Hitler soon withdrew his promised "toleration", and thereafter the Nazis joined the Communists, Socialists and Catholic Centre in opposition to the Papen cabinet, which could count only on a handful of nationalist votes in the Reichstag. In the July elections the Nazis became the largest party in the Reichstag, with 230 seats (nearly two-fifths of the entire body). Seeing that Papen would never be able to swing the electorate, Schleicher promptly decided to ditch him, and made a characteristic "deal" with the Nazis for a coalition cabinet with Hitler as Chancellor and himself as Minister of Defence. But Papen, nothing daunted by the election, had no thought of giving up the chancellorship, and now enjoyed the full support of Hindenburg. Schleicher gained nothing but the distrust of Papen and Hindenburg, and Hitler only a scornful dressing-down from the Old Gentleman, for their pains. The new Reichstag met in September only to be promptly dissolved, and Papen gaily kept office pending the November elections, in which his nationalist backers were again resoundingly defeated, while the Nazi vote dropped by some two million.† These results, coupled with Papen's obvious instability, led Schleicher

* Schleicher was succeeded as Chief of the *Ministeramt* by his friend and assistant von Bredow, who had previously been in charge of the intelligence section of the *Ministeramt*.

† Resulting in a drop from 230 to 197 in the Nazi representation in the Reichstag.

and the other cabinet ministers to insist on Papen's resignation as Chancellor. Hindenburg allowed Hitler to attempt to form a government which would command a Reichstag majority, but this proved impossible.

Schleicher was now faced with the same problem that had confronted him after Groener's resignation, except that this time it was the chancellorship into which he had to step. Thus it came about that, when his ambitious career finally carried him to the highest office, he was helpless to achieve anything. The Republic had been mortally wounded, and his old friends and supporters eliminated or alienated, by his own connivings and plottings. All the relationships on which Schleicher had depended were subverted; he himself was now in office, but Hindenburg *père et fils* were grown cold to him.

And now it was Papen's turn to play the role of which Schleicher had so long been undisputed master. Joachim von Ribbentrop and others were quietly promoting a temporary *mariage de convenance* between the Nazis and the nationalists, and a similar move was under way among the more reactionary Ruhr magnates. On January 4, 1933, Hitler and Papen met in Cologne at the home of the financier Baron Kurt von Schroeder, and discussed the entire question of Nazi participation in the government. On January 22nd, at a Berlin meeting in Ribbentrop's home, attended by Papen, Hitler, Goering, Meissner and Oskar von Hindenburg, negotiations were begun for the formation of a Nazi–Nationalist coalition cabinet.

In the meantime, Schleicher's position had become insupportable. He had vainly endeavoured to split the Nazi Party by seducing Gregor Strasser from the fold, which definitively estranged him from Hitler. Hoping to frighten his adversaries among the Junker nationalists, Schleicher next threatened to publish the details of shocking scandals in the administration of government loans in support of the East Prussian landownership. As the Junkers and the Reichswehr had always formed a close-knit community of interests, and the Hindenburgs were Junkers *par excellence*, this desperate manœuvre aroused a clamorous demand for Schleicher's resignation among those who had the President's ear, and cost him dearly in the Junker circles of the Reichswehr. Beset on all sides, and sadly aware of his lost favour with Hindenburg, Schleicher sent the tractable Hammerstein, whose personal predilections were strongly anti-Nazi, to awaken the venerable *Feldmarschall*

to the dangers of the Hitler–Papen coalition, but Hindenburg was unimpressed. With the Reichstag (as elected in November) due to assemble, on January 28th Schleicher, following Papen's precedent of 1932, asked Hindenburg for authority to dissolve it in the event of the anticipated vote of no confidence. Hindenburg brusquely cut him off and relieved him of his duties as Chancellor. Schleicher's career in office, so craftily prepared and helplessly consummated, was at an end.

Hindenburg at once sent for his "Fraenzchen", and the negotiations with Hitler for a coalition cabinet drove to their fateful *dénouement*. In a last desperate cast, Schleicher sought an alliance with Hitler looking to a Nazi–Reichswehr coalition but, as Goering piously explained on the witness stand in Nuremberg, "the Fuehrer refused, recognizing that this would be impossible, and that the intentions were not honest". Schleicher's bid did, however, help to bring together the strangely assorted group of Nazi adventurers and aristocrats of the Hindenburg entourage who were playing poker for cabinet posts. On Monday, January 30, 1933, the players picked up their chips. Adolf Hitler became Chancellor and the Third Reich was born.

Thus did the officers' corps stumble blindly through the portals of fate, bereft of the leadership which might have saved it from the disaster which awaited. In disgruntled retirement, Seeckt spoke of Nazism as the wave of the future. Groener, gallant and tenacious, could not hold out single-handed against the tide of events, Schleicher's disloyalty and Hindenburg's senility. Schleicher himself had discovered too late that pure intrigue is a *reductio ad absurdum* of purposefulness. Hammerstein showed himself no statesman. Von Rundstedt, then commanding general of the Berlin military district (Wehrkreis III), had woodenly acted as Papen's tool in forcibly evicting the Braun cabinet (Social Democratic) of Prussia in July, 1932. None of the other senior generals—Hasse, von Loetzen, von Blomberg, von Leeb, von Bock or the von Stuelpnagels—had the vision and energy to grapple with the emergency. The entire corps was ridden with overt or latent pro-Nazi sympathy, and the unconverted were satisfied to adopt a wait-and-see attitude. Thus the Republic was deserted in its hour of need, and it was only fitting that von Papen, who, almost unconcernedly, delivered the final and mortal thrust, was a former German officer of cavalry and the General Staff.

There is a general but completely erroneous notion that, once Hitler became Chancellor, all his domestic political worries were over and the path to dictatorship stretched before him unobstructed. In fact, Hitler's twelve years of power were punctuated by a series of acute and often violent crises. And on January 30, 1933, there were obstacles a-plenty for him to cope with. The least of these were his political rivals. It was a time of extremism, and the socialists, centrists and other moderates could make no new headway. Nor was there any real communist threat. As for the nationalists—Hugenberg, Seldte, Papen and the Junker bureaucrats—they were no match for Hitler in the political arena.

Nonetheless, as 1932 drew to a close the Nazi cause had appeared well-nigh lost even to its face-lifter-in-chief, Dr. Josef Goebbels. The November elections had resulted in an ominous decline in the Party's voting strength, and ensuing local elections emphasized the downward trend. These setbacks and the Party's empty treasury prompted the little *Doktor* to note in his diary (in December) that "the danger now exists of the whole Party going to pieces and all of our work having been in vain", as well as that "financial troubles make all organized work impossible".

From this pit of adversity and poverty, Hitler was rescued by the internecine strife of Papen and Schleicher, and the backing and bounty of a group of industrialists led by Gustav Krupp. In November, Krupp was promoting a petition to Hindenburg, on behalf of the Ruhr industrialists, espousing Hitler's aspirations to the chancellorship, and early in January Baron von Schroeder established the connection between Hitler and Papen which led directly to the Hitler–Papen coalition government.

Superficially, indeed, Papen appeared to have taken effective precautions against Hitlerian domination of the new cabinet. Only three Nazis—Hitler, Frick in the Interior, and Goering without portfolio—were admitted as against five holdovers from the "baron's cabinet"—Papen himself as Vice-Chancellor, and von Neurath (Foreign Affairs), von Krosigk (Finance), Guertner (Justice), and von Eltz-Ruebenach (Post and Transport). The other new members were Hugenberg (Economy and Agriculture), Seldte of the *Stahlhelm* (Labour), and von Blomberg as Minister of Defence.

Furthermore, this aggregation commanded no majority in the Reichstag, and it was apparent that another general election would have to be held. With the Ministry of Interior under his control, the Brown Shirts on the streets, and his own demagogic genius to fall back on, Hitler most of all needed money to keep the Party going, and the toleration of the Reichswehr, in order to consolidate his seizure of power.

The money problem was soon solved through the benevolence of the industrialists. On February 20th, under the ægis of Gustav Krupp and Hjalmar Schacht, some twenty tycoons—including von Schnitzler of the I.G. Farben combine and Friedrich Flick—met to hear Hitler speak at Goering's home in Berlin. One cannot charge that Hitler was much less than frank as to his intentions. "Private enterprise", he declared, "cannot be maintained in an age of democracy. . . . We must not forget that all the benefits of culture must be introduced more or less with an iron fist. . . . If the election does not decide, the decision must be brought about by other means. . . . The restoration of the Wehrmacht will not be decided at Geneva but in Germany, when we have gained internal strength. . . ." If this was not an unmistakable foreshadowing of dictatorship and military resurgence, Goering clinched the point by his sardonic assurance that "the sacrifices asked for will be easier for industry to bear if it is realized that the election of March 5th will surely be the last one for the next ten years, probably even for the next hundred years". Following these portentous harangues, the assembled magnates pledged three million Reichsmarks to the Nazi–Nationalist cause.

A few days later came the Reichstag fire, which Hitler used as a pretext to secure a presidential decree suspending the constitutional guarantees. But with all their paraphernalia of terror, the Nazis were unable to secure a majority in the election, though their vote rose to over 17,500,000 and their seats to 288 (in a house of 647). However, with the fifty-two seats held by the Nationalists, the coalition had a bare majority. Immediately the Brown Terror broke loose. Communist delegates to the Reichstag and other intransigent enemies of the Nazis (Bruening was forced to flee for his life) were hunted down, and the frightful era of concentration camps was inaugurated. On March 23, 1933, over the courageous opposition of the Social Democrats, the Reichstag committed suicide by passing the infamous Enabling Act, whereby the Hitler cabinet was empowered to govern by decree. Thereafter, in rapid and

tragic succession, there followed the suppression of all political opposition, and the subversion of the German economy, the professions, and the press and radio, in accordance with Nazi precepts. The sickening, bloody smog of the Third Reich settled over Germany.

And what of the Reichswehr during these terrible weeks? Schleicher had followed Groener into the discard,* and Hammerstein, none too deft at best, was left friendless and exposed to assault from all sides. As a comrade and fellow-traveller of Schleicher, he had lost caste with Hindenburg and the presidential camarilla. For the same reason, and irrespective of his reckless and outspoken anti-Nazism, he could count on Hitler's implacable opposition. With Schleicher's support, Hammerstein had been the instrument of frustrating Blomberg's aspirations to succeed Heye in 1929, and consequently was unlikely to find a friend in the new Minister of Defence.

For all this, Hitler was utterly dependent upon the Reichswehr's toleration, if not active support. Closely interlocked with the Junker aristocracy and carrying enormous prestige with the business and professional classes, an unmistakable military frown would have had prodigious effect throughout Germany, and would have made quite impossible such occasions as the Krupp–Schacht party at Goering's house at which the Nazi war-chest was replenished. If the senior generals had had a modicum of devotion to the Republic and firmness of purpose there is little doubt but that they could have laid Hitler low.

But devotion and purposefulness alike were quite lacking, and Hammerstein was not the man to develop an organized front. For all his charm and intelligence, he was not only politically unstable but—even more fatal—unusually lazy. Violently and even profanely anti-Nazi in speech he was and, according to Goering (testifying at Nuremberg), Hammerstein was implicated with Schleicher in a planned military *Putsch* with the Potsdam garrison during the fateful week-end preceding Hitler's appointment as Chancellor. This last-minute plot, if actual, died a-borning immediately upon Blomberg's installation as Minister of Defence. And at no time thereafter did Hammerstein embark on a methodical course of action to provide his anti-Nazi bark with a bite. As Halder puts it,

* Generalmajor von Bredow, Schleicher's trusted subordinate and successor as head of the *Ministeramt*, followed Schleicher into retirement upon the latter's dismissal as Chancellor.

Hammerstein thought he could overthrow Hitler merely by being vocally anti-Nazi, and as a result of this superficiality and levity of disposition, he accomplished nothing whatsoever. By the summer of 1933 he was discouraged and cynical, and upon occasion felt constrained to tell the officers (at Blomberg's direction) that they must set aside their doubts and "collaborate loyally with the new power".[3] For all this enforced lip service to the prevailing regime, Hammerstein's days were numbered, as he well knew. At the end of December, 1933, his imminent resignation was announced and on February 1, 1934, he was replaced as *Chef der Heeresleitung* by von Fritsch. Hammerstein was promoted to *Generaloberst* and sent to join Seeckt and Heye on the inactive list.

As Hammerstein faded out of the picture, sputtering futilely, Werner von Blomberg emerged as the leading politico-military personality of the next half-decade. Reverting to the custom of imperial times, Blomberg did not doff his uniform on taking office as *Reichswehrminister*, and for this and other reasons he played a much more direct part in the governance of the Army than had his predecessors under the Republic. It is not easy to make a just estimate of this most intriguing character's share of the responsibility for the disaster which was about to overtake the officers' corps, but there is no doubt that, from the moment of his appointment, he became the outstanding military protagonist of collaboration with Hitler.

Blomberg did not, however, owe his selection as Minister to Hitler's favour. Goering declared at Nuremberg that "von Blomberg was not known personally either to the Fuehrer or to me at that time", and that "the Reich President demanded that the office of Reich Defence Minister should . . . be in the hands of an independent person, a soldier; and he himself chose him without our having anything to do with it". This testimony was buttressed by that of von Papen, who further observed that Blomberg "enjoyed the particular confidence" of Hindenburg. Blomberg was both a Pomeranian nobleman and the *Wehrkreis* commander in East Prussia, and the agrarian Junkers were in the ascendant at the moment with the Hindenburg–Papen coterie who had turned on Schleicher and were urging Hitler's designation. According to Otto Meissner, who as Chief of the Presidential Chancellery was privy to most of the palace intrigue, Blomberg was playing with this group. Furthermore, Blomberg had many apparent qualifications for the post on merit. He was personable, had a good military

record, had been *Chef des Truppenamtes*, and was seriously considered for appointment as *Chef der Heeresleitung* in 1929. He had been to Russia and was fully familiar with the Army's clandestine activities there, and had served in semi-diplomatic capacities in the United States and as head of the German military delegation to the Geneva disarmament conference in 1932. Finally, he was near the top of the rank list in seniority.*
All of these reasons, no doubt, made Blomberg highly eligible in Hindenburg's eyes.

But if Blomberg was not a Hitler nominee, there is ample evidence that his selection was far from unwelcome to the Nazis and, in view of Hammerstein's open anti-Nazism, it is altogether probable that Hitler welcomed the appointment of Blomberg to guard against a Reichswehr *coup d'état*. Blomberg appears to have come to the Party's favourable notice primarily through his chief of staff in East Prussia, Oberst Walther von Reichenau, an exceptionally energetic and ambitious officer who was one of the earliest and most outspoken pro-Nazis in the upper levels of the officers' corps.[4] As Blomberg explains in his memoirs, "National Socialism, insofar as its main emphasis was on nationalism, was very close to me in the threatened, separated province of East Prussia", and Halder agreed that the German officers in East Prussia were chronically worried about the possibility of a Polish attack, and therefore were not unfriendly to the SA units, which might furnish useful auxiliary troops.† Reichenau represented Blomberg in dealing with the Nazis, and soon became a favourite of the Party. At the other end of the social scale, Blomberg owed many of his contacts with the Junkers to the fact that Reichenau's wife was a countess.

Blomberg, indeed, came to depend upon Reichenau in much

---

* The last published Army rank list was compiled as of May 10, 1932, on which date Blomberg was outranked by four generals other than Hammerstein—the two *Gruppenkommando* chiefs (Otto Hasse and von Loetzen, both of whom were close to retirement), von Rundstedt (of Wehrkreis III at Berlin) and von Vollard Bockelberg (Chief of the Army Ordnance Office). In October, 1932, Hasse retired, and was succeeded at Gruppenkommando 1 by Rundstedt, who was simultaneously promoted to *General der Infanterie*. Von Loetzen was succeeded at Gruppenkommando 2 by von Leeb (who had been immediately junior to Blomberg) in September, 1933. Blomberg was promoted from *Generalleutnant* to *General* (with rank predated to September, 1928, to give him seniority over Hammerstein) upon taking office as *Reichswehrminister* (January 30, 1933), Bockelberg in October, 1933 (he retired not long afterwards), and Leeb on January 1, 1934.

† In fact, when the war broke out in 1939, the SA and other para-military units in East Prussia were assembled in a corps under Generalleutnant Albert Wodrig. "Corps Wodrig", as it was then called, later became the XXVIth Corps. See page 276, *infra*.

the same way that Groener and Hammerstein had leaned on Schleicher, and when Blomberg took office as Minister he installed Reichenau as Chief of the *Ministeramt* (soon expanded and renamed the *Wehrmachtamt*), the position so long held by Schleicher and recently vacated by von Bredow. This was a strategic spot, where Reichenau was enabled to deal with all questions arising between the armed forces and the Party. So dominant a role did Reichenau assume that, when the question of Hammerstein's successor arose, Blomberg strenuously (and with Hitler's support) urged Hindenburg to select Reichenau. This effort was as characteristic of Blomberg's lack of judgment as is the reminiscence in his memoirs that "I failed because the Old Gentleman had been given some distorted information on Reichenau's personality by other people interested in that position." A simpler explanation is obvious. Reichenau was still an *Oberst*, and half a decade or more younger than the senior generals. His appointment as *Chef der Heeresleitung* would have been so flagrant a case of personal favouritism and preferment for a "firebrand" Nazi sympathizer that the whole corps of officers might have risen in protest.

As it was, Werner von Fritsch, whom Hindenburg finally selected,* was outranked by a round dozen of his colleagues.† In 1932, he had been promoted to *Generalleutnant*, and that fall he succeeded Rundstedt as Commander of Wehrkreis III at Berlin. During and after the First World War he had made a most enviable reputation as a staff officer, and was remarkable for his energy, industry and capacity for concentration. It was perhaps these qualities which led Hindenburg to pick him as a counterweight to the mercurial Blomberg, in preference to older officers such as Rundstedt and Leeb. Furthermore, although Fritsch was the traditional reactionary, stiff officers' corps type, he had no love for Hitler or his cohorts, and was determined to maintain the Army's independence of action. In this purpose, Fritsch enjoyed the full support and wise counsel of Generalleutnant Ludwig Beck, a brilliant and

* According to General Adam, Hindenburg wished to appoint von Kleist, an officer of the old *Dritte Garde* who enjoyed excellent personal contacts with the Hindenburg family. At Nuremberg, Papen claimed credit for Fritsch's selection.

† On the day of taking office as *Chef der Heeresleitung*, Fritsch was promoted from *Generalleutnant* to *General der Artillerie*. Theretofore he had been outranked (in addition to Blomberg) by the two *Gruppenkommando* chiefs (Rundstedt and Leeb), as well as Bockelberg, von Bock, Liebmann, von dem Bussche Ippenburg, Adam and five others. Rundstedt, Leeb and Bock, although they were the principal German field commanders during the Second World War, were consistently passed over for the top Army position—in 1930, 1934, and again in 1938.

sensitive officer who had succeeded Adam* as *Chef des Trup-penamtes* in October, 1933, and who was destined to become the leader of the anti-Nazi elements of the officers' corps and to sacrifice his life in the unsuccessful *Putsch* of July 20, 1942.

From the outset of the Hitler era, accordingly, there was mistrust and friction between the *Reichswehrministerium* and the *Heeresleitung*. Between Blomberg and Fritsch there was no rapport, and this coolness was to prove a major factor in the great state crisis of January, 1938. Blomberg and Reichenau were predisposed to collaborate with Hitler, as open and enthusiastic supporters. Hammerstein, Fritsch, Adam and Beck ranged from open hostility to a definitely "reserved" attitude. Inevitably, this schism at the top (which indeed reflected divided opinion throughout the officers' corps between the old-school-tie elements repelled by Nazi brashness and the firebrand crowd who were impressed by Nazism's nationalistic mass appeal) hindered the development of any decisive Army policies or attitudes *vis-à-vis* the Nazis.

Adolf Hitler took in this situation at a glance. He was acutely aware that, for his survival and the fulfilment of his far-flung dreams alike, the Army must be his, and the mingled boldness and discretion with which he approached the generals reflects his political touch at its surest. Raeder at Nuremberg described Hitler's first meeting with the generals and admirals at Hammerstein's home on the evening of February 2, 1933. In an after-dinner speech, Hitler skilfully struck the old, familiar chords. The Army was to be kept out of internal problems, and it should enjoy "an undisturbed period of development" in order to fulfil its future tasks and "prevent the Reich from becoming the sport of the other nations". He referred to Hindenburg with "particular respect", and the upshot was that those present were uncommonly pleased with the speech.

The "Bohemian corporal" was off to an excellent start in his dealings with the high brass, and after the March elections Hitler showed the same master touch in staging a dedicatory service (for the opening of the new Reichstag) at Potsdam by the tomb of Frederick the Great. Now indeed the ghost of "Old Fritz" was invoked as godfather of the new-born Third Reich. Mackensen and Seeckt emerged from retirement, and with Hindenburg, Blomberg, Hammerstein and Raeder the martial conclave was most impressive. In this theatrical setting

* Adam thereupon replaced Leeb as Commander of Wehrkreis VII (Munich) and Leeb in turn replaced von Loetzen at Gruppenkommando 2 (Kassel).

Hindenburg, *Feldmarschall* and First Soldier of the Fatherland, exhorted all present to "stand behind the government and do everything possible to support it". Hitler in reply eulogized the venerable *Reichspraesident*, and in conclusion, "with an obeisance of humility, grasped the old Marshal's hand. Magnesium flared, cameras clicked. . . . The Field-Marshal and the Corporal, the Old Germany and the New, united by a handclasp of comradeship—it was to be a theme and an event which no German was to be allowed to forget and which was to be implanted in the mind of every German child." [5]

Not the least moved of those present at the tomb was Werner von Blomberg, for whom the "*Tag von Potsdam*" assumed the proportions of a "confession of faith for the German people". The *Reichswehrminister* was, in truth, a very impressionable man. He was ambitious too, and the conjunction of the hypnotic quality of the Fuehrer with the opportunities for power and preferment which he and his programme held was quite too much for Blomberg's objectivity of mind. To be sure, on taking office Blomberg had been cautious enough to bow to the heritage of his predecessors by promising to preserve the Reichswehr as "an instrument of the state above all parties". Richenau was much less circumspect. On February 6th, Hitler's newspaper, the *Voelkischer Beobachter*, under a headline "The Reichsheer Shoulder to Shoulder with the New Chancellor", publicized this aggressive officer's declaration that "the Wehrmacht was never more at one with the tasks of the state than today" and that he was taking up his new duties as Chief of the *Ministeramt* "with the same enthusiasm which is voiced in the proclamation of the new Reich government of the German people". But Blomberg did not long lag behind in his enthusiasm for the new regime. He soon fell completely under the Fuehrer's spell, with the results disclosed by his memoirs:

> "The year 1933 brought to me an experience altogether and certainly undeserved, since I was allowed to become an assistant to the Fuehrer and to be in his immediate entourage. . . . Things I never expected to find after 1919 fell into my lap overnight: at first, faith, veneration for a man, and complete adherence to an idea; later on, a field of activities holding great possibilities for the future. . . . I pledged myself to National Socialism in 1933 because I considered its ideas promising for the future. I found that in the core of this movement everything was right."

Thus was Blomberg wooed and won to Hitler's side, and that fall, during the great Party rally at Nuremberg, this loyalty was

rewarded by his promotion to *Generaloberst*. With equal speed, if somewhat less extravagance of expression, the leadership of the German Navy capitulated. "From the very start", writes Raeder, Hitler "approached the Navy with noticeable good will, apparently because he had been informed by Admiral (Ret.) Levetzow, who joined the Party in its early stages, that . . . the Navy was filled with a united spirit and was able to produce a good record." Hitler's view of the role of the German Navy struck Raeder as conservative and sound, and the Admiral was most favourably impressed with "this vigorous personality, who was obviously most intelligent, had tremendous will power, was a master in handling people, and—as I myself observed in the early years—a great and very skilful politician. . . ."

With Blomberg, Raeder and others as firm allies, the un-converted generals uncertain and confused, and Hindenburg increasingly senescent (he was eighty-six by now), Hitler turned his attention to the scattering of his political foes and the consolidation of his dictatorship. Big business was "organ-ized" into the new scheme of things under the leadership of Gustav Krupp. The vice of tyranny was tightened with terrible rapidity—by the outlawing of all other parties, creation of the Gestapo, strangling of the trade unions, and progressive pros-titution of press and radio, law and the other professions. Local Party bosses terrorized the provinces, and the population of concentration camps multiplied.

But as opposition outside the Party was ruthlessly stamped out, dissension within was growing more acute. It was all very well for Hitler to ingratiate himself with the generals and assure them that the Wehrmacht would be the Fatherland's "sole bearer of arms", but that was not the way Ernst Roehm looked at things at all. Furthermore, those two veterans of intrigue, Schleicher and Papen, were getting restless. As spring came to Germany in 1934, it was plain that a violent political crisis was in the making.

THE REICHSWEHR AND THE ROEHM PURGE

Throughout the Nazi rise to power, the SA had been the Party's striking force and the visible vanguard of the coming terror, and when Hitler took power it was Roehm and his Brown Shirts who suppressed the Social Democrats and other political opponents of the new regime, demoralized and prosti-tuted the civil service and the professions, and generally

consolidated the tyranny. After a year of power, however, these functions were close to exhausting themselves. Restless and chafing under the yoke of inactivity, the storm-troopers were clamouring for a "second round" of revolution which would curb the prerogatives of the Junkers, the industrialists and the Reichswehr—the very complex of arch-conservatives and aristocrats who had dominated Germany for over half a century, and whose entrenched prestige Hitler had not yet ventured to challenge.

Ernst Roehm was perhaps Hitler's closest approximation to an "intimate friend", but had never been especially prominent in the Party's political leadership. He had been a regular officer of the Bavarian Army and later of the Reichswehr, but was distinctly not an "old-school" type. Plebeian, piratical, unreligious and sexually abnormal, he bitterly resented the aristocratic pretensions of the officers' corps. His intense nationalism and strongly anti-social bent found expression in a fanatical Nazism which, coupled with his very real military and organizing abilities, made him an ideal leader of the Party's "paramilitary" formations.

Ideal, that is, until the Party's internal political programme was well launched and throughout the period of widespread revolutionary violence. Thereafter, Roehm's larger purposes precipitated an immediate clash of forces. For it had long been his overriding ambition to break the power of the officers' corps and emerge as the creator of the revolutionary "people's Army", à la Trotsky. The Reichswehr was to be swallowed up in the legions of the SA, and the generals of the old guard would give way to Roehm and his lieutenants. Even for the most pro-Hitler generals such as Reichenau, Roehm's plan meant war to the death between the officers' corps and the SA leadership.

Roehm became a member of the cabinet after the elections of March, 1933, and immediately thereafter became embroiled in a series of arguments with the Reichswehr—at what rank demobilized soldiers should be taken into the SA, whether SA units should have reserve training under Army supervision, who should prepare and submit the budget for SA military training, the extent of SA representation in the Reich Defence Council, and a multitude of parallel questions. Through the winter of 1933–34 his relations with Blomberg and Reichenau steadily worsened, and in March, 1934, Blomberg emphatically protested to Hitler against the formation of SA heavy machine-

gun companies and their appearance in public in flagrant violation of the Versailles Treaty, as an unnecessary risk to the undisturbed continuance of clandestine rearmament.

As summer approached, the tension grew almost unbearable. The clamour for a "people's Army" and the overthrow of the generals was paralleled by a resurgence of economic radicalism, anti-Catholicism and a new wave of anti-Semitism; the abominable Streicher's influence was at its peak. At the same time, the lines were even more sharply drawn in the struggle for position among Hitler's lieutenants, and the result was a temporary coalition of Goering and Himmler against Roehm. In May, 1933, the Air Ministry had been established under Goering's ægis, and on August 31, 1933, tired of his undistinctive SA garb, "unser Hermann" blossomed forth in the uniform of a *General der Infanterie*. His career as an Air Force officer in the First World War and his personal ambition alike pushed him to the side of the generals in their mortal struggle with the SA, and besides, his new-born Prussian Gestapo had been in frequent conflict with the vigilante street police of the SA. As for Himmler, his SS Black Shirts were then few in number and a minor part of the SA; Roehm was their Commander-in-Chief and Himmler's superior, a situation not at all to the latter's liking. On April 1, 1934, Goering appointed Himmler as Chief of the Prussian Gestapo, and the two arch-rogues joined forces to eliminate Roehm and break the power of the SA.

As if the plot were not already thick enough, the voices of Papen and Schleicher were again heard in the land, the former from the podium at the University of Marburg, and the latter in his customary conspiratorial whisper. The general-turned-politician had gone abroad after his fall from power, but upon his return was much in evidence around Berlin, and soon there were reports that he was once again dickering with Roehm. Schleicher appears to have had in mind some amorphous "deal" which would bring him back into the cabinet as Vice-Chancellor in place of Papen, while a partial amalgamation of the Reichswehr and the SA would bring in Roehm as *Reichswehrminister*, supplanting Blomberg. How far these negotiations had proceeded is not clear, but Schleicher was playing with fire in the dry season, and the effect was to seal his own death warrant.

Papen, for his part, was increasingly vexed as the absurd powerlessness of his position as Vice-Chancellor grew more and

more apparent. His old backers among the aristocratic tycoons, too, were becoming really alarmed by the radical and menacing harangues of Roehm, Streicher, Ley and the other Nazi extremists, and were prodding Papen to take some kind of action to check their threatened excesses and expropriations. Following a precautionary visit to the now failing Hindenburg, the little man finally decided to speak out. On Sunday, June 17, 1934, at Marburg the last voice was publicly lifted for the restoration of freedom, order and sanity in Germany; the voice was that of Papen, but the words he spoke were those of his brilliant adviser Edgar Jung, who soon paid with his life for his temerity. "A free press ought to exist to inform the government with open and manly statements where corruption had made its nest," declared Papen, who went on to say that the time had come when "a statesman must step in and call a spade a spade". Goebbels at once suppressed the speech, but its general tenor became widely known, and the acclaim Papen received in "moderate" circles helped bring the crisis to a white heat.

As the storm gathered, Hitler temporized. Basically proletarian, he shared Roehm's hatred and distrust of the generals, as well as the anti-aristocratic and anti-capitalist feelings of the radical Nazis. Yet his sound political instincts told him that he was still dependent on the support of these solid centres of German power. And now an event was fast approaching which promised both supreme opportunity and great peril—the Hero of Tannenberg was dying and soon there would be a vacancy in the Reichspresidency. How would the succession be determined? To whom would the Reichswehr give allegiance? If Hitler's answers to these questions were to prevail, he indeed was in need of the Army's backing, and the issue between Roehm and the Reichswehr must finally be resolved.

On June 30, 1934, with a bloody violence which reflected the deadly pressures and murderous hatreds that underlay the political scene, Hitler struck. Leading a gang of SS Black Shirts, he descended on Roehm's temporary headquarters at Wiessee (near Munich) and directed the summary execution of his erstwhile intimate and the other SA leaders found there. Meanwhile Goering and Himmler, in Berlin, were polishing off Roehm's other chief subordinates. But the killings did not stop with the elimination of the SA chieftains; all over Germany the SS was hunting down other enemies of the regime, past, present and potential. Gregor Strasser, through whom Schleicher had

tried to split the Party in the last weeks of the Republic, died that day, as did the seventy-eight-year-old von Kahr, who had quelled Hitler's 1923 "Beer-Hall *Putsch*". Edgar Jung and Bose (another of Papen's lieutenants) were shot, but "Fraenzchen" himself was spared, perhaps out of fear that his assassination might arouse Hindenburg from the lethargy of approaching death. Not so favoured was another one-time favourite of the Old Gentleman; an SS car drew up in front of Schleicher's Berlin home, and a few moments later both the general and his wife lay dead. Nearly 400 miles away, at Constance, von Bredow was finished off.

This stark and murderous purge had a crushing effect. Papen, who in June had dared declaim Jung's winged words, in July defiled himself by accepting the post of Minister to Austria from Jung's murderers. The SA was utterly cowed. The day of Roehm's execution Hitler blandly announced that he had "relieved . . . Roehm of his position and ejected him from the Party", and under colour of this macabre euphemism appointed Victor Lutze as Roehm's successor. But Lutze was no Roehm, and the SA was never again to play a significant role in the power politics of the Third Reich.

In this respect the Reichswehr's victory was complete. As Jodl testified at Nuremberg, "after the Roehm purge we no longer had any cause for conflict with the SA", for the simple reason that the SA had been decisively and finally eliminated as a potential rival of the Reichswehr. How deeply Blomberg and Reichenau or Fritsch may have been implicated in the bloody massacre by which the Army's victory was achieved can only be surmised. Conceivably none of the military leaders was privy to Hitler's murderous plans, but Gisevius describes a meeting with Reichenau in 1935 at which the latter, "with folded arms and a significant raising of the eyebrows, told me confidentially that it had really not been a simple matter to 'work' things on June 30 so that the affair presented the surface appearance of a 'pure Party matter' ".[6]

In any event, and whatever the degree of the Reichswehr's complicity in advance of the purge, its responsibility as an accessory "after the fact" is clear enough. Despite the despicable and cold-blooded killing of two of its own leading members —Schleicher and Bredow (to say nothing of Frau Schleicher)— not a voice was raised in protest within the officers' corps except those of the discarded Hammerstein and the aged Feldmarschall von Mackensen. Goering cynically claimed that Schleicher

had been shot while reaching for his pistol and that Frau Schleicher had been hit accidentally, but the flimsiness of this excuse was the more evident in that it hardly explained the simultaneous killing of Bredow at Constance. Later on, Hitler perfunctorily "rehabilitated" Schleicher by withdrawing the accusation of treasonable intercourse with foreign powers which had furnished the pretext for the murder. Nevertheless, it was unheard of for two retired generals to be thus butchered by Nazi vigilantes, and the affair was not only a dark stain on the honour of the corps but a sign of weakness which revealed its internal rottenness and presaged the far blacker pages of its history during the ensuing decade.

For the moment, Blomberg and Reichenau were too pleased with the elimination of Roehm and the defeat of the SA to worry overmuch about the corpses of Schleicher and Bredow. Blomberg himself conveyed the cabinet's congratulations to Hitler. And yet it was portentous that it was SS squads which had liquidated both Roehm and Schleicher. Four weeks later, on July 26th, the SS was made an independent branch of the Party, and Himmler, relieved from his humiliating subordination to the Chief of the SA, was given equal status, directly under the Fuehrer. As Gisevius puts it, "with the help of the SS the Army put an end to its rival, the SA—only to find that it had nurtured the SS killers who were to strangle it".[7] Indeed, it was Goering and Himmler rather than the generals who were the real victors of June 30th, and who were soon to emerge as enemies far more dangerous than Roehm.

HINDENBURG'S DEATH AND THE MILITARY OATH OF OBEDIENCE TO HITLER

Throughout the welter and aftermath of June, 1934, death had been plucking at the ear of the *alte Herr*, who had retired to the ancestral estate at Neudeck. Papen had visited there before venturing his Marburg speech but, whatever "Fraenzchen" may have expected or hoped for, no decisive support for his bold challenge to the Nazis emanated from Neudeck when it was most needed. How much the failing *Reichspraesident* was told about the slaughter of June 30th, or how much of what he was told "registered", we will never know. A telegram to Hitler, on July 2nd, bestowed thanks and appreciation for the "determined action" which had "nipped treason in the bud". Surely the old gentleman would have been relieved that his beloved officers' corps had put down the threat of the upstart

Brown Shirts, but what of the fate of his own one-time favourite, Schleicher? Most probably he was never told, and Hitler wisely spared von Papen.

In July, Hindenburg failed rapidly, and on August 2nd the end came, near the close of his eighty-seventh year. His death marked much more than the passing of a *Reichspraesident*. Far more important, Feldmarschall von Hindenburg, *doyen* of the officers' corps, trustee for the Hohenzollerns, and enduring symbol of the *ancien régime*, was no more. To be sure, the photogenic von Mackensen, only two years his junior, was to survive for another decade, but he was little more than a museum piece, whereas Hindenburg, murky as had been his last months, remained a check on Hitler's vaulting ambition and a latent hazard to the Nazi dictatorship until the moment of his death. Now, at long last, the "lid was off". The old field-marshal's death marked the true birthday of the Third Reich.

His funeral and political testament both furnished Hitler with excellent springboards. The ceremonies at Tannenberg were a heaven-sent opportunity to play upon German susceptibility to military pomp and tradition. Hindenburg's testament, too, touched all the old chords. Once again Siegfried was slain by Hagen.[8] Once again the ghost of the "once proud, grand German Army" was invoked, and the nation was exhorted to repeat the miracle of regeneration wrought a century earlier under the leadership of Scharnhorst and Gneisenau. Nor was there any doubt that this time it was Adolf Hitler who was to furnish the guidance and inspiration, for already he had "led the German nation above all professional and class distinctions, to internal unity".

Thus endorsed by the highest authority, and strengthened in his relations with the generals by his suppression of the SA, Hitler seized the opportunity presented by Hindenburg's death. The offices of the *Reichspraesident* and Reich Chancellor were consolidated by governmental decree and merged in the person of Hitler. And for the first time since the abdication of Wilhelm II, the members of the armed forces swore allegiance and obedience to an individual rather than to the State. Following a law proclaimed on August 20th, all officers and men took the required oath:

"I swear by God this sacred oath, that I will render unconditional obedience to Adolf Hitler, the Fuehrer of the German

Reich and people, Supreme Commander of the Armed Forces, and will be ready as a brave soldier to risk my life at any time for this oath."

It is highly probable that no oath in human history has been made to serve so many purposes, or to justify so many sins of omission and commission, as that of August, 1934. Before Hitler's death and the end of the Third Reich, it constantly emerged as a seemingly insurmountable obstacle to any decisive opposition to Hitler within the officers' corps. After the collapse, hardly an officer but cited it constantly, whether sincerely or not, in defence of the terrible charges levelled against the corps.

But in August, 1934, the generals seem to have had few misgivings about the implications of the oath. True, Hitler had stamped out the last embers of liberty and democracy in Germany, but what general cared for liberty or democracy? True, the 30th of June had been a *Schweinerei*, but at least that fellow Roehm was out of the way, and now one could get down to the business of rearmament in real earnest. Certainly this man Hitler was hardly the type to which a German officer was accustomed to swear allegiance, but he seemed to have the secret of arousing the martial spirit among the young men. So far he had treated the generals with great respect, and had given every sign of devotion to the cause of German arms. Anyhow, the Old Man was gone at long last—what else was there to do? If Hitler tried to kick over the traces, the senior generals would know how to handle him—or so they thought.

So reflecting, the officers paraded their men, and read and took the oath. And thus Adolf Hitler, eighteen months after taking office as Chancellor, became the Supreme Commander —the *Oberster Befehlshaber*—of the German Armed Forces.

CHAPTER IV

REICHSWEHR TO WEHRMACHT

THE TWO and a half years from Hindenburg's death to the spring of 1937 were the most harmonious in the life of the Third Reich. Himmler was busy laying the groundwork for the aggrandizement of the SS, and was not yet ready to strike for major power. Frozen out of the police and security racket by Himmler, "unser Hermann" was happily designing uniforms for the nascent Luftwaffe, and aspired to a glorious military career borne on its wings. Relieved by the demise of Roehm and the practical eclipse of the SA and the Party extremists, the industrialists turned eagerly to the profitable and exciting business of rearmament. Politicians of the "moderate" stripe—Schacht, von Neurath, Guertner and von Krosigk—still imagined that they could exert decisive influence in the shaping of government policy.

For the generals, too, this was a time almost of honeymoon with Hitler. Their prerogatives were untouched, and the Fuehrer scrupulously refrained from interfering in the conduct of military business, while showing a most commendable—indeed, phenomenal—faculty in absorbing martial lore and lingo. All this the officers' corps found most flattering and gratifying.

At the same time, Hitler was making the corps' most cherished dreams come true. A wave of extravagant nationalism suffused Germany, and sturdy, militant young recruits flocked to the colours in droves—faster, in fact, than they could be absorbed by traditional methods. Truly the Fuehrer appeared in the guise of a political magician, and he lost no time in commencing to work his miracles. A wave of his hand in the spring of 1935: the "shackles" of Versailles were sundered, and the Luftwaffe unveiled. A shrewd gamble the following year, and German troops could once again manœuvre west of the Rhine, In the twinkling of an eye, the Reichswehr was history, and the Wehrmacht a foreboding reality.

Above all, these were the years of the armourer. In 1938 a stupefied world was to gape in frightened amazement at the

nation which had been thought so impotent barely four years earlier and which had suddenly achieved such terrifying strength. How had such a breath-taking transformation been achieved? Much of the story lay buried in the Krupp files at Essen and in the technical archives of the I.G. Farben chemical plants that dotted the Rhine valley. When, a decade later, these records were brought to light at Nuremberg, it became apparent that many of the martial fruits plucked in the thirties had ripened on trees planted in the twenties. Truly, there was a deep continuity from the Weimar Republic to the Third Reich, as the Krupps and the generals knew, perhaps better than anyone else.

WEHRFREIHEIT

Soon after the elections of March, 1933, had solidified the Nazi grip on the governmental machinery, German clandestine rearmament was greatly accelerated. Throughout the Weimar era, as we have seen, the Versailles restrictions had been constantly and deliberately evaded in a wide variety of ways, both within Germany and in countries such as Russia, Holland and Sweden that were not Treaty signatories. Beginning in May, 1933, however, rearmament proceeded on a much more methodical and calculated basis than theretofore. With no Social Democrats like Scheidemann on hand to put awkward questions in the Reichstag, Hitler no longer needed to worry about domestic opposition, and could gauge the pace exclusively in terms of the international possibilities and risks.

Before Hitler's advent, for example, the Army had not ventured to establish regular military units in excess of the ten-division, 100,000-man limits of the Treaty. The entire organization (*Gliederung*) of the Army down to companies and batteries, as well as the name, rank and assignment of every officer, was published annually in the official rank list of the German Army. The last of these enlightening volumes, however, appeared in 1932. The following year there was conspicuously none,* and for the very good reason that the activation of units above the Treaty limits had begun. Publication of the rank list would have either revealed the assignment of officers to these new units, or necessitated significant omissions. As it was, Fritsch's staff had to admonish the eager Dr. Goebbels, in July, 1934, that any announcements about rearmament,

* Secret rank lists were compiled and printed, and these are now available among the captured military documents.

including reports about enlistments and training courses, must be suppressed. A few months later all counter-intelligence officers were advised that the newly activated units could be listed in telephone and address books only under camouflaged designations, and all staff officers were ordered to avoid any open use of the designation "General Staff". The time was not yet ripe to throw off the mask, albeit the deception was wearing very thin.

In the meantime, naval rearmament did not lag behind. With the excellent rapport which Hitler and Raeder speedily achieved, the Navy had little difficulty in getting funds far in excess of what the public budget showed. During 1934 and 1935, a total of 830 million Reichsmarks was put at Raeder's disposal, of which over half was used for new ships and armaments. The treaty limitation of naval personnel to 15,000 officers and men was ignored from the inception of the "new era"; in 1934 it had already risen to 25,000, and it reached 34,000 the following year. The construction of two battle cruisers, each of some 26,000 tons displacement (the eventual *Scharnhorst and Gneisenau*), was commenced, as well as two cruisers and numerous destroyers. A prototype submarine built in Finland had already been tested at the time of Hitler's advent, and now Raeder began to collect the necessary parts for a dozen or more submarines in Kiel, so that they could be rapidly assembled in case of need or opportunity. In November of 1934 Raeder suggested to Hitler that six of these should be assembled to meet "the critical political situation" expected in the first quarter of 1935,* but Hitler replied that he would notify Raeder "when the situation demanded that the assembly should commence". This was by no means the only occasion on which Hitler was obliged to apply the check-rein rather than the spur to the military leaders.

If Hermann Goering had not happened to have been a leading World War fighter pilot as well as second man in the Nazi Party hierarchy, the Luftwaffe, as an independent arm of the Wehrmacht, might never have been born. Both the Army and the Navy had been secretly dabbling with military aviation during the Weimar years. In Germany—just as in the United States, France and Britain—the advisability of a separate and independent air force was by no means universally conceded within the military profession, nor was the scope of responsibility

---

* This was apparently an anticipatory reference to the repudiation of the Versailles restrictions the following March.

of a separate air force clearly envisaged, should it be established. When Hitler took office, there was a substantial body of opinion that the Army and the Navy should each have their own air components, and that the air arm itself should have only "basic air force training and the operational use of planes for bombing attacks ".[1]

Goering's political influence, however, settled the question in favour of a separate and coequal air force—a Luftwaffe not only independent but furiously jealous of its scope and prerogatives and bent on their constant enlargement. Of course, so long as the pretence of compliance with the Versailles restrictions was maintained, the Luftwaffe had no acknowledged official status. But Goering lost no time in commencing preparations for the eventual unveiling. He utilized his position as Minister of Aviation to expand civil aviation so as to build up a reserve of trained pilots. Training in military aviation was carried on under cover of the League for Aeronautic Sports (*Luftsportverband*). He brought into the Air Ministry as Undersecretary his old associate the Lufthansa official Erhard Milch, to lay the organizational groundwork. Soon Goering appeared in the uniform of a *General der Infanterie*, and Milch in that of an *Oberst*; the latter was speedily promoted to *Generalmajor* (1934) and *Generalleutnant* (1935). Young officers were transferred to the Ministry from the Army and Navy for flying training, and older officers to form the nucleus for future command and General Staff assignments.

It is now apparent, from papers left by Beck, that by the spring of 1934 it had been agreed in the highest circles that Hitler would repudiate the Versailles Treaty on or about April 1, 1935,[2] and thus openly acknowledge to the world the fact of German rearmament. As matters worked out, however, it was Goering's Luftwaffe which finally let—or, rather, kicked—the cat out of the bag. Early in 1935, officers began to appear on the streets of Berlin in new, grey-blue uniforms. Overhead, bombers cruised and fighters played. Fiction had been attenuated to the point of fantasy, and on Sunday, March 10th, Goering utilized a press interview with Ward Price (of the London *Daily Mail*) as the occasion to acknowledge publicly that the Luftwaffe did indeed exist. "In the future", he announced, "the distinction between our fighting force and the civilian air force will be made clear and unmistakable by badges and titles of military rank."

Thus the decade and a half of "clandestine rearmament"

came to an end. The following week-end * (March 16th) Hitler, in a proclamation "to the German people", denounced the Versailles Treaty, proclaimed the reinstitution of compulsory military service, and announced a programme for the enlargement of the Army to thirty-six divisions grouped in twelve corps.

Two months later, under the cover of a soothing declaration that Germany would continue to observe the Locarno Pact and the territorial limits fixed in the Versailles Treaty, a secret Reich Defence Law (dated May 21st) was adopted, defining the powers and responsibilities of the several cabinet ministers in preparing for the eventuality of war. In this sphere they were directed "to observe the instructions" of von Blomberg.

The other leading actor who now took his place on the stage was Hjalmar Horace Greeley Schacht. Reinstated as President of the Reichsbank by Hitler in March, 1933, and appointed Acting Minister of Economics in August 1934, Schacht was designated as "Plenipotentiary General for War Economy" under the new Defence Law, with supervisory jurisdiction over the Ministries of Economics, Food and Agriculture, and Labour. Blomberg and Schacht were directed to "effect the preparation for mobilization in closest co-operation".

This secret and purposeful reorganization was accompanied by wholesale and public rechristening of the top military positions. The "Reichswehr" itself became the "Wehrmacht". Blomberg, hitherto "Minister of Defence", was henceforth designated "Minister of War" (*Reichskriegsminister*) † and he also assumed the title "Commander-in-Chief of the Armed Forces " ‡—a title that no other German officer has ever held. § The old titles "*Chef der Heeresleitung*" and "*Chef der Marineleitung*" were abolished along with the "*Reichsheer*" and the "*Reichsmarine*". Fritsch, Raeder and Goering were each to be known as "Commander-in-Chief" (*Oberbefehlshaber*) of the Army (*Heeres*), Navy (*Kriegsmarine*), and Air Force (*Luftwaffe*) respectively. Thus the independence of the Luftwaffe was established, and Goering promptly shed his uneasy rank of *General der Infan-*

---

* The account of the events of the three days prior to the promulgation of the decree, contained in the book *Zwischen Wehrmacht und Hitler* by Halder's military adjutant (Hossbach) suggests that the exact timing of the decree was not planned in advance, and may well have been precipitated by Goering's press interview.

† Simultaneously the Ministry itself was renamed the *Reichskriegsministerium* (RKM).

‡ Blomberg's title was *Oberbefehlshaber der Wehrmacht*, as distinguished from Hitler's as Supreme Commander—*Oberster Befehlshaber der Wehrmacht*.

§ Hindenburg's leadership of the Reichswehr derived from his office as *Reichspraesident*, not his status as a retired *Feldmarschall*.

terie for the more congenial one of *General der Flieger*. Last but not least, the *"Truppenamt"* camouflage was dropped, and General Ludwig Beck, its chief, emerged as Chief of the General Staff of the Army.

The repudiation of the Versailles arms restrictions—*"Wehrfreiheit"*, as it became known in the lingo of the Third Reich—was an immensely popular action throughout Germany. To the officers' corps, above all, it was the breath of a new life. In the 100,000-man Reichswehr, perforce, promotions came slowly and retirement early, except for a very favoured few. In 1930, the average age of officers holding the rank of *Major*, *Oberstleutnant*, and *Oberst* was 41, 47·5 and 52·25 years respectively, as compared to average ages for these ranks of 35·5, 39 and 43 in 1914. By 1936, these averages were back to the approximate level of 1914, and several thousand retired officers had been reactivated. The number of generals was quadrupled and of colonels more than tripled; the 42 generals and 105 colonels of 1932 had increased to over 150 and 325 respectively in 1936.[3]

Small wonder, then, that all open and most latent opposition to Hitler in the ranks of the officers' corps was withered at the roots. A deep and genuine enthusiasm for the Fuehrer's achievements pervaded the military leadership, and many who had previously maintained a reserved attitude hastened to make public avowal of their fealty.

This new warmth of feeling was spectacularly demonstrated in the fall of 1935, when the historic *Kriegsakademie*, founded by Scharnhorst in 1810 but closed in 1920 by mandate of Versailles, was publicly ensconced in a new building. The date chosen, October 18th, was the 125th anniversary of the Academy's foundation, and great ceremony attended the occasion. The Fuehrer himself was in attendance with Goebbels and Otto Dietrich at his heels. Both the aged Feldmarschall von Mackensen and von Seeckt were on hand in full dress, as well as other venerable relics of the glorious past. Among the active military leaders present were Blomberg, Fritsch, Beck, Rundstedt, Witzleben, the newly appointed Commandant of the Academy, General der Infanterie Liebmann, and Goering and Milch from the Luftwaffe.

The exercises were graced by speeches not only by Blomberg, whose fulsome eulogy of Hitler was by now routine, but also by Beck and Liebmann, both of whom (though commoners) were highly respected senior members of the officers' corps. In their

utterances was no sign of the reserved attitude which many old-line generals had theretofore observed; both spoke out enthusiastically and devotedly for the Fuehrer. Liebmann, who had served under both Mackensen and Seeckt in the First World War, opened the proceedings by declaring:

"This memorial day comes in the year in which one of the restricting bonds of the Versailles Treaty has been torn away by your [Hitler's] actions on March 16th, and the German people have been given again their freedom of arms. . . . We realize and we are convinced in our deepest being that we have solely your determined will and your infallible leadership to thank for our freedom and—like the German people—we and the entire German Wehrmacht will show our thanks to you, our Fuehrer, through unflinching faithfulness and devotion."

Even more strikingly demonstrative of the temper of the times, and far more significant now in retrospect, was Beck's beautifully contrived speech. Three short years later Beck's was to be the leading voice in opposition to Hitler's plans for the immediate conquest of Czechoslovakia—an opposition which resulted promptly in his retirement from the Army. And in 1944 Beck was to meet his death as the central figure in the abortive *Putsch* of the 20th of July. Ever since the end of the war, Beck has been held up as the archetype of enlightened German officerdom, a courageous opponent of tyranny and a worker for peace.

Cultured, sensitive and imaginative as Beck undoubtedly was, his address to the august martial assembly betrayed him as a victim of their preconceptions and a slave to the traditions that were being celebrated. In his opening words, there cropped out that perverse militarist philosophy that regards a lost war, and a defeated and prostrate Germany, as a glorious opportunity to start again on the same terrible cycle. "The hour of death of our old magnificent Army on July 28, 1919", caused by "a dictate of twenty-seven enemy states, filled with hatred", had nevertheless "led to the new life of the young Reichswehr". The defeat of 1918 "was not, as it had been in 1806, a military failure"; rather, "the old German Army returned from the war crowned with the laurels of immortality". Therefore, in reconstructing the Reichswehr, it had been "not so important to find new ways" as to preserve those factors "which made up the tremendous military superiority of the old Army". In conclusion, Beck reminded his audience that Germany was a "military-minded nation", and exhorted the young officer-students

to remember always "the duty which they owe to the man who re-created and made strong again the German Wehrmacht and who finally struck off the fetters of Versailles".

RUHIG FLIESST DER RHEIN

But one of those fetters remained as yet unstricken—the Treaty articles requiring the demilitarization of the Rhineland. A rudimentary plan for the transfer of troops into the demilitarized zone had been prepared by Blomberg (under the code name *Schulung*) in May, 1935, but no further steps were taken for nearly a year thereafter. In the middle of February, 1936, Hitler himself brought up the idea in conferences with Fritsch and Blomberg, as well as with von Hassell, then the Ambassador in Rome, who was specially summoned to Munich for these discussions. On March 2, 1936, Blomberg issued the order for the reoccupation to the three service commanders-in-chief, and the operation was actually carried out on March 7th, under the pretext that the Franco-Russian alliance had rendered both Locarno and the Versailles restrictions obsolete.

The move was made in divisional strength, under military plans prepared by the then Oberst von Manstein, under the supervision of Beck and Fritsch. Two fighter squadrons of Goering's Luftwaffe were also moved in. But only three battalions were sent across the Rhine, and there appears to have been no thought of risking hostilities in the event of a French decision to oppose the move. For a few days there was extreme tension, and disturbing reports from the military attachés in Paris and London caused Blomberg (on the advice of his subordinates Keitel and Jodl) to propose that the three battalions be drawn back to the eastern bank of the Rhine. But Fritsch opposed the withdrawal, and Hitler rejected Blomberg's recommendation. The latter's reputation for firmness and steady nerves was not enhanced by this episode.

Hitler's confidence and Fritsch's firmness were soon vindicated. The French grumbled, but did not move, and the infant Wehrmacht won its first bloodless victory, albeit still on German soil. Once again the *Kasernen* of the Rhineland overflowed with German soldiers, and in the fall a new *Wehrkreis* and corps headquarters were established in Wiesbaden. Two years later, from one end of the Rhineland to the other, the West Wall was under feverish construction. The tempo of Europe's martial music was *accelerando*.

In 1941, when the Wehrmacht's fortunes were at flood tide, Gustav Krupp von Bohlen und Halbach delivered himself of an article describing his mental processes in the dark days of 1919. "The situation appeared almost hopeless," he wrote. But "I knew German history only too well [*sic*] . . . therefore I never doubted that, although for the time being all the indications were contrary, someday a change would come. How I did not know, and did not ask, but I believed." And accordingly "if Germany should ever be reborn, if it were ever to shake off the chains of Versailles, the Krupp concern would have to be prepared".

How Krupp, in tandem with the *Heeresleitung* and *Marineleitung* "prepared" during the Weimar years has already been sketched.[4] And in 1931 and 1932, as the Nazi shadow lengthened, Gustav Krupp began to perceive how the long-awaited "change would come". Even before Hitler became Chancellor, it was clear to those in the know that a large-scale rearmament programme was in the offing. It was in keeping with this prospect that at the end of 1932 Oberst Zwengauer, then Chief of the Artillery Department of the Army Ordnance Office, sent a New Year's greeting to the Krupp firm: "I wish to express our thanks for the excellent support which you and your staff have given us in our development work during the past year. This department is convinced that, thanks to your active co-operation and valuable advice, our armament development in 1932 has made considerable progress, which is of great significance to our intent of rearming as a whole."

And so, just as the officers' corps found itself in fundamental agreement with Hitler's political aims, so did Krupp. Indeed, the cannon king's conversion was more speedily and completely effected than that of most of the generals. At the fund-raising meeting of Ruhr industrialists on February 20, 1933, at which Hitler and Goering so clearly revealed their tyrannical intentions, Gustav Krupp took the lead in endorsing Hitler's programme, and pledged 1,000,000 marks from the Ruhr industrialists. After the March elections, Krupp fell in wholeheartedly with the march of dictatorship. As Chairman of the Reich Association of German Industry, he submitted the plan for reorganization of German industry according to the "Fuehrer-Prinzip". He organized and, until 1942, headed the so-called "Adolf Hitler Spende", a fund collected annually from every

circle of German industry, finance and agriculture for the benefit of the SS, SA, Hitler Youth, and other Party organizations. He helped to finance Alfred Rosenberg's Nazi propaganda campaign in foreign countries. Everywhere—at public meetings, industrial conferences and in print—Gustav Krupp was a vocal and enthusiastic protagonist of the Third Reich.

And now the gamble with the future on which Krupp had embarked from the inception of the Weimar era paid off, and handsomely. "After the assumption of power by Adolf Hitler", Krupp wrote, "I had the satisfaction of being able to report to the Fuehrer that Krupp's stood ready, after a short warming-up period, to begin the rearmament of the German people without any gaps in our experience." And in consequence, it was possible "to produce immediately heavy artillery, armour plate, tanks, and other arms in large quantities. . . . In the years after 1933, we worked with incredible intenseness. . . ."

In agreement with the Army, throughout the Weimar years, Krupp had concentrated on problems of design, and little or no effort had been made to build up secret stock-piles of arms. Von Seeckt had always counselled against the accumulation in peace-time of large quantities of weapons, because of their rapid obsolescence as science and technology advance. "There is only one way in which we shall be able to provide for the arming of great masses of troops," he wrote.[5] "This is to decide upon the type of arm which at any given time is the best available and then to make provision for its intensive production in case of need" by suitable arrangement "with the industrialists of the nation".

The results of this policy were sensationally successful. Indeed, the Krupp and Wehrmacht documents produced at Nuremberg reveal that the standard guns and tanks used by the German Army upon the outbreak of war in 1939 *had been developed by Krupp under the Weimar regime before the Nazis came to power*. A Krupp memorandum written in 1942 declares that "the basic principle of armament and turret design for tanks had already been worked out in 1926". And a history of the firm's activities in the field of artillery design, prepared by the Krupp department immediately concerned, discloses that, while the weapons developed in the middle twenties "must be classed as forerunners", nevertheless:

> "they made an appreciable contribution towards clarifying opinions and requirements . . . and thus entirely served their purpose. They were followed shortly afterwards by the weapons which were

finally adopted. Of the guns which were being used in 1938–41, the most important ones were already fully completed in 1933, the mortar was almost completed, and the light field gun also was ready for use."

With submarines, the story was about the same. By means of Krupp's dummy corporation in the Netherlands (the I.v.S.),[6] the prototype of the German Navy's first 250-ton submarines (*U*-1 to *U*-24) was constructed in Finland beginning in 1930; a 750-ton boat built in Cadiz, by secret arrangement with King Alfonso and Primo de Rivera, was completed and tested in 1931. This submarine was sold to the Turkish Navy in 1934, but it served as the model for the first two German "flag" U-boats (*U*-25 and *U*-26). From 1933 to 1935, the Krupp-built parts for a dozen 250-ton boats and the two larger vessels were accumulated at Kiel, where special sheds were built to permit the assemblage of six U-boats simultaneously.

The result of this pre-Hitler collaboration between the Navy and Krupp was, as a secret German naval history puts it, the "astonishing fact" that

"it was possible to commission the first submarine only three and a half months after restoration of military sovereignty on March 16, 1935, that is to say on June 29; and then, at intervals of about eight days, to put new submarines continuously into service, so that on October 1, 1935, twelve submarines with fully trained personnel were in service.

"On March 7, 1936, during the critical period of the occupation of the demilitarized zone on the western border [the Rhineland], eighteen submarines were at our disposal, seventeen of which had already passed their test period, and in case of emergency could have been employed without difficulty on the French coast as far as the Gironde."

Arms for the Wehrmacht meant profits for Krupp. The year after Hitler's seizure of power the Krupp directors were able to note, in their annual report, that "the business, for the first time after three years of losses, shows a profit". Tanks were built by the hundreds even before the repudiation of the Versailles Treaty, under the camouflage of "agricultural tractors". In 1935, Krupp net profits totalled 57 million Reichsmarks; in 1938, 97 million.

As the Wehrmacht burgeoned, Krupp's proportionate share in its construction perforce diminished. Contracts, based on designs worked out by the Wehrmacht and Krupp, were allocated to many other concerns. In sheer production capacity,

Krupp was dwarfed by the enormous Ruhr steel combine Vereinigte Stahlwerke, and rivalled by the newly assembled empire of Friedrich Flick.

But the Krupp firm never lost its symbolic pre-eminence as the "Weapons Forge" of the Wehrmacht, nor its leadership in design. Hitler continued to visit Essen and to honour Krupp publicly and treat him with greater deference than rival tycoons enjoyed. This favour was signally manifested during the war, as Gustav's health failed and his son Alfried assumed actual management responsibility. In November, 1943, a special decree—the "Lex Krupp"—recognized Alfried as the sole owner and conferred various tax and other benefits on the enterprise. No other industrial concern in Nazi Germany was ever so honoured. And, as Gustav Krupp himself stated in 1940 when receiving a "Golden Banner" from the hands of Rudolf Hess, these honours were in recognition of "a socio-political attitude which, having its roots in a 128-year-old tradition, has developed organically so as to fit into the new times, into National Socialist Germany".

I.G. FARBEN: WIZARDS OF ERSATZ

The Wehrmacht's magical resurgence involved other mysteries which remain to be unfolded. Submarines and tanks and guns are made of steel, and the words "Ruhr" and "steel" had long been practically synonymous. But since the advent of airplanes, tanks and motorized troops, steel has had two great rivals as basic ingredients of warfare: petrol and rubber. Germany was totally lacking in natural resources of either commodity. How many times during the recent war did we not read optimistic reports of the approaching exhaustion of German oil and rubber reserves, which would leave the Wehrmacht fatally crippled? How was the Thousand-Year Reich to cope with this grave weakness in its structure?

The answer lay in the great chemical plants that line the valley of the Rhine from Baden to Westphalia. Once before, during the First World War, these factories had plugged what would otherwise have been a mortal chink in Germany's armour. Cut off from access to Chilean saltpetre by the British naval blockade, and with stocks of nitrates dwindling rapidly, as early as 1915 the Kaiser's forces had been saved by Farben science and technology, through development of the famed Haber-Bosch method for the production of synthetic nitrates from air. Carl Bosch's *Badische Anilin-und Soda Fabrik* at Ludwigshaven was thus

enabled to commence the manufacture of explosives from these ersatz nitrates. Far more sensational at the time, but of less fundamental significance, was the development of poisonous gases in the laboratories of the same plants.

After the First World War, all the major chemical concerns were merged in 1926 into a single gigantic trust—the I.G. Farbenindustrie A.G.*—under the leadership of Carl Duisberg and Carl Bosch. Dyestuffs, pharmaceuticals, photographic supplies, explosives and a myriad of other products poured forth in ever-growing volume and variety. And, long before Hitler achieved notoriety, Farben scientists were wrestling with the two problems most vital to Germany's industrial self-sufficiency in case of war—the development of processes for the successful manufacture of synthetic petrol and synthetic rubber.

The petrol problem proved the easier of the two. Soon after the merger of 1926, the now-famous Farben hydrogenation process was perfected, enabling Germany's coal to be transformed into oil, petrol and other synthetic fuels and lubricants. As an excited Standard Oil official, Frank Howard, then put the matter to his president, Walter Teagle, in a confidential letter: "The Badische [the Farben Ludwigshaven plant] can make high-grade motor fuel from lignite and other low-quality coal in amounts up to half the weight of the coal. This means absolutely the independence of Europe in the matter of gasoline supply. Straight price competition is all that is left. . . . I shall not attempt to cover any details, but I think this will be evidence of my state of mind."

Thereafter Farben commenced actual production of petrol at its Leuna plant, but the process was expensive, and during the financial depression of the early thirties several Farben directors favoured abandoning the project. The critical situation led to what appears to have been the first direct contact between Hitler and the Farben management. The Farben emissaries were Heinrich Buetefisch, chief of the Leuna plant, and Heinrich Gattineau, a Farben official who was also an SA officer and personally known to both Rudolf Hess and Ernst Roehm. Soon after the election of July, 1932, in which the Nazis had doubled their vote, Buetefisch and Gattineau waited upon the Fuehrer-to-be to learn whether Farben could count on governmental support for its synthetic petrol programme in the event of the Nazis attaining power. Hitler readily agreed that Farben

* The "I.G." stands for "Interessengemeinschaft", and the name may be roughly rendered in English as "Community of Interests of the Dyestuffs Industry, Inc.".

should be given the necessary support to warrant expansion of the Leuna plant.

After the seizure of power, Farben lost no time in following up this auspicious introduction. Significantly, Farben's chosen channel was not the *Heeresleitung* but Hermann Goering's new Air Ministry. In a long letter to Goering's deputy Erhard Milch, Carl Krauch of Farben outlined a "four-year plan" for the expansion of synthetic fuel output. Milch thereupon called in Generalleutnant von Vollard Bockelberg, Chief of the Army Ordnance Office, and it was agreed that the Army and the Air Ministry together would sponsor the Krauch project. A few months later Farben received a formal Reich contract calling for the enlargement of Leuna so that production would reach 300,000 tons per year by 1937, with Farben's sales guaranteed for ten years—until June 30, 1944—on a cost-plus basis.

With the synthetic petrol programme successfully launched, Farben redoubled its research activities in the field of synthetic rubber. By 1935, sufficient progress had been made to attract favourable attention in the very highest circles. In September, 1935, Hitler's personal economic adviser, Wilhelm Keppler, informed Fritz Ter Meer, a leading director of Farben, that the Fuehrer himself, to say nothing of Blomberg and Generalmajor Kurt Leise (Bockelberg's successor), had demanded that "the problem of synthetic rubber" be dealt with "most emphatically", in order to make "fast progress in motorizing the Army". The following year, after the government had extended the usual guarantees, Farben put up at Schkopau its first plant for the large-scale production of synthetic "buna" rubber. By 1941 two more were in production and a fourth was under construction in Poland adjacent to the notorious Auschwitz concentration camp, whose miserable inmates built the plant pursuant to arrangements between Carl Krauch of Farben and Heinrich Himmler. Thus was the Wehrmacht's rubber problem solved.

The military importance of Farben's development of synthetic petrol and rubber was comparable to, if not greater than, that of nitrates in the First World War. Bureaucrats and generals alike fully realized how dependent was the Reich on the inventive genius of Farben's scientists and the management skill of Farben directors.

Largely because Farben was a widely owned stock corporation rather than a family enterprise like the Krupp concern, it presented an "impersonal" appearance to the public, and no individual Farben director achieved the world-wide notoriety

of the Krupps. Nevertheless, men like Carl Duisberg and Carl Bosch, and their successors such as Hermann Schmitz, Carl Krauch and Fritz Ter Meer, were of extraordinary stature and influence in German politico-economic affairs.

Nor did their *Weltanschauung* differ markedly from that of Krupp and the other Ruhr steel barons. As early as 1925, addressing the Association of German Industry, Carl Duisberg had called for "the strong man" who "is always necessary for us Germans, as we have seen in the case of Bismarck". A year later he insisted on "leaders . . . who can act without concern for the caprices of the masses", and by 1930 he was openly decrying democracy and trade unionism and advocating an authoritarian form of government. Small wonder that Farben was represented at the meeting of February 20, 1933, at which Hitler expounded his plan for the liquidation of democracy in Germany, and Goering, Schacht and Gustav Krupp called on the assembled industrialists for contributions to the Nazi cause in the coming elections. Small wonder that Farben made the largest payment —400,000 marks—by any single firm represented at the gathering. In July, 1933, as the grip of tyranny was being tightened by the suppression of trade unions, the prostitution of the judiciary, and the persecution of Jews and all political opponents of the new regime, Carl Bosch told some American visitors, representatives of the du Pont Company, that German industry "must support the present government to prevent further chaos". A few months later Hermann Schmitz of the Farben directorate was elected to the Reichstag as a Nazi Party nominee. In America, Farben retained the well-known publicity promoter, Ivy Lee, to combat the anti-Nazi commercial boycott and cultivate "understanding".

As was wholly natural, the relations between Farben and the Wehrmacht became increasingly intimate as the pace of rearmament quickened. In September, 1935, Farben established in Berlin a special liaison office—known as *Vermittlungstelle W*— to handle all matters in which the Wehrmacht was involved. In one highly important respect, however, Farben's military situation developed differently from that of Krupp. The latter dealt primarily with the Army and Navy through the Reich War Ministry; Farben, *per contra*, manifested an ever-growing affinity for the Air Ministry and Luftwaffe.

At the outset the Farben officials dealt principally with Milch, who supported their first big contract for the production of synthetic petrol. In 1936, however, Goering began to interest

himself increasingly in economic questions and to threaten Schacht's pre-eminence in such matters. In September of that year the Office of the Four-Year Plan was established under Goering as Plenipotentiary in Charge, and shortly thereafter Carl Krauch left the Farben management * to become Chief of the Department of Research and Development, immediately subordinate to Goering. It was a relationship which was to prove of great significance in the political crisis of 1937–38.

THE NEW WEHRMACHT

And so from the mines and mills of the Ruhr, from industrial laboratories like those of Farben, from the Fatherland's myriad country towns and teeming cities, and from the martial skills and traditions of nearly two centuries, the Wehrmacht of the Third Reich drew the breath of life and gathered strength. Its formative years were few—too few to suit the careful professional soldiers who guided its growth. A bare half decade elapsed from Hitler's seizure of power to his first use of the Wehrmacht as an offensive weapon to cow Schuschnigg in March of 1938, and but eighteen months later World War II engulfed Europe. The generals had counted on at least a full decade of preparation. The Wehrmacht of 1938–39, precociously powerful, was the product of forced feeding. Small wonder that it had suffered severely from indigestion and growing pains.

This instability permeated the topmost reaches of the Wehrmacht. Ever since Schleicher's appointment to the *Reichswehrministerium* in 1926, there had been an unsolved equation between the Ministry officials and the Army leadership. The close relations between Schleicher and Hammerstein concealed this imbalance during the last few Weimar years, but with the advent of Blomberg and Reichenau in 1933 there was a recurrence of the disease in acute form.

In the fall of 1935, the restless and ambitious Reichenau tired of his desk job at the *Wehrmachtamt*, powerful as his position there was, and procured his own transfer to the field as Commander of Wehrkreis VII in Munich.† Pro-Nazi as Reichenau had always been, his successor was destined to exert an even more corrosive influence. He was Generalmajor Wilhelm Keitel, a dull and flabby but shrewd and grasping officer. Despite or

* Krauch maintained his connection with Farben, however, as Chairman of the *Aufsichtsrat*, or supervisory council.

† Reichenau replaced General Wilhelm Adam (on October 1, 1935), who was simultaneously appointed head of the newly established *Wehrmachtakademie* in Berlin.

because of Keitel's notable lack of *élan*, he became Blomberg's valued crutch, and Keitel's eldest son married Blomberg's youngest daughter. A measure of imagination and analytical ability was brought to the War Ministry by a young newcomer to the upper levels of command, Oberstleutnant Alfred Jodl. Regarded as a brilliant and promising staff officer by Adam, Beck and others, Jodl was detailed to the *Wehrmachtamt* by Beck in 1935, but soon became an adherent of Blomberg and Keitel, much to Beck's disgust.

Under Blomberg, the military staff of the Minister of War was enlarged, notably by the establishment of a small operational planning division under Jodl which inevitably gave rise to friction between the ministry (RKM) and the planning division of the Army General Staff at OKH.* Theoretically, the RKM was supposed to co-ordinate the functions of all three branches of the Wehrmacht. In fact, however, both Raeder and Goering maintained a very independent attitude. Raeder insisted on handling naval affairs directly with Hitler, "to prevent his being instructed by von Blomberg . . . regarding Navy affairs, since that would have created the danger that, in the distribution of funds, the Navy would be short-funded as compared to the Army".[7] Goering was subordinate to Blomberg in the former's capacity as Commander-in-Chief of the Luftwaffe, but retained his coequal title of Minister of Aviation, and the RKM exercised little or no influence in Air Force matters.

In fact, one basic difficulty with the whole idea of the BKM as an interservice co-ordinating agency was that the Army was by far the most important of the three branches. This inevitably impelled the Air Force (OKL) and Navy (OKM) leaders to insist jealously on their independent status, in order to avoid being swallowed up by the Army. Just as inevitably, it resulted that the RKM was basically a second army high command, constantly overlapping the functions and threatening the prerogatives of the OKH.

Until 1938, Fritsch and Beck were able to preserve the autonomy of the OKH and independence of action in Army matters. The staff of the OKH remained far larger and more highly articulated than that of the RKM. After the *Truppenamt* was transformed into the *Generalstab* in March, 1935, the old sub-divisions of the *Truppenamt*—T 1 to T 4 [8]—were reshuffled and renamed.

* The highest headquarters of the Army bore the name *Oberkommando des Heeres*, and was commonly designated OKH. Similarly, the highest headquarters of the Air Force and Navy, respectively, were commonly referred to as OKL and OKM.

Immediately subordinated to the Chief of the General Staff were the two *Oberquartiermeister* (O. Qu.) each of whom supervised several sections (*Abteilungen*) of the General Staff. The O. Qu. I was a key position, carrying command of the operations, transport and supply sections. Until 1936 the O. Qu. I was a brilliant *Generalmajor*, Gustav Anton von Wietersheim, and from 1936 to 1938 the then Generalmajor Fritz Erich von Lewinski *gennant* Manstein, later one of the principal architects of the 1940 breakthrough in France and a *Feldmarschall* in the Russian fighting. Under the O. Qu. II and III were additional sections dealing with training, intelligence and technical and other matters.* Also subordinate to the Chief of the General Staff from 1935 to 1938 was Oberstleutnant Friedrich Hossbach, a General Staff officer assigned to Hitler as his personal military adjutant. Hossbach, who adhered to the Fritsch–Beck rather than the Blomberg wing of the High Command, was the recorder of the fateful conference of November 5, 1937, at which Hitler revealed his plans to annex Austria and Czechoslovakia, and by virtue of this record and his subsequent writings [9] has become a figure of some significance in German military history.

The Chief of the General Staff also supervised the principal Army war academy. The old *Kriegsakademie* for the training of future General Staff officers was secretly re-established on August 1, 1934, under Liebmann, who was publicly relieved of his command of Wehrkreis V in Stuttgart and ostensibly retired. After the denunciation of the Versailles Treaty the following year, the rebirth of the *Kriegsakademie* was announced, and in October, 1935, its 125th anniversary was celebrated with the ceremonies and speeches already described.

That same month, the new *Wehrmachtakademie* was established in Berlin under General der Infanterie Wilhelm Adam. This was a small and highly select institute for training promising middle-ranking officers (six from the Army and two each from the Navy and Air Force) in higher strategy and the co-ordination of the three branches of the Wehrmacht. Adam and Beck were close personal friends, and Army General Staff thinking dominated the Academy. Being an interservice institution, however, it was technically subordinate to the RKM rather than OKH.

---

* From 1935 to 1937, the second *Oberquartiermeister* (Generalmajor Rudolf Schmidt) was designated O. Qu. III. In 1937 his functions were divided; Schmidt was transferred to command the 1st Panzer Division, and Generalleutnant Franz Halder became O. Qu. II and Oberst Eugen Mueller O. Qu. III.

106

Directly subordinate to Fritsch were four other departments of the OKH, theoretically equal in status but actually narrower in scope than the General Staff. A variety of administrative, supply and recruiting functions were performed under the *Allgemeine Heeresamt* (headed by Generalmajor Fromm, who met his death during the *Putsch* of July 20, 1944, after playing a vacillating and discreditable part) and the *Heeresverwaltungsamt* (under Generalleutnant Karmann). Assignments, transfers and promotions in the officers' corps were handled by the *Heerespersonalamt* (under the influential Generalleutnant von Schwedler). But surely the most important of these four departments was the *Heereswaffenamt* under Kurt Liese, who rose from *Oberst* to *General der Infanterie* during the four years (November, 1933, to February, 1938) of his tenure. The *Heereswaffenamt* controlled all matters pertaining to the design and production of weapons and Liese's colleagues included the Army's foremost ordnance specialists, such as Becker and Zwengauer.

Under this superstructure, the German field Army grew like a mushroom. Soon after Hitler came to power, preparations were begun to transform the seven *Wehrkreise* from divisional to corps headquarters. By the time of *Wehrfreiheit* this process had been virtually completed, and in each *Wehrkreis* three divisions manoeuvred where only one had been before. Two new *Wehrkreise* had also been formed. The three cavalry divisions of the old Reichswehr were abolished, and one of these emerged as Wehrkreis VIII at Breslau, while a new Wehrkreis IX was being established at Kessel. On May 2, 1935, Goering told the foreign press correspondents that the German Army already comprised twenty-seven divisions; no doubt his calculation was based on three divisions to each of the nine *Wehrkreise*.

The announced goal of twelve corps and thirty-six divisions was rapidly achieved. Wehrkreis X was established in Hamburg in 1935. In August, 1936, Hitler ordered the extension of the term of compulsory military service from one to two years, and about six weeks later the creation of Wehrkreise XI in Hanover and XII in Wiesbaden (in the newly remilitarized Rhineland) was revealed in the published Army orders. At the end of 1936 the twelve *Wehrkreise* were commanded, in order, by von Brauchitsch, Błaskowitz, von Witzleben, List, Geyer, von Kluge, von Reichenau, von Kleist, Dollmann, Knochenhauer, Ulex, and Kress von Kressenstein, all of whom held the rank of *General*.*

* All twelve of these officers were promoted to the rank of *General* in the twelve-month period October 1, 1935, to October 1, 1936.

This multiplication of *Wehrkreise* had already required the setting up, in 1935, of a third *Gruppenkommando* (Army group headquarters) in Dresden under General der Infanterie Fedor von Bock. Bock thus joined the two previously appointed Army

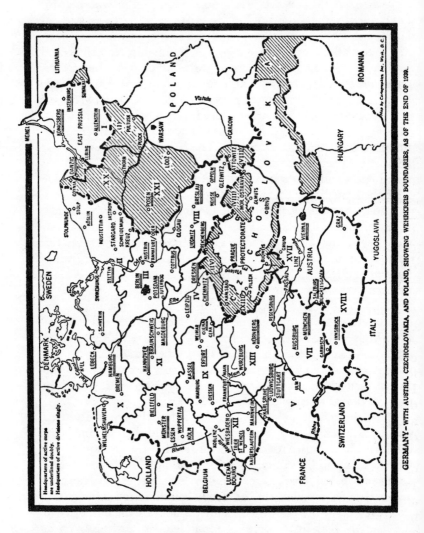

GERMANY—WITH AUSTRIA, CZECHOSLOVAKIA, AND POLAND, SHOWING WEHRKREIS BOUNDARIES, AS OF THE END OF 1938.

group commanders, Rundstedt and Leeb (to whom Bock was immediately junior in rank), as the three senior field generals—the *Heerfuehrer*—of the German Army. It was a trio that was to endure until 1942. Rundstedt, Leeb and Bock commanded the three Army groups in which the Field Army was organized dur-

ing the Polish and French campaigns of 1939–40 and the initial march into Russia in 1941.

In 1937, however, it speedily became apparent that the twelve corps–thirty-six division dimension had been an immediate, but not an ultimate, objective. During the spring of that year Wehrkreis XIII made its appearance, with headquarters at Nuremberg and commanded by General der Kavallerie Freiherr von Weichs. Geographically speaking, Germany (within the Versailles Treaty boundaries) remained permanently divided into thirteen *Wehrkreise*.

Furthermore, new formations of motorized and armoured troops were making their appearance. Generalleutnant Oswald Lutz and his Chief of Staff, Oberst Heinz Guderian, had long advocated that entire divisions of panzers should be established and used as an independent striking force. They met opposition from Beck and other conservative generals, who envisaged that tanks would be useful chiefly to support the infantry, and therefore should be organized in units not larger than brigades. During the summer of 1935, Lutz and Guderian prevailed to the extent that three panzer divisions were set up. Guderian, despite his very junior rank, was given command of one of these; Lutz, an experienced specialist in military transport, was promoted to *General der Panzertruppen* (he was the first to hold this rank),[10] and was appointed commander of a new headquarters (*Kommando der Panzertruppen*), to which all three of the armoured divisions were subordinated.

The champions of the tank divisions did not, however, win a complete victory over the old guard. Tank brigades were also formed and attached to various of the regular Wehrkreise. Likewise, three new divisions of a hybrid nature (called "light" divisions) were formed, with motorized infantry regiments and a battalion of tanks. In addition, four of the existing infantry divisions (the 2nd, 13th, 20th and 29th) were motorized.

The result of all this was a rather considerable reorganization or the motorized and armoured units, which took place in late 1937 and early 1938. Three new corps headquarters (XIV, XV, and XVI) without territorial jurisdiction were established. The motorized infantry divisions were subordinated to the XIVth and the light divisions to the XVth Corps. The *Kommando der Panzertruppen* became the XVIth Corps, and retained command of the panzer divisions. At the same time, a fourth Army Group headquarters, also non-territorial, was set up in Leipzig to command the three new corps. The new Army Group

commander was General der Artillerie Walter von Brauchitsch,* the future and last military Commander-in-Chief of the German Army. The three new corps commanders, all appointed early in 1938, were Wietersheim, Hoth and Guderian.†

The organization of the German Navy was far simpler than that of the Army and underwent less modification in the course of the Navy's growth. Under Raeder as Commander-in-Chief, the OKM was divided into a number of departments for ordnance, personnel, administration and other functions. Operational planning was handled by the Naval War Staff (*Seekriegsleitung*, or SKL), analogous to the Army General Staff, but headed by Raeder himself. Under the OKM, the several Naval group commands controlled all naval operations in specified geographical sections, except for the High Seas Fleet and the submarines, both of which, by their very nature, were too mobile for assignment to an area command and were directly subordinate to Raeder. From 1936, soon after the first U-boats were launched, to 1943, when he succeeded Raeder as Commander-in-Chief, the submarine commander was Karl Doenitz, who rose in rank during those years from *Kapitaen zur See* to *Admiral*. Admiral Rolf Carls was Commander of the Fleet from 1936 to 1938, when he was succeeded by Admiral Boehm. From 1938 on Raeder's Chief of Staff was Konteradmiral Otto Schniewind. Raeder and Doentiz were fixtures, but the other leading admirals—Schniewind, Carls, Albrecht and others—were transferred from post to post comparatively frequently. Naval expansion was reflected in the jump in the number of admirals (of all grades) from twelve in 1931 to thirty-two in 1938.

Compared to the Army, however, the Navy remained a small-time operation. Major emphasis, of course, was placed on the submarine arm, and the construction of a High Seas Fleet was undertaken only tentatively and half-heartedly. The battle cruisers *Scharnhorst* and *Gneisenau* were launched in the last months of 1936, and construction of the eventual *Bismarck* and

---

* Brauchitsch had been the commander of Wehrkreis I in East Prussia, where he was succeeded by General der Artillerie von Kuechler. The *Kommando de Panzertruppen* (later renamed the XVIth Corps) was subordinated to the new Army Group, and Brauchitsch's rank as General der Artillerie was dated back to October 1, 1935, in order to give him seniority over Lutz.

† Wietersheim and Hoth were promoted to the rank of *General* early in February, 1938, and Guderian in November of that year. In November Guderian was relieved of his corps command and assumed the office of *Chef der Schnellen Truppen* on the OKH General Staff. He was succeeded as commanding general of the XVIth Corps by Generalleutnant Hoepner, who was to be a victim of the July 20, 1944, *Putsch*.

Tirpitz was commenced during the same year. Additional capital ships were subsequently planned and laid down, but in 1939 construction was discontinued and they were broken up. Inasmuch as the Anglo-German Naval Treaty of June, 1935, authorized Germany to build its fleet up to 35 per cent of the British strength, German naval construction precipitated far less international tension than in the case of the Army and the Luftwaffe.

It was the Luftwaffe, indeed, which chiefly caused the fear which spread and deepened over Europe from 1935 on. And yet it was never as powerful as it was commonly thought to be, and eventually it proved totally inadequate for what it was called upon to do. It gave good tactical support to the Army in the early years of the war, and pressed the Royal Air Force to the limit of endurance in the Battle of Britain. But eventually it was bled to death, and Goering's grandiloquent boasts reaped a terrible harvest of destruction in the Fatherland.

From its birth, the Luftwaffe's history was stormy, commencing with Army and Navy opposition to its very existence. During the Weimar era both the *Heeresleitung* and the *Marineleitung* had endeavoured to keep abreast of developments in aerial warfare, and to utilize Germany's civilian air lines for technical research and as a reservoir of trained personnel, against the day when the Versailles ban on military aviation would be lifted or could be disregarded. In both the Army and Navy, especially in the former, were numerous officers with air experience in the First World War. Some of these men regarded the future German air arm as their personal province, and resented bitterly the advent of Goering and his favourites. In the Army, for instance, Oberst Wilberg had served most of the war on the Army Air Staff, and cherished high hopes of leading the incipient air arm. In the Navy, Captains Zander and Wenninger had headed a secret office of the *Marineleitung* for the development of naval aviation. These officers were transferred in 1933 to Goering's new-born Air Ministry, but some of them—notably Wilberg—accepted their subordination to Goering only grudgingly.

Thus the partnership of Goering with the professional soldiers was at best an uneasy one. Nonetheless, each was dependent on the other. Goering's political stature as Second Man of the Third Reich was unassailable, and it was quite apparent that the Air Force was to be his jealously guarded preserve. On the other hand, Goering was faced with the necessity of staffing his Ministry and officering his Luftwaffe—a need which could only

be met by extensive borrowing from the officers' corps of the Army and, to a lesser degree, the Navy. Some of his staff, to be sure, he was able to recruit from the civilian officials of the Deutsche Lufthansa and from old comrades of his World War I days in Richthofen's "Flying Circus". His deputy Erhard Milch and the Director of the Technical Department of the Air Ministry, the famous racing pilot Ernst Udet, came from civil life, as did von Greim, Loerzer, Christiansen, Keller and others. But upwards of three-quarters of the top-ranking leaders of the Luftwaffe—including Kesselring, Sperrle, Stumpff, Student, Jeschonnek and Wever—were transferred to the Luftwaffe from the Reichswehr or, as in the cases of Zander, Wenninger, Coeler and a few others, from the Navy.

The High Command of the Luftwaffe was born under a reversible cloak. When the Air Ministry was created in 1933, it served the double purpose of providing Goering with a cabinet office of a nature to his liking and offering a civilian "cover" for the reconstitution of a military air force, forbidden to Germany by the Versailles Treaty. When the Treaty was denounced in 1935, the RLM could have been simply rechristened the OKL. But Goering thought it advantageous to wear both hats, so that as *Reichsluftminister* he would be on an equal plane with Blomberg, to whom he was subordinate as Commander-in-Chief of the Luftwaffe.* He was also enabled to ensconce the headquarters of the Luftwaffe in his own building as part of an independent Ministry, and thus accentuate his independence of Blomberg and the RKM.

RLM and OKL, therefore, amounted to much the same thing. Milch held the title of *Staatsekretaer* (Undersecretary) of the RLM as well as his military rank in the Luftwaffe. Under Goering and Milch, the organization of the RLM-OKL roughly paralleled that of the OKH, with a *Generalstab* and half a dozen other departments for personnel, administration, supply, technical development, etc. The first chief of the *Generalstab*, the brilliant Generalleutnant Wever (chief of the training section of the *Truppenamt* prior to his transfer to the Luftwaffe in 1933), was killed in an airplane crash in 1936. He was succeeded by Generalleutnant Albert Kesselring, whose colleagues among the

---

* Goering's official status in the Nazi regime was at times somewhat anomalous. Although second man to Hitler, he never held any high position in the Nazi Party hierarchy. During 1934 his police functions passed to Himmler, and he did not invade the economic field until 1936. Only by virtue of his position as Air Minister was he a member of the Reich cabinet; his other positions were in the Prussian government or sinecures such as his title of *Reichsforstmeister* (Master of Forestry).

other department chiefs included Udet (technical development), Stumpff (personnel), Volkmann (administration), and Ruedel (anti-aircraft).

The Luftwaffe itself was organized, like the Army, on a geographical basis in six areas called *Luftkreise*. Three of these were commanded by very senior former generals of the Reichswehr, who had retired in 1932 or 1933, but were subsequently recommissioned in the Luftwaffe and given the rank of *General der Flieger*, the same rank that "unser Hermann" himself then held. These three venerable officers—Halm, Wachenfeld and Kaupisch—had all reached the rank of *Generalleutnant* in the Reichswehr in 1931–32, and were of the same vintage as Bock, Liebmann, Schleicher and Adam. The other three *Luftkreis* commanders were the much younger *Generalmajore* Sperrle and Schweickhard (from the Army), and Generalleutnant Zander (from the Navy) at Kiel. The disappointed Wilberg, as head of the *Luftkriegsakademie*, achieved only the rank of *Generalleutnant*.

Within the *Luftkreise*, the operational Air Force was organized in units called *Geschwader*, many of which were named after famous heroes (Hindenburg, Richthofen, Immelmann) or Nazi ne'er-do-wells (Horst Wessel). For a variety of reasons—shortage of materials, the imminent prospect of land warfare with contiguous neighbouring countries, and Udet's preference for fast, evasive tactics—the Luftwaffe concentrated on fighters (Messerschmitt 109s and 110s), dive-bombers (Junkers 87s, known as "Stukas"), and medium bombers (Junkers 88s, Dornier 17s and Heinkel 111s), at the expense of four-engined heavy bombers, in which the GAF remained notably deficient throughout the war.

Goering himself had fingers in too many pies and too much *joie de vivre* to give consistent guidance to his nascent Air Force, and Milch and Udet did most of the basic planning. Milch concerned himself chiefly with the administrative side, plugging for Nazi ideology but intent on ensuring good pay and living conditions and rapid promotion for Luftwaffe officers. These things, indeed, he abundantly achieved, to the extent of arousing considerable jealousy in Army circles. "Boy generals" of the Air Force flourished in the GAF as well as the USAAF. Unfortunately for the Wehrmacht, the rift between Army and Air Force ran far deeper. The Luftwaffe remained Goering's personal adornment, and never fitted into the Wehrmacht on a cooperative, not to say comradely, basis. For this misjoinder, a heavy price was destined to be paid when the chips were down.

In August, 1935, at the time his transfer from the RKM to the field was announced, von Reichenau wrote an article for *Der Angriff* in which he declared that "the armed forces of the National Socialist people can only be National Socialist", and referred to the Army and the Party as being "the two pillars" of the Reich. This figure of speech soon became a fundamental rubric in the "theology" of the Third Reich. The respective functions of the two pillars were expressed in equally "set" phrases; the Party was the "bearer of the political will of the people", while the Army was the "sole arms bearer".

While this metaphor of the pillars was by no means an empty one, in fact the Wehrmacht and the Party never formed a harmonious or smoothly working team. Anachronistic monarchism and arrogant caste-consciousness on the one hand, boorishness and thuggery on the other, made a poor basis for camaraderie. As the Wehrmacht grew, Nazi-indoctrinated youngsters permeated the lower ranks of the officers' corps. These infiltrations, and the example of the Nazi-minded senior officers such as Reichenau, divided the corps internally and weakened the hand of Fritsch and the other exemplars of the old tradition, but did little to stabilize the relations between the Wehrmacht and the Party.

Even more important than differences in social and political outlook as a cause of the cleavage was the contest for power. The assault of Roehm and the SA was successfully fended off by the Army, but the officers' corps emerged from this struggle with its escutcheon blotted by the murders of Schleicher and Bredow. For a few years thereafter the authority of the generals in matters of military policy was not seriously challenged even by the Fuehrer himself, but in 1936 and 1937 Goering and Himmler were busy fanning the embers which were to burst into blaze in the great political crisis of February, 1938.

But for all of this friction, and jockeying for power between the generals and the Party leaders, Reichenau's description of the Wehrmacht as a "pillar" of the Third Reich—and therefore of Hitler's power—was basically valid. The incontrovertible fact that the Wehrmacht supported Hitler during the consolidation of power and years of rearmament emerges strikingly even in the numerous apologias which have been written by or on behalf of the generals since the collapse of German power in 1945.

The case of Ludwig Beck is a potent and illustrative example. As the leader of the abortive anti-Hitler plots of 1938 and 1944, Beck has been dubbed a hero and martyr of the "resistance". But his worshipping biographer, Wolfgang Foerster, makes no bones of declaring that Beck welcomed the seizure of power by Hitler as an augury of the restoration of German military power.[11] During the ensuing half decade, Beck, to be sure, had his disagreements with the Blomberg–Reichenau–Keitel–Jodl coterie at OKW, but there is not the slightest evidence that he desired, much less strove for a change of regime until after the 1938 crisis. On the contrary, as we have seen, Beck added his distinguished voice to the chorus of praise for the Fuehrer at the *Kriegsakademie* in October, 1935.

Equally significant was the attitude of Hitler's military adjutant, Friedrich Hossbach, who was appointed to this post as a thirty-nine-year-old major just after Hindenburg's death. Hossbach was a trusted protégé of Fritsch and Beck, and remained loyal to them during and after Fritsch's dismissal in 1938. Surely Hossbach would be counted among the anti-Nazi officers, but he too, according to his own account,[12] "belonged to those Germans who, after the collapse of economic and internal political conditions around the turn of the thirties, put their hope for an improvement and strengthening of our total situation in the change of government brought about on January 30, 1933, under the ægis of Hindenburg". Hossbach's life as Hitler's aide was constantly troubled by the tensions among Blomberg, Fritsch and Goering, but his loyalty to Hitler remained unshaken up to the time of Fritsch's fall, and in his book he declares [13] that Fritsch, too, was loyal to the Fuehrer, though without personal devotion, and that Fritsch deprecated the rumours that he might join the clandestine "resistance movement"; Fritsch "saw no alternative to Hitler".

Hitler himself took great pains during these early years of his regime to ensure the continuing allegiance of the officers' corps. The radical wing of the Party might grumble and sneer at the "arrogant Prussian aristocrats", but the Fuehrer himself treated them with unfailing courtesy and consideration, and was especially respectful to old heroes such as Mackensen, Seeckt, and von der Schulenberg.

Even more important than these amenities, Hitler carefully avoided any interference in the conduct of military affairs. He did press constantly to accelerate the tempo of rearmament, and made the major politico-military decisions such as the

denunciation of the Versailles Treaty and the remilitarization of the Rhineland. But he kept strictly aloof from all questions of personnel and administration, and even exhibited a surprising lack of interest in the conduct of manœuvres, while in the field of planning and strategy it was the Blomberg group at the RKM rather than Hitler or the Party that tried the patience of Fritsch and Beck.

When this was the attitude of officers such as Fritsch and Beck and Hossbach, it is easy to understand why the few intransigents, like Hammerstein, failed to make any headway. There was, indeed, and as Hossbach admits, a dearth of strong leaders among the generals, and a narrowness of outlook which Hossbach himself reflects in shouldering on to Blomberg, Reichenau and Keitel the entire responsibility for the catastrophe which eventually befell the officers' corps and the nation. For, says Hossbach, the only responsibility of the generals in the face of the Nazi terror which spread over Germany and destroyed her soul was "to inform Blomberg".[14] This pitiful confession of futility, in varying forms, was constantly echoed in the courtrooms of Nuremberg and recurs again and again in the post-war apologias.

In retrospect, this abnegation of all civic responsibilities is especially contemptible because of the pathetic faith that many members of the resistance movement continued to repose in the generals, despite disappointment after disappointment. A few, such as the amazingly well-informed political exile Berthold Jacob, saw more clearly and warned that it was a fatal error to place any reliance on the Army.[15] But the prevalent attitude was more naïve and more hopeful. "Everything depended upon the attitude of the Reichswehr", writes the eminent historian Meinecke.[16] "As things are now in the Reich", declared Rauschning shortly before the outbreak of war,[17] "the only possible rebirth of the state must come from the Army . . . the Army leaders . . . are the proper leadership of the nation in time of emergency. . ." And the pages of Gisevius' account of the resistance movement are replete with interviews and attempted interviews with Brauchitsch, Halder, Kluge and other generals. "But", as Gisevius concludes, "the generals did not want to do anything." [18]

Indeed, the many points of friction between Hitler and the generals serve chiefly to underline their agreement on fundamentals. The establishment of a centralized, authoritarian regime immune to the political fluctuations of the Weimar era;

the reawakening of a strong national spirit; above all, the re-birth of German military power—these were the great purposes on which Hitler and the officers' corps were at one. These formed the base upon which the two pillars of the Reich—Army and Party—could both stand.

After the German collapse of 1945, some of the leading field-marshals, notably Rundstedt and Manstein, maintained that they "rejected", or at least subjectively disapproved, the Nazi regime from the very inception of the Third Reich. The majority of the generals took refuge in the "non-political" outlook of the officers' corps. But in their more honest and reflective moments, many prominent officers have freely acknowledged what is by now incontrovertible. Testifying at Nuremberg about the pre-war years, Generaloberst Hans Reinhardt declared that there was hardly "a single officer who did not back up Hitler in his extraordinary successes. Hitler had led Germany out of its utmost misery, both politically and economically." And General Siegfried Westphal, who had been Chief of Staff to Rommel, Rundstedt and Kesselring successively, agreed that he and most of the younger officers "placed much hope in the party" during the years before 1938.

The truth of the matter was perhaps expressed most suc-cinctly at Nuremberg by von Blomberg himself and by General-oberst Johannes Blaskowitz, both of whom declared flatly and in identical words * that "before 1938–39 the German generals were not opposed to Hitler. There was no reason to oppose Hit-ler, since he produced the results which they desired." Blom-berg, who, though vain and unstable, was nonetheless highly articulate and of a philosophical and reflective turn of mind,† later elaborated on this conclusion in a lengthy and hitherto unpublished statement: [19]

> "Hitler emphasized the 'Soldatentum', the selection of capable men, and the re-establishment of German sovereignty within the German frontiers. These were aims to which any healthy nation would give its approval after a defeat, as France had done with great success after 1870–71. . . . In the early years of his regime, Hitler stressed his adherence to the historical tradition of which the 'Tag von Potsdam' represented and continued to represent for the

---

* The precise language was formulated by Blomberg in an affidavit. Blaskowitz shortly thereafter adopted the identical expressions in an affidavit which he sub-scribed to.

† Testifying at Nuremberg, Rundstedt declared that Blomberg was "a pupil of the Steiner school of theosophy".

German people a confession of faith. During these years we soldiers had no cause to complain of Hitler. He fulfilled hopes which were dear to all of us. If the generals no longer choose to remember this, it is obviously a case of deliberate forgetfulness. No thinking soldier could shut his eyes to the fact that after 1933 rearmament commensurate with the greatness of Germany could only be carried out with Hitler's help. . . . The German people agreed with the Hitler of those days. The masses obtained tangible advantages in the matter of social justice, the labour market, and above all an increasing importance of Germany as a political body. How could we soldiers, who had continually to deal with the masses, think otherwise! Whoever asserts the contrary now is betrayed by his memory. Moreover the Hitler regime was internationally organized. How otherwise could the Pilsudski agreement and the naval treaty have been achieved? During my sojourn in London in May, 1937, as 'Coronation Delegate', I was able to ascertain everywhere indications of an improvement in the international situation vis-à-vis Germany. Until Hitler entered upon the period of aggressive politics, whether one dates it from 1938 or 1939, the German people had no decisive reason for hostility to Hitler, we soldiers least of all. He had not only given us back a position of respect in the life of the German people, and had freed all Germans from what we considered to be the shame of the Treaty of Versailles, but by the rearmament of Germany, which only Hitler could achieve, he had given the soldiers a larger sphere of influence, promotion and increased respect.

"No general raised any objection then, or offered any resistance. That would have appeared absurd to us all then, even to those who now think otherwise. The approval of the younger officers may well have been more lively and more convincing than that of the older ones, but what now appears in retrospect, to some generals, as a refusal to accept Hitler was, I am convinced, merely the traditional resistance to anything new.

". . . Not one of them retired or refused promotion because Hitler was at the helm.* I have observed, many many times, how our officers behaved personally vis-à-vis Hitler.

"Up until 1938 there was no sign of hostility. . . . We soldiers had no reason to complain. Whoever speaks now of his opposition to Hitler in the years up to 1938–1939 has been betrayed by his memory. . . .

". . . To sum up I would say that Hitler in the first period which lasted at least up to 1938 strove to obtain the trust of us soldiers, with complete success. . . .

". . . One should not repudiate that to which one formerly gave

---

* Presumably Blomberg is speaking of years before 1938. After the Munich crisis of 1938, General Wilhelm Adam retired because of disagreement with Hitler, and Beck resigned as Chief of Staff and remained on the inactive list.

approval in the main. Hitler proved fatal for the German people, but there were years, at first, when we believed that in a positive sense he was Germany's man of destiny."

Hossbach, Beck's biographer, Raeder, Blaskowitz, Westphal, and Reinhardt, to say nothing of the contemporary documentation, provide compelling support for Blomberg's analysis and conclusion. Hitler played his hand with consummate skill and patience and bided his time. As long as the generals' aims and plans paralleled his own, there was nothing to be gained by challenging their prestige and prerogatives. Rather it was the better part of wisdom to be gracious and bestow honours. And thus it came about that Werner von Blomberg rose to be the first *Feldmarschall* of the Third Reich—a promotion that was soon to prove his undoing.

THE FIRST *FELDMARSCHALL* OF THE THIRD REICH

On April 20, 1936, Adolf Hitler celebrated his forty-seventh birthday. As the *Voelkischer Beobachter* put it, the anniversary was a day of "festival for the whole German people . . . and, above all, for the soldier of the young German Wehrmacht". In the morning, the military leaders appeared before the Fuehrer to offer their congratulations. Fritsch was absent because of slight injuries sustained while riding, but Blomberg, Raeder and Goering were on hand with Rundstedt as Fritsch's representative. To Blomberg's good wishes Hitler replied in a short speech based on the familiar "two-pillars" theme.

But more than verbal felicitations were to mark the day. Hitler seized upon the occasion to announce the promotion of Blomberg and the three service chiefs—Blomberg received the baton of a *Generalfeldmarschall*, Fritsch and Goering the rank of *Generaloberst*, and Raeder that of *Generaladmiral*. The Fuehrer declared that by these promotions he was honouring "the entire Wehrmacht, every individual officer and soldier". But behind each of them lay its individual story.

According to Hossbach, the idea of promoting Blomberg originated with Hitler, who at first wanted to give him the hitherto unknown rank of *Reichsmarschall*, but discarded this idea in favour of a promotion to *Feldmarschall*. It is illustrative of the Fuehrer's still deferential attitude toward the military leaders that Hitler did not act on these promotions until after full consultation with them. Indeed, to the acutely rank-conscious officers' corps the appointment of the first *Feldmarschall*

since the First World War was a matter of very major moment. From the days of the Kaiser, the only three surviving *Feldmarschaelle* were the seemingly indestructible Mackensen and the *ci-devant* Duke Albert of Wuerttemberg and Crown Prince Rupert of Bavaria. To Blomberg's elevation the objection was raised that the coveted baton should only be awarded for wartime service, but here Hitler's reading in military history stood him in good stead, and he accurately observed that the great von Schlieffen himself had been made a *Feldmarschall* during the peaceful year 1911, and that Wilhelm II had so honoured five other officers during years of peace.* So Blomberg attained the highest rank, never achieved by the great Seeckt, and became the first *Generalfeldmarschall* of the Third Reich.

The promotion of Fritsch to *Generaloberst* required no breach of precedent, inasmuch as his three predecessors in command of the Reichswehr—Seeckt, Heye and Hammerstein—had all taken this rank. Fritsch did suggest that the three senior Army generals—Rundstedt, Leeb and Bock, who commanded the three Army groups—should also be promoted, or that at least Rundstedt, as the oldest active officer, should be so honoured. But, perhaps because of fear that the Luftwaffe and Navy might then feel slighted, it was finally decided to promote only the chief of each of the three services.

For Hermann Goering, the occasion was not an unmixed pleasure. Incredibly vain and constantly preoccupied with uniforms and insignia, he was furiously jealous of Blomberg's new and exalted status. Yet it must have eased his mind that now at least he could wear one more star than his three venerable "coaches", Halm, Wachenfeld and Kaupisch. Furthermore, his own promotion enabled him to advance his deputy, Milch, to the rank of *General der Flieger*.

The rank assumed by Raeder was in many ways the most interesting and indicative of the latent tensions of the festive day. He had held the rank of *Admiral* ever since 1928, and in the German naval hierarchy the only higher rank was *Grossadmiral*, the naval equivalent of *Feldmarschall* and previously held only by a handful of others, including von Tirpitz and Albert Wilhelm Heinrich, Prince of Prussia. But Raeder, who hated

* In addition to Schlieffen, Wilhelm II gave promotions to *Feldmarschall* to von Loë, von Hahnke, Count Gottlieb Haeseler and Frhr. Kolmar von der Goltz. In 1900 Waldersee was made a *Feldmarschall* before departing to command the allied forces in China during the Boxer Rebellion. In fact, there had been a number of other such instances; von Roon and von Manteuffel, for example, were both made *Feldmarschaelle* in 1873, Gneisenau in 1825 and Yorck von Wartenburg in 1821.

Goering, also feared him, and the canny Admiral was far from anxious to share Goering's jealousy with Blomberg. So the obsolete Dutch rank of *Generaladmiral* was revived for the occasion, as a close equivalent of that of *Generaloberst*.

During the next two days there were other honours for the great of former years. By a special decree, Blomberg bestowed on the ageing Seeckt and the long-dead Prince Eugene of Savoy the title of "National Hero". And Hitler also made Seeckt the honorary chief (*Chef*) of the 67th (Spandau) Infantry Regiment.* Truly those were halcyon days for the Wehrmacht, reminiscent of its status in imperial times.

So impressively did the Wehrmacht loom during these years that many observers were led to conclude that it had snatched the leading role from the Party. The distinguished historian Alfred Vagts, for example, wrote in September, 1935, that [20] "the National Socialist Party has ceased to be a formidable rival of the Army . . . the reign of the Party is over."

Events were soon to prove how far this estimate was wide of the mark. In 1934 Goering and Himmler had sided with the Army in order to dispose of Roehm. Two years later events again began to press them together in another strike for power, and this time the generals were to be numbered among the victims. The honeymoon was over, and in 1938 the "two pillars" of the Reich were to tremble in the great political crisis which brought about the downfall of both Blomberg and Fritsch and dealt a mortal blow to the unity and power of the officers' corps.

* Hitler thus adopted a practice which was later utilized to honour Mackensen, Blomberg, Rundstedt, Fritsch and von Epp.

CHAPTER V

THE BLOMBERG–FRITSCH CRISIS
OF 1938

In a showcase of the Pentagon Building in Washington, there has reposed since the war a field-marshal's blue baton. It bears an inscription from the Fuehrer to "the First Field Marshal of the Luftwaffe", and the date, February 4, 1938. Its former owner, Hermann Goering, carried it when he sat as president of the military "Court of Honour" which tried and acquitted Generaloberst Freiherr von Fritsch on a morals charge in March, 1938. Goering carried it again at Fritsch's funeral in October, 1939, after the latter fell in the front lines before Warsaw. He carried it until July, 1940, when Hitler gave him a better and bigger baton, signalizing his promotion to the newly created rank of *Reichsmarschall*.

This discarded bauble, picked up by American troops at Goering's summer headquarters at Berchtesgaden, attracts little attention from passers-by, but it and its history symbolize almost perfectly the second great military crisis of the Third Reich. Hitler's political skill, frustrating Goering's ambition while gratifying his vanity; the disunity of the Wehrmacht; above all, the moral and political bankruptcy of the officers' corps—all these things are mirrored in the extravagant decoration and pretentious dedication of Goering's blue baton.

During the week preceding Goering's elevation, Blomberg was dismissed from his post as *Reichskriegsminister* and retired to inactive duty—"*ausser Dienst*", in German military parlance—and Fritsch was relieved as Commander-in-Chief of the Army and suspended from duty pending his trial. The events of that week have gone down in history as "the Blomberg–Fritsch affair", but far more was at stake than the fate of these two individuals, august as were their respective stations. This was, indeed, the second major political crisis of the Third Reich, and its outcome was more significantly decisive, even though bloodless, than that of the Roehm massacre in June, 1934. By the elimination of Fritsch and the simultaneous reorganization of the High Command of the Wehrmacht, Hitler broke the power

of the officers' corps and reduced it to a leaderless, divided and impotent condition.

The focus of this crisis was the struggle for control of the military power of the Third Reich, and Hitler's victory was a decisive turning point in history. But the scope of the conflict which exploded openly in February, 1938, included more than the military field. The economic power which Schacht had wielded was also at stake and Schacht went down to defeat along with Fritsch. Ribbentrop replaced von Neurath as Foreign Minister on the same day that Goering received his baton. The edge of the storm even touched the world of sports, and engulfed a famous international tennis-player.

Blomberg and Fritsch were linked by fate and fell simultaneously, but not in a common disaster. Blomberg was the individual victim of his own instability, Goering's vanity, and the sanctimonious caste-feeling of the officers' corps. His departure, the result of an unorthodox marriage, would not in itself have significantly altered the balance of power as between Army and Party.

But Blomberg's going offered Hitler, as well as Himmler and Goering, a pretext and opportunity, which they were not slow to seize, for an assault upon the entrenched power of the generals. Fritsch was the symbol of this power; he and his supporters were overwhelmed and outwitted, and Hitler emerged from the fray in direct control of the Wehrmacht, with the new Commander-in-Chief of the Army, von Brauchitsch, in a well-nigh helpless position. Beck, Adam and a few others continued to strive for a measure of independence, but before the end of the year Beck and Adam were also retired, and the only remaining opposition thereafter took the form of half-hearted protests, resignations and clandestine plotting.

The first signs of the storm that was brewing were noticeable as early as April, 1936, the very month in which Hitler celebrated his birthday by promoting the four top military leaders. That month Goering received a far more tangible reward than his elevation to *Generaloberst*; he was designated as Co-ordinator for Raw Materials and Foreign Exchange, a post which immediately brought him into conflict with Schacht as General Plenipotentiary for War Economy. Two months later, on June 17, 1936, Himmler succeeded in consolidating his authority over the entire German police system. With the SS and the police both under his personal command, Himmler was ready to take up the game which Roehm had played unsuccessfully—

the creation of a military force outside the Wehrmacht. Little by little, armed SS units began to encroach upon the Wehrmacht's prerogative as "sole arms bearer of the Reich".

Hitler aside, accordingly, the ambitions of Goering and Himmler were the underlying causes of the power crisis, and Schacht, Blomberg and Fritsch were the quarry. Goering did not dispute Himmler's leadership of the police, and Himmler gave Goering a free field for his campaign to supplant Schacht. In the military field, the Goering–Himmler axis was a *mariage de convenance*; both aspired to supreme power, but they chose different avenues of access, reflecting their contrasting social backgrounds, Goering wanted to lead the officers' corps; Himmler, like Roehm, aimed to destroy it.

But it would be a mistake to over-emphasize the importance of Goering and Himmler in the total picture. Over the scene loomed the figure of Hitler and the shadow of war. For all his political genius and demoniac power, the Fuehrer was an impatient and desperate gambler. Schacht and Fritsch—and even Blomberg—were not setting a rapid enough pace, and Hitler chafed under their warnings that the time to strike was not yet at hand. German aerial exploits in the Spanish Civil War fed his ego; Austria was invitingly feeble; the democracies were soft and could be bluffed again and again. In the privacy of the Obersalzberg, the Fuehrer fulminated against the generals as "medieval knights" and the industrialists as "stupid fools who cannot see beyond the wares they peddle". Besides—horrible thought!—he might die before these slow coaches got their nerve up. There was no time to lose, and whoever stood between him and his plans must be swept away. And that was just what Hitler accomplished on February 4, 1938.

GOERING *v.* SCHACHT

Hjalmar Horace Greeley Schacht was the first victim of the pressures which were building up as Germany waxed stronger. This self-righteous and stiff-necked individual was and remains the most enigmatic and controversial person of the pre-war years. He had served as President of the Reichsbank during the Weimar era up to 1930, when he resigned and joined the right-wing opponents of Bruening. Authoritarian and strongly nationalistic by disposition, he found much to his liking in the National Socialist programme, but did not join the Party. After the Nazi successes in the 1932 elections, Schacht swung openly to their side and he acted as "banker" at the fund-raising

meeting of industrialists at Goering's home in February, 1933. Shortly thereafter, at Hitler's suggestion, Hindenburg reappointed Schacht to the Presidency of the Reichsbank.

Using the credit of the Reichsbank, Schacht at once embarked upon a broad programme to reduce unemployment by public works. Soon the now famous *Autobahnen* were spreading across Germany. His other major task was the financing of the expanded rearmament programme, for which purpose Schacht resorted to short-term commercial bills guaranteed by the Reichsbank.* Schacht's methods served their purpose, and he rapidly emerged as the dominant figure in the economy of the Third Reich. In August, 1934, he became Minister of Economics, and in May, 1935, Plenipotentiary-General for War Economy under the Reich Defence Law.

In these multiple capacities, Schacht shared with Blomberg the main responsibility for rearmament and, as Schacht himself wrote in May, 1935, "the accomplishment of the armament programme with speed and in quantity is *the* problem of German politics, and everything else should therefore be subordinated to this purpose, so long as the main purpose is not imperilled by neglecting all other questions". But this last qualification was vitally important; Schacht insisted on working within the framework of his own economic principles. The printing presses must not be worked to inflationary extremes; imports of raw materials must be limited to what could be procured by German exports under the barter arrangements which Schacht called his "New Plan". In short, "Germany's rearmament had to fit into the framework of the New Plan—or break it".[1] It did not fit, and it broke not only the New Plan but Schacht's power as well.

In November, 1935, Schacht advised Blomberg that it would not be possible to augment the Wehrmacht's foreign purchases of copper. Warnings such as this, coupled with his standoffishness and ill-concealed contempt for "economic amateurs", were beginning to undermine his favour with the Fuehrer. At about this time, Schacht also protested sharply against the Party's purchases of foreign exchange to support its propaganda activities abroad, but Hitler refused to back him up. As a result, on April 4, 1936, Schacht was relieved of all authority in connection

* These were the well-known "Mefo bills", drawn by Army contractors on the "Metallforschung G.m.b.H." (Metal Research Company), a concern with very little capital, but whose bills were guaranteed by the Reichsbank for discount three months after the date of issue.

with foreign exchange control, and Goering was appointed Co-ordinator for Raw Materials and Foreign Exchange.

Within a matter of weeks the newspapers were reporting that Schacht and Goering were in violent controversy, and that Blomberg had intervened in Schacht's behalf and to restore a semblance of harmony.[2] At a series of conferences in May, 1936, under Goering as chairman, and attended by Schacht, Blomberg and Schwerin von Krosigk (Reichsminster of Finance), the differences between Goering and Schacht were thrown into bold relief. The former pressed strongly for increased public borrowing and rapid expansion of the production of synthetic substitutes (*Ersatzstoffe*) in order to render Germany economically self-sufficient. Schacht countered by stressing the dangers of inflation and criticized the production of high-cost substitutes for commodities which could be procured more economically by importation.

But Schacht was fighting a losing battle. Early in September he learned that Hitler proposed to use the annual Party rally at Nuremberg as the occasion to announce the launching of a vast programme for national self-sufficiency. He beseeched Blomberg to "warn the Fuehrer against this step" and predicted that:

"If the Fuehrer emphasizes this in front of the masses in Nuremberg he will receive a great amount of applause from the audience, but with it he will bring failure to the entire commercial policy. There is only one thing in our present needy position: *the promotion of exports. Every threat against foreign countries*, however, will bring about contrary results.

"We have had reverses in the field of fuels . . . there will not be large amounts of rubber. The Renn process in the field of ores is meeting great difficulties.

"If we now shout our decision to make ourselves economically independent, then we cut our own throats, because we can no longer survive the necessary transition period. . . .

"If the food supply of the people is not to be endangered, the Fuehrer must refrain from his plan."

The warning fell on deaf ears. Two days later Goering appeared at an economic cabinet meeting armed with a memorandum from Hitler supporting Goering's programme. The budding economic potentate preened himself and coolly informed Schacht that "Frederick the Great . . . was in his financial behaviour a strong inflationist". At Nuremberg Hitler announced the Four-Year Plan for economic self-sufficiency, and in October formal decrees were promulgated establishing the Office of

126

the Four-Year Plan, and designating Goering as Plenipotentiary, with authority to issue decrees and directives for "the
strict co-ordination of all competent authorities in Party and
state". A memorandum to Goering from Hitler directed that
self-sufficiency for the contingency of war should be based on
developing the necessary plant capacity in Germany for the
production of such vital war materials as rubber, petrol and
explosives.

If the Four-Year Plan flew in the face of the principles for
which Schacht had been contending, it was wholly to the liking
of the I.G. Farben directorate. As between Goering and
Schacht, there was no question where Farben stood. The contacts between Farben and Schacht had been conspicuously few,
whereas its relations with the Luftwaffe had grown steadily
more intimate. For years, Farben had been staking its future on
synthetic products, particularly petrol and rubber. So it came
as no surprise that one of the leading Farben directors, Carl
Krauch, was shortly appointed Chief of the Department for
Research and Development in the Office of the Four-Year
Plan. For the first six months of the four-year period, the projects of the plan envisaged investments of nearly one billion
Reichsmarks; approximately two-thirds of this entire amount
was used for Farben products. There was, indeed, ample reason
for Schacht's complaint that "industrialists and businessmen
crowded into Goering's ante-room in the hope of getting orders
when I was still trying to make the voice of reason heard".[3]

Quite apart from the repudiation of Schacht's policies, Hitler's mandate to Goering brought about an overlapping authority between Goering and Schacht that was bound to prove un-
workable. This caused Blomberg, who was anxious to keep the
peace between them, great concern. In December, 1936, a
memorandum from the RKM pointed out that Schacht had
been authorized in 1935 to "direct economic preparations for
the eventuality of war", while Goering's new task was "to put
the entire economy in a state of readiness for war within four
years". After describing this situation as "untenable", the
RKM paper proposed a redefinition of their respective spheres
which would have left Schacht's power substantially intact.

No such solution was forthcoming, and the conflict grew more
and more acute. Late in January, 1937, Schacht threatened to
resign, and in February he informed Blomberg that he would
suspend his activities as Plenipotentiary for War Economy pending clarification of his and Goering's responsibilities. Blomberg

appealed to Hitler to "induce Dr. Schacht, whose co-operation as Plenipotentiary is of great significance, to resume his former activities". But Schacht remained "out on strike" until June and deigned only to inform Blomberg that the Wehrmacht budget for 1937 would have to be held down to ten billion Reichsmarks, and to send Goering a long essay on the necessity of curtailing the Four-Year Plan and postponing further rearmament until the raw-material shortages were ameliorated and stockpiles built up.

In July, 1937, a temporary truce was effected. Goering and Schacht signed a memorandum, distributed only to the higher officials, which declared that the "basic questions" are "hereby settled" and that their respective tasks "are being solved in closest mutual co-operation". In fact, nothing had been settled. Within three weeks thereafter, Goering issued a decree relating to iron-mining which was a patent invasion of Schacht's authority as Minister of Economics. Schacht protested in a long letter to Goering dated August 5, 1937, in which he bluntly declared that "your foreign-exchange policy, your policy regarding production, and your financial policy" are "unsound".

At the same time, Schacht hied himself to the Obersalzberg and put his resignation in Hitler's hands. Embarrassed by the possibility of unfavourable reactions abroad, the Fuehrer asked Schacht to stay in office for two more months, to which the latter consented. An unyielding reply from Goering to his protest about the iron-mining question, however, exhausted Schacht's patience. On August 26th he wrote to Goering that he hoped the Fuehrer would soon "place the further direction of economic policies solely in your hands", and early in September Schacht took leave from the Ministry of Economics.

A final meeting between Goering and Schacht on November 1st failed to break the impasse, and two weeks later Schacht submitted a written resignation as Minister of Economics to Hitler, who accepted it (as well as Schacht's earlier resignation as Plenipotentiary-General for War Economy) on December 8th. Hitler designated Goering himself as Schacht's successor, but this was only a temporary measure, and Goering's appointment was not made public, as it had already been decided to appoint Walther Funk as Minister of Economics on January 15, 1938. As matters worked out, Funk's appointment was slightly delayed by the Blomberg–Fritsch crisis, and was finally announced on February 4th, along with those of Ribbentrop, von Brauchitsch and others.

In order to cushion the shock to world opinion, Hitler insisted that Schacht retain the title of Minister without Portfolio, as well as the Presidency of the Reichsbank. In the latter capacity he continued to exercise some influence on financial policy, but his share in the rearmament and economic mobilization programme was negligible as, indeed, it had been since his open break with Goering early in 1937.

With Schacht's replacement by Goering, all semblance of economic restraint on the rearmament programme was cast off. As early as December, 1936, Goering had informed a large audience of industrialists and government officials that: [4]

"The battle we are approaching demands a colossal measure of production capacity. No limit on rearmament can be visualized. The only alternatives are victory or destruction. If we win, business will be sufficiently compensated. . . . We live in a time when the final battle is in sight. We are already on the threshold of mobilization and we are already at war. All that is lacking is the actual shooting."

This inflammatory language aroused no protests among the businessmen. On the contrary, 1937 was for German industry the year of war mobilization plans. These embodied the programme and methods for an immediate speed-up in the production of war materials in the event of war, as well as plans for defence against bombing attacks. The mobilization of German economy was symbolized by a ritual which gave the principal industrialists a semi-military status. In March, 1937, Blomberg ordered the establishment of a "leadership corps" for military economy:

"The war economy leaders [*Wehrwirtschaftsfuehrer*] shall be the responsible collaborators of the Wehrmacht in preparing and carrying out the mobilization of the armament industry and in the conduct of war. . . . Their tasks . . . in connection with rearmament place them in a position corresponding approximately to that of reserve officers on active duty."

Truly Schacht's defeat was utter, and the principal reason for it is plain. His own colleagues among the industrialists lent him no support, and preferred to bask in Goering's smile and enjoy the profits and emoluments of the Four-Year Plan. The more cautious were informed by "unser Hermann" that "they had an outlook the size of a lavatory seat", and the objects of his contempt dared only to cringe. We cannot here pass judgment on the measure of Schacht's guilt; at least he never cringed and he was no fool. He sought to turn the clock back, but he did not want to see it smashed. Fundamentally Goering was right

about the narrow range of vision of the German industrial tycoons—they, like the other leaders of German society, failed the Fatherland in its hour of greatest need. The verdict of history will support most of the damning, if self-righteous, conclusions thus formulated by Schacht: [5]

"My attempts to hold up the wheel of tyrannous government under Hitler failed. . . . I am not raising any question of blame in connection with those who thought but did not act as I did. I merely place the fact on record that no help of any sort came from them; neither from the class-conscious workers, nor from the disciplined military; nor from the liberal bourgeoisie; nor from scientific circles; nor even from the Church."

GOERING AND HIMMLER *v.* BLOMBERG AND FRITSCH

While Schacht was learning his bitter lesson in the course of open conflict with Hitler and Goering, the surface relations between these two worthies and the top generals remained relatively untouched. Some forewarnings of Goering's jealousy, however, became visible to the sensitive observer soon after the Roehm purge. Such an observer was Major Friedrich Hossbach, Hitler's military adjutant and a faithful protégé of Fritsch and Beck. [6]

At first, Goering's military vanity manifested itself chiefly in childish outbursts in matters of protocol. At the Nuremberg Party Rally in September, 1934, for example, a larger dinner was given at the Hotel Deutscher Hof for all the visiting generals and admirals. Hossbach, in charge of the seating for the occasion, followed strict military seniority, a procedure which resulted in Goering's chair being farther from the head of the table than was his wont or pleasure, and caused an angry protest to which Hossbach did not yield.

The following year Hossbach, on returning from his summer vacation, discovered that Hitler's Air Force adjutant, previously an officer junior in rank to Hossbach, was now Oberstleutnant Bodenschatz, who had served with Goering in the Richthofen days. Bodenschatz, on the basis of his senior rank, asserted precedence over Hossbach in Hitler's *Adjutantur*, and Hossbach was unable to get any backing from Blomberg, who was reluctant to offend Goering. Fritsch, however, was determined that the Army should not be outranked in Hitler's personal entourage, and, after a firm expression to the Fuehrer, had Hossbach promoted to *Oberstleutnant*, with rank retroactive to August 1, 1934, which gave Hossbach seniority over Bodenschatz. Goering was

wild with rage and Blomberg was a very worried man, but Fritsch was unyielding and, with the unexpected help of Rudolf Hess (who as Third Man in the Party had his own reasons to be jealous of Goering's status as Second Man), the Army carried the day over the Luftwaffe, and Bodenschatz was transferred back to the Air Ministry. Such was the childish level at which the mortal duel began.

After Blomberg's promotion to *Generalfeldmarschall*, however, Goering's jealous resentment deepened. As Blomberg succinctly puts it in his memoirs, Goering "resented the fact that he was not the first soldier of the Reich, but shared second rank with two others". Furthermore, by 1937, Blomberg was flying very high, wide and handsome. He gave many of the orations on state occasions such as Seeckt's funeral. He addressed large groups of workers in the munitions plants, telling them that wage increases must be sacrificed to national security, and describing the conduct of "so-called labour leaders" during the First World War as "treason". And, as we have seen, he intervened in Goering's struggle to oust Schacht in a manner not helpful to Goering's purpose.

Abroad, too, Blomberg was increasingly to the fore, at the expense of the chafing Goering. The latter wanted to represent Germany at the coronation of George VI in London; Blomberg was sent instead.* Then—crowning insult—at the manœuvres in Italy during the fall of 1937 Blomberg dared to contradict Goering in the presence of Mussolini! † "Unser Hermann" eyed the incautious *Feldmarschall* ever more narrowly and bided his time. In a few more months his own fat hand would clutch the only baton in the Wehrmacht.

If Blomberg, as Goering's prime quarry, was largely the victim of his own rank, such was not the issue between Himmler and Fritsch. Heinrich Himmler had been given the title *Reichsfuehrer SS* in 1929, and that was all the rank he wanted. This sinister yet sentimental creature, obsessed with primitive fancies, was utterly lacking in the magnetism and genius for "terrible simplification" that gave Hitler his apocalyptic stature. Yet this unspectacular man had an awful directness which even the

* According to Goering's biographer, he actually flew to London but was persuaded by Ribbentrop to return to Germany before his presence became known. See Frischauer, *The Rise and Fall of Hermann Goering*, pp. 133–135.

† Interestingly enough, the subject of dispute was the Tukachevsky trial, which Goering declared had weakened the Russian military machine. Blomberg, who had been in Russia during the Tschunke–Niedermayer days, contradicted Goering flatly, declaring that Goering underestimated the strength of the Soviet regime.

Fuehrer failed to match, and it may be that Himmler left the uglier and deeper scar on the face of Europe. Of Hitler's early associates, only Himmler and Goebbels (excluding late-comers such as Martin Bormann) grew steadily in power throughout the years of the Third Reich, but the highly intellectual *"kleine Doktor"* was cast of much lighter metal than Himmler.

If Himmler was personally unimpressive, he was patient, implacable, and above all single-minded. He did not, like Goering, pride himself on his versatility, or preen himself as a "Renaissance type". Rather, he concentrated on the pursuit of naked power with a terrible intensity tempered only by a shrewd caution which kept him from overplaying his hand. With a sure and cold eye he observed Goering's tendency to dissipate his remarkable energies in dilettantism, and his incurable weakness for the trappings, rather than the essence, of power. He sensed the decline in the importance of the *Gauleiter* and other purely Party officials such as Hess, as revolution crystallized into regime. And he noted Hitler's increasing absorption with foreign and military affairs, and gauged his own tactics accordingly. With utmost skill, Himmler utilized the Roehm affair not only to eliminate his superior and most dangerous rival, but also to push Goering out of the field of police and internal security and into the military arena which the Fuehrer regarded as his own preserve, and where Goering could at best hope to be second man. Thus a sort of power vacuum was opened in the internal management of the Reich, and this vacuum Himmler proceeded to fill with his chosen engine, the SS. And so it was that the Third Reich more and more became the SS State[7] as Himmler tightened his grip on the internal controls.

The grip tightened slowly. Contrary to popular impression, the SS was not a major component of the Party during its revolutionary period. When Himmler took over the leadership of the SS on January 6, 1929, its total membership was only 280. It was supposed to constitute the "elite corps" of the Party, and at the time of the seizure of power, it still numbered only some 50,000. Eligibility for membership in the SS was governed by strict standards and superstitions; height, complexion, facial structure, and racial background were the principal determinants, and all marriages of SS men were subject to organizational approval.

Thus early Himmler showed his capacity to put into literal and terrible execution the racist notions that Hitler spouted chiefly for political purposes. The Fuehrer's undoubtedly sin-

cere predilections for blue-eyed "Aryans" and antipathy to Jews did not deter the practical politician in him from using the club-footed, stunted Goebbels as his close adviser, or from granting Milch "absolution" of his part-Jewish ancestry. But for Himmler there was no such half-way house. Hitler might declaim at the Obersalzberg about the social uselessness of the superannuated and incurably diseased; Himmler would establish the system for their "disposal". Hitler might rant against the Jews and threaten them with extinction; Himmler was the man to carry it out—not as a chore, but as part of the noble mission of the SS. "This is a page of glory in our history," Himmler told his SS generals at Posen in 1943. "Most of you know what it means when one hundred corpses are lying side by side, or five hundred or one thousand. To have stuck it out and at the same time . . . to have remained decent fellows, that is what has made us hard."

Such was the man who, as soon as he had cemented his control over the entire police and internal security system of the Reich, turned his formidable talents to the destruction of the officers' corps. He did not repeat Roehm's mistake of attacking too soon, or seek to accomplish his end with one blow. Roehm had risked too much by stepping faster than Hitler's tempo and had forced the Fuehrer to choose between him and the Reichswehr before Hitler was ready to challenge the generals. Himmler was ready to gear himself to Hitler's pace, and to strike with him, rather than striving to force his hand.

The immediate issue between Himmler and the Army, which led Himmler to seek Fritsch's downfall, related to the size and role of the armed SS units—the so-called *SS Verfeugungstruppen*, later to be known as the Waffen-SS. The establishment of these avowedly military SS formations threatened, just as had the SA under Roehm, the Wehrmacht's prerogatives as "sole arms bearer of the Reich". Nevertheless, Hitler supported Himmler in this regard, partly because it was a cardinal, and politically sound, point of principle with him that the Wehrmacht should under no circumstances be used to put down internal disturbances. In Hitler's own words: [8]

> "It is necessary to maintain . . . a state military police capable of representing and imposing the authority of the Reich within the country in any situation.
>
> "This task can be carried out only by a state police which has within its ranks men of the best German blood and which identifies itself unreservedly with the ideology at the base of the Greater German Reich. . . .

"We must never again tolerate that the German Wehrmacht based on universal conscription should be used against its own compatriots, arms in hand, when critical situations arise in the interior. Such a step is the beginning of the end. . . . Our history contains sad examples of this. The Wehrmacht in the future is intended for all time for use solely against the Reich's foreign enemies."

Up to 1937, Fritsch and Blomberg succeeded in keeping Himmler's military inclinations within fairly reasonable bounds. By January of that year, the entire SS consisted of approximately 210,000 men, but its armed strength was limited to three regiments—the SS Regiments "Leibstandarte Adolf Hitler" (motorized) in Berlin, "Deutschland" in Munich and "Germania" in Hamburg—and two or three independent SS battalions. In addition, the SS included about 3,500 armed and militarized concentration camp guards, known as the "Death's Head Units" (*Totenkopfverbaende*). The SS had also adopted its own system of unit designations and ranks—regiments were called *"Standarten"* and their commanders (the equivalent of an *Oberst* in the Army) *Standartenfuehrer*, battalions were called *Sturmbanne*, companies *stuerme*, etc. SS generals bore titles of rank such as *Brigadefuehrer* and *Obergruppenfuehrer*.[9]

For all this fine system of uniforms and ranks, however, the entire armed strength of the SS at the end of 1936 amounted only to the equivalent of one Army division, and this was too little to satisfy Himmler. Early in 1937 he began to press Fritsch and Blomberg for an increase, especially for the purpose of policing the borders of the Reich against "penetration by communists, saboteurs and adventurers". A discussion early in March between Fritsch and Himmler led to "no positive results". Fritsch was firmly opposed to any enlargement of the armed SS units, and Blomberg supported his objections. On March 22nd, at a conference in which Goering also participated, the Army categorically rejected Himmler's request to establish an SS "border protection corps". But Himmler was obviously ill-disposed to let the matter rest, and in May Blomberg expressed grave misgivings to Keitel concerning the constant development of the SS.[10] Unfortunately for Blomberg, events were soon to show that Keitel was far from a safe repository for such confidences.

Sharp as was this disagreement over the SS border units, the fundamental source of the hostility between the SS and the officers' corps lay far deeper. It lay deeper even than Hitler's

need for an armed force which could be relied upon, more firmly than the Wehrmacht, to back up the Nazi regime and the Party's policies by force. At bottom, the conflict between Fritsch and Himmler was a struggle for the allegiance of German youth.

For throughout modern German history the Army had not only been the core of the Reich in terms of power politics, but had become a basic social institution and a major educational force as well. The indoctrination to which all German conscripts were exposed during their period of military service was the foundation of the national outlook to which Beck referred in his 1935 speech before the *Kriegsakademie*, in describing Germany as a "military-minded nation". The officers' corps in general and the ranking military leaders in particular were the objects of the veneration so inculcated and the beneficiaries of the scale of values thus established.

The resumption of compulsory military service in 1935 threw into bold relief the issue whether the Army should continue to exert the dominant influence over the hearts and minds of young Germans. With Nazism had come the *Hitler-Jugend*, the Reich Labour Service (*Arbeitsdienst*) and other high-pressure youth organizations, as well as the Party itself, with its special formations such as the SA and SS for adult Germans. Inevitably, Hitler, Himmler and other Party leaders looked on the period of compulsory military service as an unwelcome and dangerous break in the Party *cursus honorum*. The crucial and all-important issue was whether young Germany should learn to worship the old, established gods or the new deities of Nazism. The Army struggled to reawaken the spirit of Moltke and Schlieffen—of a rigid military elite. The Party, through Goebbels, Rosenberg, Himmler and Hitler himself, preached new and violent doctrines in many respects incompatible with the old orthodoxy. And Himmler's essential aim was to rip off the mantle of prestige which had so long adorned the officers' corps, and drape it over the black uniform of the SS.

The battlefield on which Fritsch and Himmler met was, in short, an ideological one. Prussianism or neo-paganism; emperors and field-marshals or the Fuehrer of the Thousand-Year Reich and his attendant archangels—this was the symbolic paraphernalia of the struggle for power between the Party and the officers' corps. And in this struggle it was Hitler and Himmler rather than Goering, and Fritsch rather than Blomberg, who were the chief antagonists.

THE WEHRMACHT IN THE SPANISH CIVIL WAR

To this deadly play of German power politics, an additional explosive element was added by the outbreak of civil war in Spain. For several years theretofore, Spanish generals and other nationalist agents had been in contact with, and successfully seeking support from, both Hitler and Mussolini. General Sanjurjo, who had led an unsuccessful revolt against the Republican government in 1933 and later fled from Spain, visited Berlin early in 1936 and was cordially received by the Fuehrer. When Generals Mola and Franco launched the rebellion in July, 1936, accordingly, German and Italian support, both economic and military, was immediately available.

Italian military airplanes, in fact, were dispatched to aid Franco in Spanish Morocco immediately before the opening hostilities. German Junkers transports appeared during the early days of the war, and rendered Franco vital assistance by ferrying some fifteen thousand Moroccans and soldiers of the Spanish Foreign Legion from Morocco to southern Spain. During August more German planes arrived, substantial quantities of military supplies were sent to Franco from Germany via Portugal, and the "pocket" battle cruiser *Deutschland* appeared off Ceuta. In September, Oberstleutnant Warlimont, an OKH General Staff officer, was appointed Plenipotentiary Delegate of the Wehrmacht in Spain.

The German Army, however, pursued a cautious policy in Spain. Von Fritsch and Beck saw much risk and little advantage from involvement, and strongly opposed committing any substantial number of regular troops. For political reasons, however, Hitler and Mussolini desired to support Franco, and Goering was more than willing to advertise the power of the Luftwaffe and test its new planes under combat conditions. German participation in the Spanish war thus became primarily a Luftwaffe affair, and an additional source of friction between Hitler and the Army leaders.

Under the ægis of the GAF, German volunteers in large numbers began arriving in Spain in November, 1936. Some 6,500 men were landed at Cádiz and transported to Seville, where they furnished the nucleus of the so-called "Condor Legion". Warlimont returned to Germany, and Generalmajor Hugo Sperrle was detailed by Goering to command the Legion, which at the outset comprised several squadrons each of bombers (Junkers 52s) and fighters (mostly Heinkel 51s), and half a

dozen batteries of anti-aircraft guns, including prototypes of the famous German 88s that were later to prove of great value to the Afrika Korps as anti-tank weapons.[11]

The Spanish insurgents had been counting on a speedy victory, more by way of a *Putsch* than a protracted civil war. When the Republican government showed unexpected will and ability to resist, and particularly after December, 1936, when Russian and other international help for the Loyalists started to materialize, Franco's demands for increased German and Italian assistance grew louder. Early in December, Goering revealed to a group of his principal subordinates (Milch, Kesselring and Udet, among others) that Mussolini had suggested that Germany and Italy each send a full division of ground troops to Spain.[12] Goering was highly excited: "The general situation is very serious. Russia wants war. England rearms speedily. . . Peace until 1941 is desirable. However, we cannot know what the future holds. We are already in a state of war; it is only that the shooting has not yet started." Obviously Goering was much more "in the know" than the Army leaders: "Feldmarschall von Blomberg will be informed by the Fuehrer tomorrow."

The Army viewpoint prevailed, however, and no regular German division was sent to Spain. In December, 1936, and January, 1937, the Condor Legion was reinforced with Air Force personnel, a few specialist Army units and "volunteers", but its total strength never exceeded some 20,000 men. The cruisers *Karlsruhe* and *Koeln* joined the *Deutschland* in Spanish waters, and the chief of the Wehrmacht intelligence section, Admiral Canaris, went to Spain in January to organize a counter-intelligence service. But reinforcements for Franco's ground troops were provided chiefly by the Italians. Despite the so-called "gentlemen's agreement" for non-intervention in Spain, some 40,000 Italian troops joined Franco during January and February, and before the end of the war this number was approximately doubled.[13]

So far as the Wehrmacht was concerned, January, 1937, was the month during which the decisive lines of policy in Spain were laid down. Franco's requests for aid resulted in an Italo-German military conference in Rome on January 14th. The German delegation was led by Goering, but the upshot of his meeting with Mussolini was that no more German personnel would be sent to Franco, and that Germany's further contribution would be made in military supplies only. These were sent, in substantial quantities, during the early months of 1937.

For neither the Italians nor the Condor Legion was their Spanish adventure any picnic. The Italians, indeed, promptly suffered a disastrous rout at Guadalajara in March, 1937. The Germans fared much better, but were unable to maintain air superiority after the appearance of new Russian planes over Madrid in December, 1936. Late in May, 1937, the *Deutschland* was hit and severely damaged by Loyalist planes. Like a neurotic, cruel child the German fleet "retaliated" by senselessly shelling the coastal town of Almería, inflicting many civilian casualties, and foreshadowing far darker pages in the annals of the Wehrmacht.

Not to be outdone, Sperrle soon let loose his Junkers bombers against Spanish towns and villages behind the Loyalist lines. The raid on Guernica, immortalized by Picasso, occurred during the summer of 1937. Though a town of a few thousand inhabitants only. Guernica was a religious and cultural symbol of the Basque country, which perhaps explains its selection as a target for devastation. Early in 1938 the Legion inaugurated a series of daytime bombing attacks against Barcelona. Thus was sounded the prelude to the terrible symphony of urban destruction during the Second World War.

For the most part, however, the planes of the Condor Legion were used for tactical support of Franco's ground forces, and planes and artillery alike made a major contribution to his eventual victory. So that other senior officers of the Luftwaffe could profit by the experience, Goering rotated the command at yearly intervals, Sperrle, promoted to *Generalleutnant* and then to *General der Flieger* within a year, returned to Germany in November, 1937, to take command of the air fleet (Luftflotte 3) based at Munich. His successor, Generalleutnant Volkmann, held command until November, 1938. Volkmann likewise won promotion to *General der Flieger*, and was thereafter put in charge of the *Luftkriegsakademie*. The last commander of the Legion, Generalmajor Wolfram von Richthofen, had served as Chief of Staff to both Sperrle and Volkmann. But by that time Hitler and the generals alike were preoccupied with much larger matters than the Condor Legion or even the Spanish Civil War itself.

HITLER SHOWS HIS HAND: NOVEMBER 5, 1937

By the end of 1937, Hitler the demon was beginning to get the upper hand of Hitler the shrewd and ruthless politician who had successfully ridden the whirlwind of revolution into unchallenged political leadership of Germany. One cannot deny that

the state of the world played into the demon's hands. It was not merely that the structure of Versailles had collapsed like a house of cards at his first touch, and that rearmament and remilitarization of the Rhineland had been easily achieved by bold action; for these things there was undeniably some justification. But to Hitler's cold eye it was plain that the whole world of Geneva and Locarno was cracking up. In the Far East, Japan had overrun Manchuria and pushed deep into China. In open defiance of the League of Nations, Mussolini's tawdry conquest of Abyssinia had laid the mantle of empire on the shoulders of the unenthusiastic Victor Emmanuel. Day after day in Spain and Spanish waters, the dictators were openly flouting the "gentlemen's agreement". The prestige of the League of Nations dwindled to the vanishing point, and deep cracks serrated the "united front".

Punch-drunk and disillusioned, would not the lacklustre leaders of the democracies yield to a combination of threats and decisive action? So reasoned Hitler and rightly, as 1938— the year of *Blumenkriege* and umbrellas—was abundantly to prove. Hitler the political genius sensed that it was time to start; Hitler the demon never knew when to stop.

Did the generals know that Hitler was possessed of a demon? Should not any self-respecting General Staff officer have read his Fuehrer's writings? According to Blomberg's post-reflective memorandum, while many of them may have read *Mein Kampf*, he himself "had the impression that the book was a piece of propaganda for his own inner struggle". Furthermore, "We soldiers . . . had learned too much from the First World War to be able to follow what we considered a fantasy. The later gigantic circulation of the book was due to a forced sale. I am of the opinion that there were far more owners than credulous readers of Hitler's book."

This impression that *Mein Kampf* was merely a propaganda exercise was undoubtedly strengthened by Hitler's temperate and courteous relations with the generals prior to 1938. Rearmament and the reoccupation of the Rhineland, as we have seen, won their enthusiastic support, nor is there any evidence that either step was regarded as dangerously reckless. To be sure, in May, 1935, at the time of *Wehrfreiheit*, Blomberg had requested Fritsch to study the possibility of a *Blitzkrieg* against Czechoslovakia, and this had worried Beck to the extent of stimulating him to write a staff memorandum pointing out the folly of such an adventure in view of the certain intervention of

other countries. But nothing came of the project at that time, and no other efforts (if, indeed, this was such) to steer German staff work toward aggressive military action were made during the next two years. The strategic plans and studies with which the General Staff of OKH occupied itself were defensive in character, and followed the general pattern of staff work common to most countries. Not until the outbreak of the Spanish Civil War was any political pressure for military adventurism exerted, and even then Fritsch and Beck were able to prevent any full-scale German involvement.

These cautious policies continued to prevail through the summer of 1937. In June the annual "directive for the preparation of the armed forces" was approved by Blomberg and circulated to the three services. The opening paragraphs of this directive stated that: [14]

> "The general political situation justifies the supposition that Germany need not consider an attack from any side. Indications of this are, in addition to the lack of desire for war in almost all nations, particularly the Western powers, the lack of preparedness for war of a number of states and of Russia in particular.
> "The intention to unleash a European war is held just as little by Germany."

Very different this was from Goering's excited speeches to his Air Force generals six months earlier! Nevertheless, the Wehrmacht was not to be caught napping, either by the enemy or fortune's nod. The directive continued:

> ". . . the politically fluid world situation, which does not preclude surprising incidents, demands constant preparedness for war on the part of the German armed forces,
> (a) to counterattack at any time.
> (b) to make possible the military exploitation of favourable opportunities should they occur."

Accordingly, the three services were directed to prepare for two major eventualities, each based on the hypothesis of a simultaneous attack on Germany from both east and west. The first assumed the opening of war by a surprise French attack, in which case the Wehrmacht would deploy its principal strength in the west; the plan to meet this attack was given the cover-name "Red", and was known in German staff circles as *"Fall Rot"* (Eventuality Red). The second plan—*"Fall Gruen"* (Eventuality Green)—envisaged "a surprise German operation against Czechoslovakia in order to parry the imminent attack of a

superior enemy coalition". For this purpose, only a light screen of troops would be left in the west to hold against a French attack, while the bulk of the German forces would speedily overrun Bohemia and Moravia, thus depriving Russia of air bases and eliminating "for the duration of the war" any "threat by Czechoslovakia to the rear of operations in the west".

In addition to these two basic staff studies, there were special situations to be prepared for. Otto, the Habsburg scion, was growing up and getting his picture in the papers. The thought of a revived Habsburg empire gave comfort neither to Hitler nor to the generals. With that literal-mindedness which often exposed German intentions during the war, this "eventuality" was dubbed "*Sonderfall Otto*" (Special Eventuality Otto) in the secret archives. "Armed intervention" in order "to compel Austria by armed force to give up a restoration" was to be buttressed by "making use of the domestic political dissension of the Austrian people," culminating in "a march . . in the general direction of Vienna" in the course of which "any resistance will be broken".

Spain was likewise a danger spot. "*Sonderfall Richard*" was directed to the danger of conflict between Germany and "Red Spain". But "preparatory deliberations to meet this eventuality are to be instituted only by the Navy". The Army and Air Force would do no more than assist "White Spain with material and personnel, as has been the procedure up to now".

So ran Blomberg's directive of June, 1937, and if not precisely a platform for world federalism, neither did it project any immediate threat to world peace. Rather it faithfully reflected the patient, yet amoral, viewpoint of the German General Staff officer—to build strength and conserve resources for *der Tag*, which would surely come but not necessarily soon.

Yet, as the autumn of 1937 chilled the air, the international temperature rose. The Spanish fighting stirred strong emotions everywhere. The Wehrmacht grew like an adolescent boy; Mussolini attended its manœuvres in September, as did delegations from England and Hungary. And on November 5, 1937, Hitler—the Hitler of *Mein Kampf*—spoke.

He spoke to a small and select circle. Blomberg, Fritsch, Goering and Raeder were there, as well as von Neurath, the Foreign Minister. Fortunately for history, Hitler's military adjutant Hossbach, newly promoted to *Oberst*, was also present, and it is from his account, written five days later, that our knowledge of this historic conference is derived.[15]

The conference opened in Berlin a little after four o'clock in the afternoon, and lasted over four hours. The atmosphere, though tense, was orderly; discussion was general, and conflicting views were freely expressed. But Hitler the demon was undeniably manifest in what transpired.

Hitler first explained that the subject was so important that security required its discussion in the select circle present, rather than in the cabinet. What he had to say, declared the Fuehrer, should "be looked upon in the case of his death as his last will and testament". He launched at once into a favourite subject—*Lebensraum*. The German economic and social problem could not, he reasoned, be solved either by economic autarchy (limited possibilities in the sphere of raw materials, and virtually none in that of foodstuffs) or by increased international trade (British domination of the sea lanes and instability of the export trade). Therefore "The only way out . . . is the securing of greater living space. . . . Should the security of our food position be our foremost thought, then the space required for this can be sought only in Europe. . . . It is not a case of conquering peoples, but of conquering agriculturally useful space. . . . The question for Germany is where the greatest possible conquest could be made at lowest cost." In determining this question "Germany must reckon with its two hateful enemies, England and France, to whom a strong German colossus in the centre of Europe would be intolerable". Accordingly:

"The German question can be solved only by way of force, and this is never without risk. The battles of Frederick the Great for Silesia, and Bismarck's wars against Austria and France, had been a tremendous risk and only the speed of Prussian action in 1870 had prevented Austria from participating in the war. If we place the decision to apply force with risk at the head of the following expositions, then we are left to reply to the questions 'when' and 'how'."

Thus the Fuehrer proceeded from generalities to particulars. In any circumstances, he declared, Germany must strike no later than the years 1943–45. By then, rearmament would be at its peak of efficiency; thereafter, weapons presently being produced in quantity would be obsolescent and the secrecy of "special weapons" would be endangered.* Furthermore, the

* In all probability this is an early reference to forerunners of the V-2 rocket. General Franz Halder informed the writer that he had witnessed experiments with the propellant fuel for V-2s in 1938, and his diary entry for September 26, 1939, refers to long-range rockets, with a one-ton explosive charge, under development at Peenemuende and probably ready for use in three to four years.

economic strain of supporting a large army would lower both the standard of living and the birth rate, and the Nazi movement and leaders would age. If he lived so long, said Hitler, it would be "his irrevocable decision to solve the German space problem no later than 1943–45".

But opportunity might knock much sooner. The "social tensions in France" might "lead to an internal political crisis of such dimensions that it absorbs the French Army and thus renders it incapable of employment in war against Germany". Alternatively, France might become "so tied up by a war against another state that it cannot proceed against Germany". In these inviting circumstances, who were the intended victims of German might?

On this score Hitler left no room for doubt. "For the improvement of our military and political situation it must be our first aim, in every case of entanglement in war, to conquer Czechoslovakia and Austria simultaneously, in order to remove any threat from the flanks. . . . The annexation of the two states to Germany . . . would constitute a considerable relief, owing to shorter and better frontiers, the freeing of fighting personnel for other purposes, and the possibility of constituting new armies up to a strength of about twelve divisions."

As for the risks of intervention by the great powers, if a "planned attack" were carried out in 1943–45. Hitler felt that probably England and perhaps France were in the course of "writing off" Czechoslovakia. But he was laying great store by the possibility that the Spanish war and tension in the Mediterranean might soon lead to war among Italy, France and England; should this occur, the Fuehrer had "firmly decided to make use of it at any time, perhaps even as early as 1938". Here was no fantasy about *Lebensraum*. Here was the imminent possibility of war, and Hitler's audience was now thoroughly aroused.

The mention of Spain led Hitler to further interesting observations. He neither expected nor desired an early end to the war: "From the German point of view a 100 per cent victory by Franco is not desirable; we are more interested in a continuation of the war and preservation of the tensions in the Mediterranean." A complete Franco victory would spell the end of Italian intervention, whereas its continuation (especially Italian control of the Balearics) might be expected to embroil England and France in Mediterranean hostilities. This, in turn, would

offer Germany the opportunity to "dispose of the Czechoslovakian and Austrian questions".

Unfortunately for history, Hossbach's record of the discussion which followed Hitler's exposition is sketchy. Raeder's reaction, if indeed he spoke, is not mentioned. Goering merely observed that the prospect of these enterprises made it "imperative to think of a reduction or abandonment of our military undertaking in Spain", and to this suggestion Hitler agreed in principle but postponed any final decision until a later time.

Blomberg, Fritsch and Neurath, however, all resisted the Fuehrer's thesis. Both of the military men opined that France would be able to cope with Italy without losing its margin of superiority on the Franco-German frontier. Blomberg was especially emphatic; German fortifications in the west were of "very small value", and the four new motorized divisions "which had been laid down for the west would be more or less incapable of movement". Furthermore, the Czech fortifications "had assumed the character of a Maginot Line . . .which would present extreme difficulties to our attack".

Perhaps to draw Hitler out, Fritsch adverted to the staff study of a possible *Blitzkrieg* against Czechoslovakia—*Fall Gruen*—called for under the 1937 military directive. Fritsch had planned to go on leave abroad on November 10th, and after his return to carry out the study during the winter. Should he relinquish his leave, in view of what Hitler was contemplating? Hitler replied that "the possibility of the conflict was not to be regarded as being so imminent", and told Fritsch to take his vacation. Neurath then interjected his view that "an Italian–English–French contest was not as near as the Fuehrer appeared to assume". This elicited from Hitler a statement that "the date which appeared to him a possibility was the summer of 1938".

The foregoing is the essence of the famous "Hossbach protocol", and little additional information about this extraordinary meeting has, or is likely to, come to light. Of the participants, Hitler and Fritsch were dead by the end of the war, and Blomberg died early in 1946 without having thrown any new light on the episode.*

Goering, Raeder and Neurath, however, all gave testimony at Nuremberg about the meeting. Goering declared that Hit-

---

* At Nuremberg Blomberg was questioned briefly about the conference. He declared that he had attended many previous meetings at which Hitler "gave his fantasy free play", but that the meeting of November 5, 1937, stood out in his memory because Hitler spoke of the possibility of war at specific future times.

ler told him, just before the conference, that its purpose was to bring pressure to bear on Fritsch to speed up rearmament. The Fuehrer hoped that Blomberg would co-operate in exerting this pressure, and wanted Neurath present so that things would not look "too military". Raeder, testifying subsequently, supported Goering's story and added a personal post-inference that Hitler also wanted to "scare" Neurath out of his office as Foreign Minister, and replace him with Ribbentrop. Both Goering and Raeder strove to give the impression that the conference was intended chiefly for "dramatic effect", and that the talk was not taken seriously by them. Neurath, on the other hand, pinpointed the meeting as the first occasion at which Hitler's aggressive plans became apparent. As a result, Neurath was much upset "both physically and spiritually", and sought out Fritsch and Beck two days later to discuss the affair.

It is, of course, quite probable that Goering, and possible that Blomberg and Raeder (both of whom were on far closer terms with Hitler than Fritsch and Neurath), had heard Hitler express himself similarly on previous occasions, and were thus less susceptible to surprise and alarm. Goering's story, however, does not ring true. Understanding the relations between and respective qualities of Blomberg and Fritsch as he must have, it is inconceivable that Hitler could have relied on Blomberg to "high-pressure" Fritsch, and as Hossbach's record shows, Blomberg was in fact quite open in his opposition to Hitler's programme. Indeed, Hossbach, the only other witness to the occasion, has subsequently declared [16] that Blomberg and Fritsch not only debated with Hitler but strongly attacked Goering's handling of the Luftwaffe, much to the latter's discomfiture.

At all events, other records completely dispel the impression, sought to be created by Goering and Raeder, that the meeting of November 5th was a casual affair intended for "moral effect". As Jodl's diary reveals, records of Hitler's presentation were made not only by Hossbach but by Keitel (based, no doubt, on information furnished by Blomberg) and Goering as well. Goering immediately prepared a directive to the Chief of the General Staff of the Air Force (Stumpff) and Jodl himself proceeded to develop "ideas" and "deployment orders" for submission to Keitel and Blomberg. And on December 13th Hitler approved a report "concerning the military execution of the intentions developed by him on November 5th". At the same time the portion of the June directive to the armed forces

dealing with *Fall Gruen* (the invasion of Czechoslovakia) was superseded by a new version drafted as a result of the November 5th conference.

Nor was Fritsch's account of the meeting such as to cause Beck to take the matter lightly. Beck had been repeatedly giving warning, in staff memoranda, against the folly of premature involvement in war. In June, 1937, he had visited France, and his informal discussions with Daladier, Pétain and Gamelin had given him some hope of a Franco-German *rapprochement*. Thoroughly aroused by the events of November 5th, Beck delivered himself of a long critique of Hitler's thesis. The notion of inevitable war by 1943-45 he characterized as "superficial", and the possibility of France's internal political collapse as "wishful thinking". As for a Franco-Italian war, this would not divert French strength sufficiently to justify German aggression.

At Nuremberg a procession of field-marshals and generals— Brauchitsch, Leeb, Rundstedt, Halder and Manstein, among others—took the stand to swear that they had no contemporaneous knowledge of the November 5th conference. No doubt some of these officers spoke the truth. But the impression thus sought to be conveyed—that knowledge of these events did not pass outside the circle of immediate participants—is sufficiently exploded by the available records and normal inferences. By direct evidence, as we have seen, Keitel, Jodl, Beck and Stumpff were informed by Blomberg, Fritsch and Goering. The preparation of the revised directives must have involved a considerably wider circle of officers. It is also worth noting that, according to Jodl's diary, on January 21, 1938, "on the occasion of the end of the national political training course", Hitler talked "for two and a half hours to the generals about his conception of history, politics, national unity, religion, and the future of the German people". Unfortunately, no other record of this speech has come to light; who was present and precisely what transpired we do not know. It is probable, however, that much of what Hitler had said in November he repeated in January.

Three months after the conference of November 5, 1937, Blomberg, Fritsch and Neurath were all out of office.* These were the three who had ventured openly to oppose Hitler at the meeting. It is easy to infer that their opposition was the direct and principal cause of their downfall, but, especially in the case

---

* Although Neurath, relieved as Foreign Minister, was given the empty title President of the Secret Cabinet Council.

of Blomberg, this is undoubtedly an over-simplification. There can be little question, however, that the impressions Hitler gathered from their critical comments were a powerful contributing factor in the profound convulsion which was about to grip the Third Reich.

THE FALL OF GENERALFELDMARSCHALL WERNER VON BLOMBERG

Generalfeldmarschall von Blomberg was a widower, but his life was brightened by a secretary of whom he had long been very fond. Toward the end of 1937, he entertained seriously the thought of marrying the lady, whose name was Fraeulein Eva Gruhn. This project presented more difficulties than would have been the case in a social milieu less rigid than the upper reaches of the German officers' corps. Fraeulein Gruhn was neither wealthy nor well-born according to the prevailing standards of the corps. Moreover, she was a lady with a "past" which could hardly survive inspection through the lorgnette of respectability. Quite definitely, this was not the sort of marriage that a *Feldmarschall* and ranking member of the officers' corps could embark upon without risking serious repercussions.

The moonstruck, unstable Blomberg, however, did not count his costs. On December 15, 1937, according to Jodl's diary, he became "highly excited" for some unaccountable reason, "apparently a personal matter", and retired for a week "to an unknown place". On December 22nd, however, he appeared on schedule to deliver the funeral oration for Ludendorff at the *Feldherrnhalle* in Munich. Hitler was present, and after the ceremonies he and Blomberg conferred briefly but privately. Early in January, rumours of Blomberg's impending second marriage began to circulate, and on January 12, 1938, the nuptials were celebrated with little ostentation, but with the Fuehrer himself and Goering as witnesses. The honeymoon was soon interrupted by the death of Blomberg's mother, and by January 20th the *Feldmarschall* was back at his desk in Berlin.

In the meantime, the gossips and scandalmongers had been having a field day with the name and reputation of the new *Frau Feldmarschall*. Unpleasant, mocking telephone messages from anonymous callers were received at the RKM and OKH, and the generals began to grumble about Blomberg's having "disgraced" the officers' corps by a *mesalliance*. Unhappily for Blomberg and his bride, the rumours were not without foundation; some years earlier Fraeulein Gruhn's mother had made

147

her massage *salon* into a very interesting place and the police had interfered, with unfortunate results for both mother and daughter. The police dossier reached the desk of Count Helldorf, chief of the Berlin police, at about the time of Blomberg's return from his honeymoon.

Aware that he was handling dynamite, Helldorf took his dossier to Keitel. Here at least Blomberg might have expected loyal and discreet support. Not only was Keitel his immediate and principal subordinate; his daughter had married Keitel's son. According to Gisevius' account,* however, Keitel failed to warn Blomberg of his peril and refused to take any hand in the matter whatsoever. Furthermore, with either incredible stupidity or utter disloyalty, Keitel suggested that Helldorf take the dossier to, of all people, Hermann Goering!

At all events, when Hitler returned to Berlin from his week-end in Bavaria on Monday, January 24th, Goering lost no time in putting in an appearance. Hossbach was also present. Goering roundly declared that it was a shame the way the generals were talking about the affair, and that there was no disgrace in Blomberg's having married "a simple girl". The next day, however, the three were again in conference, and the tone of the conversation had entirely changed. Hitler announced that Frau von Blomberg had a "bad reputation"; Goering criticized the *Feldmarschall* for having revealed to him and to the Fuehrer before the wedding only that the lady "had a past". Hitler attacked the prudery of the officers' corps and praised Blomberg's loyalty—he would be sorry to lose Blomberg. He also revealed to the shocked and angry Hossbach that there was another dossier which implicated Fritsch in homosexuality, and that the latter would also have to resign.

At noon Goering went off to Blomberg's office and confronted him with the charges against his new wife. The shattered *Feldmarschall* offered to separate from her, but Goering replied that this would not eliminate the necessity for his resignation. Goering then returned to Hitler and announced that Blomberg "had admitted all". At noon of the following day, January 26th, Keitel informed Jodl, in strictest confidence, that Blomberg had been dismissed.

The behaviour and motives of the several actors in this weird sequence remain somewhat obscure to this day. It has not in-

---

* Gisevius and Helldorf were both participants in the anti-Hitler group which attempted the *Putsch* of July 20, 1944, and were in frequent contact at the time of the Blomberg–Fritsch crisis. See *To the Bitter End*, pp. 219 *et seq.*

frequently been suggested that Goering (or Goering and Himmler) deliberately lured Blomberg into the marriage in order to bring about his dismissal. The factual basis for this appealing inference is slender. Certainly, however, the discovery of the police files on the unhappy Fraeulein Gruhn, coupled with the snobbish outrage of the generals, presented Goering with a golden opportunity to eliminate the man who stood athwart his rise to the highest military rank, an opportunity which Goering seized with ruthless alacrity.

In these dire straits, Blomberg found no true friends among his brother officers, with most of whom he had lost personal contact. Fritsch and Hossbach took the surprisingly liberal view that Blomberg's marriage was his personal affair, but Fritsch was simultaneously involved in an even uglier mess and was powerless to aid Blomberg had he so desired, and Hossbach's devotion was to Fritsch rather than to Blomberg. Keitel, as we have seen, actually betrayed Blomberg, whether by design or ineptitude. Reichenau, who, like Keitel, could hope for promotion as a result of Blomberg's misfortune, did nothing for his former superior. In his memoirs Blomberg wrote: "I have a good memory of Reichenau although he, too, was no exception to the conventional attitude the generals adopted toward me after my departure; I had really expected different treatment from him because of his independent personality." Beck, from whom one might have expected a less rigid attitude, shared the conventional attitude of outrage. On January 28th, after Blomberg's departure, Beck read Keitel a lecture on the social ethics of the officers' corps, thus summarized in Jodl's diary:

> ". . . the situation with regard to the wife of the *Feldmarschall* affects the top of the Wehrmacht. Telephone calls from her friends are supposed to have reached the generals from public houses in which they celebrated the social rise of their 'colleague'.
>
> "One cannot permit the highest-ranking soldier to marry a whore; he should be forced to divorce the woman or else be taken off the list of officers; he could no longer be the commander of even a regiment. The commanding generals would have to submit their point of view to the Fuehrer."

Such, indeed, was the general opinion of the officers' corps.*

* Illustrative of the tense feelings at the time is an episode referred to by Jodl in his diary entry for February 2, 1938. General Wilhelm Adam, then head of the *Wehrmachtakademie* in Berlin, attended a reception given by the Swiss Ambassador at the end of January, at which Blomberg's marriage was a principal subject of gossip. Hans Frank, at that time Reichsminister without Portfolio, came up to

But there was neither need nor opportunity for representations to Hitler. By this time, Blomberg was already on his way to Capri, and a few days later the Fuehrer curtly informed the generals "that he alone and not the officers' corps is entitled to judge and decide in this matter". The Bavarian corporal was beginning to act the *Oberster Befehlshaber* in good earnest.

Hitler himself seems to have had mixed feelings about the Blomberg affair. Though not much given to personal fondnesses, Hitler always disliked to change the faces in his entourage, once he had become accustomed to them. It is inconceivable that Frau von Blomberg's "past" troubled him one whit, and more than probable that he would willingly have rejected the demands of Beck and other generals for Blomberg's dismissal, if for no other reason than to assert his own supreme authority, and if Blomberg's individual fate had been the only thing at stake. Hitler decided otherwise, and let Blomberg fall, primarily because he saw the episode as a springboard to a definitive subjection of the officers' corps. No doubt he was also annoyed with Blomberg's lack of enthusiasm for warlike adventures, but this was a secondary factor. Since he was determined to remove the real obstacle to his complete power—Fritsch—by a sordid and false accusation which would arouse and offend the officers' corps, it was advantageous to Hitler and characteristic of his tactics to utilize the Blomberg "scandal" to becloud the issue, confuse the public and divide the generals. If a field-marshal could commit so grave an indiscretion, one could much more readily believe that a general—even a Fritsch—might have been guilty of a moral lapse.

But if Hitler's attitude toward Blomberg was devoid of personal animus, this did not make his dismissal less of a surprise to the latter, who seems to have had no premonition of disaster's approach. It did, however, greatly ease the circumstances of his departure. While informing Blomberg of his dismissal on January 26th, according to Jodl's mawkish diary entry: "The Fuehrer, by his superhuman kindness, succeeded in comforting the *Feldmarschall*; he told him: As soon as Germany's hour comes, you will be at my side, and everything which happened in the past will be forgotten." Indeed, Blomberg's impression at the time was that he was only being given a year's "vaca-

---

Adam and made sneering remarks about Blomberg's enjoying the sunshine of Capri with his young wife. Adam replied, "Blomberg isn't our *Feldmarschall*, he is your *Feldmarschall*", implying that Blomberg had long been more of a Nazi than an Army officer.

tion". In his memoirs he refers to "the very far-reaching promises which were given to me in case of war and for the time
of my return after a one-year vacation abroad", and declares
that "during my last interview in January, 1938, the Fuehrer
spontaneously promised me with the greatest emphasis that I
would take over the supreme command in wartime". Relying
on these assurances, Blomberg abandoned any thought of resisting his removal or demanding an opportunity to justify his
conduct before a military court of honour, and agreed to his
own immediate disappearance from the German scene. He
conferred with Hitler twice (on January 26th and 27th), discussed the selection of successors to himself and to Fritsch, and
left Berlin the evening of January 27th.

Lulled by Hitler's honeyed words, Blomberg and his new
bride hied themselves to Capri and relaxed in the warm
Italian sun. His tragi-comedy was nearly finished, but a
moment of burlesque was interjected before the final curtain.
A young naval officer assigned to the *Wehrmachtamt*, Kapitaen-
leutnant von Wangenheim, became fired with officious zeal
and took off for Capri in hot pursuit of the bride and groom.
Raeder had asked him to convey to Blomberg the advice that he
divorce "this woman", but Wangenheim had in mind a more
definitive solution. He reached Capri on January 31st, and
promptly appeared before Blomberg and "tried to put a pistol
into his hand". For this idea the honeymooning *Feldmarschall*
had no stomach, and rejected the proffered weapon with the
observation that Wangenheim "apparently held entirely different opinions and a different standard of life". The frustrated
Wangenheim returned to Berlin to find himself the subject of
vast disapproval. Keitel was furious because Wangenheim,
though a member of his staff in the *Wehrmachtamt*, had gone
without his permission. Jodl noted in his diary that "the
attempt made by Wangenheim has probably been made with
the best of intentions, but shows an extraordinary arrogance on
the part of this young officer who believes it his duty to be the
guardian of the honour of the officers' corps . . . everything had
to be done to avoid a suicide, the Fuehrer succeeded in that and
the adjutant [Wangenheim] could have destroyed everything".

Throughout this hectic last week of January, no official word
of Blomberg's resignation had been made public, though Berlin
was buzzing with rumours. By February 1st the foreign press was
carrying confused accounts of the crisis, but definite confirmation of Blomberg's departure was not given out until February

4th, when a broad governmental reorganization was announced. Buried in the pages describing the new set-up was a brief dispatch which quoted Hitler's farewell letters to Blomberg and Fritsch. To the former, Hitler expressed his thanks for loyal services during the past five years and for Blomberg's contribution to the building of the new Wehrmacht.

With this graceless word of thanks, Blomberg utterly disappeared from the scene. The January, 1938, issue of the official RKM monthly *Die Wehrmacht* had carried a full-page photograph of Blomberg as a cover-piece. He was never pictured in its pages again. The March issue was entirely devoted to the Luftwaffe, and carried on its cover a picture of Goering, complete with field-marshal's baton. Blomberg's name was stricken from the Army rolls, and was never again carried in the rank lists.

If, despite all this, Blomberg continued to rely on Hitler's promises, his final disillusionment was not long delayed. His congratulatory telegram to Hitler after the Austrian *Anschluss* went unanswered. He wandered around Italy for some months and then took a trip to the Dutch East Indies, completely out of contact with doings at home. When he finally returned to Germany he was met with a "curtain of silence drawn around my person and my activities", and was indirectly informed that the promises made to him "could no longer be realized". He offered his services when war broke out in September, 1939, but without success. And so he lived quietly and in complete obscurity in a small Bavarian village near the Tegernsee throughout the war, the end of which he survived by less than a year.

In this enforced retirement, Blomberg committed to paper lengthy and wandering memoirs, largely concerned with personal trivia but touched here and there with revealing reflections. Despite the broken promises, Blomberg's confidence in Hitler as a "great captain and omniscient statesman" remained intact through most of the war. His philosophizing, or theosophizing, even led him to accept his own dismissal as justified by the very nature of Hitler's Reich:

"I began to understand that a good and—considering the prevailing form of government—sufficient reason for my removal was to be found in the totalitarian principles which governed the state. . . .

"Hitler and his party wanted total power in their hands; no secondary powers, no independence of action, no centrifugal ex-

pression or diversionary tendencies could be tolerated, only the totalitarian, indivisible, untrammelled power could prevail. This had been accomplished everywhere except in the armed forces. Direct command functions were in the hands of a soldier, myself; the Fuehrer held only indirect command powers. This created distrust."

One can hardly gainsay the accuracy of this diagnosis; what is distressing is Blomberg's near-reconciliation to the concepts that caused him to be discarded. After the war, to be sure, Blomberg was able to speak [17] of Hitler's "mistakes as a statesman and soldier, his cruel injustice and intolerance, and the shameful crimes which were committed in his name, and probably on his orders". But this awakening came so late that it can hardly be counted to his credit.

On the other hand, there is no justification for making Blomberg the prime whipping-boy for all the sins and misfortunes of the officers' corps, as so many of his brother officers have tried to do during the years since the war. At Nuremberg and elsewhere a veritable parade of senior German officers sought to fasten on Blomberg the principal blame for Hitler's subjection of the generals, and even for Germany's misfortunes in war.* There was blame in abundance to be shared by all; Blomberg was a convenient and welcome target chiefly because of his leading role in the early days of the regime, his loss of personal contact with his former colleagues, and his mésalliance. In fact, he was devoted to Hitler but not to the Party, and his resistance to Party pressures on the Army was by no means a total failure. His own self-defence, written at Nuremberg, is not unpersuasive in this respect:

". . . Hitler on several occasions approached me with the idea of training the SA as a reserve formation. He gave in to my objections and accordingly the political importance of the SA disappeared gradually, and the three regiments of the Waffen-SS were *not* increased in my time—in spite of heavy pressure on the part of Himmler. To what extent I was successful in keeping the Wehrmacht free from the influence of the Nazi Party, and from being linked up with it, has not been realized. . . . In my time the Wehrmacht stood in no sense behind the Party, but took its stand

---

* A notable and curious (in view of the hostility between Blomberg and Goering) exception was Goering's deputy, Milch, who testified at Nuremberg (Vol. IX, *Trial of the Major War Criminals*, p. 91): "Blomberg was in a position to resist Hitler and he had done so very often, and Hitler respected him and listened to his advice. Blomberg was the only elderly soldier who was clever enough to reconcile military and political questions."

independently alongside it. The Party often sought to change this situation but did not succeed, because Hitler listened to me in those days, which can be confirmed not only by me but by all who know the facts.

". . . Had I been a spineless tool in the hands of Hitler, as some generals now assume, then he probably would have dealt differently with me. Up to January, 1938, I served my Supreme Commander, Hitler, loyally according to my oath and conviction, and before that I prevented much planned interference in the affairs of the Wehrmacht. On the other hand, objections to Hitler as head of the state did arise, since justice toward all Germans was often violated. Toward the Party and its leaders I experienced, like many Germans, a feeling of distrust. Since life only seldom offers easily solved equations, a choice had to be made between various solutions. . . . The other generals heard nothing of my protests and showdowns with Hitler."

In fact, despite his adulation for Hitler, Blomberg's political outlook did not mirror the Fuehrer's, but rather embodied old and deep currents of thought common to many Junker nobles. Like von Seeckt, he favoured a close and permanent relation to Russia, and advocated the eventual partition of Poland. He was anti-Japanese and, again like Seeckt, pro-Chinese; in 1934 he sent a military mission headed by von Falkenhausen to advise Chiang Kai-shek. He hoped for an understanding with "conservative elements" in England and believed that, once this was achieved, the power of France could safely be ignored. He had a poor opinion of Italy as a military ally. In domestic politics he was a typical authoritarian and, like most officers, anti-Semitic, although he "did not approve of the methods employed" by the Nazis against the Jews. He believed war to be inevitable, but desired a decade of peace to build up Germany's industrial capacity and military power so that a long war could be sustained.

All this is characteristic of the German military mind, and it is probably a fair evaluation of Blomberg to say that he was distinctive in temperament rather than mentality. For a German officer he was unusually articulate, flexible and broad in his personal contacts. These qualities and his professional competence were diluted by an instability and impressionability which undermined his capacity for leadership, and which Hitler exploited with his usual skill in wringing the worst out of every man.

But it scarcely becomes the generals who led Hitler's march of conquest and connived or winked at his hideous atrocities to

point the finger of scorn at Blomberg. Whether Blomberg would have signed his name or lent his authority to the terrible register of criminal orders and directives that stained the history of the Wehrmacht after his departure is an interesting but academic question. He was not put to the test; many of his fellows, including some of his bitterest critics, were tested and failed. What happened after Blomberg passed from the scene is their responsibility and their shame, not his.

THE FALL OF GENERALOBERST FREIHERR VON FRITSCH

Blomberg's prestige depended entirely upon the personal favour of Hitler, and his fall signified little in the power crisis of 1938. Fritsch, on the other hand, had never enjoyed Hitler's favour. He was stiff and reserved—a *Generalstabscharakter* (in Raeder's phrase) in whose presence Hitler was invariably uneasy. Nor had Fritsch achieved a unique leadership within the officers' corps comparable to that of Seeckt. His outstanding professional ability and devotion to the Army had, however, made a considerable impression, he was generally respected and admired, if not revered, and his authority as Commander-in-Chief and official spokesman of the Army was unquestioned. In Hitler's eyes, Fritsch was the quarry and Blomberg the decoy, and upon the elimination of Fritsch the Fuehrer now bent his ruthless energies.

Fritsch left Germany for a vacation in Egypt a few days after the fateful conference of November 5, 1937. He appears to have been shadowed by Himmler's agents in the course of his trip, but no untoward incidents occurred, and he returned to Berlin shortly before the celebration of Blomberg's marriage, worried about Hitler's warlike tendencies but unsuspecting of an approaching catastrophe. Presumably Himmler or Goering put the *dossier* on Fritsch into Hitler's hands shortly after the latter's return from Bavaria on January 24th. At all events, Hitler was in possession of it the next day when his long conference with Goering and Hossbach took place and, according to Hossbach's account, was already persuaded that it established Fritsch's guilt of homosexual offences under Section 175 of the German criminal code.

Despite Hitler's orders to the contrary, Hossbach went to Fritsch that evening and informed him of the contents of the *dossier* and of his grave peril. Fritsch categorically denied the charge, and Hossbach carried his denial back to Hitler the following morning of Wednesday, January 26th. Hossbach

also insisted on Fritsch's behalf that the Army Commander-in-Chief should be given an opportunity to appear before the Fuehrer and deny the charges in person.

The opportunity was extended late in the evening of the same day, but in a manner hardly calculated to advance Fritsch's cause. Himmler and Goering were also present, as well as an odoriferous and theretofore obscure individual named Schmidt. As Fritsch was in the course of denying the accusation, Schmidt was introduced into the room and identified Fritsch as the person whom he had observed commit a homosexual offence some years earlier. Hitler suspended Fritsch from his position of Army Commander-in-Chief and Fritsch, humiliated and apparently too stunned for a convincing display of righteous anger, returned to his apartment at the Bendlerstrasse. Goering appeared in the room where Hossbach had been waiting and dramatically declared that Fritsch's guilt had been established beyond question. Hossbach continued to insist that Fritsch be given a chance to clear himself, and succeeded in having Beck summoned to the Chancellery despite the late hour. After conferences both with Hitler and with Fritsch at the latter's apartment, Beck put forward a demand for a trial of the charges before a military court of honour, but Hitler did not immediately give his consent, and this issue was not resolved that evening.

Circumstances now conspired to Hitler's advantage. Fritsch was a lifelong bachelor who was not known to have ever had much to do with the opposite sex, and a very reserved man. He was thus especially vulnerable to accusations of this type, and his situation was greatly worsened by the fact that the gossip about Frau Blomberg had turned out to be not unfounded. Finally, he did not help his own cause by incautiously revealing to Hossbach that he had been in the habit of giving food to one or two boys of the *Hitler-Jugend* at his Bendlerstrasse apartment. Although this was not an uncommon practice at the time, and Fritsch's behaviour was later proved to have been wholly innocent, at the outset it lent colour to the charges and caused even Hossbach some anxiety. And the entire concatenation of circumstances gave others pause, even within the officers' corps. Beck was at first inclined to believe the charges, and Blomberg commented just before his departure for Capri that Fritsch was not a "woman's man".

The result of all this was that, even if Fritsch had been the type of man to rally the generals behind him to meet Hitler's attack

(which he was not), his personal situation was so beclouded as to make such a move very difficult. Fritsch himself was slow to realize that anything more was at stake than a ghastly mistake about his own person. Furthermore, he was inept at political in-fighting, and most of his colleagues in the higher levels of the officers' corps were no better equipped. Thus Hitler was able to deflect the attention and energies of Fritsch and his supporters to the proposition that Fritsch be accorded opportunity to clear his name before a court of honour; in the meantime Hitler proceeded with a sweeping reorganization of the Wehrmacht's leadership, almost unopposed. The officers' corps was defeated before its members realized that they, and not Fritsch alone, were the real targets of Hitler's assault.

Like Blomberg's dismissal, Fritsch's suspension was held *in camera* for nearly ten days, while rumours flew thick and fast. The day (Thursday, January 27th) after the confrontation with Schmidt, Hitler summoned Keitel, treated him in a confidential and flattering manner, and said that he planned to supplant Fritsch, and that he wanted a new Army adjutant who, unlike Hossbach, "will be my and your confidant and not the confidant of the other departments". Keitel and Jodl agreed that "the man most suited to be the Fuehrer's adjutant" was a *Major* named Schmundt. The following day, Hitler advised Keitel of the nature of the charge against Fritsch. The Reichsminister of Justice, Guertner, was called into the picture, and Hitler directed that Guertner, the legal division of the Wehrmacht, and the SS should all proceed to a full investigation of the Fritsch case. Guertner and the military lawyers promptly recommended that a trial be held and in this they were supported by von Rundstedt as the senior active Army officer.

In the meantime, Generaloberst Freiherr von Fritsch had been subjected to the unheard-of indignity of interrogation at the hands of the Gestapo at their Albrechtstrasse headquarters, a procedure which he unwisely had consented to. Hossbach, too, had suffered the axe. While at lunch with the Fuehrer on January 28th, Hossbach's own subordinate at OKH, Major von Ziehlberg, informed him by telephone that he had been relieved as adjutant to the Fuehrer. Hossbach's emotional description[18] of the immediately ensuing scene between himself and Hitler chiefly serves to illustrate the magnetic grip which the Fuehrer was able to fix on men in his entourage, even when their opinions and traditions were in strong conflict with his

own. Schmundt reported the next day, beginning a tour of duty as adjutant which was to last until the bomb exploded at Hitler's headquarters on July 20, 1944; Schmundt was one of the few who perished from the blast.

The official announcement of Fritsch's dismissal, like that of Blomberg's, was published on February 4th, together with a brief letter of thanks for past services. No mention was made in the press of the charges against Fritsch, but Hitler described them the same day to a hastily assembled and secret meeting of all the leading generals, with what Liebmann described as "crushing effect". Following this meeting, Brauchitsch and Rundstedt urged the generals to take no "hasty steps", but return to their posts and await the outcome of court-martial proceedings.

For Hitler did not dare reject the demand that Fritsch be allowed to stand trial. At the end of January, Fritsch retained Graf von der Goltz as his counsel, and a methodical investigation of the charges got under way. Himmler and Heydrich had contrived their case well enough for a *coup d'état*, but not for a judicial proceeding. It was soon discovered that Schmidt was a sordid and convicted blackmailer, who had stuffed the Gestapo files with accusations of sexual perversion against numerous prominent persons. Among them were Funk (soon to be appointed Minister of Economics), a former ambassador, the SS police-president of Potsdam, and the famous international tennis star, Baron Gottfried von Cramm.

Some of the charges were apparently true, others highly questionable or totally unfounded. The opening of these files had, at all events, disastrous consequences for the unhappy von Cramm. Returning to Germany from Italy after a six-months tournament tour abroad, his scheduled triumphant reception was suddenly cancelled, and he was arrested by the *Kriminalpolizei* a few days before the opening of Fritsch's trial. In all probability, the purpose was to establish the "truth" of at least one of Schmidt's charges.*

Schmidt's accusation against Fritsch was that he had seen the Army Commander-in-Chief commit an offence with a *Lustknabe* near the Potsdam railroad station in November, 1934. Thereafter, Schmidt declared, he had successfully blackmailed the general, who paid him a substantial sum of hush money at a

* Von Cramm was arrested on March 5th, and convicted under Section 175 on May 14th. He was sentenced to one year's imprisonment, but was paroled on October 16, 1938.

rendezvous in the Lichterfelde quarter of Berlin. But numerous items in Schmidt's story in the Gestapo files did not fit Fritsch, and the pre-trial investigators were eventually able to unearth a retired Rittmeister von Frisch living in Lichterfelde, who admitted that he had been the actual culprit and victim of Schmidt's extortion.

No doubt frightened out of his wits by the Gestapo, Schmidt now declared that there had been both a Fritsch and a Frisch episode, and on this implausible footing the case went to trial at the Preussenhaus in Berlin on March 10, 1938. Goering, newly a field-marshal and thus ranking officer of the Wehrmacht, presided, flanked by Raeder, the new Army Commander-in-Chief von Brauchitsch, and two judges of the *Reichskriegsgericht* (Supreme War Tribunal), Drs. Selmer and Lehmann. Public and press were excluded. Schmidt repeated his accusations, but before much further progress was made Goering announced a suspension of the hearings. The day before Schuschnigg had ordered the Austrian plebiscite, and Hitler had decided on invasion to achieve *Anschluss*. The march of conquest had begun, and the commanders-in-chief were wanted at their posts.

The trial was resumed on March 17th, and concluded the following day. Schmidt tried to stick to his impossible tale of two occurrences, but after Frisch had admitted his involvement, and it became apparent that Frisch's story tallied with Schmidt's original accusation against Fritsch, Schmidt broke down and admitted that there was a Frisch affair but no Fritsch affair. Goering, who by that time had little to lose from the acquittal of Fritsch, posed as the fair-minded judge and excoriated Schmidt for his wanton prevarication. The tribunal announced the acquittal of Fritsch "for proven innocence", and the proceedings were closed. The court made no effort to explore the background of the false accusations, so the role of Himmler and Heydrich was not disclosed.

Thus was Fritsch's personal honour vindicated, but what of the broader issues? Hitler had won his goal weeks earlier. Brauchitsch was now the Commander-in-Chief of the Army, and Fritsch found himself merely a *Generaloberst* with an unblemished reputation but no command. The machinations of the SS were suspected by a few, but not generally realized even among the generals, to say nothing of the officers' corps as a whole. Fritsch had finally realized, as had Beck, Hossbach and several others, what a crushing defeat the Army had suffered

at Hitler's hands. What counter-measures did Fritsch and his supporters contemplate?

By interesting coincidence, Fritsch had been assigned to the *Heeresleitung* at the time of Seeckt's dismissal in 1926. At that time Fritsch had unsuccessfully advised Seeckt to rally the Army behind him and seize power. Faced with his own crisis, Fritsch brooded over the same idea, but never got beyond brooding, despite the urgings of Hossbach. His principal concern continued to be his own personal and public "rehabilitation" and the exposure and punishment of the SS and Gestapo plotters whose spurious charges had led to his downfall. But his political archaism is well illustrated by the fact that the only direct action he ever took was his attempt to challenge Himmler to a duel with pistols. It is doubtful that the challenge ever reached the little black schoolmaster,* and, in any event, such a naïve and unimaginative tactic was foredoomed to failure.

But even had he chosen to act more boldly, Fritsch's chances of success were meagre. By the time his name had been cleared, he had no strong cards left to play. The annexation of Austria had greatly enhanced Hitler's prestige, both with the public and throughout the officers' corps. The Luftwaffe was under Goering's thumb, and little or no support against Hitler could be expected from Raeder. Even in the Army there was no unanimity, despite the deep disaffection the episode had stirred in Beck, Adam, Hossbach and a few others. Keitel and Jodl had swung completely to Hitler's side. Brauchitsch was in no mood to jeopardize his new post as Army Commander-in-Chief. Among the field commanders, there were a number who followed Reichenau's pro-Nazi orientation, either by conviction or because they had fallen heir to better assignments as a result of the reorganization of the High Command at the time of Fritsch's dismissal.

Fritsch rightly gauged the prospects of a *coup d'état* and his own capacity to lead one as well-nigh hopeless and settled back into embittered retirement. His friends in the officers' corps took up a collection to provide him with a house in Berlin; while it was being readied, Fritsch stayed at a small estate at Achterberg in the Lueneburg Heath.

In June, Hitler exculpated Fritsch in a speech before the

---

* It has been said that Fritsch turned the note over to Rundstedt, as *doyen* of the officers' corps, for delivery to Himmler, and that Rundstedt gave it the "pocket veto".

commanding generals at Swinemuende. According to Lieb-mann's account, the Fuehrer was at his cleverest. He gave every appearance of honest regret that a terrible misunder-standing had damaged Fritsch, while an adroit reference to the Hitler Youth episode left a feeling of doubt. As for Fritsch's reinstatement, that was out of the question, as the Fuehrer had told the German people that Fritsch's health had failed, and could not go back on his story.

Fritsch's public "rehabilitation" took place on August 11, 1938, when he was made *Chef* of Artillery Regiment 12, which he had commanded a decade earlier. This was an honour previously conferred only on Seeckt, Mackensen and Blom-berg, but for Fritsch it was more funeral than triumph. The ceremonies took place at the Gross-Born parade-grounds near Schwerin in Pomerania. A letter from Hitler was read, and Brauchitsch made a courteous speech. In his reply, Fritsch was so discreet as to pay tribute to the *vorwaerts stuermenden Geist* of Adolf Hitler's Reich. That evening the *Wehrkreis* commander, Blaskowitz, gave a large party in Fritsch's honour. The next day, Fritsch was back at Achterberg. In February, 1939, he moved to the "gift house" on Albertininstrasse in the Zehlendorf sector of Berlin. A more fitting gift was the great Moltke's desk from the Bendlerstrasse, used ever since by the chiefs of the General Staff and of the *Heeresleitung*.

Fritsch's last year was a weird and pathetic sort of half-life. Regiments are commanded by colonels, not senior generals, and Fritsch's designation as *Chef* of an artillery regiment was sup-posed to be strictly honorary. Fritsch would not have it so. He watched his regiment's training manœuvres, and reported to it during the Czech crisis in the autumn of 1938. After he moved to Berlin there were a few months of separation. But he declined invitations from Spain and South America to act as a military adviser, and clung to his remaining Army con-tacts in Germany. And in August, 1939, as war loomed, he rejoined his regiment, by then already stationed in East Prussia. A few weeks later, he met his death from a Polish machine-gun bullet in a field on the outskirts of Warsaw.

RKM TO OKW

Thus was the downfall of Fritsch and Blomberg accom-plished. Their elimination, however, left Hitler with problems as well as augmented power. Who was to succeed these men in their exalted posts? Goering was flushed with victory and

vanity, and Reichenau was eager to grasp the prize which had once before eluded him. On the other hand, the elevation of either of these worthies might well touch off an explosion among the disillusioned and rebellious elements of the officers' corps. In addition, Blomberg's departure opened up the possibility of reorganizing the top command structure of the Wehrmacht, and this aggravated the already sharp tensions and rivalries among the three branches of service. The situation called for all the Fuehrer's genius for political manœuvre, and once again he rose to the emergency.

The most pressing question was that of a successor to Blomberg. Hossbach, before his dismissal, recommended Rundstedt and Beck to the Fuehrer, as well as Graf von der Schulenburg, an elderly retired general who had been the Crown Prince's Chief of Staff during the First World War. According to Hossbach's account, Hitler took kindly to the idea of Schulenburg, who had become a strong Nazi, and authorized Hossbach to make inquiries. But when he telephoned to Schulenburg in southern Germany, Hossbach was told that Himmler's adjutant, of all people, had already been in touch with Schulenburg,* and that for reasons of health the old gentleman could not undertake the journey to Berlin.

In the afternoon of January 27th, Hitler discussed the probability of Fritsch's departure with Keitel, and on this occasion too Schulenburg was mentioned, together with Rundstedt, Reichenau, and Joachim von Stuelpnagel, a leading general of the old Reichswehr who had preceded Rundstedt as Commander of Wehrkreis III in Berlin, retiring at the end of 1931. All three, however, were rejected, Stuelpnagel as "not loyal", Reichenau as "too jumpy and superficial" and Rundstedt as "told old and worn out", an ironic commentary on the man who was to be the leading German field commander throughout the war.

In fact, the question of Blomberg's successor had been decided earlier that day, and on the recommendation of Blomberg himself, when he bade the Fuehrer farewell. Hitler asked for his opinion on the matter, and Blomberg proposed Goering on the basis of rank. Hitler, however, declared that Goering lacked both patience and diligence and was too self-indulgent.

---

* Schulenburg, who was then seventy-two, had been an honorary officer in the SS since 1934, and since 1936 had held the rank of *Gruppenfuehrer*, so it was not unnatural for Himmler's office to contact him. The episode does, however, show that Himmler was in close touch with Hitler's thinking and action on the top military appointments.

Thereupon Blomberg suggested that the Fuehrer himself take the post. Whether or not Hitler had had this solution in mind all along, this was in fact the upshot; the same afternoon Hitler informed Keitel that "the uniform and concentrated leadership of the Wehrmacht is sacred and untouchable to me, and I myself will take it over with your help".

Superficially it may appear extraordinary that Blomberg should have sponsored the very men who had just destroyed his own career. At the time, however, Blomberg was counting on Hitler's promise to restore him to office at some future date. Furthermore, Blomberg was in no mood to suggest any Army general for the position. Goering had very cleverly emphasized to Blomberg that it was the generals themselves who, because they disapproved the marriage, had forced Hitler's hand, and Blomberg completely swallowed this half-truth. His reaction was highly personal but quite understandable.*

The decision personally to assume Blomberg's office left Hitler with the problem of doing something to assuage Goering's ambition. The obvious answer was to promote him again, and this was, accordingly, the reason for the field-marshal's blue baton which now reposes in the Pentagon Building. Thus Goering failed in his quest for supreme military power and won only the trappings of rank, but Hitler gauged his man shrewdly, and "unser Hermann" was enormously pleased to be the one and only *Feldmarschall* of the Wehrmacht.

The reorganization of the High Command structure, however, was a more complicated problem. Beck lost no time in pressing the Army's claim to leadership within the Wehrmacht. The day after Blomberg's departure, Beck told Jodl that the Army was "the most decisive factor in Germany . . . must conduct the war", and declared that the Luftwaffe should be abolished as an independent arm and subordinated to the Chief of the General Staff of the Army.

But Goering was an insuperable obstacle to any such move, and Hitler's decree of February 4, 1938, did little to alter the relative status of the three services. Rather, it served to clinch his own personal control of the entire Wehrmacht.

In form, the decree abolished the *Reichskriegsministerium*. In practical effect, its name was changed to *Oberkommando der Wehrmacht* (OKW). By this device, no doubt, Hitler meant to stress that his own relationship to the Wehrmacht would not be

---

* These obvious inferences were confirmed by Blomberg in June, 1945, when he was interviewed by Fritsch's one-time defence counsel, Graf von der Goltz.

that of a civilian minister, but rather one of direct and personal command. Accordingly, the decree declared:

> "From now on I take over directly the command of the entire Wehrmacht.
> "The former *Wehrmachtamt* in the RKM will come directly under my command. . . .
> "At the same time, the OKW takes over the responsibilities of the RKM. . . ."

Thus the supreme commands of the three services (OKH, OKM and OKL) were subordinated to the OKW in place of the defunct RKM, and directly to Hitler instead of indirectly through Blomberg. Keitel's *Wehrmachtamt* disappeared as an independent bureau, and became the OKW. Keitel himself became a sort of chief of staff to Hitler—indeed it was originally proposed that he carry the title "Chief of the General Staff of the Wehrmacht". At the last minute, however, Hitler decided that this was "not important enough", and Keitel emerged as "Chief (*Chef*) of the Supreme Command of the Wehrmacht (OKW)". Unlike Blomberg, however, Keitel had no independent prerogatives of command—he was Hitler's executive agent, and issued orders only in the name of the Fuehrer.

This decree, while it fixed the authority of Hitler and Keitel, did little to set at rest the jockeying for position among the services. Goering retained his independent Air Ministry (RLM), and with his exalted rank remained uncontrollable except by Hitler. Raeder soon made a bid, albeit unsuccessful, for an independent naval ministry. Early in March, the OKH presented a formal memorandum which would have given the Army definitive leadership of all the armed forces, and transformed the OKW into a directorate for national economic and social mobilization in the event of war. Goering encouraged Keitel to oppose this vigorously, and in April the OKW submitted a counter-memorandum, drafted chiefly by Jodl, which stressed the "universality" of modern warfare, and the necessity for an over-all direction, free from domination by any one branch. In a pseudo-philosophical appendix, the OKW declared: [19]

> "Despite all attempts to outlaw it, war is still a law of nature which may be channelled but not eliminated. It serves the survival of the race and the state's assurance of a historical future.
> "This high moral purpose gives war its total character and its ethical justification."

In the end, the interservice situation was left substantially unchanged. By a further decree in June, 1938, the OKW was confirmed as a personal "working staff" to the Fuehrer in his capacity as Wehrmacht Commander-in-Chief. Its personnel was inter-service but predominantly from the Army; nevertheless, the top Army officers of OKW, such as Keitel and Jodl, worked at arm's length rather than intimately with the OKH, so that the Army's influence in OKW was not strong.

As it finally took shape, the OKW comprised four principal departments. Most important was the *Fuehrungstab* (WFA), with its component National Defence Section (*Landesverteidigungsabteilung*), which was the operational planning organ of the Wehrmacht. Jodl continued to head the National Defence Section, but Keitel felt the need of a more senior officer to take over the WFA. The choice was Generalleutnant Max von Viebahn, an excellent staff officer who had served as Leeb's Chief of Staff at Kassel and as Commander of the 34th Infantry Division at Koblenz. Viebahn's nerves, however, proved quite unequal to withstanding the tensions and jealousies between the OKW and OKH. He soon fell into difficulties with Keitel, and was relieved of duty after about six weeks.* Jodl took over Viebahn's post, and Warlimont, who had served both in Spain and in the RKM, replaced Jodl.

The other three major departments were intelligence and counter-espionage (*Auslandsnachtrichten und Abwehr*) headed by Vizeadmiral Canaris, the department for general Wehrmacht affairs (AWA) under Oberst Reinecke, and the economic staff under Generalmajor Thomas. In addition, the Army inspector of communications (Generalmajor Fellgiebel) was given authority in this field by the OKW throughout the armed services.

The decree of February 4, 1938, transmuting RKM into OKW, and the military personnel changes of that day, were presented to the German press as part of a vast, general reorganization of the leadership of the Third Reich. "*Strongest Concentration of All Powers in the Fuehrer's Hands*", screamed the headlines of the *Voelkischer Beobachter*. The news of Blomberg's and Fritsch's retirements "for reasons of health" was half buried in the welter of announcements, and their pictures were not used, though photographs of more than two dozen other

---

* Viebahn was hospitalized for nervous disorders in late March or early April, 1938. He later recovered and held several staff and command assignments, but none of major importance.

generals and officials, some of distinctly minor stature, were carried.

The Fuehrer's assumption of direct military command was, of course, given primary emphasis in the press. Treated as almost equally important, however, was the simultaneous establishment of a new governmental body called the Secret Cabinet Council (*Geheime Kabinettsrat*). In his decree, Hitler described its purpose to be "for my guidance in the conduct of foreign policy". Neurath, replaced as Foreign Minister by Ribbentrop, was designated President of the Council; all other members were *ex officio*, and included Keitel and the three service commanders-in-chief, and Ribbentrop, Hess, Goebbels and Lammers. But despite its impressive sound and great publicity, the Secret Cabinet Council was nothing but a false front. Its real purpose was to divert foreign attention from the military crisis, and maintain Neurath's prestige abroad despite his replacement by Ribbentrop. The Council never held a single meeting or transacted any business whatsoever.

Beyond the military reshuffle and Ribbentrop's accession to the Foreign Ministership, the remaining major personnel announcement was that of Walther Funk as Economics Minister. This was mere official confirmation of the state of affairs which had existed since Schacht's retirement the previous year. A reorganization of the Ministry's structure was also publicized, with long lists of little-known names. The Foreign Ministry announced the recall of three well-known diplomats—von Hassell from Rome, von Dirksen from Tokyo, and von Papen from Vienna. It was the end of his official career for the first, but Dirksen was sent to London to replace Ribbentrop, and the indestructible Papen was soon up and doing again in Turkey.

All in all, February 4th appeared as a wonderful grab-bag day, with promotions, transfers and retirements for nearly everyone. Thus did Hitler cover up the lethal struggle for military power which had brought all this about.

BRAUCHITSCH, CAPTIVE COMMANDER-IN-CHIEF

Assuredly there were inconsistencies and ironies aplenty in the events surrounding February 4, 1938. In a Continental nation where the Army had always been dominant, an airman was field-marshal and outranked all the Army generals. The first Minister of War and Field-Marshal of the Third Reich, rejected by his comrades of the officers' corps, helped subject

them to his own most ruthless rivals. A respected Commander-in-Chief of the Army was removed on an unproven morals charge the same day that Funk, whose sexual tastes had long been suspect, was elevated to cabinet rank. But still another paradox rounded out the list. Blomberg was cashiered for marrying below his station; Walther von Brauchitsch, who was selected to succeed Fritsch, insisted on simultaneously divorcing his wife, and accepted help from Hitler and Goering in making his new domestic arrangements! Small wonder that he proved a shadow Commander-in-Chief, carrying little influence either with Hitler or with his high military colleagues.

From the moment of Fritsch's suspension, there were two leading candidates for his position—Reichenau and Brauchitsch. The former had been Commanding General of Wehrkeis VII in Munich since 1935; he was still quite junior in rank, but, as the leading pro-Nazi among the generals, stood high in Hitler's favour. Brauchitsch was considerably senior to Reichenau, but was nevertheless outranked by nine other generals.* However, he had been given command of the new Army Group 4 (for mobile and mechanized troops) in Leipzig upon its creation in 1937, and thus held a higher command than several of his colleagues who had theretofore preceded him on the rank list.†

Between these two men the Fuehrer's choice wavered for a week.[20] At the outset (January 28th), he favoured Reichenau, once again in accordance with Blomberg's parting counsel. In his memoirs, Blomberg wrote:

"When I left in 1938, I suggested to the Fuehrer that either General von Brauchitsch or General von Reichenau be appointed as successor to General von Fritsch. On that occasion, I emphasized that Reichenau was the more reliable National Socialist of the two. To my surprise—and probably to Reichenau's disappointment—the Fuehrer appointed Brauchitsch. I believe that Reichenau would have been more successful in combating the

* Blomberg and Fritsch were the only Army officers who held a rank higher than *General*. Upon their departure, there were twenty-six *Generale* with dates of rank ranging from Rundstedt (October 1, 1932) to Keitel (August 1, 1937). Rundstedt, Leeb and Bock (at the top of the list in that order) commanded Gruppenkommandos 1, 2 and 3, and Brauchitsch (tenth) commanded Gruppenkommando 4. Reichenau stood twenty-second on the list, which, in addition to four *Gruppenkommando* and thirteen *Wehrkreis* commanders, included the two war college commandants (Liebmann and Adam), Keitel, Beck and five OKH staff generals (Lutz, Becker, Pogrell, Heitz and Liese). On February 1, 1938, eight more *Generalleutnante* were promoted to the rank of *General* (Gossler, Wietersheim, Schroth, Kuntze, Halder, Schwedler, Schobert and Busch).

† For example, List and Knochenhauer, who were *Wehrkreis* commanders.

distrust the Party felt towards the 'reactionary' Army and thus much tension would have been avoided during World War II."

But even the supine Keitel opposed the selection of Reichenau, knowing how badly the other senior Army generals would regard such a choice. Keitel mentioned Leeb and Brauchitsch, and promptly (January 28th) asked the latter to come to Berlin "in order to submit several questions to him, e.g., whether he would be able to bring the Army closer to the Reich and Reich ideology, to choose a Chief of the General Staff with the same qualities, and to go along with the top organization". Brauchitsch apparently offered no objection on the first and third points, but the idea of replacing Beck was not revived until several months later. The next day, after a meeting with the Fuehrer, Brauchitsch was "ready to agree to everything". On Sunday, January 30th, Jodl noted that "Goering is very much in favour of Brauchitsch and not of Reichenau". But "the latter is in Berlin and phones Keitel continuously, he would like to see the Fuehrer".

That same Sunday, however, sex reared its ugly head again. Brauchitsch had revealed that he was planning a divorce, and Keitel summoned Brauchitsch's son "in order to send him to his mother" and secure her agreement to her distinguished husband's plan. On Tuesday, February 1st, Brauchitsch and Keitel jointly waited upon Goering, where, according to Jodl, "the family situation of Brauchitsch is under discussion. Goering is going to examine this and then will have an opinion about Brauchitsch, if the results of the investigation are satisfactory. Brauchitsch's son returns with a very dignified letter from his mother."

Apparently Goering as self-appointed judge of domestic relations found nothing to condemn. Following his selection as Commander-in-Chief, Brauchitsch proceeded to divorce his wife and marry the daughter of a Silesian official. According to Halder and others,[21] Hitler provided Brauchitsch with the necessary funds to make a settlement with his first wife. Thus was erased the stain which Blomberg's *déclassé* affair had laid on the honour of the officers' corps.

However, a last-minute hitch of a quite different kind threatened Brauchitsch's elevation. At some point in the discussions he had been asked to consent to certain transfers and mandatory retirements among the senior Army generals. On February 2nd, Jodl learned that the day before Brauchitsch

had insisted on an opportunity to reflect on these personnel changes: "This again makes his appointment as Commander-in-Chief of the Army insecure, because personnel changes above all are a *sine qua non*. The Fuehrer has always desired them. . . . Therefore, Brauchitsch has been asked to come to Berlin again. . . . If Brauchitsch does not agree, then the Fuehrer will take Reichenau after all."

The situation became increasingly delicate. Jodl advised Keitel "to be extremely careful when effecting any change in personnel, in order to avoid irreparable damage. . . . We cannot afford to lose our best leaders . . . only what is absolutely necessary may be changed." Nevertheless, upon his return to Berlin for another meeting with Goering (who "asked that this discussion should take place in his presence") and Keitel, Brauchitsch agreed "to nearly all of the important changes, the greatest part . . . he would have effected on his own initiative". Apparently this was not good enough for Hitler and Goering. The following morning (February 3rd), Jodl found Keitel "greatly depressed", because:

> "The Fuehrer and Goering dislike increasingly the idea of appointing Brauchitsch and are more in favour of Reichenau. General Keitel does not see how he can bear all this. He is thoroughly convinced that this appointment would lead to the third, and most intolerable, shock to the Army.
>
> "General Keitel would have to bear the responsibility, and it would be said that he chose this solution, or at least that he did not prevent it, and he would have to keep silent and be unable to say how hard he fought against the decision.
>
> "I support his opinion; everything must be attempted to prevent this disaster.
>
> "A great number of the old elite group will leave; General Beck will not stay, and General Halder will not agree to be Chief of the General Staff under Reichenau, as they would not be able to co-operate."

Accordingly, Keitel requested another conference with Hitler. Early that afternoon he triumphantly informed Jodl: "The fight has been won. The Fuehrer has decided to appoint Brauchitsch. We two are greatly relieved. Now it can be hoped that we will be able to weather the heavy shock which the Army has suffered." And the following day Walther von Brauchitsch, newly promoted to *Generaloberst*, became Commander-in-Chief of the German Army. Reichenau received a consolation prize; he was named to succeed Brauchitsch as Commander of Gruppenkommando 4 at Leipzig.

The mandatory retirements to which Brauchitsch gave his consent were seven in number, including six (nearly a quarter)* of the *Generale*. The leading name was that of von Leeb, who was retired from the command of Gruppenkommando 2 with the honorary (*charakterisierte*) rank of *Generaloberst*. Two *Wehrkreis* commanders bit the dust—the northern aristocrat von Kleist and the Bavarian aristocrat Franz Kress von Kressenstein. The other three *Generale* were Lutz (the first *General der Panzertruppen*) von Pogrell (Inspector of Cavalry), and Liese (Chief of Army Ordnance), and the seventh victim Generalleutnant von Niebelschuetz (Inspector of Army Schools).

Who selected these officers, and what was the basis for their dismissal, has been the subject of much speculation. At that time Hitler was acquainted with very few generals, and it seemed highly unlikely that his individual predilections played much of a part. Certainly Hitler and Goering had numerous reports from the SS and Party about the personalities and behaviour of all the generals. It seems probable that these reports, no doubt reflecting unfavourably on the more aristocratic, religious or outspokenly anti-Nazi officers, played a part in the process, and that the matter was handled by Goering, working through Keitel and Brauchitsch. In addition to whatever part Himmler's dossiers may have played, there was an apparent desire to retire enough generals to "loosen up" the top of the ladder and make possible the promotion of several generals of definite pro-Nazi sympathies.

With these two over-all considerations in mind, the selections seem to have been made by scanning the rank list and picking out individuals who fitted the pattern. Among the Army group commanders, Rundstedt stood especially well with Hitler; Leeb was both senior to Bock and strongly Catholic,† so Leeb was picked for retirement. Lutz was elderly, and had already lost preeminence in the development of the mobile troops when Brauchitsch was jumped over him on the rank list and given command of the new Army Group 4. Of the *Wehrkreis* commanders, Kleist was a strong monarchist and close to the Hindenburg family; both Kleist and Kressenstein were "oldline" aristocrats. Niebelschuetz was anti-Nazi and of the same general stamp.

* Excluding the eight promoted to this rank on February 1, 1938.

† According to Jodl's diary entry for February 3rd, General Halder's situation was rendered uncertain at this same time "on account of his strong Catholic connections", but Keitel succeeded in overcoming these objections.

But it would be a mistake to regard these dismissals as primarily a purge of dissident generals. Both Leeb and Kleist were later recalled to service, and became leading field commanders and *Feldmarschaelle* during the war. All of the others, except Kressenstein, were likewise recalled to duty, although they did not serve in prominent capacities. The objections against Kressenstein seem to have been more fundamental; he was called to deputize for Weichs as commander of Wehrkreis XIII during the Munich crisis when Weichs went to the field, and for Schobert in Wehrkreis VII at the outbreak of war in 1939. But on this second occasion he was relieved within a few days, in his belief on Hitler's direct order.* However, neither Kressenstein nor any of the other generals then retired ever suffered persecution or harassment from the Nazis in later years.

There is no question, however, that the vacancies thus created were used to advance the careers of generals openly friendly to Hitler. List, who moved up to Leeb's Army group command, and Busch, Schroth, Guderian and von Schobert, who replaced Kleist, Kressenstein, Lutz and Reichenau, respectively, were all regarded at the time as pro-Nazi. Reichenau's own promotion to Brauchitsch's old post was also a patent manifestation of this policy.

In addition to replacing the seven who were retired,† a number of significant reassignments were simultaneously ordered. The Army Personnel Office was a key spot, inasmuch as all promotions, transfers and retirements were handled there. So its chief, General von Schwedler, was made a *Wehrkreis* commander (succeeding List), and Keitel's younger brother Bodwin, then an *Oberst*,‡ was appointed in Schwedler's place. In the Army General Staff, the brilliant Manstein was relieved as O. Qu. I and sent to command an infantry division. He was replaced by General Franz Halder (theretofore O. Qu. II), and Halder in turn by Generalleutnant Heinrich von Stuelpnagel.

In addition to supervising the reorganization of the Army

---

* This information is derived from the author's interview with Kressenstein at Planegg near Munich in April, 1949. The interview was primarily revealing of the depths of Kressenstein's ignorance of the reasons for his retirement.

† Liese was replaced as Chief of Ordnance by General der Artillerie Becker, who had been Liese's principal deputy in charge of munitions-proving. Pogrell was replaced as Inspector of Cavalry by General der Kavallerie von Gossler, and Niebelschuetz as Inspector of Army Schools by Generalmajor Brand, but these inspectorates were soon abolished, and Gossler retired in the spring of 1939.

‡ Bodwin Keitel was promoted to *Generalmajor* a month later.

High Command, Feldmarschall Goering made a few alterations in his own Luftwaffe. The three "elder statesmen"— Halm, Wachenfeld and Kaupisch—were retired to inactive duty, along with the disgruntled Wilberg.* The territorial organization of the Luftwaffe was changed from the former six *Luftkreiskommandos* to three *Luftwaffengruppen*. Gruppe 1 (Ost) in Berlin was commanded by General der Flieger Kesselring, Gruppe 2 (West) in Brunswick by Generalleutnant Hellmuth Felmy (soon promoted to *General der Flieger*), and Gruppe 3 (Sued) in Munich by General der Flieger Sperrle. Several new staff divisions were also established and Bodenschatz, Ruedel, von Greim, Jeschonnek, Kammhuber and others received promotions or improved assignments.

All these organizational and personnel changes in the Army and Air Force alike were given full publicity in the press following their announcement on February 4th. They helped to convey the impression that what had happened was merely a normal, albeit unusually extensive, administrative reorganization of the Wehrmacht and the Foreign and Economics Ministries, rather than a decisive shift in the focus of military power.

Indeed, several otherwise well-informed journalists went so far as to imply that Hitler had suffered a defeat, insofar as Brauchitsch and Keitel were officers "of the old school" and would insist on moderate policies.[22] And if a few inquiries in Army circles would have destroyed any such illusions about Keitel, Brauchitsch's feet of clay were better shod and not so easily discernible.

Had the officers' corps retained any cohesion and political sagacity, or had Brauchitsch possessed any real loyalty or firmness, of course he would not have accepted a permanent appointment as Commander-in-Chief under the circumstances. To serve temporarily, pending the outcome of Fritsch's trial, would have been defensible. But Brauchitsch allowed himself to be chosen as permanent successor to a man against whom the charges were unproven and soon demonstrated to be a shameful and deliberate fabrication. This selfish and short-sighted decision immediately made Brauchitsch's own position vulnerable and deprived him of any moral leadership among the generals.

* Two more Luftwaffe *Generalleutnante*, Karlewski and Niehoff, were retired at the same time. All of these officers (except, perhaps, Wilberg) were recalled to duty in the Army (not the Luftwaffe) during the war.

Thus, as so many times thereafter, Hitler successfully exploited the ambitions of individual generals. To achieve his new position, Brauchitsch stooped to the meanest concessions and put himself under permanent obligation to Goering and Keitel as well as to Hitler. For this dismal surrender of principle for position, the officers' corps paid soon and dear.

The officers' corps had traditionally prided itself on its "honour", but in February and March of 1938 it suffered, without resisting, the most unheard-of indignities. They were well symbolized by Goering, clutching his baton and sitting in judgment on Fritsch's morals and Brauchitsch's marital affairs, and dictating the retirement of elders of the corps such as Leeb. Where was the spirit of Moltke and Schlieffen?

By 1938, it was no longer pervasive. The weaknesses of Brauchitsch, ambitious chiefly for rank and station, were prevalent rather than exceptional. Fritsch might be dishonoured and Leeb discarded, but the other two most senior *Generale*, Rundstedt and Bock, were glad to accept promotions to *Generaloberst* a few weeks later. Indeed, the list of officers who received promotion or advancement in command or staff assignments as a result of or at the time of the Blomberg–Fritsch crisis is an excellent index of the moral bankruptcy of the corps—Brauchitsch, Rundstedt, Bock, List, Reichenau, Keitel, Gossler, Wietersheim, Schroth, Halder, Schwedler, Schoberg, Busch, Guderian, Hoth, Manstein and a dozen or more at lower levels.

Outwitted, demoralized and bribed, the officers' corps was soon faced with the terrible issues of Europe on the eve. Dismayed as some of them were by Hitler's reckless surge, scarcely any of the remaining active generals, other than Beck and Adam, were willing to stake their careers on their convictions. As Beck wrote to Brauchitsch in July, 1938,[23] "History will indict the highest leaders of the Wehrmacht with blood-guilt if they do not act in accordance with expert and statesmanlike knowledge and conscience. Their duty of soldierly obedience finds its limits when their knowledge, conscience and responsibility forbid the execution of an order." The officers' corps was not without its Cassandra, but conscience and responsibility were hopelessly atrophied—the rotten fruit of years of mental and moral malnutrition.

But it would be a mistake to regard the generals' acceptance of the Blomberg–Fritsch *coup* as solely attributable to ineptitude and timidity or the vanity of individuals. Its more fundamental portent was that the community of interest between Hitler

and the Wehrmacht was strong enough so that even this rude blow failed to shatter it.

The officers' corps had seen the Nazis overthrow the Republic and establish a ruthless dictatorship. They had seen their comrades Schleicher and Bredow murdered, Fritsch fall victim to a foul attack, and seven of their most respected members rudely pensioned off.

But they also saw in Hitler the leader of a Party which had established a strong and seemingly unshakable government, and which eagerly provided the wherewithal for rearmament without any need for explaining and justifying everything to the Reichstag. They saw the factories of Germany humming and pouring out the armaments needed to reconstitute the Wehrmacht. They observed approvingly that Hitler was a "realist" with scant respect for the sanctity of treaties; they shared Hitler's intention ultimately to put the Wehrmacht to use.

All these things were more important to the generals than the fate of Fritsch, the fear of Himmler, or the humiliations suffered at the hands of Goering. Basically, the reason the Army did not take a firm stand behind Fritsch was that it did not want to take a decisive stand in opposition to Hitler. Their differences with Hitler were those of manners, methods and timing. These were minor compared to the identity of major purpose.

CHAPTER VI

BLUMENKRIEGE: AUSTRIA AND CZECHOSLOVAKIA

THE UNPLEASANT memory of the Fritsch disaster might not have faded so rapidly had not the Wehrmacht immediately become preoccupied with even weightier matters. Even before Fritsch's trial and acquittal, Austria was swept into the black pit of Nazism. A few weeks later Hitler and the generals were engrossed in military plans for the destruction of Czechoslovakia. Within less than a year after the portentous meeting of November 5, 1937, Hitler had achieved his initial aims without spilling the blood of a single German soldier.

For this was the time of the "flower wars" (*Blumenkriege*). "Not bullets but flowers greet our soldiers," chanted Doktor Goebbels, as German tanks rolled toward Vienna and Prague. Seyss-Inquart and Henlein were blazing the trail of infamy for the Quislings and Lavals of the war years. Their treason, the shadow of Luftwaffe wings, the fear of German *Macht*—these were the arms with which Hitler won his flower wars.

It was as well for the Wehrmacht that these weapons were sufficient. In 1938, the panzer divisions were few in number, recently assembled, and half trained. Despite Goering's bluster, the Luftwaffe was far from ready for serious combat. The western fortifications were little more than embryonic. The soil in which the flowers of the *Blumenkriege* grew was a sludge of fear and bluff.

ANSCHLUSS

At Nuremberg, a veritable procession of generals entered the witness box to declare that the German march into Austria caught them entirely off guard. The Fuehrer had given them no foreknowledge of his intentions. "It came as a complete surprise to me", declared Brauchitsch.[1] "I had to draft the orders for this [operation] myself. . . . I had 4 or 5 hours altogether to do it in", lamented Manstein.[2] Rundstedt was at an Iron Cross ceremonial in Breslau, and learned of the occupation only after it "had actually taken place".[3] List, Keitel and Jodl confirmed the utterly unexpected character of the entry.

Here, at least, the generals were telling the truth. List, however, could not resist the temptation to embellish it: "This is a particularly typical example of how little Hitler informed the generals of his intentions, and how secret his intentions were kept." [4] In point of fact, it was nothing of the sort. Hitler did not forewarn the military leaders for a very simple reason—he himself was not forewarned. The timing of the Austrian invasion was not predetermined by Hitler, but was precipitated by Chancellor Schuschnigg's surprise order calling for an Austrian plebiscite on the question of his nation's future. To frustrate Schuschnigg's *coup*, Hitler for the first time called on the Wehrmacht to march beyond German borders.

But if Schuschnigg's action upset Hitler's time-table, this does not mean that Hitler had not fixed on the annexation of Austria as a primary aim, or that his intentions were known only to a few. This goal was stated on the very first page of *Mein Kampf*: "German Austria must be restored to the great German Motherland" because "people of the same blood should be in the same Reich". Himself an Austrian, Hitler brought the Austrian Nazi movement under his own control, and encouraged it to revolutionary behaviour. When Chancellor Dollfuss' government imprisoned several Austrian Nazis, Hitler countered by placing a thousand-mark tax on German tourist travel to Austria, a measure very injurious to the Austrian economy. In July, 1934, the Austrian Nazis attempted a *Putsch*, in the course of which Dollfuss was murdered. Mussolini manifested acute displeasure at the prospect of a Nazi *coup*, and assembled Italian troops near the Brenner Pass. The *Putsch* failed, and the Austrian government, now headed by Schuschnigg, outlawed the Nazi Party.

Frustrated by this fiasco, Hitler realized that a more deliberate and cautious policy was in order. To execute it, his choice fell upon the ubiquitous and incorrigible von Papen. "Fraenzchen" was still quivering under the impact of the Roehm purge, in which several of his close associates had been murdered and his own life threatened. But pride was not one of Papen's long suits, and he eagerly exchanged the inhospitable atmosphere of Germany for a spell of Viennese *Gemuetlichkeit* by accepting the post of Minister to Austria. At the same time, Papen warned Hitler that *Anschluss* could be achieved "only on the basis of a slow, peaceful evolution", and that German Nazi interference in Austrian internal politics would not be conducive to this end.

Accordingly, Hitler's letter of appointment to Papen condemned the assassination of Dollfuss, and expressed a desire to change the Reich's "strained" relations with Austria into "normal and friendly channels". In May, 1935, Hitler, speaking before the Reichstag, renounced any intention "to interfere in the internal affairs of Austria, to annex Austria, or to conclude an '*Anschluss*' ". And on July 11, 1936, Hitler entered into a public Austro-German "accord" which recognized "the full sovereignty" of Austria, and barred all "direct or indirect influence" in "internal political conditions". In return, the accord embodied an Austrian agreement that her "policy toward Germany . . . shall be constantly guided by the principle that Austria recognizes herself to be a German state". Furthermore, secret clauses of the accord permitted German subjects in Austria to establish their own Nazi organizations and to wear the swastika.

From Hitler's and Papen's standpoint, all this was a façade and a tactic. Papen's Military Attaché, Generalmajor Muff, was an old associate of Blomberg's, and promptly established close contact with the Nazi-minded elements of the Austrian Army. In private and semi-official talks with diplomats in Vienna, the habitually indiscreet Papen made no bones about the fact that his mission was to weaken the Austrian government and pave the way for ultimate *Anschluss*. He stayed in close touch with Captain Leopold, the leader of the outlawed Austrian Nazi Party, while recommending to Hitler "on the tactical side, continued, patient psychological treatment, with slowly intensified pressure directed at changing the regime". Hitler continued to finance the Austrian Nazis, who organized provocative demonstrations and maintained a clamour for representation in the Austrian government.

In due course, the pressure was felt, and Schuschnigg started to yield. "Nationalist" Austrians and Nazi sympathizers such as Guido Schmidt and Glaise-Horstenau entered the cabinet. Thousands of Nazis were amnestied. At the same time, Schuschnigg sought to build up a counter force by permitting some monarchist activity, and Otto of Habsburg's stock enjoyed a temporary rise on the diplomatic exchange. This, no doubt, was the precipitant of *Sonderfall Otto* in Blomberg's directive to the Wehrmacht in June, 1937.[5]

All in all, Papen's methods were bearing fruit, and by the end of 1937 Hitler gauged the time to be ripe for a stepping-up of the war of nerves. In November, 1937, Austrian police uncovered

a secret plan of action emanating from Rudolf Hess, which paralleled very closely Hitler's pronouncements at the secret conference of November 5, 1937.[6] According to the Hess plan, the time for action in Austria was close at hand. Italy, France and England were preoccupied in the Mediterranean; Czechoslovakia was already weakened by the Sudeten problem. The Austrian Nazis, therefore, should start demonstrations which would provoke Schuschnigg to repressive measures, and these, in turn, would give Hitler the needed pretext for an ultimatum and for the German Army to march in.

Papen, in the meantime, was evolving new steps to bring the Austrian government increasingly under German domination. Early in January, 1938, he proposed to Schuschnigg the idea of a visit to Hitler at Berchtesgaden to iron out "differences and misunderstandings" between the two governments. He further recommended that Schuschnigg bring an additional representative of the Austrian nationalists into the cabinet for the special purpose of acting as a political liaison officer between Austria and Germany, and for this position he proposed the name of Artur Seyss-Inquart, an able lawyer, a pronounced nationalist, and a devotee of *Anschluss* who also enjoyed Schuschnigg's confidence to a considerable degree.

Just as these plans were developing, the Blomberg–Fritsch crisis broke, and on the evening of February 4, 1938, Papen received a telephone call from Berlin informing him that he had been recalled and that his mission to Vienna was at an end. Deeply disappointed, Papen repaired immediately to Berchtesgaden, and broached to Hitler his notion of a visit from Schuschnigg. The Fuehrer reacted with great interest and enthusiasm. He did not reinstate Papen, but requested him to go back to Vienna and remain in charge of the Embassy until after the proposed meeting had taken place. Upon his return, Papen met with no objection from Schuschnigg, and the meeting was scheduled for February 12, 1938, at Hitler's Berchtesgaden headquarters, the "Berghof" on the Obersalzberg.

It was at this meeting that the Wehrmacht first became directly involved in Hitler's efforts to overthrow the Austrian government. By elaborate stage management and offensive blustering, the Fuehrer undertook to frighten Schuschnigg out of his wits and secure his signature to maximum concessions. In accordance with this design, when Schuschnigg was met by Papen at the Austro-German border on the morning of February 12th, Papen greeted the Austrian Chancellor with

the information that some of Hitler's generals would also be present at the Berghof.

There is a legend that Hitler selected the most fearsome-looking generals to cow Schuschnigg with their scowls. To be sure, the jowled and brooding Sperrle might well have qualified on this basis of selection. Nor is there any question but that the generals were called in to provide a minatory *mise en scène*. But the three individuals were picked for less theatrical reasons. Keitel, as Hitler's chosen military stooge and *chef de cabinet* of the Wehrmacht, was a logical selection. The other two, Reichenau and Sperrle, were the Army and Air Force commanders of the South German area bordering on Austria.*

Upon his arrival at the Berghof, Schuschnigg was made acquainted with the generals, and was then ushered in for a long private conference with Hitler. The Fuehrer was not in a pleasant mood. He made no precise demands, but roundly abused Schuschnigg as a "traitor to Austria", and declared that he was determined to bring the Austrian question to an immediate solution, if necessary by the use of military force.

After two hours of Hitlerian harangue there was a pause for lunch, at which the generals reappeared on the scene. After the meal, Schuschnigg was taken to see Ribbentrop, who laid on the table a document containing the German demands. These called for a general Austrian amnesty, legalization of the Austrian Nazi Party, and the appointment of Seyss-Inquart as Minister of the Interior. The document was presented as an ultimatum, and both Ribbentrop and Papen advised Schuschnigg to sign at once.

The unhappy Schuschnigg was now hustled back to Hitler, who demanded immediate acceptance of his demands "or else I will order the march into Austria". Schuschnigg demurred on the ground that he was not empowered to sign, and that the agreement would have to be presented to President Miklas. Hitler flung open the door, bellowed for Keitel, and told Schuschnigg to wait outside. Twenty minutes later Schuschnigg was recalled, and Hitler declared: "For the first time in my life I have changed my mind! You must sign the demands that I have made upon you, then report them to President Miklas, and within three days from now Austria must fulfil the agreement; otherwise things will take their natural

---

* Reichenau had been in command of Wehrkreis VII (Munich), and apparently had not yet moved to his new Army group command at Leipzig. Sperrle commanded Air Group 3 (South) at Munich.

course." An hour before midnight Schuschnigg signed the agreement, bade Hitler and the generals farewell, and returned to Vienna with Papen.

In order to ensure that Miklas would approve the protocol signed by Schuschnigg, Hitler now ordered Keitel to maintain military pressure by sham manœuvres and other deceptive measures. As organized by Keitel, Goebbels, Admiral Canaris (Chief of Intelligence of the OKW) and Jodl, these included airplane flights and mountain troop exercises at the border, "phony" radio traffic between Berlin and Munich, and the spreading of rumours—such as the suspension of troop furloughs, the assemblage of rolling stock in southern Germany, and the recall of Generalleutnant Muff to Berlin—that the Wehrmacht was preparing to move into Austria.

On February 14th, Jodl noted in his diary that the effect of these measures "is quick and strong", and that "in Austria the impression is created that Germany is undertaking serious military preparations". At all events, on February 16th the Austrian government announced the appointment of Seyss-Inquart and the amnesty, and two days later the Austrian Nazis were "legalized". Well content with his achievements, Franz von Papen took his skis and headed for Kitzbuehel for a well-earned vacation.

But the Schuschnigg regime was mortally wounded, and the Austrian Republic had less than a month to live. Seyss-Inquart was no sooner installed as Minister of the Interior than he headed for Berlin and a series of conferences, on February 17th, with Hitler, Himmler, Ribbentrop and Frick. Upon his return to Vienna, Seyss-Inquart started to work on his plans for bringing the Austrian Nazis into greater power.

Schuschnigg, however, was sore and kicking against the pricks. In his speeches he constantly stressed the inviolability of Austrian sovereignty, proclaimed that there would be no further concessions to Germany, and left no doubt that he had acted under pressure at the Berghof. Seyss-Inquart and Papen both warned him that such talk was bound to lead to trouble. Reports of all this filtered back to Hitler; on March 3rd, accordingly to Jodl's diary, the Austrian question was again regarded as "critical", and Hitler was considering the dispatch of one hundred German officers to Austria to bring the Austrian Army around to acceptance of an *Anschluss* accomplished by the Wehrmacht.

Wriggling desperately, Schuschnigg decided to "go to the

country" and win a demonstration of popular support. On Wednesday, March 9th, he announced that a nation-wide plebiscite would be held the following Sunday, March 13th. The question to be submitted was "Are you in favour of an independent, social, Christian, German and united Austria?"

The possibility of a heavy "yes" vote, which would have strengthened Schuschnigg and put back the possibility of *Anschluss*, together with the early date set for the voting, threw Hitler into a high state of alarm and indignation. He was "determined not to tolerate it", and summoned Goering to the Reichschancellery for consultation on counter-measures during the evening of March 9th. At the same time he recalled Reichenau, who, as a prominent sportsman, had gone to Cairo for a meeting of the Olympic Games Committee. Reichenau's successor as Commander of Wehrkreis VII, General von Schobert, was also summoned, as well as the Austrian Minister Glaise-Horstenau, who happened to be in Germany.

The following morning, Reichschancellery and Bendlerstrasse buzzed with the toings and froings of excited generals. Keitel was summoned to appear before Hitler at ten o'clock. Before leaving his office, he consulted Viebahn and Jodl. The conferees recalled that Blomberg's directive of June, 1937, had included *Sonderfall Otto*.[7] After Keitel left, Jodl fished out the directive and then followed his chief to the meeting with Hitler.

Keitel soon left the Reichschancellery and hotfooted it back to the Bendlerstrasse, where he immediately sought out Beck, and demanded to know what detailed mobilization and other tactical plans had been developed at OKH for the carrying out of *Otto*. Beck held out empty hands: "We have prepared nothing, nothing has been done, nothing at all." As Jodl explained later, *Otto* was "a theoretical plan and drafted solely for the event of a Habsburg restoration, and as such a restoration was not expected for the moment, the OKH had done virtually nothing about it."

In this extremity, Beck picked up Manstein, who had not yet left OKH to assume his new divisional command, and the two hurried off to the Reichschancellery, arriving in Hitler's office at about eleven o'clock.* Hitler declared again that the Schuschnigg plebiscite must be forestalled, and that preparations

---

* Brauchitsch's whereabouts at this time are something of a mystery, but apparently he was not in Berlin, or for some other reason was unavailable, despite the statements of Kielmansegg, Gisevius and others that he was in Berlin participating in the Fritsch trial. See *supra*, p. 158.

should be made for a march into Austria. None of the generals interposed any objection. Time was pressing; the troops would have to march at the latest on Saturday, and it was already Thursday. Beck then proposed that the troops of the two *Wehrkreise* (VII, Munich, and XIII, Nuremberg) bordering Austria, together with the 2nd Panzer Division (Wuerzburg), should be mobilized at the Austrian border on an "improvised" basis. This plan was approved in the course of a two-hour conference, and at one o'clock Manstein returned to the Bendlerstrasse to draft the necessary orders. This task he completed shortly after six o'clock that evening, and the mobilization was set in process.

The VIIth and XIIIth Corps were both subordinated to Gruppenkommando 3 at Dresden, commanded by General-oberst von Bock. For purposes of the invasion, Bock's head-quarters was now designated the Eighth Army, and all troops taking part in the operation were put under Bock's command. These included primarily the troops of Schobert's VIIth and Weich's XIIIth Infantry Corps, and Guderian's new XVIth Corps command for motorized troops, to which were sub-ordinated the 2nd Panzer Division under Generalmajor Veiel and Hitler's motorized SS bodyguard, the SS Leibstandarte Adolf Hitler, under Sepp Dietrich. Various other SS and police units were also attached to the Eighth Army, as well as miscel-laneous squadrons of the Luftwaffe, which were assembled in Bavaria under Sperrle. His forces comprised a few pursuit and ground-attack aircraft, but principally transport, recon-naissance and courier planes.

By Friday evening, March 11th, preparations were virtually complete. Ribbentrop being detained in London, Neurath had returned to temporary control of the Foreign Office. The Navy had ordered all ships back to Germany. At noon, Hitler had issued a formal directive to the Wehrmacht embodying the military dispositions previously arranged, and announcing that "if other measures prove unsuccessful, I intend to invade Austria with armed forces to establish constitutional conditions and to prevent further outrages against the pro-German population". The troops were admonished that their behaviour must be such as to "give the impression that we do not want to wage war against our Austrian brothers. It is in our interest that the whole operation shall be carried out without any violence but in the form of a peaceful entry welcomed by the population. Therefore, any provocation is to be avoided. If,

however, resistance is offered, it must be broken ruthlessly by force of arms."

Hitler was worried, however, not so much about Austrian resistance as about Mussolini, who had peered protectively over the Brenner Pass at the time of the abortive Dollfuss *Putsch.* Now he dispatched a long, personal letter to the Duce, recalling German support for Italy during the Ethiopian campaign, and promising that the Brenner would be an inviolable and permanent frontier between Germany and Italy. Greatly to Hitler's relief, Mussolini acquiesced in the new shape of things with good grace. Late in the evening of March 11th, the new German Ambassador to Italy, Prince Philip of Hesse, advised Hitler by telephone that "Il Duce accepted the whole thing in a very friendly manner. He sends you his regards." Schuschnigg had been in touch with Rome, but had been advised that Mussolini regarded Austria as "immaterial to him". To Mussolini, Hitler returned his most effusive and almost frenetic thanks, later embodied in the famous telegram: "Mussolini, I shall never forget this!"

At a quarter to nine on the evening of March 11th, Hitler signed the order directing that the occupation of Austria be carried out, beginning at daybreak of the 12th. Jodl dispatched a supplementary order later that evening, directing that any Czechoslovak units encountered in Austria were to be regarded as hostile, but "the Italians are to be treated everywhere as friends, especially as Mussolini has declared himself disinterested in the solution of the Austrian question". All was now in readiness for the morrow.

In the meantime, the diplomatic pot had been bubbling furiously, and political activity in Vienna was at fever pitch. Franz von Papen, recently returned from his skijoring at Kitzbuehel and packing for his departure from Vienna, rushed (on Thursday the 10th) to urge Schuschnigg to call off or modify the plebiscite; Seyss-Inquart took the same line. The next morning Glaise-Horstenau arrived, fresh from his conference with Hitler. He and Seyss-Inquart presented themselves to Schuschnigg and delivered a virtual ultimatum; the plebiscite must be postponed for several weeks, and so altered that it would lead to the same results as the Saar plebiscite—union with Germany. Schuschnigg was shaken; he called a cabinet meeting for two o'clock that afternoon (Friday), and soon it was decided to rescind the order for the plebiscite. This news immediately reached Hitler and Goering, closeted

in the Reichschancellery. The Fuehrer showed signs of hesitation about proceeding with the march-in. Goering, however, urged that the time was ripe, and telephoned Seyss-Inquart. Calling off the plebiscite would not suffice; Schuschnigg must resign, and Seyss-Inquart must be appointed Chancellor, with a predominantly Nazi cabinet, including Ernst Kaltenbrunner, the head of the Austrian SS, in charge of "internal security". All this must be announced by half-past seven that evening; otherwise the German troops would march. Within an hour, Schuschnigg had resigned.

The pressure now shifted to the President of Austria, Miklas, who balked at appointing Seyss-Inquart as Chancellor. He was treated to successive visits from the German Military Attaché, Generalleutnant Muff, and Hitler's personal economic adviser, Wilhelm Keppler. But the old President was stubborn; the ultimatum expired and Hitler gave the order to launch the occupation at daybreak Saturday morning. Papen was called to Berlin by plane. Goering sought to "cover" the invasion by proposing that Seyss-Inquart, as the new Chancellor, send Hitler a telegram requesting German intervention to preserve orderly conditions. Whether or not Seyss-Inquart, who assumed the chancellorship just before midnight, ever authorized such a message, it was promptly publicized in Germany as justifying the military occupation. Schuschnigg awoke on Saturday to find his home encircled by SA troops; he remained a prisoner until the collapse of the Third Reich in May, 1945.

Thus the Austrian citadel was captured by an "inside job" several hours before the first German troops crossed the frontier. The Wehrmacht had accomplished its mission by mobilizing, and giving point and power to the threats hurled by Hitler and Goering through Muff, Keppler, Glaise-Horstenau, and Seyss-Inquart. The Austrian Army had been ordered not to resist but rather to welcome their German brothers-in-arms. Now that the time for military action had come, attack was unnecessary and a parade was in order.

Early on the morning of the 12th, hundreds of German planes rose from Sperrle's Bavarian airfields. Some circled lazily over Vienna, Linz and other Austrian cities dropping leaflets hailing the return of the Ostmark to the German Fatherland. Others came down at Austrian airports, to disembark high German officials. Heinrich Himmler was in the vanguard; he landed at Aspern airport near Vienna at about three o'clock in the morning, and was greeted by Ernst Kaltenbrunner. Had the Austrian

people known of Himmler's plans for their country, the on-coming German troops might have had a far less sunny welcome.

Not all of the Army units were able to jump off on schedule on Saturday morning, and Guderian's motorized troops, assembling at Passau, had an especially difficult time. The 2nd Panzer Division had to come from Wuerzburg, 200 miles away, and the SS Leibstandarte from Berlin. Generalmajor Veiel did not reach Passau with the main body of his troops until Friday midnight; he arrived with no maps and no petrol. Baedekers had to do for maps, and fuel dumps had to be commandeered. The jump-off was scheduled for eight o'clock Saturday morning, but it was after nine when the vanguard of Guderian's forces crossed the border. His tanks and vehicles were decked out with flags and greenery by way of celebration.

By lunch-time Guderian had arrived at Linz. Here he encountered Himmler, Seyss-Inquart, and Glaise-Horstenau, who had come up from Vienna to meet Hitler. These worthies asked Guderian to block off the roads and the market-place for Hitler's arrival, and Guderian, thankful for a breather for his hard-pressed and half-trained forces, halted and deployed them as traffic policemen. Hitler did not appear at Linz until late in the afternoon. From the balcony of the Rathaus Seyss-Inquart delivered a fulsome and fawning welcome, and Hitler a maudlin, self-intoxicated harangue. At nine in the evening Guderian resumed his march, and reached Vienna with elements of his troops in the small hours of Sunday morning.

The infantry divisions made their way in more slowly on Saturday, Sunday and Monday. The popular welcome appeared to be genuine, and there were no serious contretemps. To assuage Czech apprehensions, no large units approached the Czech–Austrian border, and as a sop to Austrian pride a few small Austrian Army formations crossed the border into Germany to make the *Anschluss* appear slightly more bilateral. On Wednesday the 15th there was an enormous Austro-German military parade in Vienna.

Meanwhile, the Austrian Republic had ceased to exist. On Sunday the 13th of March, the day which had been scheduled for the Schuschnigg plebiscite, President Miklas resigned, and the *Anschluss* was officially ordained. Austria became a province (Ostmark) of the Reich. To tidy up the face of things, a plebiscite was announced on the question of *Anschluss*, to be held in April. The Austrian armed forces became a component of the Wehrmacht and passed under the direct command of von

Bock; all Austrian officers and men took the oath of allegiance to Hitler. Seyss-Inquart was appointed *Reichsstatthalter*, or Chief of the Civil Administration, for Austria.

Supplementary decrees followed in rapid succession extending the Four-Year Plan, Himmler's police power, the Nuremberg racial decrees, and other Nazi measures to Austria. The April plebiscite, as was expected and planned, produced a nearly unanimous vote of approval for the annexation. Seyss-Inquart's authority did not long withstand the pressures of ambitious German Nazis. Buerckel, Gauleiter of the Saar and Palatinate, was appointed High Commissioner, and Seyss-Inquart was forced into second place; later Buerckel was replaced by Baldur von Schirach. Decisive power flowed more and more into Himmler's hands.

As a demonstration of German *Macht*, the occupation of Austria was not an unqualified success. To be sure, one could see that the General Staff's capacity for prompt and precise tactical execution had survived the lean years since 1918. Beck and Manstein successfully improvised a concentration of forces on short order; Bock, Weichs, Schobert and Guderian assembled their troops nearly on schedule, and Sperrle accomplished what little the Luftwaffe was called on to do by way of demonstration and transport.

Guderian's motorized "dash" to Vienna, however, was not the impressive demonstration of the new German armour that it was meant to be. According to his own recollection, some 30 per cent of his panzers came to grief on the roads.[8] Jodl described the march-in rather more caustically:[9] "Seventy per cent of all the armoured vehicles and lorries were stranded on the road from Salzburg and Passau to Vienna, because the drivers had been taken from their recruit training for this task."

For all this Guderian had many explanations. The march was long and unexpected; snow was encountered between Linz and Vienna; the panzer arm was young and the troops had just begun their training in company strength. But these excuses were in part a confession that German armour was not yet ready for war, and to the lay eye the stranded tanks along the roadside betokened weakness. Even to some professional eyes, it was certainly not commendable. Generaloberst Fedor von Bock had no words of praise for Guderian's march. Furthermore, the stark and humourless Bock took a very dim view of the flags and sprigs of green on the tanks; these were most unmilitary.

Apart from the lessons learned, the annexation of Austria appreciably strengthened Germany's military situation. The Swiss and Italian frontiers of Austria held no perils; the Czech, Hungarian and Yugoslavian borders opened new avenues for a *Drang nach dem Osten*. The situation of Czechoslovakia was enormously weakened. Bohemia and Moravia now lay almost encircled by the Reich, caught between Silesia to the north and the Ostmark to the south. Furthermore, the Czechs had made little effort to fortify the Austrian approaches, preferring, naturally enough, to strengthen themselves on their German borders.

These strategic advantages far outweighed the gains by way of military man-power. The population of Austria was only 7,000,000, and its Army (the *Bundesheer*) correspondingly small. Still, the German Army itself as yet numbered only forty-odd divisions, so the Austrian increments were not to be sneezed at.

As the top Army command for the Ostmark, a new Army Group (*Heeresgruppe*)* 5 was established in Vienna. Two new *Wehrkreise*—XVII in northern and XVIII in southern Austria —were also set up. The Luftwaffe followed suit by adding a fourth Air Fleet with headquarters in Vienna.

Bock's archaic and arrogant Prussian personality was not well suited to the Austrian climate, and he returned to his old Army Group 3 command at Dresden before the end of March. As Commander-in-Chief of Army Group 5, the choice fell on General Wilhelm List, a Wuerttemberger who had headed a military delegation to Austria during the Schuschnigg regime. List was succeeded as Commander-in-Chief of Army Group 2 (Kassel) by General Wilhelm Adam.†

Within the two Austrian *Wehrkreise*, four new German Army divisions—two infantry divisions in Wehrkreis XVII and two mountain divisions in XVIII—were formed, principally from Austrian troops. A large number of German officers were transferred to both staff and command assignments in Austria in order to assure a rapid and effective assimilation. The Austrian officers were taken into the regular German rank lists, and a number of Austrian units were sent to Germany for training exercises.

Within these new formations there seems to have been an

---

* In 1938, the old *Gruppenkommandos* were redesignated *Heeresgruppen*.

† Adam had been Commandant of the *Wehrmachtakademie*, which was closed when he was transferred to Kassel. List had succeeded Leeb as Commander-in-Chief at Kassel only a few weeks before he was called to Vienna.

effort made to divide the highest positions about equally between German and Austrian officers. If List was German, his opposite number in the Luftwaffe (Commander of Air Fleet 4) was the former Commander-in-Chief of the Austrian Air Force, General Alexander Loehr. General der Infanterie Kienitz, a newly promoted German, was appointed Commander of Wehrkreis XVII at Linz, but an Austrian, General der Infanterie Beyer,* was given command of Wehrkreis XVIII at Salzburg. Beyer's Chief of Staff was a German, and Kienitz' an Austrian, Oberst Lothar Rendulic, who had been expelled from the Army under Schuschnigg because of his open support of the outlawed Austrian Nazis. Two of the new divisional commanders were German and two Austrian.

After the *Anschluss*, Guderian's XVIth Motorized Corps headquarters and the SS Leibstandarte returned to Berlin. The Military Attaché, Muff, whose duties were terminated by the annexation, was also sent home to the Reich and rewarded for his performance with promotion to the brevet (*charakterisiert*) rank of *General der Infanterie*. Generalmajor Veiel's 2nd Panzer Division, however, remained in Vienna, directly subordinated to List's Army group headquarters. The Army group also held direct command of a new "light" (*leichte*) division, formed from Austrian cavalry components. The former quarters of the 2nd Panzer Division at Wuerzburg were used to assemble and train the new 4th Panzer Division.

The annexation of Austria, accordingly, brought to the Wehrmacht a tidy tactical increment and a strategic windfall. The generals were well pleased. Little had been risked and not a shot fired in anger. Hitler blew his trumpet, the Wehrmacht marched around the walls, and the walls came tumbling down.

There is no evidence that any ranking officer of the Wehrmacht manifested any opposition whatever to Hitler's decision to utilize the Schuschnigg order for a plebiscite as a basis for forcing the *Anschluss* by military pressure. Barely four months earlier, Beck had unsparingly criticized Hitler's policies as outlined at the November 5, 1937, conference.[10] But in March, Beck, like all the other generals, collaborated promptly and effectively in bringing off the *coup*. When Guderian was summoned by Beck to receive orders for assembling the motorized troops, Beck remarked that if there was to be an *Anschluss*, this seemed to be the propitious moment.[11]

No doubt Beck believed, and correctly, that the proposed

* Beyer had been Inspector-General of the Austrian Army.

Czech adventure involved far graver risks of Anglo-French or Russian intervention than did the *Anschluss*. Then, too, the Austrian question was precipitated so suddenly and resolved so rapidly that there was no time for latent opposition, if any, to develop. But it is highly unlikely that there was any such opposition. Sentiment in favour of *Anschluss* was overwhelming throughout the Wehrmacht.

"CASE GREEN"

"After the annexation of Austria", Jodl's diary tells us "the Fuehrer mentions that there is no hurry in solving the Czech question, because Austria has to be digested first." The digestive process was a brisk one. Barely a month after Hitler's triumphant return from Vienna, the generals of the Bendlerstrasse were hard at work on plans for the conquest of Czechoslovakia—plans which were given the name "Case Green", in accordance with the terminology of Blomberg's 1937 directive.

Ever since 1925, German–Czech relations had been governed by the Locarno Treaty. By 1938, the Czechs were understandably sceptical that Hitler would be governed by the spirit and promises of Locarno. The *Anschluss* did less than nothing to assuage those doubts, but Hitler and Goering were at great pains to reassure the Czechs that they had nothing to fear. To Mastny, the Czech Minister to Germany, Hermann Goering gave his *Ehrenwort*. We may safely accept Goering's own evaluation of his word of honour, as he put it at Nuremberg eight years later: "An explanation was desired for the moment and in connection with Austrian events. I could conscientiously assure him on my word of honour that Czechoslovakia would not be touched then, because at that time no decisions had been made by us, as far as a definite time was concerned with respect to Czechoslovakia or the solution of the Sudeten problem."

But these decisions were reached soon enough. The Wehrmacht's "state of preparation" for an attack on Czechoslovakia was reported to Hitler by Keitel and Jodl on April 21, 1938. The next day the Fuehrer's new military adjutant, Major Rudolf Schmundt, recorded in summary a conference between Hitler and Keitel at which the "political aspects" and "military conclusions" of the Czech situation were outlined. Hitler ruled out a "surprise attack out of a clear sky without any justification" because "hostile world opinion" would lead to a "critical situation". Therefore, military preparations should be premised either on "action after a period of diplomatic clashes,

which gradually come to a crisis and lead to war", or, preferably, "lightning-swift action as the result of an incident, for example, assassination of the German Ambassador in connection with an anti-German demonstration". In either event, the attack must take the form of a "lightning-swift blow", because: "Politically, the first four days of military action are the decisive ones. If there are no effective military successes, a European crisis will certainly arise. Accomplished facts must prove the senselessness of foreign military intervention, draw allies into the scheme (division of spoils!) and demoralize *Gruen*" (Czechoslovakia).

For the time being these discussions were confined to the OKW, and neither OKH nor the other services were consulted. Hitler went off to Berchtesgaden; Keitel consulted with Jodl, but since Hitler had set no time-table, their deliberations were leisurely.

At the Wilhelmstrasse, however, anti-Czech operations were stepped up. Ever since 1935, the German Foreign Office had been subsidizing the Sudeten German Party in Czechoslovakia to the tune of 15,000 marks monthly. In March, 1938, Ribbentrop brought the Sudeten Party under his direct and absolute control. Konrad Henlein, the Sudeten leader, was ordered to maintain constant contact with the German Legation at Prague, and he agreed that the dictates of Ribbentrop should be "exclusively decisive for policy and tactics of the Sudeten German Party". On March 28th, Henlein came to Berlin to receive direct instructions from Hitler, and the next day Ribbentrop, assisted by Weizsaecker and other high officials of the Foreign Office and the SS Racial Office, laid down the law to Henlein, Karl Hermann Frank, and other Sudeten representatives. The essence of the new policy was for the Sudeten Germans to make far-reaching and gradually increasing demands upon the Czech government, and avoid reaching any agreement, so as to provoke a crisis.

Fifth-column activities within Czechoslovakia were complemented by efforts to disrupt the ties between the Czechs and England and France. In May, the Wilhelmstrasse dispatched Henlein to England to visit Sir Robert Vansittart and other British leaders. Under Weizsaecker's coaching, Henlein was to "try to create the impression in London that the Czechoslovakian state is gradually decomposing, in order to discourage those circles that still consider it practical to uphold the structure of this state".

Immediately after the Henlein trip to England, the military pot began to boil in good earnest. Hitler, still enjoying the spring season at the Obersalzberg, was beginning to fancy himself as a "great captain", and to intrude himself into the professional deliberations of the generals. On May 16th, Schmundt, who had accompanied his Fuehrer to Salzburg, wired an inquiry to OKW for the numbers of the divisions on the Czech border that would be "ready to march within twelve hours, in the event of mobilization". In reply, Oberstleutnant Zeitzler (later Chief of the General Staff of the Army) of OKW listed ten infantry divisions and one mountain and one armoured division, all stationed in Bavaria, Saxony and Silesia. The next day Zeitzler was furnishing Hitler with details concerning the Czech fortifications. And on May 20th, Keitel dispatched to the Obersalzberg a new general directive for *Gruen*, prepared by Jodl.

The opening paragraphs of Jodl's draft paralleled closely Hitler's oral directions to Keitel a month earlier. It was not intended to smash Czechoslovakia in the near future without provocation; the necessary political and diplomatic conditions would first have to be established. When war came, substantial victory would have to be achieved within four days to forestall Allied intervention. To this end, as Jodl laid it out, the mass of the Army would be employed against the Czechs, and only screening forces would be left in the west. A simultaneous and ruthless blow by air and ground was to destroy the Czech Air Force and pierce the fortifications, after which "the bulk of the Army has the task of frustrating the Czech plan of defence, of preventing the Czech Army from escaping into Slovakia, of forcing a battle, of beating the Czech Army, and of occupying Bohemia and Moravia speedily". This remained throughout the basis of the Wehrmacht's strategic plan.

The day after Keitel sent the new directive off to Hitler, the Czech government called up one class of reserves and specialist troops, and reinforced the garrisons in the Sudeten region bordering Germany. Municipal elections were scheduled for May 22nd, and Henlein's forces were provoking riots and disorder throughout the Sudetenland. In addition, there were rumours of German troop movements and concentrations near the Czech border. The Czech Chief of Staff, General Krejci, informed the German Military Attaché in Prague, General Toussaint, that he had some information of the assemblage of "ten or twelve German divisions" near Dresden.

In fact, no such concentration had taken place, and the

Wehrmacht was as yet far from ready to attack. But Keitel admitted to the British press representatives that "routine" troop movements had in fact occurred. Barely three days earlier Zeitzler had informed Hitler that twelve divisions could march immediately in the event of mobilization. It may be that some news of the German plans leaked out and gave rise to the rumours that alarmed the Czechs, who in any event needed the reserve troops to restore order on the eve of elections in the Sudetenland.

Be that as it may, the Czech mobilization, though partial and explicable, caused a minor European crisis and enraged Hitler. Jodl noted in his diary that the Czech actions "lead to a loss of prestige for the Fuehrer, which he is unwilling to tolerate". Echoes of the ill-starred Schuschnigg plebiscite! This time Hitler was not yet prepared to strike immediately against a far doughtier and more formidable antagonist than Austria. But the Czech mobilization furnished the stimulus and pretext for an internal and secret decision to crush the Czechs at the earliest opportunity.

In consequence, Hitler promptly summoned Henlein to report and receive new orders, and then quit the Obersalzberg and hastened to Berlin to confer with Brauchitsch and Keitel and speed the military preparations. On May 28th the Fuehrer called Goering, Brauchitsch, Beck, Keitel, Raeder, Ribbentrop and Neurath to the Reichschancellery, inveighed against the Czech mobilization, and declared his "unshakable will that Czechoslovakia shall be wiped off the map". Two days later, Jodl's *Gruen* directive was signed by Hitler and distributed to the three service chiefs. The preamble, however, had been significantly altered. It now read: "It is my unalterable decision to smash Czechoslovakia by military action in the near future. . . . Accordingly, the preparations are to be made at once." Keitel's covering memorandum declared that the execution of *Gruen* "must be assured as from October 1, 1938, at the latest".

Fall Gruen was a subject which proved especially provocative of evasiveness and worse among the German generals who testified at Nuremberg. List, who commanded the army scheduled to invade Czechoslovakia from Austria, declared that he learned of the plan only "one or two days" before the actual occupation of the Sudetenland. Leeb, who commanded another invasion army, insisted that his only military objective was to occupy "a border area . . . twenty to thirty kilometres

deep", in the face of the directives calling for an assault to the heart of Bohemia to entrap and destroy the Czech Army. Brauchitsch went so far as to assert that "no plan existed" for the occupation of Czechoslovakia.[12] In fact, plans and preparations proceeded apace throughout the four-month period from the "smash directive" of May 30th until the Munich settlement at the end of September.

Two more military planning conferences with Hitler took place early in June, and for the second of these a series of memoranda were prepared on the armament of the Czech forces and the progress of German fortifications on the French frontier. By the middle of July, the Italian government had learned of the German plan and even the approximate proposed timing. At about the same time, OKH distributed a new and highly secret schedule of summer manœuvres to meet the special needs of the plan of attack and leave the troop units suitably disposed at their conclusion. Early in August, the German Air Attaché at Prague was secretly reconnoitring the Sudetenland for flat areas that could be used as landing-fields for German planes. Plans were drawn up for the establishment of ten Army headquarters; five of these armies were to carry out the attack in Czechoslovakia and the other five were to protect the western frontier and the areas bordering on Poland. The commanders-in-chief, chiefs of staff and operations officers for the ten armies were selected, and their major component units prescribed. Elaborate mobilization schedules were drawn up.

By the latter part of August, the preparations were well advanced and the "Sudeten crisis" approached fever pitch. Hitler made a demonstrative tour of inspection of the western fortifications, and then went off to Nuremberg for the annual Nazi Party Rally. Under Goebbels' able guidance, this was made the occasion for a series of inflammatory and provocative speeches to whip up a war spirit and lay the psychological and political basis for the onslaught. Soon after the close of the rally, the Czech government ordered a partial mobilization, and on September 15th Neville Chamberlain grabbed his umbrella and flew to Berchtesgaden.

From this point on, diplomatic and military activities were inextricably intertwined. But to understand the complex of forces at work within Germany, it is necessary to review what had been going on within the higher circles of the Wehrmacht since the promulgation of the May 30th directive.

On May 30th, Jodl recorded in his diary the issuance of the *Gruen* directive, and then noted that "the whole contrast becomes acute once more: the Fuehrer's intuition that we *must* do it this year, and the opinion of the Army that we cannot do it as yet, as most certainly the western powers will interfere, and we are not as yet equal to them". Jodl's observation was accurate; another major conflict between Hitler and the generals was in the offing.

In this affray, the leading protagonist of the opposition to Hitler was General Ludwig Beck, who by this time had had eight years of education in the Fuehrer's ways and objectives. Beck had been the regimental commander at Ulm in 1930 during the trial of three of his subordinate officers for prohibited pro-Nazi activities, and had sensed the impact of Nazi nationalism among the juniors of the officers' corps. He had welcomed Hitler's seizure of power, and had publicly extolled the Fuehrer after the achievement of *Wehrfreiheit*. But during the Fritsch affair, many of the scales had fallen from Beck's eyes, and by the spring of 1938 he was thoroughly alarmed over Hitler's headlong foreign policy, as well as by the accumulating evidence that Hitler was bent on destroying all semblance of independent leadership in the Wehrmacht.

Beck's own position, however, was far from strong. His attitude in support of Fritsch had aroused Hitler's distrust, while the *Anschluss* had greatly enhanced Hitler's prestige throughout Germany. Between Beck and Keitel there was no common ground. Furthermore, Beck had few opportunities for direct access to Hitler, since Brauchitsch stood above him in the chain of command. As for Brauchitsch, Beck soon realized that this was a slender reed to lean on, and no relation of mutual confidence developed between the two.

But if Beck could not approach the Fuehrer directly, he could at least write staff memoranda and record his views. Indeed, the pen was almost the only weapon on which Beck could lay his hands. He had resorted to it on previous occasions, most notably after the conference of November 5, 1937.[13] Now, in the spring and summer of 1938, his dissenting opinions poured forth in profusion.[14]

The first of these was dated May 5, 1938, and was delivered to Brauchitsch two days later. Presumably it was stimulated by news of the instructions to proceed to implement *Fall Gruen*

which Hitler had conveyed to Keitel two weeks before. The gist of Beck's case was that, in the event of an attack on Czechoslovakia, Germany could count on no reliable or strong allies, and would face the united hostility of England and France backed by the "arsenal" of the United States, as well as of Russia. For such a struggle the Wehrmacht was quite unready, and the war economy was insufficient. Accordingly, for the time being the Czech problem could be approached only within the framework of a solution acceptable to England and France.

Three weeks later Beck attended the meeting of May 28th, at which Hitler announced his "smash Czechoslovakia at the first opportunity" policy. Beck took careful note of Hitler's arguments, which not only ranged the familiar ground of *Lebensraum*, autarchy, the weakness of France and the menace of Czechoslovakia, but anticipated the events of 1940 by emphasizing Germany's strategic need to control the coastline of Belgium and Holland. Beck immediately prepared a memorandum of refutation, which he read orally to Brauchitsch on May 30th. He conceded Germany's need for more territory and that Czechoslovakia, unduly inflated by the Versailles *Diktat*, must eventually be reduced in size. But he repeated his earlier arguments about the danger of Anglo-French intervention and Germany's unreadiness to face a general war. Furthermore, declared Beck, the OKH was not being consulted sufficiently, and Hitler was moving rapidly toward "untenable propositions" which might "seal Germany's fate".

The same day that Beck laid these views before Brauchitsch, Hitler signed the revised *Fall Gruen* directive, requiring that preparations for the Czech attack be completed by October 1st. This precipitated another memorandum from Beck dated June 3rd, which criticized the new directive as "militarily unsound" and based on an over-estimate of the Army's strength. But neither this nor the earlier memoranda produced the slightest effect on the situation; preparations in line with the *Gruen* directive were continued, and there was no sign of hesitancy on Hitler's part.

By early summer, Beck must have realized the futility of his writing memos to Brauchitsch, however cogent the contents. Either Brauchitsch was not relaying or utilizing Beck's views in conference with Hitler, or he was presenting them half-heartedly or ineffectually. In July, Beck concluded that other and more vigorous measures were called for, including concerted action on the part of all the senior generals.

As a basis for these new moves, Beck prepared another memorandum, the last of the series, dated July 16th. Execution of the *Gruen* directive, he warned, would lead to world war, to a war unwanted by the German people, and to catastrophe for Germany. Victory over Czechoslovakia in a few days, as postulated by Hitler, would be impossible, and Anglo-French intervention a certainty. The western front could not possibly be held with the available troops. It was the responsibility of the military leaders to prevent such a disaster.

In a handwritten draft of this document, Beck had stated that he, as Chief of the General Staff, was unable to carry out *Gruen*. This declaration was replaced in the final version by a sharp demand that preparations for war be stopped. Beck further declared that the *Oberquartiermeister* and all the section chiefs of the General Staff shared his views. In conclusion, Beck proposed that Brauchitsch call a meeting of all the commanding generals, and discuss the situation with the Navy and Luftwaffe commanders, after which a united front against war should be presented to Hitler.

In presenting his memorandum to Brauchitsch, Beck supplemented his document with the oral observation that, if Hitler proved adamant, the generals should resign in a body. Their action would be supported by all "upright civil officials", he predicted. Three days later, Beck was again closeted with Brauchitsch, with detailed and strong recommendations of the methods by which the *démarche* to Hitler should be made. At long last—unhappily, much too late—it had begun to dawn on Beck that he was confronting a problem far broader and deeper than how to put an end to *Fall Gruen*. At last he realized that the menace of war was not simply a momentary, mad idea of Hitler's, but was an intrinsic part of an evil and dangerous political and social system. Beck was face to face with the Third Reich itself.

Accordingly, his proposals to Brauchitsch on July 19th went far beyond anything that he had yet written. The Army generals must seek allies among the surviving better elements, including the "good generals" of the Luftwaffe, civilian ministers, and even the more respectable and reasonable Nazi Party officials. All these should be warned of the perils of the situation. So reinforced, and avoiding any appearance of conspiracy, the coalition should meet the SS and the radical Party leaders head-on and "re-establish orderly conditions". There was to be no *Putsch*, and Hitler would remain; the keynote was

reform: "For the Fuehrer, against war, against 'boss rule', peace with the Church, free expression of opinion, an end to the 'Cheka', restore justice in the Reich, cut in half contributions to the Party, no more building of palaces, housing for the people, Prussian cleanliness and simplicity". This was a platform that Groener might have written. The pity of it was that Beck, no more than his brother generals, had had the vision to support Groener in the latter's hour of need. By 1938 the odds against dissidence and reform were overwhelming, and Beck was about to drink the same cup of lonely and impotent righteousness that Groener had drunk in 1932.

During the balance of July, Beck continued to press his views upon Brauchitsch and give vent to them among his colleagues. Generalleutnant Heinrich von Stuelpnagel, the O. Qu. II, helped work out the plans. Ribbentrop and Himmler, Beck thought, were egging Hitler on to war. Goering, however, "was not a warmonger" and might be approached. As for timing, Hitler might perhaps be more willing to listen to reason toward the end of September, after the hysteria of the Nuremberg *Reichsparteitag* had tapered off. The *démarche* would undoubtedly cause acute political tension and possibly domestic violence. Therefore, General von Witzleben, the Commander of Wehrkreis III in Berlin, and Count Helldorf, the Berlin police chief, should make joint preparations to preserve order.*

Early in August, it became known to Beck that Hitler was planning to address the generals on August 15th, at the Jueterbog Army review. This, Beck felt, called for a speed-up in his preparations; the generals should meet at once to lay the basis for collective action and prepare to meet Hitler's arguments. He pleaded his cause vigorously with Brauchitsch, and the latter was thus prevailed upon to call a meeting of all the commanding generals on August 4th.

Distrusting Brauchitsch's firmness and powers of expression, Beck prepared a speech for Brauchitsch to deliver at the meeting, and to use in subsequent discussions with Hitler. It consisted chiefly of analysis of the military situation and probable attitude of each country that might be involved in a European crisis, in order to demonstrate Germany's isolated position. England was confronted with an Italian threat in the Mediterranean, wanted quiet in Europe, and was not in good military

* Beck, Witzleben and Helldorf were all later involved in the attempted *Putsch* of July 20, 1944.

repair. However, she would follow the French on the Czech problem, her "imperial resources" gave her the depth for a long war, and she could count on American logistic support. France, bound by treaty to support Czechoslovakia, was "the strongest military power in Europe", with manifold superiority over Germany. By the fifth day of mobilization she could put on the western front three times as many divisions as Germany could muster. Germany was quite unable to hold the French in the west while fighting the Czechs in the south-east. America was a country of tremendous military potential, and her attitude was irretrievably favourable to England. Poland was interested in detaching the Teschen area from Czechoslovakia, but the Poles hated Germany and could not be counted on to side with Germany against France and England. In Russia the purges had weakened the Army, but in a long war she would be a powerful enemy. Japan was preoccupied in China, and in no position to aid Germany against Russia, England or the United States. Italy was ill prepared for war and could give Germany no decisive relief; General Pariani (the Italian Chief of Staff) was especially opposed to war with England and France. Belgium, normally neutral, was subject to Anglo-French pressure, and would surely allow the French to march through and threaten the Ruhr.

For all these reasons, Germany could not possibly prevail in a world war in her then state of preparation. The question was not one of peace or principle, but of timing; *the German Army would not be ready until 1941*. The generals' judgment of the military situation must govern, and Brauchitsch must demand that Hitler act in accordance with their views.

It was a forceful speech, but Brauchitsch was not the man to deliver it. He called the generals together, but did not read the speech, and left it to Beck to take the lead. Beck thereupon read his memorandum of July 16th to the assemblage, making a very deep impression.

General Wilhelm Adam immediately rose to support Beck's views and, as the general who would be in command on the western front in the event of war, stated that the fortifications were totally inadequate. Under the *Gruen* directive calling for the concentration of the Army against Czechoslovakia, Adam complained, he would have in the west only five active divisions, four reserve divisions, and the over-age troops of the Landwehr. This pitiful force would be speedily overrun by the French. "I paint a black picture", declared Adam in conclusion, and

198

added that he was quite prepared to repeat his views to Hitler in person should the opportunity present itself.

Thus encouraged by Beck and Adam, Brauchitsch ventured to remark that he shared their apprehensions. Beck then asked whether any of those present held opposing views. None were expressed, and there was obviously general agreement with Beck's analysis.

Now, if ever, was the moment for the generals to translate discussion into a programme for effective action. But as soon as the conferees reached this point, their unanimity was broken. Apprehensive they all might be, but too many of them were dazzled by Hitler's past triumphs, or beholden to him, or ambitious, or fearful of the consequences of open opposition. Reichenau declared that the great decision of war or peace was for the Fuehrer to make. Busch, another outspokenly pro-Hitler general, spoke of obedience and the oath of loyalty. Few of the other generals were prepared to join in the steps proposed by Beck and seconded by Adam, although von Kluge did suggest that, if Hitler pushed matters to the point of war, all the *Generale* should resign. Brauchitsch failed to press the matter to a conclusion, and the meeting broke up with no decisions taken and no problems solved.

Brauchitsch did, however, show Beck's July memorandum to Hitler. The Fuehrer's reaction was characteristic; who else had seen the document? The principal result was to confirm Hitler's distrust of Beck, and this soon led to the latter's virtual exclusion from performance of his duties as Chief of Staff. With Hitler's encouragement, Brauchitsch avoided Beck and started to deal directly with Beck's immediate subordinate, General Franz Halder, the O. Qu. I. Relations between Brauchitsch and Beck grew increasingly tense as the latter, without surprise but with bitterness, concluded that Brauchitsch not only would give in to Hitler but was preparing to put Beck on the shelf at the very moment of crisis.

When Hitler learned that Beck's memorandum had been read to the commanding generals, he took a highly unorthodox but very characteristic step. He had long felt that many of the older generals were both over-cautious and untrustworthy, but that he could hope for more enthusiastic and unquestioning support from younger generals like Guderian and Manstein and, later on, Rommel, Dietl, Model and others. In private conversation, Hitler declared that he would take Czechoslovakia with the old generals, and then tackle France with a

new crop. Many of the "new crop" were scheduled to be assigned as chiefs of staff to the commanders-in-chief of the ten armies which were to be constituted under the plans for *Gruen*.

On August 10th, Hitler summoned to meet with him at the Berghof all the Army chiefs of staff (except Beck), the chiefs of staff of the four Luftwaffe groups, and several other young but highly placed General Staff officers. Neither Brauchitsch nor any of the commanding generals were invited. This circumvention of the commanders-in-chief and direct recourse to their subordinate *Chefs* was unheard of and an obvious and intentional slap at the older generals. It was a breach of military protocol which Fritsch would never have tolerated, and which Hitler would not have dared to attempt a year earlier.

Protocol counted for a great deal in the German Army, and accordingly it was an ill-at-ease and puzzled group of staff officers that sat down to lunch that day with Adolf Hitler at the Berghof. Among those present were Manstein, Wietersheim, Salmuth, and Ruoff from the Army chiefs of staff, as well as Jodl from OKW and Jeschonnek from the Luftwaffe General Staff.*

After lunch, Hitler held forth for nearly three hours on *Weltpolitik*. By way of unacknowledged reply to Beck's memorandum, he discussed each European country, in the course of an analysis leading to the conclusion that England and France would not attack Germany to save Czechoslovakia.

The results, from Hitler's standpoint, were anything but satisfactory. As the ranking officer present,† General Gustav Anton von Wietersheim challenged Hitler's conclusions about Anglo-French non-intervention, and topped off his reply by quoting General Adam's observations of the previous week that the western fortifications could hardly be held for three weeks. At this point Hitler lost his temper, and declared that if this were the fact, "the whole Army was good for nothing. I

---

* Some of these officers, such as Wietersheim and Manstein, held field commands at the time but were scheduled to become chiefs of staff (Wietersheim to Adam and Manstein to Leeb) to Army group or Army commanders when the mobilization for the Czech attack took place. The other Army chiefs-of-staff-designate, in addition to those named above, were von Apell, Hollidt, Viebahn, Sodenstern, Model, Felber and Bernard. Presumably most of these were also present, as well as the four air group chiefs of staff. Jeschonnek, then only an *Oberstleutnant*, held a position in the Luftwaffe General Staff corresponding to that of Jodl at OKW.

† Wietersheim had been promoted to *General der Infanterie* on February 1, 1938. The other officers present (excluding Hitler's adjutants) ranged from *Oberstleutnant* to *Generalleutnant*.

assure you, General, the position will not only be held for three weeks but for three years." On this dissonance the meeting broke up, much to the distress of Jodl, reflected in his diary:

"The cause of this despondent opinion, which unfortunately enough is held very widely within the Army General Staff, is based on various reasons.

"First of all, it is restrained by old memories; political considerations play a part as well, instead of obeying and executing the military mission. That is certainly done with traditional devotion, but the vigour of the soul is lacking because at bottom they do not believe in the genius of the Fuehrer. And one does perhaps compare him with Charles the XIIth.

"And since water flows downhill, this defeatism may not only cause immense political damage, for the opposition between the generals' opinions and those of the Fuehrer is common talk, but may also constitute a danger for the morale of the troops. But I have no doubt that somehow the Fuehrer will be able to boost the morale of the people in an unexpected way when the right moment comes."

But if Hitler had convinced neither the commanders nor their chiefs of staff, no more had they succeeded in checking his pursuit of his own intuition. At the Jueterbog review on August 15th, he again addressed the generals, and reiterated his imminent intention to "solve the Czech question by force". There was no show of opposition, and Beck saw the handwriting on the wall. By this time he was Chief of the General Staff in name only, and three days later he asked Brauchitsch to relieve him of his duties in that capacity. Hitler accepted his resignation with alacrity but insisted that his resignation should be given no publicity, and Beck, like Fritsch limited by personal reticence and false patriotism, would have no demonstration. One can but sadly wonder whether the news of an open breach at so high a level might not have at least prompted Neville Chamberlain to think twice before reaching for his umbrella.

But, as von Hassell observed, Beck was "pure Clausewitz, without a spark of Bluecher or Yorck".[15] On August 27, 1938, Beck summoned his *Oberquartiermeister* and section chiefs of the OKH General Staff to his office in the Tirpitzufer, read them a short lecture on the historic "independence" of the General Staff, and quietly departed. He resigned as Chief of Staff but remained, for the time being, on the active list, hoping for a field command. He had been true to the dictates of his mind, but lacked the fire and force to transmute dangerous thought into bold action.

During the last few months of his tenure, Beck had been in touch with a number of those who were, or were later to be, members of the German "resistance group"—among others Schacht, Witzleben, Gisevius and Oberstleutnant Oster, an officer of Admiral Canaris' OKW intelligence service. When Beck resigned as Chief of Staff, according to Gisevius,[16] he assured this group that his successor, General Franz Halder, was equally determined to oppose Hitler's aggressive plans. As we shall soon see, Halder proved to be a man who moved in many directions at once—or, better, a man incapable of moving steadfastly in any single direction. In fact, it was not Halder who picked up the torch where Beck had dropped it, but Adam.

In many ways, it was remarkable that Wilhelm Adam was still in the Army at all in August, 1938. Already past sixty, Adam was one of the half-dozen oldest generals, and he and Leeb were the two most senior Bavarian members of the officers' corps.* He was known as the "father" of the German mountain troops, and was most highly regarded as a professional soldier. Had Adam chosen to play along with Hitler, there is little doubt that he would have become a field-marshal and one of the leading German field commanders during the war.

For all of his ability, Adam had never been in the good graces of the Nazis. He had been Chief of the *Truppenamt* under Hammerstein, and was thus tainted in Hitler's eyes as an associate of both Schleicher and Hammerstein. Beck had replaced him as Chief of the *Truppenamt* in the fall of 1933, when Adam was transferred to the command of Wehrkreis VII in Munich. Two years later he was relieved of his command to make room for Reichenau, and his retirement seemed probable. However, Blomberg and Fritsch needed an experienced general to head the new *Wehrmachtakademie* at Berlin, and Adam was persuaded to take the assignment. The purpose of the *Wehrmachtakademie* was to train a limited number of staff officers from the Army, Navy and Air Force in inter-service strategy and the handling of combined operations.† This was an important but hardly a

* After the retirement of Blomberg, Fritsch and Leeb in February, 1938, there were only three remaining active generals senior to Adam: Rundstedt, Bock and Liebmann.

† There were ten pupils, six from the Army and two each from the Navy and Air Force. Only staff officers of proven ability at the rank or equivalent of lieutenant-colonels and colonels were admitted to the school. During the year 1937–38, six officials of civilian ministries closely involved in the war effort were added. The jealous "independence" of the Navy and Air Force was an obstacle to the school's effective functioning.

spectacular task, and Adam, despite his high rank and reputation, sank into relative obscurity.

Because of his past associations and seniority, Adam was a likely candidate for retirement, along with Leeb, Kleist, Kressenstein and the others, at the time of the Blomberg–Fritsch crisis. But for some reason he was not included in the list, although he himself was outraged by the affair and asked Beck for his release. Within a few weeks, however, a new Army group was created at Vienna as a result of *Anschluss*, and List's transfer to Vienna left a vacancy in the Army group at Kassel. Beck, foreseeing new tensions and in desperate need of strong allies, prevailed upon Adam to take the command at Kassel. That Beck was able to effect Adam's appointment is an interesting sign that Hitler's control of Army appointments was not yet close or complete.

By virtue of Adam's new position, he was the logical choice to be Commander-in-Chief of the German forces on the western front under the plans for *Gruen*. And as soon as preparations for *Gruen* got under way, Adam constantly and vigorously maintained that the west could not be held against the French with the resources at his disposal.

On June 26, 1938, Adam was summoned to the Berghof to give Hitler a personal report on the progress of construction of the West Wall.[17] This was an undertaking in which the Fuehrer took deep personal interest, and which he had committed to the charge of the famous Dr. Fritz Todt, then Inspector of General Construction. Before the meeting, Hitler's adjutant (Schmundt) told Adam that Hitler was anxious about the matter and that Adam would be well advised to make a favourable report. This had chiefly the effect of irritating the blunt old Bavarian, who promptly went in and told Hitler that the West Wall "did not amount to much yet". Hitler blew up and declared angrily that Todt was working hard on the problem and that "nothing is impossible for Todt".

At the meeting of all the commanding generals on August 4th, Adam promised Brauchitsch and Beck that he would tell Hitler, at the first opportunity, his pessimistic estimate of the chances of holding the west against the French. Adam's views were, as we have seen, relayed to the Fuehrer by General Wietersheim at the Berghof on August 10th, with unpleasant results. But Adam himself did not again see Hitler in private until the end of that month.

On August 26th, Hitler, accompanied by Jodl and other

officers and civilian officials, commenced a tour of inspection of the western frontier and Todt's fortifications. Adam joined the Fuehrer's special train at Aachen on the 27th, and accompanied him all the way to the Swiss border, where the party arrived on the 29th. Everywhere the SS and *Hitler-Jugend* were out in force, and the tour took on the air of a triumphal procession. Despite the fact that many families had been evicted from their lands and homes to make way for the West Wall, there was every evidence of loyal enthusiasm.

Hitler was easily intoxicated by such display, and the occasion was anything but propitious for another remonstrance. Nevertheless, once he found himself in Hitler's private car, Adam lost no time in bringing matters to an issue, in a direct and almost peremptory manner to which the Fuehrer was, by then, quite unaccustomed. Adam found Hitler surrounded not only by generals but by Himmler, Hierl (an old-time Nazi and head of the Reich Labour Service), Todt and other government and Party bigwigs. With exceptional boldness, Adam requested Hitler to dismiss from the car Himmler and all the other civilians, so that Adam could address Hitler personally and in the presence of his military colleagues only.

This unprecedented approach provoked sneers from Hitler and Himmler, but Adam carried his point, and the civilians were banished. Adam then launched into a comprehensive report on the weakness of the German position in the west, and an argument against the risks of war which *Gruen* entailed. He reminded Hitler that the latter had repeatedly predicted that the French and England would not interfere. On the contrary, Adam declared, they would be at war as soon as the first German shot was fired against the Czechs, and the French would soon break through.

An almost hysterical scene ensued. Hitler interrupted to say that he had no time to listen to such nonsense, and then emitted a flood of statistics on steel production and other economic matters purporting to show that Germany was stronger than France and England taken together. Adam sarcastically rejoined that *if* all Hitler said were true, then he (Adam) was quite wrong and should never have raised the issue. At this point Himmler and the other civilians re-entered the car, and heated argument gave way to cool stiffness.

Despite his outspoken opposition, Adam was left in command on the western front. But Hitler had the bit in his teeth and was not to be checked. He grew increasingly excited as the

trip progressed, and many of his entourage were almost equally swept up in the wave of enthusiasm. Jodl, for example, noted in his diary at the end of the tour: "The impression of the attitude of the population, as well as of the work done, is tremendous—the work done in the short period is colossal. It is a pity that we could not have started work four weeks earlier. At the end the Fuehrer says, 'The man who does not hold these fortifications is a scoundrel.' And to General Adam he says, 'I only regret that I am the Fuehrer and Reichschancellor, and that therefore I cannot be the Supreme Commander of the Western Front.'"

Hitler simply would not listen to reason, and that was the only weapon Beck and Adam had employed. By the end of August it was plain that they had failed. On the last day of the month, Hitler approved a memorandum of Jodl's on timing the attack so as to achieve optimum air–ground co-ordination, in which it was declared that "*Gruen* will be set in motion by means of an 'incident' in Czechoslovakia which will give Germany provocation for military intervention". A few days later Hitler was off to the *Reichsparteitag* at Nuremberg, Henlein was busy manufacturing "provocations" in Czechoslovakia, and events were hurtling uncontrollably toward war, some other kind of showdown, or—Munich.

MUNICH AND THE "HALDER PLOT"

In truth, there was already considerable evidence to support Hitler's "intuition" that the British government, in particular, was anything but anxious to go to war to support the French alliance with Czechoslovakia. Early in June, the London *Times* had counselled the Czechs to hold a plebiscite in the Sudetenland, and to allow such areas as so desired to join the Reich. Two months later, Lord Runciman arrived in Prague to lend his "good offices" toward a settlement between the Sudeten Germans of Henlein and the Prague government. The atmosphere was heavy with the scent of appeasement.

As we have seen, Henlein was in no sense a free agent, but merely the creature of Hitler and Ribbentrop. Even before Runciman reached Prague, Ribbentrop's deputy, von Weizsaecker, had sent out instructions to the effect that "German co-operation with the Runciman mission is out of the question. It goes without saying that Runciman must not be relieved of the anxiety that the Czech question might take a dangerous turn, if Runciman's proposals do not satisfy the Sudeten

Germans." But this policy led Henlein to overplay his hand. He insolently absented himself from the negotiations, and his representative, Karl Hermann Frank, treated them as unimportant and openly predicted a "forceful solution". The German Foreign Office was obliged to admonish the Henlein group that they had been instructed "to appear to negotiate seriously".

If the English appeared to be softening, and the Henlein gang were willing puppets, Hitler's bid for other Continental allies met with little success. As Beck had predicted, the Italians had no stomach for a war, and even the Hungarians, with long-standing territorial "claims" against Czechoslovakia, were hesitant. The Hungarian Regent, Admiral Horthy, visited Hitler at Berlin during the latter part of August. The Fuehrer was anything but subtle; as Weizsaecker expressed his attitude, "Whoever wanted to join in the meal would have to participate in the cooking as well." But the Hungarian military position was not strong, and they were worried about counter-action on the part of Yugoslavia in the event of war. Although the meeting led to discussions between the German and Hungarian Chiefs of Staff (Halder and Fischer) early in September, nothing of importance developed, and Halder was careful to give the Hungarians no inkling of the planned timing of *Gruen*.

But Germany's obvious and painful diplomatic isolation had no more effect on Hitler than the forebodings of Beck and Adam. Flushed with confidence after his tour of the western frontier, the Fuehrer summoned Brauchitsch and Keitel to the Berghof on September 3rd to review the military plans for the attack.

By this time, the plans were in an advanced stage of development. The Army High Command had about forty-eight trained regular divisions at its disposal, of which three were armoured and four others motorized.* However, three infantry divisions were stationed in East Prussia, and their removal would have both jeopardized the secrecy of the plan and left East Prussia unprotected against a possible Russian or Polish attack. Accordingly, at best forty-five regular divisions were available to carry out *Gruen* and guard the western front

* Of the remaining forty-one, there were thirty-four infantry divisions, three mountain divisions and four light divisions, which were more mobile than infantry and included an armoured battalion. A fourth armoured division had been mobilized at Wuerzburg after the *Anschluss*, but was in a rudimentary stage of training.

These could be supplemented by the three SS regiments, the reserves, and the over-age troops of the Landwehr.

The *Gruen* plans called for an extraordinary concentration of these forces on the borders of Bohemia and Moravia, in a ring from Silesia in the north around to Austria in the south. Five regular infantry divisions were to be left with Adam, who was to protect the western front with these five plus four reserve divisions and some fourteen Landwehr divisions. All or nearly all of the remaining forty regular divisions, including all the armoured and mobile troops, were to surround and overrun the Czechs. The Luftwaffe, too, would leave a minimum defensive force in the west, while the bulk of its strength was to be employed simultaneously with the Army thrust into Czechoslovakia, to destroy the Czech Air Force and Army supply bases, immobilize the Czech Army, and paralyse the Prague government.

Surprise and the camouflage of troop movements were to be achieved chiefly by extensive and nation-wide summer and fall manœuvres. In East Prussia, Kuechler's First Corps was to hold early fall exercises, to which foreign military observers and attachés would be invited. At all the great manœuvre-grounds in the rest of Germany—Grafenwoehr, Jueterbog, Grossborn, Neuhammer and elsewhere—the armoured, motorized and reserve divisions would train during August and September. There were fortress warfare exercises on the western front, and mountain manœuvres in Bavaria and Austria.

As the time for attack approached, the divisions were to be swiftly and secretly moved to "exercise areas" near their jumping-off points. When the day for the attack (known as "X-day") was fixed, the troops would move rapidly to the jumping-off points, and strike, in close co-ordination with the Luftwaffe, at the appointed hour ("Y-hour").

Under the plans drawn up by Brauchitsch and Halder, the entire Army would pass over into a war-time order of battle comprising one Army group and ten Army headquarters. The Army group, under Adam, would command all forces on the western front. Under him would be three armies: the Seventh Army, in the south along the Rhine; the First Army, based on Wiesbaden, to defend the Rhineland and the West Wall opposite France; and the Fifth Army in the north opposite the Low Countries. On paper the formation of an Army group and three armies looked formidable enough. But it was impressive only on paper, as these headquarters would have at their

disposal only the five regular divisions, four reserve divisions and Landwehr troops allotted to the west.

Two more of the ten armies had a purely defensive role. In East Prussia, Kuechler's forces were to be grouped under the Third Army headquarters. Across the Polish Corridor, in Pomerania, a Fourth Army was to be established as an additional safeguard against a Polish move, but its subordinate formations would be almost entirely reserve and Landwehr.*

The other five armies were grouped concentrically around Bohemia and Moravia. The Second Army was based in Upper Silesia, in position to strike south across the narrow "waist" of Czechoslovakia, just west of the border between Moravia and Slovakia. The Eighth Army was concentrated in the Dresden area, north from Prague. The Tenth Army was drawn up along the extreme western frontier of Bohemia; its headquarters were east of Nuremberg in the Grafenwoehr area. The Twelfth Army, based at Passau, covered the south-eastern frontier of Bavaria and the Austrian border north of Linz. The Fourteenth Army, at Vienna, was opposite the Second Army in Silesia, ready to attack north into Moravia.†

The selection of generals to be commanders-in-chief of these armies was an extraordinary reflection of the iron-clad rule of seniority in the officers' corps, still holding firm against the political and personal predilections of Hitler and the Nazis. Not only was the dissident Adam designated Commander-in-Chief of the Army Group in the west. Beck, who had resigned as Chief of Staff but not from the active list, was named to command the First Army in the Rhineland. This army, facing the French at the most probable place for a French attack, was at once the most important and most vulnerable of the three armies in the west. The Fifth Army was to be commanded by Liebmann, and to lead the Seventh Army the choice fell upon General der Infanterie Freiherr Seutter von Loetzen, who had been in retirement since 1933.‡

In the east, Kuechler's designation to command the Third Army was entirely logical, despite his relatively junior rank, as he had been in command in East Prussia since the spring of

---

* It has not been possible to piece out an entirely complete divisional order of battle on the basis of the available documents, and it is possible that one or two regular infantry divisions were to be included in the Fourth Army.

† There were no armies numbered 6, 9, 11 or 13.

‡ Von Loetzen had preceded Leeb as Commander-in-Chief of Gruppenkommando 2 at Kassel, and presumably had special familiarity with the defence problem in the west.

1937. But the selection for the Fourth Army in Pomerania was another interesting echo of days gone by, for it was none other than Hammerstein, who had been living in complete retirement since his replacement by Fritsch in 1934.

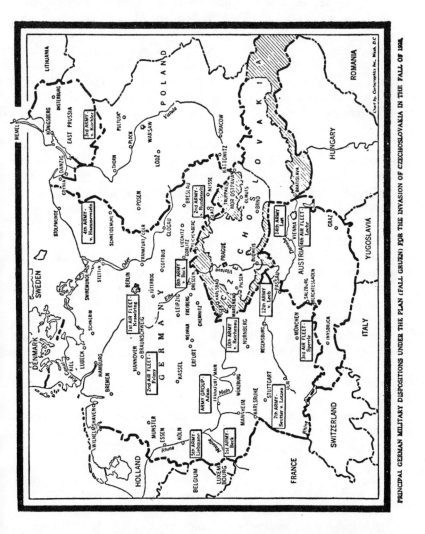

PRINCIPAL GERMAN MILITARY DISPOSITIONS UNDER THE PLAN (FALL GRUEN) FOR THE INVASION OF CZECHOSLOVAKIA IN THE FALL OF 1938.

In the south, List was to lead the attack of the Fourteenth Army from Vienna, where he was already stationed. Rundstedt headed the Second Army in Silesia, and Bock, the Eighth Army in Saxony, where he had been the principal commander since 1935. Reichenau was posted to the Tenth Army. To

lead the Twelfth Army, von Leeb was recalled to duty. As Leeb had had no headquarters or staff since his retirement at the time of the Blomberg–Fritsch crisis, a special "Working Staff Leeb" was established at Munich during the summer of 1938 under Manstein, who was to be Leeb's Chief of Staff, and from this staff the Twelfth Army headquarters developed.*

The five armies ringing the Czechs, under the OKH plan, would comprise about thirty-seven divisions, or about four-fifths of the ground forces available for *Gruen*. The strongest forces were to be gathered on the north in Rundstedt's Second Army and on the south in Leeb's and List's Twelfth and Fourteenth Armies, and the basic strategy was that Rundstedt and List would push toward each other with the objective of meeting between Olmuetz and Bruenn, thus pinching off and isolating Bohemia and Moravia from Slovakia, and encircling the Czech Army. Parachute troops under Generalleutnant Kurt Student were to be dropped in front of Leeb's army to hasten its advance.

But when Brauchitsch and Keitel met with Hitler at the Berghof on September 3rd, the Fuehrer was not satisfied. He thought that the Czech defences opposite Rundstedt would be the strongest, and that it was an error to stake so many divisions where they might be stopped, and thus risk a "possible repetition of Verdun" which would involve "bleeding to death for a task which cannot be accomplished". List's thrust from Austria, Hitler thought, would be hampered by poor transport facilities. His solution was to strengthen Reichenau's Tenth Army, assembling under him all the armour and motorized troops, and thrust due east into the "heart of Bohemia" toward Prague.

The disagreement was not at once resolved, and two days later Hitler went off to the Nuremberg rally, where Keitel joined him. The excitement of the rally had its usual effect of reinforcing Hitler's self-confidence to the point of intoxication, and he grew increasingly scornful of generals whose cautions he resented and whose military plans he found defective. On September 9th, Brauchitsch and Halder were summoned to Nuremberg for a showdown conference, which lasted from ten in the evening to nearly four o'clock the following morning.

* In summary, therefore, the eleven major field commands (Army group and ten armies) were held by the six senior active generals (other than Brauchitsch)—Rundstedt, Bock, Liebmann, Adam, List and Beck—plus three equally or more senior retired officers—Hammerstein, von Loetzen and Leeb—plus Reichenau and Kuechler.

The meeting opened with a long defence by Halder of the OKH plan. As Halder saw it, a speedy victory could be achieved only by preventing a Czech retreat eastward into Slovakia, and for this objective the best medicine was the pincer movement between Rundstedt on the north and Leeb and List on the south. The main push was to be made by Rundstedt, who should be able to reach Olmuetz by the second day of the offensive. If, contrary to expectations, Rundstedt were stopped, there would be no "bleeding to death" on the fortifications. The Army's strategic concentrations were flexible. List would be coming up from Austria in the rear of the Czech position. Leeb, after breaking through to the north, should turn east and "race for Bruenn [Brno]. This operation will definitely succeed", declared Halder.

Hitler was unconvinced. "There is no doubt that the planned pincer movement is the most desirable and should take place", he admitted, but "its success is nevertheless too uncertain to be depended upon". If one looked at the problem from the Czech point of view, the necessity of holding the Silesian frontier was clear, in order to avoid being cut in two. Therefore, the strongest fortifications and best troops would be facing Rundstedt. Furthermore, if Rundstedt succeeded in breaking the defence line, the distance to his objective was not great and could easily be traversed by infantry; therefore, he had no real need for the motorized division (the 2nd Division) which had been assigned to him.

Accordingly, Hitler argued, while the pincer move should be attempted, it should not be the sole reliance. In addition, Reichenau's Tenth Army should be strengthened for a drive east to Prague. Rundstedt and Leeb should each give up a motorized division (the 2nd and 13th Divisions) to Reichenau, who would then have a highly mobile eight-division army, including one armoured, one light and three motorized divisions, with three infantry divisions in support. The two motorized divisions taken from Rundstedt and Leeb could be replaced by bringing down two additional infantry divisions (the 9th from Giessen and the 30th from Luebeck) in trucks. Rundstedt, List and Leeb would then do the pinching, Reichenau the pushing, and Bock's relatively weak Eighth Army would supplement Rundstedt's effort.

This episode marked Hitler's first direct incursion into the sphere of military tactics. Munich soon made the issue between him and Halder an academic one. But at the

conference, Hitler made his decision prevail, and the new troop dispositions were made accordingly. As Keitel later put it to Jodl, the Commander-in-Chief of the Army and the Chief of the General Staff sustained a "defeat" at the hands of the former corporal.

The revised plan also meant a more important role in the campaign for Hitler's favourite, Reichenau, whose Tenth Army was strengthened by two motorized divisions and would make one of the two major assaults. Within Reichenau's army, the major attacking strength was concentrated in Guderian's XVIth Corps, to which were subordinated the 1st Panzer Division and the 13th and 20th Motorized Infantry Divisions. Guderian had been specializing in the development of armoured tactics since 1928, and had made a favourable impression on Hitler soon after the seizure of power, when he demonstrated mobile and armoured units to the Fuehrer. Aggressive and able in promoting the importance of the panzer arm, he had clashed with Beck and developed a rapport with Blomberg and Reichenau which led to his rapid promotion over the heads of scores of his brother officers.* The vicissitudes of his "armoured dash" to Vienna in February apparently did not harm his standing with Hitler, and now he was entrusted with the *Schwerpunkt* of Reichenau's attack.

Having thus established his dominance of the High Command, Hitler returned to politics and propaganda. The Nuremberg rally became a vehicle for the emotional mobilization of Germany and the demoralization of the democracies. Goering sneered at the compatriots of Smetana and Dvořák as a "miserable pygmy race without culture". The same day (September 10th) Weizsaecker forwarded instructions to Henlein that provocative incidents in the Sudetenland were to be brought rapidly to a "climax". On September 12th, Hitler brought the *Reichsparteitag* to a close with a venomous anti-Czech speech calling for "self-determination" in the Sudetenland, and the next day Henlein delivered an ultimatum to the Prague government calling, among other things, for the removal of all Czech police from the Sudetenland. Prague ignored the Henlein demands, and called up eight classes of

* At the time of the seizure of power Guderian was a junior *Oberstleutnant*. In 1935, though only an *Oberst*, he was given command of the 2nd Panzer Division, and in 1936, was promoted to *Generalmajor*. On February 4, 1938, he was again promoted to *Generalleutnant* and took command of the new XVIth Corps of armoured divisions. In November, 1938, he was designated *Chef der Schnellentruppen*, and promoted to *General der Panzertruppen*.

reserves to quiet the tumult in the Sudetenland and guard the border. Henlein and his cohorts fled to Bavaria, and called upon all able-bodied Sudeten Germans to follow him and join their strength with the Germans for the "liberation" of the Sudeten area. The world awoke to the realization that Europe was trembling on the verge of a general war.

The officers' corps, too, was in a high state of alarm. It was plain to any professional soldier that the western front could not be held against a determined French attack, and Hitler had given the generals repeated assurances that *Gruen* could be carried out without Anglo-French intervention. It was the validity of this assumption that Beck and Adam questioned. By mid-September, however, it began to appear that Hitler was planning to proceed regardless of what action England and France might take. In a meeting with Jodl on September 8th, Generalleutnant Heinrich von Stuelpnagel, the O. Qu. I, observed "that for the first time he wonders whether the previous basis of the plan is not being abandoned. It has been assumed that the western powers would not interfere decisively. It begins to seem now as if the Fuehrer will stick to his decision even though he may no longer be of this opinion."

Stuelpnagel's fears were widely held, and even Jodl admitted to himself "that I am worrying too". Reports of defeatism among the generals soon reached Hitler, who promptly administered a terrific dressing-down to Keitel. The results were colourfully recorded by Jodl in his diary entry for September 13th:

> "As a result of his bad experiences General Keitel makes a very excited speech to his . . . department chiefs. The accusations on account of defeatism made to the Fuehrer are now extended to the OKW too. Reports on the defence conversation Canaris–Pariani, and a memorandum of the Economic Defence Staff about the strength and invulnerability of the British armament industry are the unjustified reasons for this. . . . General Keitel emphasizes that he will not tolerate any officer in the OKW who takes to criticism, scruples and defeatism.
>
> "He informs me between ourselves that a record was submitted to the Fuehrer, apparently by the Luftwaffe (General Kitzinger) of a conference of General Hansen [of OKH] in July, in which he made by no means hopeful remarks abou tthe situation in the west.
>
> "The Fuehrer knows furthermore that the Commander of the Army has asked his commanding generals to support him in order to open the Fuehrer's eyes about the adventure in which he has

decided to engage. He himself has unfortunately no more influence on the Fuehrer.

"Thus a cold and frosty atmosphere prevailed in Nuremberg and it is highly unfortunate that the whole nation is behind the Fuehrer with the exception of the leading generals of the Army."

But if he had his private worries, there was no question where Jodl stood as between the Fuehrer and his doubting brother officers:

"Only by actions can they repair the damage which they have caused through lack of strength of mind and lack of obedience. It is the same problem as in 1914. There is only one disobedience in the Army and that is that of the generals and it has its final reason in their arrogance. They can no longer believe and no longer obey because they do not recognize the Fuehrer's genius; part of them still see in him the corporal of the world war, but not the greatest politician since Bismarck."

Among those who were far less sanguine of the Fuehrer's genius than Jodl was the new Chief of the General Staff, Halder. A stuffy, schoolmasterish, unimpressive little man, Halder was, like Brauchitsch, constantly torn between ambition and anxiety. Just as Brauchitsch had cut the ground from under Fritsch by stepping into the latter's position and accepting the conditions laid down by Hitler and Goering, so had Halder connived at the circumvention of Beck and slipped willingly into his place. But if Halder's moral fibre was little stronger than that of Brauchitsch, Halder was the more opinionated and prideful, and he was not bound by personal obligation to Hitler and Goering, as was his chief. He profoundly distrusted Hitler's judgment of the international situation, and deeply resented being overruled by Hitler in the sphere of military questions, in which Halder had undoubted competence.

Soon after he took over from Beck, Halder established contact with Schacht, Oster and Gisevius, and entered into discussions of how Hitler could be headed off or removed from power. These talks led to the first organized "resistance" within the officers' corps, feeble and evanescent as the effort proved to be. The other principal military figure in the "plot", if it merited the expression, was General der Infanterie Erwin von Witzleben, Commanding General of the IIIrd Corps and *Wehrkreis* headquarters at Berlin.

The essence of the "Halder plot" was a plan for the seizure of governmental power by a military *Putsch*, centring in Berlin. Witzleben's role, therefore, was to ensure support for the *Putsch*

from the troops in the Berlin area. He succeeded in bringing into the plan Generalmajor von Brockdorff-Ahlefeldt, Commander of the 23rd (Potsdam) Infantry Division.* The cooperation of Helldorf, the police chief of Berlin, was also assured. The general outlines of the plan had been developed before the conclusion of the Nuremberg rally on September 12th.

For all that the German military machine was unready, inadequate and shot through with disaffection, Hitler showed no signs of slackening the pace. While at Nuremberg, he signed an order subordinating the *Reichsarbeitsdienst* to the Army as of September 15th. Hundreds of Sudeten Germans were crossing into Germany to join Henlein's Freikorps. It became increasingly apparent that Hitler was moving on a time schedule under which the blow would fall on or about September 30th.

Then, just at the moment when the recklessness of Hitler's course was awakening the widest apprehensions within the Reich, Neville Chamberlain came to the Fuehrer's rescue. Late in the evening of Wednesday, September 14th, the German radio announced that Chamberlain and Hitler would confer at the Berghof on the following day. Just seven months had elapsed since Schuschnigg's ill-starred visit, and once again Keitel was ordered to be in attendance.

Before Keitel left Berlin for Berchtesgaden, he sat down with the Chiefs of Staff of the Army and Air Force (Halder and Stumpff) to consider "what could be done if the Fuehrer insists on advancing the date [for *Gruen*], owing to the rapid development of the situation". It was the unanimous judgment that this could not be done, chiefly because the railway schedules that had been worked out for the movement of troops and supplies could not be altered at such a late date. Jodl noted that "the new railway schedule is effective only as of September 28th. Thus we are bound to the date which the Fuehrer has chosen." Furthermore, all the remaining time was needed for work on the West Wall. This conclusion was telephoned to Major Schmundt at the Berghof; Schmundt, in turn, reported to Jodl that "the conference with Chamberlain progressed extremely favourably".

From the German standpoint, this was no overstatement. The Press had already carried reports that England and France were urging Beneš to agree to a plebiscite in the Sudetenland.

* Rundstedt, Commander-in-Chief of the Army group headquarters at Berlin, had no connection with or, so far as appears, any knowledge of the "plot".

Chamberlain came to Berchtesgaden with neither leverage nor a plan. It was patent that his intention was to bargain concessions for peace, and the only question was how much could be extorted. It was a situation made to order for Hitler. Plebiscites, he told Chamberlain, were now out of the question. The predominantly German border areas of the Sudetenland must be annexed outright to Germany; the more evenly mixed regions should be given a cantonal status à la Suisse, and Czechoslovakia "neutralized" by termination of the French and Russian alliances. The meeting lasted only three hours; Chamberlain agreed to confer again at Godesberg on the 21st or 22nd, and left Berchtesgaden, apparently in the best of spirits.

The Berchtesgaden meeting caused an immediate lessening of tension in Germany and, indeed, everywhere except Czechoslovakia. Preparations for *Gruen*, however, were not discontinued; on the contrary, the railways were ordered to begin a secret accumulation of empty rolling-stock, the border guard was strengthened, and arrangements were completed for the withdrawal of the labour contingents from the West Wall.

In the meantime, Chamberlain spent Saturday the 17th "selling his deal" to a divided British cabinet, and the 18th conferring with Daladier and Bonnet, who had flown to London from Paris. At the conclusion of these talks, the British and French governments advised Beneš to accept Hitler's terms.

Prague was stunned; the Czechs had been counting on the French alliance as on a bond secured by French flesh and blood. Beneš and his colleagues stalled for forty-eight hours but finally, during the evening of the 21st, capitulated and accepted the terms. But while the eyes of the world were glued on Prague, the script for the next scene in the drama was being written elsewhere. Hitler's cynical prediction to Keitel in April ("division of spoils!") proved mercilessly accurate. The Hungarians, with Italian backing, came forward with their claims, and the Poles, with incredible shortsightedness, set up a shout for the Teschen area. Hitler promptly concluded that, if he could get so much so easily, he could get still more. In preparation for the Godesberg meeting, a long list of additional points was drawn up, including further territorial demands, demobilization of the Czech Army, destruction of all Czech fortifications, and even the "cessation, immediately, of all military intelligence work against Germany. Violation will be considered a breach of neutrality".

And so, when Chamberlain arrived at Godesberg on the

22nd, with London's shouts of "Good old Neville" still ringing in his ears, he found a Fuehrer whose thinking had passed far beyond the Berchtesgaden stage. Cantons and international commissions were now as dead as plebiscites. Here was a map showing all the areas which Hitler was determined to annex; the other prepared demands were also presented in the manner of ultimatum, with a "due date" of October 1st, the very date that had been planned for the consummation of *Gruen*.

A very disgruntled Chamberlain returned to his hotel in Godesberg to brood. Stuelpnagel, who was in Godesberg with Keitel, telephoned to Berlin that preparations for *Gruen* were to go forward, including the transport to the west of the four reserve divisions assigned to bolster Adam's defences. Hitler and Chamberlain exchanged written communications on the 23rd, but met only for a short leave-taking in the evening. Chamberlain flew back to London the morning of the 24th, and the British and French governments transmitted the new demands to Prague without, however, any pressure on the Czechs to accept.

Now began the period of greatest tension. The Czechs ordered general mobilization, and the French called up half a million reserves. The British High Seas Fleet put to sea, and in London anti-tank ditches were dug and sandbag walls thrown up. On the 26th, President Roosevelt sent an appeal for a negotiated settlement to Hitler, but that evening the Fuehrer reiterated his demands for outright annexation before a monster gathering at the Sportspalast in Berlin. Chamberlain continued the nightmarish cycle with his well-known speech of September 27th, in which he mused wonderingly that all this trouble could come to England because of a "far-away country", and opined that England should only go to war for "larger issues" than the threat of a strong country to destroy a small one. As October 1st approached, it seemed that war was certain.

And so it seemed to Halder, Witzleben, Schacht and the others who were preparing the Berlin *Putsch*. It was a small circle, and their plans were not developed in any detail. Bockdorff-Ahlefeldt's troops would seize the Berlin governmental buildings, and Witzleben would establish a temporary military regime. Peace would be assured, the tyranny ended and a parliamentary regime re-established.* According to

---

* Winston Churchill, in *The Gathering Storm* (p. 313), after mention of the Witzleben–Halder plans, states that "of other less violent but earnest efforts of the

Halder's calculations, Hitler's presence in Berlin was essential, so that he could be sequestered and put out of reach of working mischief. Hitler had returned to Berlin after Godesberg, war loomed, and by September 28th, Halder and Witzleben decided the time had come to strike. Halder endeavoured to draw in Brauchitsch, and Witzleben went to his headquarters, ready to start the troops in motion for the *Putsch*. But they had reckoned without Hitler's suppleness of tactics and the western allies' almost hysterical anxiety to avoid war at all costs.

Indeed, Hitler appears to have kept his own intentions flexible up to the last moment. Undoubtedly, what he most wanted was to bargain, cajole and frighten England and France into washing their hands of the Czechs, so that the Wehrmacht could overrun their country, whether by battle or forced capitulation. The Godesberg demands had precipitated a touch-and-go crisis, but Hitler seems to have remained confident that in the end the western powers would give him his way. Consequently, the preparations for *Gruen* were never carried through to a finish. The five Army headquarters in the west, Pomerania and East Prussia seem never to have been actually set up, and on September 26th, Keitel and Brauchitsch "stopped the intended approach march of the advance units to the Czech border, because it is not yet necessary and because the Fuehrer does not intend to march in before the 30th in any case".

On the 27th, however, it again appeared that Hitler really meant business. The five Army headquarters ringing Bohemia

General Staff to restrain Hitler there can be no doubt. On September 26, a deputation, consisting of General von Hanneken, Ritter von Leeb, and Colonel Bodenschatz, called at the Chancellery of the Reich and requested to be received by Herr Hitler. They were sent away. At noon on the following day, the principal generals held a meeting at the War Office. They agreed upon a memorial which they left at the Chancellery. This document was published in France in 1938." As source, Mr. Churchill cites an article by Professor Bernard Lavergne in *L'Année Politique Française et Etrangère* of November, 1938. He describes the memorial in terms approximating the views of Beck and Adam.

The author doubts the authenticity of this story. (1) Leeb testified at Nuremberg, both before a Commission of the International Military Tribunal in 1946 and at the later trial in which Leeb himself was a defendant, in April, 1948. He made no mention of such a *démarche*. (2) On the date in question, Leeb was presumably at Passau in command of the Twelfth Army. *Trials of War Criminals before the Nuernberg Military Tribunals*, Vol. X, p. 622. (3) The combination of Hanneken, Leeb and Bodenschatz for a *démarche* to Hitler is incredible. Bodenschatz was a close personal friend of Goering's who had recently been made a *Generalmajor* in the Luftwaffe and was a most unlikely candidate for a mission of protest. Hanneken was a very junior *Generalmajor* in the Army, and an officer of no particular stature. The alleged combination of these two with the very senior Leeb does not make sense, and the whole story is out of keeping with the protocol of the officers' corps.

and Moravia were all functioning by this time, and shortly after noon Hitler directed that the assault units (about seven divisions) should start moving from their "exercise areas" to the jumping-off points for the attack. That evening he ordered the five regular divisions in the west to be ready for deployment in the area of the West Wall. He also ordered, for propaganda purposes, an enormous evening parade of motorized troops through Berlin. From all eyewitness accounts, the popular reaction to this display manifested less than no enthusiasm for war.

So matters stood on September 28th, which Jodl described in his diary as the "most difficult day". France and England were clearly ready to let Hitler have the Sudetenland by international compact, but not by ultimatum; Hitler seemed determined to act unilaterally. France, England and Czechoslovakia were mobilizing, while in Germany *Gruen* was coming to a sort of half-hearted fruition. Brauchitsch was imploring Keitel "to do everything in his power to persuade the Fuehrer not to transcend Sudeten German territory". Halder and Witzleben were on the verge of attempting their *Putsch*. Chamberlain was seeking the good offices of Mussolini to restrain Hitler, and President Roosevelt was issuing new appeals. On the sidelines, Poland and Hungary were waiting eagerly for such crumbs as might fall from Hitler's table.

In retrospect, it appears that Hitler's strategy was to push things to the limit of endurance, hoping to create a situation in which he could safely take unilateral action against the Czechs. If this should prove impossible, he could at least rest assured that there would be a constant flow of appeals for peace, coupled with concessions, which he could accept with the appearance of magnanimity and which would gain him most of his objectives. The more intransigent his apparent intentions, the greater the concessions were likely to be.

And this is precisely what happened. On September 28th a French proposal for a "big-four" conference was transmitted to Germany by Mussolini. The Czechs and their Russian ally were left out in the cold. Hitler, Mussolini, Chamberlain and Daladier would dispose of the problem and, it was perfectly clear, Hitler's demands would be substantially gratified. At the peak of his bargaining position, Hitler the political genius agreed to a quadripartite meeting to be held at Munich the next day; Hitler the demon was not yet in full sway. Chamberlain was able to interrupt his ominous report to Parliament

with the "good news" that Hitler had consented to negotiate further. He boarded his plane for Munich a national hero, calling to the crowd, with what now is seen as incredible fatuity, "If at first you don't succeed, try, try, try again." And he added, "This time it will be all right."

The news of the Munich conference swept the "Halder plot" into the dustbin. For Germany it was peace with victory, and Hitler's prestige rose to new heights. Neither with the public nor among the generals or their troops would any support for a military *Putsch* have materialized. Indeed, from Halder's standpoint, the "plot" was obsolete for reasons more fundamental than impracticability. When asked whether he had abandoned his plan because of Hitler's departure from Berlin, he replied * that this was not the governing consideration at all. The purpose of the *Putsch* was to prevent war; the announcement of the Munich conference made it clear that there was to be no war; therefore, there was no longer any reason to have a *Putsch*. *Quod erat demonstrandum*. The "Halder plot" was not, in his mind, an anti-Hitler plot at all. It was a plot to prevent a war which Halder believed Germany would lose. A peaceful victory was a highly desirable outcome, and now it would be a splendid thing to be Chief of the General Staff of the German Army.

And so, with all domestic opposition silenced and frustrated, Adolf Hitler travelled to Munich and put his signature to the Munich agreement of September 29, 1938. Mussolini supported his demands, and Chamberlain and Daladier had no stomach for any serious dispute. Hitler was able to write his own ticket. The occupation of the Sudetenland was to commence on October 1st, as *Gruen* contemplated and as Hitler had insisted at Godesberg. Four zones were marked on a map; these were to be occupied between October 1st and 7th. Additional territory "of preponderantly German character" was to be specified by a quadripartite "international commission" and occupied by October 10th. Czechoslovakia's new boundaries were guaranteed by England and France, and were to be subsequently guaranteed by Germany and Italy, but only "when the question of the Polish–Hungarian minorities in Czechoslovakia has been settled". Thus the little jackals got their scraps of the spoils. It was indeed a great day for the Fuehrer, and Jodl ecstatically confided to his diary that "the genius of the Fuehrer and his determination not to shun even a

* During a conversation with the author on December 12, 1947.

220

world war have again won the victory without the use of force. It is to be hoped that the incredulous, the weak, and the doubtful have been converted and will remain so."

With the wisdom of hindsight, the newspapers of the Munich days make sad reading. Experienced foreign correspondents wrote that the four-way conclave had inaugurated a new and better era in European diplomacy, while Goering rubbed his fat hands with almost lecherous pleasure at the signing ceremony, crowds wept in the square of ancient Prague, and Chamberlain vaporized about "peace in our time" and preened himself as a modern Disraeli.

And yet there can be little doubt that Chamberlain and Daladier accurately gauged the temper of the French and English people. The people wanted peace; Hitler wanted to crush Czechoslovakia; both had their wish. The *New York Times* was right to say, as it did, that no man should criticize the upshot unless he was prepared to pay the price of a different one. Few were, and it was the guilt of Chamberlain and Daladier that they, who should have known and told the people what they were buying and at what a price, did not know, were incapable of leading, and merely reflected popular apprehensions and misapprehensions.

For it is clear in retrospect that the price of a better outcome would not have been nearly so high as was generally feared at the time, and that the price paid for Munich was staggering, as the *Times* also and rightly declared. Chamberlain's use of the old nursery rhyme was tragically apt. He did try, try and try again, but each time he tried to do precisely the wrong thing, and the tragedy is that he succeeded. The conclusion is inescapable that at Berchtesgaden, Godesberg and Munich the western powers kicked away a golden opportunity to put an end to the menace of the Third Reich, and struggled frantically to give Hitler an opportunity to do later what he could not possibly have done in 1938.

As witness we need only turn to Jodl, who, whatever his faults, was an exceedingly able soldier. Testifying at Nuremberg, he flatly stated:[18] "It was out of the question with five fighting divisions and seven reserve divisions in the western fortifications, which were nothing but a large construction site, to hold out against 100 French divisions. That was militarily impossible."

Adam's judgment that the west could not be held, in short, was not only correct but glaringly obvious to anyone who knew

the basic military facts. *Gruen* simply was not a plan seriously designed to cope with the event of Anglo-French intervention; its only hope of successful consummation was that Czechoslovakia would be the only enemy belligerent. No matter how shoddy and dispirited the French Army might have been in 1938, as it proved to be in 1940, there is no question but that it could have marched with ease through Adam's pitifully small forces and uncompleted defences. To be sure, the German armies in the south might in the meantime penetrate Czechoslovakia, but by the time they were well into Bohemia they would have had a hard time getting out. The French forces, if handled with some measure of decision, let alone *élan*, would already have been deep in Germany.

In almost every other vital respect, the Third Reich was unready for a major conflict. London shivered in fear of a rain of bombs which almost certainly would never have come, and at worst would have been a drizzle. The Luftwaffe, like the Army, was concentrated against Czechoslovakia, and there was little to spare for the defence of the west and nothing for a bombing offensive. Farben's buna programme had just been fairly launched, but synthetic rubber was not yet on hand in anything like sufficient quantities. Nor was the output of synthetic aviation petrol up to war-time requirements, and under the stress of *Gruen* the Air Ministry was obliged to buy large quantities of tetraethyl lead (essential in the manufacture of high-octane petrol) from the Ethyl Export Corporation. In July, 1938, Carl Krauch of I.G. Farben pointed out to Goering numerous deficiencies in the government's programme for the production of explosives, poison gas, rubber and petrol, and a revised and enlarged schedule (the so-called "Karinhall Plan") was drawn up. Even Farben's skill in the development of synthetics needed time to bring its promise to fulfilment, and the fall of 1938 was decidedly too soon.

In the light of all these circumstances, which must have been as apparent to Hitler as to the generals, the true inwardness of his policy and of *Gruen* becomes clear. The threat to Czechoslovakia was real and based on ready force, but as regards England and France, it was a policy of bluff and bluster. Beck and Adam were exposing the weakness of Hitler's hand, and the more cogent and unanswerable their arguments, the greater was the Fuehrer's rage, for no one likes to have his bluff called, especially when everything he has is at stake.

For by the middle of September, after Nuremberg *Reichs-*

parteitag fulminations, Hitler was, as Beck had predicted, in an "untenable position", and if Chamberlain and Daladier, instead of clutching the umbrella, had stood firm, Hitler's position and future would have rapidly become insupportable. The threats and declarations of "unalterable intention" were by then so categorical and numerous that, if their hollowness were exposed and Hitler forced to back down, he would not have been able to threaten again. The next time it would have been the old story of "Wolf, wolf!" Hitler, and indeed all Germany, would have realized that conquest by mere menace was no longer possible, and that there would be no more *Blumenkriege*. Beck and Adam would have been vindicated instead of made to appear as ludicrous prophets of a doom which Hitler's genius converted into triumph. The pillars of the Third Reich itself would have trembled, and the whole edifice of tyranny might well have toppled.

Just as certainly, if Hitler, cornered by his own recklessness, had launched *Gruen* in desperation and in defiance of a determined Anglo-French-Czech coalition, it would have spelled the end of the Third Reich and the German menace. With French troops pouring in from the west, with Adam, Beck and Wietersheim—the three key figures in the western command—convinced of the insanity of the struggle and perhaps openly rebellious, with Witzleben and Halder launching their *Putsch* in Berlin, with Hammerstein, Kluge and many other commanders disaffected or hopeless, with latent opposition in other governmental circles, and with a populace anything but eager for war, there must have ensued a collapse disastrous to Hitler's fortunes.

How did the French and British military chiefs gauge the situation? What estimates did they lay before the French and British cabinets? As of this day we do not know. During the war which soon followed, and which Munich made inevitable, German military security was not good and British military intelligence was superb. Furthermore, according to Halder and Gisevius,[19] during September an emissary (Boehm-Tettelbach) was sent to England to tell the British that the German Army would not support Hitler in a general European war. It seems out of the question that the British and French governments did not know, at least in outline, the available strength of the German Army and Air Force and the incredible weakness of the German position in the west, or the schisms and dissension within the German High Command.

Perhaps one day we will learn more about this. In mitigation of what now appears as an inexcusable and fateful error of judgment and collapse of moral purpose, one must bear in mind the distressing disrepair of British arms, and the desperate clutching of all peoples for continuation, at whatever cost, of a peace which had endured for twenty years. But, as Winston Churchill declared in the House of Commons immediately after Munich, the western powers had "sustained a total and unmitigated defeat".

And it was not only the western powers who were victimized. From Munich the path led straight to Prague, to Poland and to the war and all its consequences. It is, perhaps, poetic if infernal justice that it is the Soviet Union, insultingly and stupidly excluded from the Munich settlement, that has presently profited most from the timorous blundering of Chamberlain and Daladier. Certainly there has never been a more compelling demonstration that the road to hell is paved with the good intentions of small men of little faith.

THE FALL OF PRAGUE

On October 1, 1938, the German forces ringing Bohemia and Moravia started converging on Prague. Their immediate objectives were more limited. In the next ten days they would occupy only the Sudeten areas to be annexed to Germany under the Munich settlement. Then there was a pause of five months before they resumed their advance. But from the very outset of the march their destination was Prague and their purpose the total destruction of Czechoslovakia. Thomas Masaryk was dead, and Beneš quit his native land immediately after Munich. Little enough remained of the state they had built so painfully and lovingly, and soon the remnants would be swallowed up.

Pursuant to the Munich agreement, Leeb's troops occupied Zone I, in southern Bohemia, during the first two days of October. Bock moved into Zone II, in the northern extremity of Bohemia, on October 2nd and 3rd. Zone III, much the largest of the four, comprised the western portion of Bohemia, including Karlsbad, Eger and Asch; Reichenau's units marched in on October 3rd, 4th and 5th. Zone IV, in northern Moravia, was taken by Rundstedt on October 6th and 7th.

By this time the international commission had specified the additional territory to be annexed, and all four armies moved forward again, as well as List's, which occupied a strip of

southern Moravia. Substantially all the Czech fortifications were included in the annexed regions, and any defence of the remainder was quite hopeless; the major cities of Pilsen, Bruenn, Olmuetz and Budweis were all within a few hours' march of the new border, and even Prague was less than forty miles from the northern boundary.

Nor were these the only mutilations that Czechoslovakia suffered. The shattered state was unable to resist the Polish demand for cession of the Teschen region. Hungary's claims were committed to Ribbentrop and Ciano for "arbitration", and on November 2, 1938, by their decision, a strip was peeled from southern Slovakia and awarded to Hungary.

All this, if deplorable, was nonetheless within the letter and contemplation of the Munich accord. Hitler had, furthermore, proclaimed that the Sudeten question represented the last territorial claim that Germany would make in Europe. But even during the ten days of the Army's advance into the Sudetenland, plans were being made for the continuation of its march.

Adolf Hitler allowed himself but a few days to enjoy the triumph of Munich. On the morning of October 3rd he arrived at Asch, where he was met by Guderian, who furnished his Fuehrer with a field-kitchen breakfast. Unhappily, there was meat in the soup; the vegetarian Hitler munched apples and requested a change in the menu for the remainder of his visit. At Eger the following morning the meal was more to his liking, and he picnicked happily with Reichenau, Guderian, Keitel, Henlein, Himmler and other favourites. Hitler travelled through the Sudetenland under the protection of an escort battalion commanded by a then little-known *Oberst* whose military writings the Fuehrer had read and admired. His name was Erwin Rommel.

Guderian observed Hitler's mood as one of satisfaction that war had been averted. But the satisfaction, if genuine, was short-lived. From the Sudetenland he took his way to Saarbruecken, where, in a speech on October 9th, he sharply admonished the English to "drop certain airs which they have inherited from the Versailles epoch". Germany, Hitler declared, "cannot tolerate any longer the tutelage of governesses", and British politicians would be well-advised to stop putting their noses into purely German problems. Furthermore, should such men as Churchill, Eden or Duff Cooper come to power in place of Chamberlain, they would make common cause with

"that Jewish-international foe" and launch a world war. Therefore, the construction of the West Wall must be pushed forward with increased vigour.

As a rule Hitler, in action and private conversation, manifested a healthy respect for the English. But, beyond a doubt, he was very much annoyed with them after Munich. Later in October he twisted the lion's tail again in a speech at Weimar. Why? Had not Chamberlain come three times to Germany to give in to Hitler's demands?

These questions puzzled and troubled Chamberlain no end. They also puzzled Guderian, who sipped tea with the Fuehrer after the Weimar speech. Hitler explained that Chamberlain had been "dishonest" during their negotiations at Godesberg. Also, the British were impolite and condescending. Nevile Henderson's dress when he visited the Chancellery was inexcusably sloppy!

Whether or not these explanations satisfied Guderian, they were surely superficial. What really appears to have exasperated Hitler is that Chamberlain insisted on giving, instead of letting Hitler take. Furthermore, Chamberlain had not given Hitler what he really wanted—i.e., all of Bohemia and Moravia.

Indeed, Hitler seems to have toyed with the notion of disregarding the Munich-fixed boundaries and marching right on to Prague. The operation would have presented few military difficulties within Czechoslovakia. The Czech Army had pulled back out of its fortifications in the Sudetenland and was in a helpless position. Some twenty-four German divisions were in the Sudetenland. At about the time of his Saarbruecken speech, Hitler asked Keitel to determine what reinforcements would be necessary "to break all Czech resistance in Bohemia and Moravia". Keitel consulted the five Army group commanders; * List and Reichenau asked for nothing; Rundstedt and Bock requested each an additional motorized division, and Leeb two motorized divisions and an armoured brigade. The Luftwaffe thought that its presently available forces were adequate. Keitel forwarded these views to Hitler, adding that

* The Germany "Army" was a war-time headquarters which (in contrast to "Army groups" and "corps") did not exist in the peace-time establishment. Consequently, when it was determined that the occupation of the Sudetenland was to be "peaceful", the "Army" headquarters established under *Gruen* were dissolved. Rundstedt, Bock, Reichenau and List reverted to their peace-time status as the Commanders-in-Chief of Army groups 1, 3, 4 and 5 respectively. Leeb, who had been called back from retirement, had no permanent Army group; his headquarters in the Sudetenland was redesignated "Heeresgruppe z.b.V." (Army Group for Special Purposes), and was dissolved in the latter part of October.

"OKW believes it would be possible to commence operations without these reinforcements in view of the present signs of weakness in Czech resistance".

However seriously Hitler may have entertained such intentions, their fulfilment was postponed. The treachery of such a move would have been so appalling and shocking to world opinion that Hitler wisely laid it aside for the time being. During the latter part of October, most of the German divisions in the Sudetenland were withdrawn and returned to their home stations. At the same time, Hitler issued an interim directive to the Wehrmacht requiring that preparations be made "to smash at any time the remainder of Czechoslovakia if her policy should become hostile toward Germany". Should this highly improbable contingency occur, the objective was to be "the swift occupation of Bohemia and Moravia and the cutting off of Slovakia".

The Sudetenland thus followed Austria into the alimentary canal for "digestion". It was a population increment to the Third Reich of some 3,500,000 souls * and a strategic gain of enormous proportions. The bloodless capture of the Czech fortifications and the destruction of Czech military power served to release at least twenty-five German divisions for employment elsewhere in the event of war.

Munich spelled death not only to the Czech state but to the military careers of Beck and Adam, as well as another and crushing defeat to the "conservative wing" of the officers' corps. It was characteristic of Beck's somewhat abstract cast of mind that, although he had resigned as Chief of Staff rather than carry out *Gruen*, he did not wish to leave the Army. It was known that Rundstedt, who was sixty-three years old, was planning to retire, as he in fact did on October 31, 1938.† Bock was to be transferred to Berlin to replace Rundstedt in command of Army Group 1, and Beck aspired to the command (Army Group 3 at Dresden) thus vacated by Bock. But Hitler, not unnaturally, refused to approve Beck's designation because of "lack of mutual confidence", and on October 19th Beck submitted his resignation from active duty. At the end of the month he was retired with the *charakterisiert* rank of *General-oberst* and went to live in Berlin-Lichterfelde, where he described himself in private correspondence as a "corpse in a beautiful

* The annexed Sudeten regions were added to the four *Wehrkreise* (IV, VIII, XIII and XVII) bordering on Czechoslovakia.

† In March, 1939, Rundstedt was designated *Chef* of the 18th Infantry Regiment

coffin". In November he wrote a last memorandum, in which he opined that Germany would not be attacked unless she herself attacked, but that, in the event of a world war, Germany would surely lose because "the Wehrmacht has feet of clay". Beck then buried himself in military history until, after war had indeed come to Germany, he became active in the resistance groups.

In contrast to Beck, General Adam made no effort to remain in service. On October 16th, immediately after the reserve divisions had been sent home from the western front, Adam submitted his resignation. It was promptly accepted; no doubt it would have been requested in any event. At the end of the year he, like Beck, was made a *charakterisiert Generaloberst*. Adam retired to his home in Garmisch-Partenkirchen, where he lived in complete obscurity until his death in 1949.

The simultaneous retirement of Rundstedt and Adam, and the transfer of Bock to Berlin, left vacancies in the Army group commands at Frankfurt-am-Main (2) and Dresden (3). Likewise, a new Army group headquarters (6) was established at Hanover. These top field commands were filled, in accordance with traditional German military practice, by the three generals next in order of seniority. Blaskowitz went to Dresden, Witzleben to Frankfurt and Kluge to Hanover.* The corps commands which they vacated were filled respectively by Strauss, Haase and Foerster.† At the same time Keitel reaped the reward of subservience by his promotion to *Generaloberst*. In the Luftwaffe, Milch was similarly honoured.

With the two most prominent dissident generals thus eliminated, and with the Army poised to crush the remains of Czechoslovakia at the first opportunity, the Wilhelmstrasse now took the centre of the stage in the *Drang nach dem Osten*. The strategy of Ribbentrop and Weizsaecker was to drive a diplomatic wedge between the Czech provinces of Bohemia and Moravia and the eastern province of Slovakia, so that the Prague government would collapse at the merest touch. Independence for Slovakia! Not only would this put an end to the Prague regime; as a German Foreign Office official (Woermann) wrote immediately after Munich: "An independent Slovakia would be a weak political organism, and hence would

* Leibmann was senior to all three of the appointees, but was slated for retirement, which occurred within a few months. Knochenhauer was senior to Witzleben, but was in poor health and died the following year.

† Foerster had been promoted to *General der Pioniere* in April, 1938, and Strauss and Haase were both promoted to the rank of *General* on November 1, 1938.

lend the best assistance to the German need for pushing forward and obtaining space in the east."

Now the hardening of Hitler's outlook and strategy, foreshadowed in his Saarbruecken and Weimar speeches, started to pervade the entire body politic of the Third Reich. On November 9th, the Secretary of the German Legation in Paris, vom Rath, was shot and mortally wounded by a Jewish refugee named Grynspan. With Hitler's approval, Goebbels and Heydrich set in motion the bestial pogrom in Germany which became known as "Crystal Week" because of the enormous quantities of broken glass in Jewish shops and homes. Synagogues were burned, shops looted and homes set afire. Some Jews were killed, many injured and thousands arrested. When it was found that most of the broken windows had been insured by "Aryan" insurance companies, Goering convened a meeting of high officials (Goebbels, Heydrich, Funk, von Krosigk and others) to cope with the unexpected problem. The state confiscated all insurance moneys payable to Jews, a fine of one billion marks was levied upon the Jewish communities, and new measures were decreed to "eliminate Jews from the economic life of Germany and Austria" and "Aryanize" their properties.

Many Germans were horrified; no doubt many of the generals were disgusted too. But none did anything about it; not a voice was lifted in open protest. And yet Crystal Week was surely the first in a series of suicidal mistakes which led to the ultimate collapse of the Third Reich. The shock to world opinion did much to dissipate the atmosphere of Munich and awaken even the Chamberlains to the true nature of the evil with which they were at grips. Hitler's demon was rapidly becoming his master, and his political genius broke through ever more rarely.

At the turn of the year another portent was observed. Hjalmar Schacht made a last effort to assert his authority as President of the Reichsbank—a post which he still occupied despite his resignation as Minister of Economics a year earlier. The first of his famous "Mefo bills", issued in 1934, were about to mature. In January, 1939, Schacht submitted a memorandum to Hitler calling for a curtailment of the tremendous armament expenditures in order to meet the bills and prevent inflation. The result was his immediate dismissal from the Reichsbank, where he was replaced by Funk. Schacht retained the empty title of Reichsminister without Portfolio, but he had

lost all influence and ceased to play any effective part in the affairs of the Third Reich. He left Germany for a tour of India and Burma, from which he returned, just before the outbreak of war, in August, 1939.

In Italy, too, Mussolini was becoming dizzy from Hitler's intoxicating breath. Anti-Semitism, and the goose-step *sub nomine passo romano*, were taken up, albeit half-heartedly. In December, and in the presence of the French Ambassador, the Italian Chamber of Deputies erupted with belligerent shouts for the annexation of Savoy, Nice, Tunis and Djibouti.

For the first few months after Munich, despite these ominous signs, Chamberlain and Daladier hewed manfully to the Munich pattern. Early in December, Ribbentrop and the French Foreign Minister, Bonnet, went through the hollow ritual of a "good neighbour" declaration. In January Chamberlain and Halifax went to Rome to cultivate the Duce. With Munich fresh in Fascist minds and Franco on the verge of victory, the Duce was condescending and vague to the plenipotentiaries of His Britannic Majesty. Mussolini and Ciano smirked openly behind the Englishman's backs, and Ciano noted in his diary Mussolini's comment that "these men are not made of the same stuff as Francis Drake and the other magnificent adventurers who created the Empire. They are, after all, the tired sons of a long line of rich men." To which Ciano added, "The British do not want to fight."

In the meantime, Germany had ostentatiously failed to proceed with the quadripartite guarantee of the new Czechoslovak borders contemplated by the Munich accord. In December, Weizsaecker was pointing out to Italian and Hungarian diplomats that "Czechoslovakia's future is in Germany's hands, and a guarantee from any other power would be worthless". Shortly thereafter, two trusted Nazi agents, Keppler and Veesenmayer, were sent to stimulate and support the Slovakian separatist movement. The Prague government was rickety and their task was not difficult. By March the fruit was ripe, and the Slovakian leader, Tiso, was summoned to Berlin. The Fuehrer was by now the Lord of Central Europe, and his edict was brief and blunt:

> "It was not a question of days but of hours. If Slovakia wished to make herself independent, Hitler would support this endeavour and guarantee it. If she hesitated and did not wish to dissolve the connection with Prague, he would leave the destiny of Slovakia to the mercy of events, for which he was no longer responsible."

For the Slovaks, it was Hobson's choice. On March 14th, the Slovakian diet in Bratislava declared its independence. Hungarian troops, by prearrangement between Hitler and Horthy, occupied Ruthenia, the eastern tip of Czechoslovakia.

While the Prague regime was being done to death, its aged President, Hacha, was brought to Berlin to officiate at the funeral of his own state. After hours of harassment at the hands of Hitler, assisted by Goering, Ribbentrop and Keitel, Hacha put his signature to a document incorporating Bohemia and Moravia in the Third Reich as a "protectorate".

Even before Hacha succumbed, German troops were within the protectorate-to-be. For the Wehrmacht, the occupation was no more than an exercise, and the only enemy the wintry weather. In December, Hitler had issued a supplemental directive specifying that preparations for the "liquidation of the rest of Czechoslovakia" were to be made "on the assumption that no resistance worth mentioning is to be expected". Therefore "the action must be carried out by the peace-time units only, without reinforcement from mobilization". It was of cardinal importance that "to the outside world it must clearly appear that it is merely an act of pacification and not a warlike undertaking".

So it was simply a matter of assembling and supplying the troops of the *Wehrkreise* bordering Bohemia and Moravia for the short march into the rump state. Blaskowitz, the new Army group commander in Dresden, occupied Bohemia, and List took Moravia. Planes from Kesselring's, Sperrle's and Loehr's air fleets demonstrated and soon settled on the Czech airfields.

This was the last of the Wehrmacht's *Blumenkriege*, but this time the flowers were lacking as well as the bullets. Silence and despair greeted Blaskowitz as his troops marched into Prague. Hitler was nervous about his own personal safety, and consulted Rommel, who was again in command of the escort battalion. The nerveless Rommel, however, advised his Fuehrer to "get into an open car and drive through the streets to the Hradschin without an escort".[20]

The Fuehrer acted on Rommel's suggestion, to the astonishment and grudging admiration of friendly and hostile observers alike. From the Hradschin he issued on March 16, 1939, a formal decree establishing the Protectorate. Autonomy in name was coupled with complete German control in fact. Von Neurath was taken out of cold storage and appointed "Reich Protector". As in the case of Austria, Himmler

promptly moved in; this time his chosen representative was Konrad Henlein's former deputy, Karl Hermann Frank.

In Slovakia, domestic autonomy was not as completely crushed, but German military, diplomatic and economic domination was assured. Under the "Treaty of Protection" of March 23, 1939, in return for a German guarantee to protect Slovakian independence and territory, Germany secured unlimited rights to garrison troops and build military installations. Slovakian military and diplomatic activities were to be conducted "in close agreement" with Germany. A confidential protocol to the Treaty laid the basis for extensive economic controls in line with German needs.

In "justification" of the final destruction of Czechoslovakia, German diplomacy reached a new level of cynical mendacity. Weizsaecker promptly instructed all German diplomats abroad to declare that action had been taken "with the full agreement of the Czechoslovakian government". A few days later, when the French Ambassador Coulondre came to protest the blatant violation of the Munich accord, Weizsaecker insultingly refused "to enter into any discussion of this matter" because: "Legally regarded, there was an agreement between the Fuehrer and the Czechoslovakian President. The Czech President had come to Berlin according to his own desire and had immediately stated . . . that he wanted to place the fate of his country in the hands of the Fuehrer." Weizsaecker scornfully suggested that the French government should not "be more Catholic than the Pope and mix into affairs which rightly were settled between Berlin and Prague".

Indeed, Hitler had succeeded in making everyone but himself look ridiculous. At Munich, his internal opponents such as Beck and Adam were discredited because the Anglo-French opposition which they predicted failed to materialize. Instead, the English and French were bluffed into abandoning a position in support of the Czechs which they could have successfully maintained, in return for empty promises that Germany had no further territorial demands in Europe. They were left morally committed to guarantee a Czech state which was no longer militarily defensible or politically viable. The events of March 15, 1939, laid bare the utter worthlessness of the bargain they had made.

Small wonder that the bewildered and embittered Chamberlain swayed like a tree buffeted by shifting winds. On the day Hitler entered Prague, he declared in Parliament that the

secession of Slovakia had "put an end by internal disruption to the state whose frontiers we had proposed to guarantee, and His Majesty's Government cannot accordingly hold themselves bound by this obligation". Two days later, however, in a speech at Birmingham, Chamberlain discarded the umbrella and brought to a close the unhappy era of appeasement. Something must have brought home to him the enormity of his miscalculation and the extent to which he and his country had been gulled. Angrily he recounted Hitler's assurances on which he had relied: "I shall not be interested in the Czech state any more and I can guarantee it. We don't want any Czechs." Then, rhetorically, "How can these events this week be reconciled with these assurances. . . . Is this the last attack upon a small state or is it to be followed by another? Is this in fact a step in the direction of an attempt to dominate the world by force?"

By the end of the month Chamberlain was satisfied that he knew the answer to these questions. With the occupation of Moravia and military domination of Slovakia, the borders of German *Macht* had crept ominously around Poland, just as, one year earlier, the *Anschluss* had achieved the virtual encirclement of Bohemia and Moravia. Now all of western Poland lay between the upper jaw of Prussia and Pomerania and the lower of Silesia, Moravia and Slovakia. "Poland's existence is intolerable, incompatible with the essential conditions of German life," von Seeckt had written in 1922.

On March 29, 1939, Chamberlain announced in Parliament his government's intention to double the size of Britain's Army. Two days later he took an even more fateful step:

> "I now have to inform the House that . . . in the event of any action which clearly threatened Polish independence and which the Polish government accordingly considered it vital to resist with their national forces, His Majesty's government would feel themselves bound at once to lend the Polish government all support in their power. They have given the Polish government an assurance to this effect.
> "I may add that the French government have authorized me to make it plain that they stand in the same position in this matter as do His Majesty's government."

Even as Chamberlain spoke, the basic OKW directive for the conquest of Poland was taking shape. "Peace with honour" had already decomposed. For "peace in our time", there remained only a half-life of five months.

CHAPTER VII

BLUMENKRIEG TO BLITZKRIEG

As FATE would have it, the *Tirpitz* was launched at Wilhelms-haven on April 1, 1939,* the day after Chamberlain's speech in Parliament by which the Polish guarantee was proclaimed. Hitler, who spoke at the launching from behind a bullet-proof glass screen, was in a rage. Both March and April of 1939 were truly months of the lion. Harbingers of the Apocalypse hurtled into the European scene almost daily; every bud of spring seemed to shroud a dragon's tooth.

Barely a week after Prague fell, the pocket battleship *Deutschland* put into Memel with a seasick Fuehrer and a Raeder eager for a small slice of the glories of the *Blumenkrieg*. This venture had been planned since November, 1938, under the code name "Transport Exercise Stettin". Hitler was no sailor, and the Memel territory could have easily been occupied by Kuechler's troops in East Prussia, but the faithful Raeder was overdue for attention and acclaim; Memel was made "a special task of honour of the Navy". The Lithuanians were helpless to withstand the German claim that Memel was an *alte deutsche Burg*, and another 1,000 square miles were added to the Third Reich. At the launching of the *Tirpitz*, Raeder was again honoured by his promotion to *Grossadmiral*.

The Mediterranean waves were even wilder than those of the Baltic. On March 26th, Mussolini put his dictatorial stamp of approval on the demands against the French which had been shouted in the Italian Chamber in December. Three days later Madrid fell to Franco, and the Republican cause in Spain was lost. Then, to cap the climax, on April 7th Italian troops invaded and overran Albania, adding another "jewel" to the rather shabby collection in Victor Emmanuel's imperial crown.

All this, however, was as nothing compared to the storm which began to gather over Poland. Much diplomatic history had to be unwound to enable Hitler to make a *casus belli*. At Locarno in 1925, Germany and Poland had agreed to the arbitration of

---

* The *Bismarck* had been launched on February 14, 1939. The *Bismarck* was commissioned in 1940, and the *Tirpitz* in 1941.

any disputes that might arise. In 1934, Hitler and Pulsudski had approved a non-aggression pact between the two countries. Twice in 1937 and twice in 1938 Hitler or Ribbentrop had reaffirmed the non-aggression pact, and at the height of the Munich crisis Hitler had vowed that Germany had "no further territorial problems" in Europe.

A month later the first rumblings were heard. On October 24, 1938, Ribbentrop took lunch at Berchtesgaden with the Polish Ambassador, Lipski. The exchange was pacific in tone, but Ribbentrop for the first time put forward the suggestion that Danzig (a "free city" under League of Nations control, with a predominantly German population but of vital importance for Polish maritime commerce) should be reunited to the Reich, and that Germany should be granted an extra-territorial road and railroad across the Polish Corridor from Pomerania to East Prussia. Lipski replied that he "could see no possibility of an agreement involving the reunion of the Free City with the Reich", and this view was soon confirmed by the Polish Foreign Minister, Josef Beck.

In January, the discussion was moved to a higher level; Beck went to Berchtesgaden to see Hitler. The Fuehrer was suave; because of the Russian menace "a strong Poland was an absolute necessity for Germany". However, Danzig was "a German city", and "sooner or later it must return to the Reich". When Beck replied that this was "a very difficult problem", Hitler hastened to reassure him that "there would be no *fait accompli* in Danzig". Beck, however, was not satisfied, and told Ribbentrop the next day that "for the first time he was in a pessimistic mood", because he "saw no possibility whatever of agreement over the Danzig question".

Hitler still had other fish to fry before it was Poland's turn in the pan. Ribbentrop visited Warsaw later in January and made a soothing speech, and on January 30th Hitler, in the Reichstag, hailed the fifth anniversary of the 1934 non-aggression pact and declared that "the friendship between Germany and Poland has been one of the reassuring factors in the political life of Europe".

So matters rested until after the fall of Prague and the establishment of the Czechoslovakian Protectorate. They then took a sharp turn for the worse. On March 21st, Ribbentrop summoned Lipski and complained about the Polish Press and student demonstrations. Furthermore, the failure of the Poles to evince a "positive reaction" to the Danzig question "had made an unfavourable impression" on Hitler. Ribbentrop also

advised that Beck should come to Berlin to discuss Danzig, and that "the talk should not be delayed, lest the Chancellor come to the conclusion that Poland was rejecting all his offers". Lipski promptly reported to Warsaw that "Germany has resolved to carry out her eastern programme quickly. . . . In these circumstances the conversation acquires very real importance, and must be carefully considered in all its aspects." Two days later, the annexation of Memel occurred.

Lipski's message indeed stirred Beck to action, but he went to London, not Berlin. The result was Chamberlain's assurance to Poland given in the Commons on March 31st, followed by an Anglo-Polish communiqué stating that "the two countries were prepared to enter into an agreement of a permanent and reciprocal character".

This rebuff was quite enough for Hitler and Ribbentrop, who promptly abandoned the negotiations with Poland. As was customary when matters reached this stage, Weizsaecker was brought into the picture. On April 5th, he instructed the German Ambassador at Warsaw "not to go into any further discussions . . . we must prevent Poland from throwing the ball back to us". The next day he received Lipski, and declared that "we have suddenly heard the rattling of the sabre in Poland. The offer by Hitler to the Poles was made once; the future will tell whether Poland has acted wisely in spurning it." On April 28th, in the Reichstag, Hitler threw off the mask and denounced both the German-Polish pact of 1934 and the Anglo-German naval treaty.

Weeks earlier, however, it had become apparent that a new crisis was in the making, and the diplomatic pot started to boil in Rome, Washington and Moscow as well as Berlin, Warsaw and London. On April 15th, Goering was in Rome, and pointed out to Mussolini and Ciano how greatly the conquest of Czechoslovakia had strengthened the German military position *vis-à-vis* Poland; Germany could now attack from two flanks, and the Polish industrial districts were barely a half-hour's flying time from German airfields. By fall Germany would be able to count on a monthly production of 280 planes of the new Junkers 88 type; "in nine months or a year the situation for the Axis, from a military standpoint, would be more favourable . . . the Axis was very strong and could defeat all possible opponents in a general conflict". Thus mutually encouraged Germany and Italy signed the "Pact of Steel" in Berlin on May 22nd.

On the day of the Mussolini–Goering–Ciano meeting, Roose-

velt sent a public appeal to both the Fuehrer and the Duce asking them to allay the word's fear of war by guaranteeing that neither country would undertake further aggression for the next ten or more years. Hitler's riposte was skilful, if disingenuous; he proceeded to circularize some twenty countries, not including Poland, with an inquiry whether they felt threatened by Germany. As was to be expected, the replies were in the negative, including those from Yugoslavia, Greece, Denmark, Norway, Holland, Belgium and Luxembourg, all of whom soon enough had cause to feel differently. Upon learning that the little Baltic country of Latvia was exhibiting signs of caution in answering the German inquiry, Weizsaecker sent a brusque message to the German Ministry in Riga; if the question was not promptly answered "with a downright 'no' we should have to add Latvia to those countries which are making themselves wilful accomplices of Mr. Roosevelt". Thus was Latvia frightened into declaring that she was not frightened.

Meanwhile, the English were not sitting idle. On April 27th, Chamberlain announced the introduction of conscription for military service, a violent wrench from traditional British policy. On May 12th, the Anglo-Turkish Agreement was ratified. Likewise, on April 15th talks had been commenced between the British Ambassador in Moscow and Foreign Minister Litvinov. And thus emerged the great question of the spring and summer of 1939: Confronted with the ever more hopeless impasse between France, England and Poland on the one hand, and Germany and Italy on the other, what would Russia do?

Russian intentions speedily grew increasingly obscure. After the fall of Prague, the Moscow government had unsuccessfully proposed a six-power conference. Litvinov had been the principal protagonist of the "united front" against Fascism, but Russia's exclusion from Munich had aggravated the Soviet's distrust of the western powers. Chamberlain's assurance to Poland was little better received in Moscow than in Berlin, for the Russians regarded it as indicating that England preferred the Polish to the Soviet alliance, and was still bent on excluding Russia from the European political scene.[1] Nevertheless, when the conversations with the British opened at Moscow, Litvinov proposed an Anglo-Russian-French mutual-assistance agreement. The British government did not react with enthusiasm.

The very next day the Russian Ambassador in Berlin called on Weizsaecker for the first time in many months, and declared that "for Russia, there is no reason for not living with Germany

on a normal footing. And from normal, relations might become better and better." It was the first straw in the wind. On May 3rd, Litvinov was relieved as Foreign Minister and replaced by Molotov. And on May 30th, despite all the ranting in *Mein Kampf* and a myriad of speeches and writings against the bestial Jewish Bolsheviks, the German Foreign Office instructed their Ambassador in Moscow that, "contrary to the policy previously planned, we have now decided to undertake definite negotiations with the Soviet Union".

Thus was the Russian policy of Seeckt revived by Hitler. Its second life was to be short, but long enough to accomplish what Seeckt had foretold: the destruction of Poland by Germany with the help of Russia. And it was decisive for the issue of peace or war. After May 30th, the critical questions were: Would Russia and the western powers revive the united front, or would Hitler succeed in unsaying all that he had said since 1920 and neutralize Russia by treaty? If the latter, how soon would Hitler determine to strike at Poland, and would the western powers then honour their guarantee, or yield as they had at Munich? If England and France stuck to their word backed by guns, would the German officers' corps allow Hitler to lead Germany into a world war, or would the generals attempt to stay his hand?

THE OFFICERS' CORPS ON THE EVE OF WAR

The upper levels of the officers' corps had gone through great upheavals during the period of the *Blumenkriege*. The year 1938 had witnessed the retirement, voluntary or involuntary, of Blomberg, Fritsch, Rundstedt, Leeb, Adam, Beck, Lutz, Kleist, Kressenstein, Pogrell and Liese. On April 30, 1939, Liebmann retired, and two *Wehrkreis* commanders—Geyer and Ulex—went on the inactive list at about the same time. Shortly thereafter Knochenhauer died.* Thus, seven of the ten most senior generals, and sixteen of the top thirty, were removed from the active list.

Of these, only Rundstedt, Leeb and Kleist were recalled to major commands when war came. Blomberg, Adam and Beck had placed themselves (in Blomberg's case involuntarily) irretrievably beyond the pale. So had Fritsch, for whom there remained only a brief and ghostly reappearance and death during the Polish campaign. Liebmann commanded an army on the

---

* Geyer was replaced as commanding general of Wehrkreis V by General der Infanterie Richard Ruoff, Ulex in Wehrkreis XI by General der Artillerie Emil Leeb, and Knochenhauer in Wehrkreis X by Generalleutnant Peter Weyer.

western front for the first few weeks of the war, but then was again deactivated. None of the others was a major figure. None of the generals who had been retired before 1938 was allowed to return to a leading role, though Hammerstein, like Liebmann, briefly held an Army command on the western front. Others, such as Joachim von Stuelpnagel, Falkenhausen, von Vollard Bockelberg, Kaupisch and Gruen, served only for a short time or in secondary positions.

None of these discarded generals was in a position to assert leadership or any substantial influence as the crisis approached. Hammerstein had failed in 1933, and had been silent since that time. Blomberg was under a cloud, and Adam and Beck were discredited by Hitler's successes in the face of their dire predictions. Fritsch's political limitations had led to his downfall, and he was a broken man. None of the others was sufficiently prominent or capable to grapple with large issues.

With the inclusion of Rundstedt, Leeb and Kleist, accordingly, the active senior generals of the officers' corps, as war approached, were: *

	Command	Rank	Age
1. von Brauchitsch	C.-in-C. Army	Genobst. 4.2.38	59
2. von Rundstedt	Temporary ret.	Genobst. 1.3.38(1)	64
3. von Bock	Army Group 1	Genobst. 1.3.38(2)	59
4. von Leeb	Temporary ret.	Genobst.† 1.3.38(3)	63
5. Keitel	Chief, OKW	Genobst. 1.11.38	57
6. List	Army Group 5	Genobst. 1.4.39	59
7. Blaskowitz	Army Group 3	Gen. d. Inf. 1.12.35(1)	56
8. von Kluge	Army Group 6	Gen. d. Art. 1.12.35(2)	57
9. von Witzleben	Army Group 2	Gen. d. Inf. 1.3.36	58
10. Dollmann	Corps IX	Gen. d. Art. 1.4.36(2)	57
11. von Kleist	Temporary ret.	Gen. d. Kav. 1.8.36(1)	58
12. Becker	Chief, Army Ordnance	Gen. d. Art. 1.10.36(1)	?
13. von Weichs	Corps XIII	Gen. d. Kav. 1.10.36(3)	58
14. von Reichenau	Army Group 4	Gen. d. Art. 1.10.36(7)	56
15. Heitz	President, Military Court	Gen. d. Art. 1.4.37(1)	61
16. von Kuechler	Corps I	Gen. d. Art. 1.4.37(3)	58

Among these men there was little breadth of outlook or unity of purpose. With few exceptions they were not men of strong individuality, and as a group they were profoundly afflicted with the occupational mental diseases which environment traditionally visited on the officers' corps—true children of *Gross Lichterfelde*. The impact of the rigid seniority system of the German

---

* The listed officers are those who had reached the rank of *General* prior to the Blomberg–Fritsch crisis.

† When Leeb was retired in February, 1938, he was given the *charakterisiert* rank of *Generaloberst*. Upon the outbreak of war he was given straight rank as a *Generaloberst*, with date of rank March 1, 1938, just below Bock on the rank list.

Army is clearly to be seen in the right-hand column; except for the two retired "elders" (Rundstedt and Leeb) and Heitz, all fell within the four-year age bracket fifty-six to fifty-nine.

None of these senior generals stood out as an acknowledged leader. Brauchitsch, as might have been expected from the circumstances surrounding his selection as Commander-in-Chief, had proved far less able to influence Hitler than the much-blamed Blomberg. The ineffable Keitel was nothing but a tool —a ceremonial attendant and military secretary to Hitler. Becker and Heitz were never in the forefront. The remaining twelve were the highest field commanders—the *alte Feldherrn*— of the Army, and it will be useful to take a look at some of them as individuals.

The dean of the officers' corps, ever since von Loetzen's retirement in 1933, was Gerd von Rundstedt, a Prussian military aristocrat of impeccable vintage. The son of a general and a graduate of *Gross Lichterfelde*, Rundstedt boasted an impressive mien and bearing and an acknowledged ability which fully supported his seniority. Although he had proved himself in staff as well as command, he had become "typed" as a field commander; consequently, he was not a "Bendlerstrasse general", and, like Bock and Leeb, was repeatedly passed over when Army commanders-in-chief were in the making. Although not altogether indifferent to politics and civilian pursuits, Rundstedt rarely allowed his actions to stray beyond the manœuvre-ground. He was strong on the field of battle, but quite incapable of taking the helm in affairs of state.

Next in age, Wilhelm Ritter von Leeb* had even less to offer in times of stress. He was a strait-laced and incurious Bavarian Catholic, whose professional competence had been manifested chiefly in excellent studies of defensive position warfare. Unquestionably a devout man, with an outspokenly devout wife, he was singularly ill fitted for the violent power fracas of the Third Reich. There was more than a touch of Beck's caution in Leeb, which eventually found documentary expression, but, in political terms, he was a man without hormones.

The third of this trio of elders, Fedor von Bock, was the *reductio* almost *ad absurdum* of the Prussian *Geist*. Almost, but not quite. His mind was closed to everything but the most immediate consequences of "soldiering for the king", but his fana-

* Despite the "Ritter von", Leeb was not noble-born ; his title derived from the patent of knighthood carried by the Bavarian order, Militaer-Max-Joseph, which had been conferred on him. Therefore, his younger brother was simply Emil Leeb.

tical absorption in his profession, his energy and his utterly nerveless physical courage carried him to the highest levels that he himself could imagine or desire. Like Rundstedt the son of a Prussian general, Bock was born and brought up at the old fortress of Kuestrin on the Oder. Frederican Prussianism was deeply ingrained in his character; he was a violent nationalist, a stern disciplinarian and intent only upon strengthening the Army and advancing his own military career, in which he was distinguished by industry and determination more than brilliance. His arrogance and unmitigated Prussianism sometimes amused but more often irritated his colleagues, and his contempt for politicians or, indeed, civilians of any description did not endear him to the Party. Nevertheless, his singleminded devotion to military matters gave Hitler little cause for distrust, and, after the retirement of Rundstedt and Leeb, Bock stayed on active duty as the senior field commander of the Army.

During the Polish and western campaigns, and the initial attack on Russia, the entire German Army was divided into three Army groups, of which the commanders were, at all times up to the end of 1941, Rundstedt, Bock and Leeb. Their seniority and supremacy in the chain of command set them above their fellows and, had they been versatile, flexible and resourceful men, they could have wielded enormous influence in the Reich. Instead, this critical moment in German history found men at the top of the rank list who were, to be sure, ambitious, energetic and skilled in military science, but whose other faculties were either still-born or atrophied from disuse. The officers' corps respected their seniority and attainments, but did not listen to them in times of crisis because they had nothing to say. Rundstedt's bearing, to be sure, impressed Hitler in the early years, and he was consulted when the selection of a successor to Fritsch was in question. But Rundstedt merely echoed Keitel's opposition to Reichenau, and did nothing to pull the Army's leadership out of the morass into which Hitler, Goering and Himmler had plunged it.

Few of the other senior generals had much more to offer. Reichenau was still firmly harnessed to the Nazi chariot as, to a lesser degree, were List and Dollmann. The last-named was an artillery specialist of no particular consequence, but List had won high favour and promotion to *Generaloberst*, and his experience in Austria and Slovakia presaged his later conquest of the Balkans.

Basically neuter in their orientation within the Third Reich

were Blaskowitz, Weichs and Kuechler. None of these had acquired influence or special prestige within the officers' corps. The same was true of Kleist, whose antediluvian monarchism had led to his retirement during the Blomberg–Fritsch crisis, and who did not return to active duty until just before the outbreak of war.

In fact, out of the entire list of sixteen senior generals, there were by 1939 just two who might perhaps have exhibited the sense of responsibility and strength of mind to offer opposition to Hitler. These were Kluge and Witzleben. Guenther von Kluge, unfortunately, was not sufficiently endowed with either quality. At the generals' meeting of August 4, 1938, Kluge had supported Beck and Adam and proposed a mass resignation if Hitler forced matters to the point of war. Thereafter, Kluge retained some peripheral contacts with the resistance group building up around Schacht and Beck. He was willing to listen and sincerely worried, but he never went beyond a nervous vacillation which accomplished nothing.

Erwin von Witzleben was a more determined man. At the time of Munich, as Commander of the Berlin *Wehrkreis*, he had been the linch-pin of Halder's abortive *Putsch*, and he remained in close contact with Schacht, Beck, Gisevius and the other "conspirators" after Halder drew in his revolutionary horns. In 1939, however, there was little that Witzleben could do. The resignations of Beck and Adam left Witzleben isolated, and his transfer from Berlin to Frankfurt, although a promotion, removed him from the centre of decision. Finally, Witzleben, for all the courage which eventually led him to his death in 1944, did not rise above his brother generals in political aptitude.

Below this group of sixteen seniors on the rank list were about twenty who attained the rank of *General* in 1938 and 1939 before the outbreak of war. Nearly all of them were in their middle fifties; a few were older, while Guderian and Fromm, who were promoted unusually rapidly, were only fifty-one. Among them were a number—including Schroth, Schobert, Busch and Guderian—who were strongly pro-Hitler, but none who were firm opponents. Wietersheim, one of the ablest, had crossed Hitler at the Obersalzberg in August, 1938, and paid for it with loss of favour and the end of his hopes for promotion. Halder was constantly exasperated by the interference of the OKW generals in Army planning, but was in no mood for another attempt at a *coup d'état*. His O. Qu. I, Heinrich von Stuelpnagel, was an able and courageous officer who lost his life in the 1944

242

plot, but in 1939 he had neither the rank nor the opportunity for effective opposition on his own initiative.

Throughout the entire list of generals there were few, if any, who could accurately be described as "personal favourites" of Hitler. Indeed, too much has often been made of the "favourite general" idea—more than the truth warrants. As we have already observed, Hitler was not much given to this sort of thing. True, he regarded generals such as Keitel and Reichenau as more dependable than such as Leeb or Kressenstein, and it was not hard to fall into disfavour, as Beck, Adam, Wietersheim and others soon learned. Some he regarded as abler or more progressive than others, as he showed in November, 1939, when Guderian was again promoted (to *General der Panzertruppen*) and, at Hitler's personal insistence, was relieved as commander of the XVIth Corps, and required to devote his full time to his staff duties as co-ordinator (*Chef*) of all motorized troops.

Indeed, prior to the outbreak of war, Hitler's contacts with individual generals, outside of the OKW and OKH chiefs, were relatively infrequent. He regarded generals as somewhat stodgy technicians, essential to the execution of his grand designs but quite unfit to participate in their conception. A Guderian or a Rommel might attract his favourable attention as a military innovator or a "perfect specimen", but this did not make them his confidants.

But if there were no generals who won Hitler's ear and few who wanted or dared to brook his wrath, there were first-class military minds among the officers' corps. Seeckt had bequeathed an excellent cadre to the generals of the thirties. The formidable command talents of Rundstedt and others ensured good tactical discipline. The imaginative tactical exploitation of motor and armour was made possible by Lutz, Guderian and other specialists. The over-all planning of the campaigns, however, was for the most part the work of a few brilliant staff generals chosen not by Hitler but by the normal processes of selection within the General Staff. Most of them were generals of middle and lower rank, in their late forties and early fifties, who had served extensively in the OKH General Staff or as chiefs of staff to the senior field commanders. Manstein, Halder, Heinrich von Stuelpnagel, von Sodenstern, Paulus, Blumentritt, Wietersheim until he fell from grace, Viebahn until his nerves gave way—these were the planners, the "bright young men" of the German High Command. Jodl too, despite his bedazzlement by the Fuehrer, was of the same stamp; he left OKW and

went on field duty after Munich, but was scheduled for recall to OKW in the event of war.

At the lower reaches, the military proficiency of the officers' corps was not as uniformly good. With the enormous expansion of the Army, Seeckt's cadre was stretched thin. The after-effects of the lean times of Weimar could not be completely eradicated in six years. Furthermore, the younger officers were closer to the temper of the times, and pro-Nazi sentiment was much more intense and widespread than among the senior officers.

In short, 1939 found the officers' corps leaderless and disunited. Much of its professional competence had been retained, but the quality was uneven; it was not a vintage wine. In terms of social consciousness, the corps had even retrogressed. Most of the elders had learned nothing since the Kaiser's abdication, and many of the juniors had succumbed to the lure of Nazism. Faced with times which were sadly out of joint, the officers' corps had neither skill nor will to mend them.

THE WEHRMACHT ON THE EVE OF WAR

The Army that the officers' corps led in 1939 was still suffering from the effects of forced growth. There were not enough experienced non-commissioned officers to go around in the mushrooming units. Many of the rank and file were half trained.

Nonetheless, enormous progress was made during the last year before the war. By 1939, the first three panzer divisions were three years old, and had come a long way since the stumbling procession to Vienna of February, 1938. Most of the regular infantry divisions of the peace-time Army were in an excellent state of training. The reserves were building up rapidly in quantity and quality. The officers and non-coms were energetic and devoted, and the morale of the troops, on the whole, was excellent.

Organizationally, the Army changed very little after the Blomberg–Fritsch crisis and the creation of the OKW early in 1938. Halder enlarged and ramified the OKH General Staff into twelve sections under five *Oberquartiermeister*. Heinrich von Stuelpnagel, as O. Qu. I, supervised five sections (1, 5, 6, 9 and 10), including the important operations section, headed by Oberst von Greiffenberg. Generalmajor Sixt von Armin, the O. Qu. II, directed the two sections (4 and 11) devoted to training of officers and men. As O. Qu. III, Oberst Stapf was charged with the sections for Army organization (2) and technical matters (8). More important was, or could have been, the

O. Qu. IV, Generalmajor von Tippelskirch, in charge of Army intelligence (Sections 3 West and 12 East) and the military attachés. Generalleutnant Erfurth, as O. Qu. V, was the official Army historian (Section 7).

Outside of the General Staff, the OKH signalized changing times by the abolition of the Inspectorate of Cavalry and the designation of Guderian as *Chef der Schnellen Truppen*. As war loomed, the importance increased of the General Army Office *Allgemeines Heeresamt*), which controlled the reserve units and the inspectorates. Its chief, Friedrich Fromm, was promoted to *General* in April, 1939, and rivalled Guderian's record of rapid advancement. At the OKW, Warlimont substituted for Jodl as chief of operations while the latter went to the field as an artillery officer.

One particular shortcoming of the High Command warrants special mention. The excellence of its staff work did not extend into the field of intelligence. This was not primarily due to the fortuitous circumstance that the OKW intelligence section was a focal point of anti-Nazism in the Wehrmacht, with its chief, Admiral Canaris, as well as Oster and others in close touch with the resistance groups. Rather it was due to the tendency, characteristic of other armies, of the officers to regard intelligence work as beneath their dignity. This shortsightedness was destined to cost the Wehrmacht dear.

Likewise, the importance of the war academies declined. The *Wehrmachtakademie* was abolished when Adam, its first and only commandant, was transferred to Army Group 2 in March, 1938. The *Kriegsakademie*, so ostentatiously reopened in 1935, was temporarily closed on the outbreak of war in 1939. When Liebmann, its first commandant, retired in May, 1939, he was the fifth-ranking general on the active list. His successor was Eugen Mueller, a brilliant staff officer but a mere *Generalmajor*. The expansion of the Army in war-time created enormous demand for staff officers, and the institution Scharnhorst had fathered, when reopened in 1940, became a training-school for the many rather than an academy for the pick of the crop.

The official structure of the field Army was not altered after the augmentations consequent upon the annexations of Austria and Bohemia-Moravia. Six Army groups, eighteen corps and fifty-one divisions (thirty-nine infantry, of which four were motorized, plus five armoured, three mountain and four light) were listed in the official order of battle.[2]

In fact, however, the summer of 1939 witnessed a very

substantial enlargement of the Army as the reserves were called up and new formations established. By September, five new corps (numbered XIX, XXI, XXII, XXVII and XXX) had been established, bringing the total of corps headquarters to twenty-three.

At the same time, fifteen new divisions of reservists and two of regular troops,* numbered between 50 and 79, were mobilized.† In August, 1939, another twenty-two divisions of over-age (Landwehr) troops were called up.‡ Finally, just before the outbreak of war, fourteen more divisions were assembled from replacement units.§ Another armoured division was also put together at the last moment.‖ In addition, there was the equivalent of about a division of SS motorized troops, an independent cavalry brigade and various other odds and ends.

Accordingly, if one were concerned with the total strength "on paper" of the German Army at the end of August, 1939, it might be said to have comprised about 106 divisions. This was about double its peace-time strength. Totals of this kind are usually misleading and rarely useful unless broken down into their components. As a bare total, however, this figure is sufficiently accurate; General Halder, in his diary entry for August 22, 1939, referred to German "available forces" totalling 102 divisions. Jodl, however, in his testimony at Nuremberg, declared that Germany entered the war with "some seventy-five divisions".[3] This estimate must have been based on the regular and reserve divisions, and have disregarded or heavily discounted the third and fourth "waves" of Landwehr and replacement divisions.

In practice, of course, the total effective strength of an army can be gauged only in the light of how its units are disposed and what use can be made of them on initiative or to counter enemy action. When war came, most of the third- and fourth-wave divisions were used for static defence on the western front, and some were along the Dutch and Belgian borders, separated from hostile forces by miles of neutral territory. It might fairly be concluded that Germany entered the war with some seventy di-

* From the border commands at Kuestrin and Trier.

† These seventeen divisions were called the "second wave", and the peace-time divisions the "first wave" (*Welle*).

‡ These divisions, chiefly manned by men over thirty-five years of age, were the so-called "third wave", and were numbered between 199 and 246.

§ The "fourth wave" of divisions, numbered between 251 and 269.

‖ Actually the sixth in order of formation, but ultimately designated the 10th Panzer Division, as the four light divisions were converted into panzer divisions during the winter of 1939–40 and given the numbers 6 to 9.

visions fit for first-line use, and thirty-five more which were suitable, in varying degrees, for static defence in the West Wall, guarding neutral borders, protection of lines of communications and other secondary missions.

The strength of the Luftwaffe upon the outbreak of war cannot be as accurately determined. A leading authority on the German Air Force, Wing-Commander Asher Lee, declares [4] that "its first line strength expanded from 1,000 aircraft in 1935 to about 4,000 in the summer of 1939". This is considerably higher than the figure given by Kesselring on the witness stand at Nuremberg.[5] Kessselring, at the time in question, was not at the Air Ministry, but, as commander-in-chief of one of the four air fleets and former Chief of Staff, his information should have been reasonably accurate. He estimated the Luftwaffe's total strength at "approximately 3,000 aircraft", comprising some forty groups (at about thirty planes to a group) of bombers, thirty of fighters, and ten to twelve of dive-bombers, as well as reconnaissance and naval aircraft.

Whatever the precise strength in numbers of airplanes may have been, there is no question but that the Luftwaffe had grown rapidly in both strength and combat efficiency since the Munich crisis. Quite a number of its generals and thousands of pilots and ground crews had had several years of combat experience in Spain. These returned to Germany after the end of the Spanish Civil War in March, and at about the same time there was an additional increment from absorption of the Czechoslovakian aerial resources. All along the line—recruitment, training, airplane design and manufacture, and air defence—there was great progress during the last year of "peace".

This was especially true with respect to fighters and fighter-bombers. The Heinkel 51, Henschel 123 and Arado 68, which had been built in large numbers in the Luftwaffe's infancy, were already obsolescent by 1938. By 1939, they had been largely replaced by the Messerschmitt 109, a single-engined type which remained a basic fighter and interceptor model throughout the war, and the Junkers 87 dive-bomber, more familiarly known as the "Stuka". Against a good interceptor the slow Stuka was helpless, but it was an accurate dive-bomber and, against the weak Polish and French Air Forces, proved invaluable for ground attack.

In bombers the picture was not so bright. The twin-engined medium bombers used in 1939 were chiefly the Dornier 17 "flying pencil" and the Heinkel 111, neither of which proved

adequate. The Junkers 88, the standard long-range bomber during the war, was available by 1939 only in small numbers, and did not see service in Poland. Good as it was, the twin-engined Junkers 88 was not a true heavy bomber.

The lack of four-engined bombers, was indeed, one of the Luftwaffe's most critical shortcomings. But there was little need for such a type during the first year of the war, so its absence was not keenly felt. According to Milch,[6] the production of four-engined bombers was stopped by Goering, acting upon the recommendation of Kesselring (then Chief of the General Staff of the Luftwaffe), on April 29, 1937. The expense of such craft, particularly in terms of critical metals, was high, and for Continental land warfare it was determined that a larger investment in fighters and medium bombers would be preferable. This was also in line with the tactical ideas of Udet, who favoured speed rather than fire-power or armour as a defence against interceptors and flak. Later in the war, as Kesselring put it, "the absence of a four-engined bomber became extremely awkward".

Apart from these deficiencies in bombers, the principal weakness of the Luftwaffe was that in 1939 the reserves of aircraft, to replace losses in the operational squadrons, were very scanty. Fortunately for Goering, there were no heavy losses prior to the Battle of Britain. According to Asher Lee's estimate, at the outbreak of war Germany was producing about 800 combat planes per month. Of these, however, nearly half were obsolescent Heinkel 111s and Dornier 17s; the balance was chiefly comprised of Messerschmitt 109s, with some Stukas and twin-engined Messerschmitt 110s, and an increasing volume of Junkers 88s. This was ample to maintain and, indeed, to expand the Luftwaffe in the early days of easy victories, but its sufficiency was due to the weakness of the opposing air forces and the long months of "phony war".

Organizationally, the Luftwaffe changed little between February, 1938, and the fall of 1939. Early in 1939, however, a number of personnel changes were made in the General Staff and Air Ministry. Stumpff was replaced as Chief of the General Staff by one of Goering's favourite officers, Hans Jeschonnek, barely forty years old and newly promoted to *Generalmajor*.* Simultaneously Milch inserted himself more directly into Luft-

* Stumpff replaced Ruedel, the flak expert, as Chief of Air Defence, but a year later, Stumpff was appointed Commander-in-Chief of the Air Fleet in Norway, and Ruedel resumed his old position.

waffe administration by taking the title of Inspector-General (replacing General der Flieger Bernhard Kuehl *) in addition to his position as Under-secretary at the Air Ministry. Ernst Udet, by now a *Generalleutnant*, was given the resounding title of *Generalluftzeugmeister* and put in charge of aircraft production.

Milch, Jeschonnek and Udet were the three most important subordinates of Goering in the general planning and centralized command of the Air Force. Others who had Goering's ear included his old associates of the Richthofen days, Bodenschatz, Greim and Loerzer. The first-named, promoted to *Generalmajor* in 1938, can best be described as Goering's Keitel. Greim, who became a *Generalleutnant* in 1939, was Chief of Personnel. Loerzer had piloted the plane in which Goering flew as an observer in World War I, and was Goering's oldest war-time friend; by 1939 he was Reich Air Sports Leader, a *Generalleutnant* and commander of an air division, but usually he was at Goering's side as personal confidant.

In the operational commands of the Luftwaffe, few changes were made. Kesselring, Felmy, Sperrle and Loehr continued in command of the four air fleets at Berlin, Brunswick, Munich and Vienna, respectively. Kurt Student developed the paratroopers. Zander, a former naval officer, had been in charge of coastal and naval aviation; in 1939 he was retired as *General der Flieger* and Generalleutnant Hans Geissler, also a naval transferee, took over the coastal command. Other leading air generals were Bogatsch, Dessloch, Kammhuber, Keller, Klepke, Pflugbeil, Quade, Richthofen, Volkmann, and the anti-aircraft specialist Weise.

The air generals were a very much more mixed and, on the whole, a younger group than the Army commanders. The nobility was spread thin; von Greim and von Richthofen were the only ones rejoicing in the prefix that so pervaded the list of Army generals. Those who had come over from the Reichswehr, such as Felmy, Kesselring, Kuehl, Loehr, Quade, Ruedel, Sperrle, Stumpff and Weise, were the same age as or only slightly younger than their Army opposites. But the "irregulars"— Greim, Milch, Loerzer and Udet, for example—were all still in their forties. And, for the most part, the former Army officers shed their old associations and joined the Luftwaffe in spirit as well as body; there was little or no cohesion between the air generals and the Army officers' corps.

But, whatever the shortcomings in cohesion and co-operation

* Kuehl became Chief of Training and Education at the Air Ministry.

between the German Army and Air Force, in bombers and aircraft reserves, in trained staff officers and non-coms, and in other fields, German strength on land and in the air had reached formidable proportions by the summer of 1939—especially formidable in comparison to the opposing resources of the Allies. The French Army, including trained reserves and colonial troops, was larger in numbers, but woefully deficient in both matériel and *esprit*. The Poles had little but heroism and obsolete infantry and cavalry masses. The French had long since been outstripped by Germany in the air. The Royal Air Force was gaining rapidly on the Luftwaffe, but was not yet nearly abreast.

On the high seas, however, the picture was reversed. Raeder could not have hoped to draw even with the Royal Navy short of a decade. He was allowed little more than half the necessary span, and 1939 found the German Navy less than a quarter built and far inferior, in striking power, not only to the Army but also to the adolescent Luftwaffe.

The upper levels of the naval officers' corps were correspondingly thin. At the end of 1938, there were under Raeder only five who had reached the rank of *Admiral*. Of those, the two most worthy of notice were Admiral Rolf Carls, who had been Commander-in-Chief of the High Seas Fleet until 1938 and thereafter headed the regional command in the Baltic, and Admiral Hermann Boehm, who succeeded Carls in command of the fleet.* Doenitz, still in command of the U-boat fleet, was promoted to *Konteradmiral* in 1939. Another powerfully placed officer was Otto Schniewind, promoted to *Vizeadmiral* in 1939, who, from November, 1938, until June, 1941, served as Raeder's Chief of Staff.† The other naval officers destined to play leading parts during the war had not, prior to its outbreak, risen to the highest ranks or top positions in the narrow hierarchy.

The Navy had never been much of a drawing card for the nobility, and by 1939 it was overwhelmingly bourgeois. Of thirty-two admirals of all grades, only four were "vons". Like the Army generals, however, the admirals were rather elderly men. Raeder was sixty-three (a year younger than Rundstedt), while Carls, Boehm and the other senior admirals were in their middle fifties.

---

* The three other *Admiraele* were Albrecht, Saalwaechter and Witzell.
† Schniewind's exact title was Chief of Staff of the Naval War Staff and Chief of the *Marinekommandoamt*.

German naval policy reveals, perhaps as clearly as anything else, the shift that took place in Hitler's thinking after Munich. From 1933 to 1938, the German Navy had made no plans looking toward a high seas fleet which could rival that of England. The battle cruisers *Scharnhorst* and *Gneisenau*, the three pocket battleships, and even the heavy battleships *Bismarck* and *Tirpitz*, were designed and laid down with France and Russia much more in mind than England. With the English, indeed, the Anglo-German naval agreements presupposed that Germany would not compete.

After Munich, however, Hitler raised his sights, and told Raeder that the possibility of war against England would have to be the basis of future naval construction. Raeder, according to his later memoranda and interrogations, told Hitler that, even with maximum effort, the German Navy could not possibly be ready to engage Britain before 1945 or 1946.

On the assumption that five or six years of peace (at least with England) was assured, Raeder, at the end of 1938, developed a new plan of naval construction, known as the "Z Plan". This plan called for the completion, by 1945, of six additional heavy, Diesel-powered battleships, eight heavy and four light cruisers, two aircraft carriers and 126 submarines. The necessary enlargement of the naval bases and shipyards at Wilhelmshaven, Bremen, Hamburg and Kiel, as well as the fortification of Heligoland, was set in motion at the same time.

It was the Kaiser and von Tirpitz all over again. On May 20, 1939, speaking at Brunswick to a Hitler Youth rally, Raeder declared that "capital ships alone are able to win or defend the supremacy of the seas". Some months earlier the basic premises of the Z Plan had been embodied in a "Draft Study of Naval Warfare against England". Raeder submitted it for comment to Admiral Carls, then commanding the High Seas Fleet. In response Carls observed that he was in "full agreement with the main theme of the study", and went on to declare: [7]

"1. If, according to the Fuehrer's decision, Germany is to acquire a position as a world power, she needs not only sufficient colonial possessions but also secure naval communications and secure access to the ocean.

"2. Both requirements can only be fulfilled in opposition to Anglo-French interests.... It is unlikely that they can be achieved by peaceful means. The decision to make Germany a world power therefore forces upon us the necessity of making the corresponding preparations for war.

"3. War against England means at the same time war against the Empire, against France, probably against Russia as well as a large number of countries overseas, in fact against a third or a half of the whole world.

"It can only be justified and have a chance of success if it is prepared *economically* as well as *politically* and *militarily* and waged with the aim of conquering for Germany an outlet to the ocean." *

But the imminence of war, as the Polish crisis deepened, put an end to these grandiose designs. Raeder was obliged to scrap the Z Plan and face war with a surface fleet inferior even to the French. The *Bismarck* and the *Tirpitz* were not yet completed; the *Scharnhorst* and *Gneisenau* had been commissioned but were not yet fully "shaken down". Of the three pocket battleships, the *Deutschland* and *Graf Spee* were ready for action, but not yet the *Scheer*. Two heavy cruisers, the *Bluecher* and *Hipper*, were in commission, and the *Prinz Eugen* was nearing completion. There were five light cruisers—*Koenigsberg*, *Nuernberg*, *Koeln*, *Leipzig* and *Karlsruhe*. In addition, and serviceable for training and coastal use, there were the two old battleships, *Schlesien* and *Schleswig-Holstein* and the light cruiser *Emden*. There were no aircraft carriers and only one—the *Graf Zeppelin*—was completed during the war.

Faced with the overwhelming Anglo-French superiority, such a fleet could not venture on the high seas *as a fleet*. The vessels could be used in the narrow waters of the Baltic, for nearby landing operations (as they were in Norway), and, singly or in small groups, as commerce raiders. Beyond this, as Raeder gloomily observed in a memorandum written the day Britain declared war, the German surface forces "can do no more than show that they know how to die gallantly and thus are willing to create the foundations for later reconstruction". Thus did Raeder, on the eve of the most disastrous war in German history, echo Beck's words at the dedication of the *Kriegsakademie* in 1935: "Just as the greatest defeat of the Prussian Army became the foundation for its marvellous resurrection, so the hour of death of our old magnificent Army on July 28, 1919, led to the life of the young *Reichsheer* . . . only in that way is losing ennobled by the pride of a glorious fall."

With the scrapping of the Z Plan, German naval policy was again concentrated on expansion of the submarine arm. The estimates of German U-boat strength in September, 1939, as

* Undoubtedly, Carls meant the North Sea coasts of France, Belgium and Holland.

given by Raeder and Doenitz at Nuremberg (forty-eight commissioned, of which about thirty had completed their tests and fifteen were capable of operations in the Atlantic), are considerably lower than those established by the captured German naval documents. These [8] seem to establish conclusively that fifty-seven submarines had been completed by September 3, 1939. However, not more than half were large enough and sufficiently broken in for action in the Atlantic. In fact, eighteen were sent into action against England at the start of war, and three others put to sea in the Baltic to support the operations against Poland. In his memorandum of September 3, 1939, Raeder stated that "about twenty-six boats are capable of operations in the Atlantic; the submarine arm is still much too weak, however, to have any decisive effect on the war".

As of the time he wrote, Raeder's judgment was probably correct. A large building programme, however, was well under way, and by the spring of 1940, the number of ocean-going U-boats had been doubled. As matters developed, the outcome of the struggle between the U-boat and Allied commerce was not to be determined so much in terms of numbers as by a race between submarine design and anti-submarine technique and tactics. The airplane, radar, sonar and other new devices soon changed the whole nature of submarine warfare.

Such, in outline, was the strength of the three arms of the Wehrmacht as war approached in 1939. Behind it lay the economic and scientific resources of the Third Reich which Schacht and, since 1937, Goering had been responsible for mobilizing on a war economy basis.

Goering, to be sure, had been thumping the tub for war mobilization indefatigably and enthusiastically ever since the end of 1936, when he had told the industrialists [9] that war was already at hand except for the "actual shooting", and had promised them that in the event of victory, "business will be sufficiently compensated". Early in 1937 he had launched the Reich upon an enormous project, *sub nomine* the Hermann Goering Works, to end Germany's dependence on imported Swedish iron ore by exploiting the low-grade ore deposits in the Salzgitter region. "Iron is the decisive raw material to win freedom and space for the people," he declared.

After Munich, violent efforts were made to shoot adrenalin into the armament build-up. On October 14th, Goering called in his chief economic subordinates, and announced that Hitler had ordered him "to carry out a gigantic programme compared

to which previous achievements are insignificant". Within the shortest possible time, "the Air Force is to be increased fivefold", the Navy should expedite its armament, and "the Army should procure large amounts of weapons at the fastest rate, particularly heavy artillery and tanks".

At this same meeting another note was struck which, to many of the industrialists, was a siren song: "The Sudetenland has to be exploited with all means. . . . Czechs and Slovaks will form German dominions. They must be exploited to the utmost." Magnates like Krupp, Flick and the Farben directors foresaw the prospect of economic *imperium* on a scale never before imagined.

The *Anschluss* and the conquest of the Sudetenland had already offered opportunities for economic aggrandizement. The Farben interests had been, perhaps, the most rapacious of all. Within a month after *Anschluss*, Farben was equipped with the first of a series of "new order" programmes—"The New Order of the Major Chemical Industries of Austria". The first goal of this plan was for Farben to absorb the largest chemical enterprise in Austria—the gunpowder plant Skodawerke Wetzler A.G. To induce the Nazi government to support their claim, Farben underlined the "necessary" replacement of Jews by Aryans in the management, and the need for integrating the Austrian chemical industry with the Four-Year Plan.

Much the same thing happened in Czechoslovakia. The Czech chemical trust, the Prager Verein, owned plants at Aussig and Falkenau in the Sudetenland which Farben was eyeing as early as April, 1938. Once again, the Jew and the Four-Year Plan were trotted out and, soon after Munich, the Farben directors were "negotiating" with the Prager Verein for the "sale" of the Sudeten plants. In November, by dint of arrogant threats, the transaction was consummated.

Farben's behaviour was typical rather than unique. The principal Austrian metal works—the Berndorfer Metallwarenfabrik (originally founded by Arthur Krupp, a relative of the Essen Krupps)—was taken over by Krupp, with Goering's assistance, soon after *Anschluss*. As the Krupp historian put it, the Berndorfer acquisition was "a pleasant consequence of the annexation". In accordance with the extended Four-Year Plan, Berndorfer was soon turning out munitions and other war materials for the Wehrmacht. Friedrich Flick used the pressure of the Aryanization laws and the Sudeten occupation to expand his coal reserves from the holdings of the Petscheks, a Jewish

family of Prague and Aussig. The leading German banks, and especially the Dresdner Bank, were entrusted by Goering with the task of gaining control of the most important Czech industries, and the Dresdner Bank itself took over the big Czech chain of banks, the Boehmische Escomptebank.

In essence if not in form, men like the Farben and Krupp directors, Flick, Rasche of the Dresdner Bank, and Pleiger of the Hermann Goering Works, were part and parcel of the Wehrmacht just as much as Rundstedt, Milch and Raeder. Some of them, such as Carl Krauch of Farben, held high official positions in addition to their private industrial capacities. Many of them enjoyed closer relations with the Party leaders than did the generals. Goering, especially, maintained close relations with the business world; Flick, Rasche and certain other business leaders were also on singularly good terms with Heinrich Himmler.

By 1939 the Wehrmacht was, at bottom, the creature of all the leading Germans—generals, admirals, Party leaders, diplomats and business magnates—whose ambitions depended on German military domination of the Continent, and the effective use of German power for conquest. All of these protagonists of *Macht* had, to paraphrase the Krupp historian, found "pleasant consequences" from the victories of the *Blumenkrieg*. All were ready for another helping, and most were willing to let Hitler decide when to ask for more.

The aims and views of these men did not much depend on whether or not they wore uniforms. In April, 1939, Carl Krauch, in his capacity as "Plenipotentiary-General of Minister President Feldmarschall Goering for Special Questions of Chemical Production", submitted a "work report" in which he declared:

"When on June 30, 1938, the objective of increased production in the spheres of work discussed here was given by the *Feldmarschall*, it seemed as if the political leadership could determine independently the timing and extent of the political revolution in Europe and could avoid a rupture with a group of powers under the leadership of Great Britain. Since March of this year, there is no longer any doubt that this hypothesis does not exist any more. The economic war against the anti-Comintern powers under the leadership of Great Britain, France and the U.S.A., which has already been conducted secretly for a long time, has now been finally opened; as time passes, it will become more and more severe.

"At Wilhelmshaven, the Fuehrer expressed his determination not to remain passive in view of this policy of encirclement which

for the time being is economic and political but is aiming ultimately at military isolation.

*   *   *   *   *

"By the policy of encirclement manifested by the enemy, a *new situation* is created:

"It is essential for Germany to strengthen its own war potential as well as that of its allies to such an extent that the coalition is equal to the efforts of practically the rest of the world. *This can be achieved only by new, strong and combined efforts by all of the allies, and by expanding and improving the greater economic domain* corresponding to the improved raw material basis of the coalition, *peaceably at first*, to the Balkans and Spain.

"*If action does not follow upon these thoughts with the greatest possible speed, all sacrifices of blood in the next war will not spare us the bitter end which already once before we have brought upon ourselves owing to lack of foresight and fixed purposes.*"

Compare Krauch's memorandum with the one written by Admiral Carls a few months earlier [10] giving, as the justification for war "against a third or a half of the whole world", the aim of "conquering for Germany an outlet to the ocean". Or compare it with Goering's speeches to the businessmen and Hitler's to the generals. Despite all the clashes of temperament and judgment—despite the caution which made the generals and admirals want to hold back until 1943, or 1944, or 1945, and the demon which drove Hitler to force his luck and betrayed his own malignant but phenomenal political genius—these men were at one in their aim. They wanted to make the world their own, and they were prepared to smash it if they could not have their way.

"CASE WHITE"

The next step along the way, toward which the Fuehrer was already pointing, was Poland. Just as the General Staff plan for the invasion of Czechoslovakia had been given the covername *Fall Gruen*, so the plan for the destruction of Poland was dubbed *Fall Weiss* (Case White). The OKW directive which first bore the name was issued on April 3, 1939, just after Chamberlain's verbal guarantee of Poland and Hitler's angry reply at the launching of the *Tirpitz* at Wilhelmshaven.

There were, however, a few antecedents. Late in November, 1938, the existing military directives, covering the protection of German frontiers and preparations for the liquidation of the remainder of Czechoslovakia and the occupation of Memel, were supplemented by one for the occupation of Danzig. This project

was to be covered under the name "Transport Exercise Stolp-muende" and its governing hypothesis was "a *quasi-revolutionary* occupation of Danzig, exploiting a favourable political situation, *not a war against Poland*". The occupation was to be effected by troops from Keuchler's Ist Corps in East Prussia, possibly with a naval landing in support.[11] This directive was issued soon after Ribbentrop had put forward to Lipski the idea that Danzig should be reunited with Germany, no doubt with the hope that the Poles might wobble and that provoked incidents could be exploited to "justify" a German occupation.

Hitler's efforts to persuade the Poles to sanction the annexation of Danzig came to nothing, and in February and March Germany's war machine was brought closer to mobilization. Officers from the OKH ordnance department toured the Farben explosives plants, and a new production plan, called the "Rapid Plan", was instituted to give priority to the particular explosives most needed in the immediate emergency. On February 18th, a new mobilization directive for the civil administration was issued, which carefully distinguished three different stages of mobilization: (*a*) the "period of tension" (advance measures to lay the basis for mobilization, without provoking foreign reactions), (*b*) "X-case" (mobilization of the armed forces, and perhaps general mobilization, but without public announcement and camouflaged as far as possible), and (*c*) "Mob-case" (mobilization, with public announcement, on a general basis). This directive was to become effective on April 1, 1939.

The sequence of events which led directly to the *Weiss* directive occurred during the last ten days of March. On the 21st, Ribbentrop had, for the first time, pressed Lipski sharply on Danzig, and Lipski had gone to Warsaw to stress the urgency of the problem. On March 25th, Hitler departed from Berlin, leaving a memorandum of information and instructions for Brauchitsch. Danzig was the first item: [12]

> "Lipski will return from Warsaw on Sunday, March 26th. He was commissioned to ask whether Poland would be prepared to come to some terms with regard to Danzig. The Fuehrer left Berlin during the night of March 25th; he does not wish to be here when Lipski returns. Ribbentrop shall negotiate preliminarily. The Fuehrer does *not* wish, however, to solve the Danzig problem by the use of force. He would not like to drive Poland into the arms of Great Britain by doing so.
>
> "A military occupation of Danzig would be considered only if

257

Lipski gives a hint that the Polish government could not take the responsibility toward their own people to cede Danzig voluntarily and the solution would be made easier for them by a *fait accompli*."

Here, then, was the true reason for the preparations being made for "Transport Exercise Stolpmuende". It was a characteristically Hitlerian analysis—characteristic especially of his low regard for the representatives of parliamentary governments. For once, however, the Fuehrer had badly misgauged his immediate opponents and intended victims. The Polish government was far from looking for a *fait accompli* in Danzig or elsewhere. And while Hitler was concerned to avoid driving Poland "into the arms of Great Britain" over the Danzig question, Chamberlain was getting ready to issue his "assurance", and soon Colonel Beck was in London cementing the Anglo-Polish *entente*.

As late as March 25th, accordingly, it is clear that Hitler had not yet decided that the time was ripe to go beyond the Danzig question and attack Poland herself. It is equally clear that Hitler planned to destroy Poland at the first opportunity. These matters, too, were dealt with in the memorandum for Brauchitsch:

> "For the time being, the Fuehrer does not intend to solve the Polish question. However, it should now be worked on. A solution in the near future would have to be based on especially favourable political conditions. In that case Poland shall be knocked down so completely that it need not be taken into account as a political factor for the next decades. The Fuehrer has in mind as such a solution a boundary advanced from the eastern border of East Prussia to the eastern tip of Upper Silesia."

In fact, as we have seen, the English guarantee to Poland immediately and powerfully stimulated Hitler's desire to "solve the Polish question". Still smarting from English intervention in the Czech situation, he was enraged anew by Chamberlain's *démarche* of March 31st. Danzig took second place in his thinking, which gravitated rapidly toward the goal of a speedy and definitive "settlement" with Poland.

The military *point de départ* for the Polish venture was the directive *Fall Weiss*, circulated in five copies under a covering memorandum by Keitel, dated April 3, 1939.[13] Keitel's memorandum informed the three commanders-in-chief that the "Directive for the Uniform Preparation for War by the Wehrmacht for 1939–40" would be reissued by the middle of April. Parts I (Frontier Defence) and III (Danzig) of the directive

258

would remain unchanged as to "basic principles". A new Part II (*Fall Weiss*) was enclosed with the memorandum. It began with the declaration that "the present attitude of Poland requires . . . the effecting of military preparations to exclude, if necessary, any threat from this direction forever". The succeeding section on "Political Requirements and Aims" read as follows:

"German relations with Poland continue to be based on the principle of avoiding any quarrels. Should Poland, however, change her policy towards Germany, based up to now on the same principles as our own, and adopt a threatening attitude towards Germany, a final settlement might become necessary, notwithstanding the pact in effect with Poland.

"The aim then will be to destroy Polish military strength, and create in the east a situation which satisfies the requirements of national defence. The Free State of Danzig will be proclaimed a part of the Reich territory at the outbreak of the conflict, at the latest.

"The political leadership considers it its task in this case to isolate Poland if possible, that is to say, to limit the war to Poland only.

"The development of increasing internal crises in France and the resulting British cautiousness might produce such a situation in the not too distant future.

"Intervention by Russia so far as she would be able to do this cannot be expected to be of any use for Poland, because this would imply Poland's destruction by Bolshevism.

"The attitude of the *Baltic States* will be determined wholly by German military exigencies.

"On the German side, Hungary cannot be considered a certain ally. Italy's attitude is determined by the Berlin–Rome Axis."

The ensuing "military conclusions" reflected Hitler's increasing preoccupation with Anglo-French interventionism: "The great objectives in the building up of the Wehrmacht will continue to be determined by the antagonism of the 'Western Democracies'. *Fall Weiss*' constitutes only a precautionary complement to these preparations. . . . The isolation of Poland will be more easily maintained, even after operations have begun, if we succeed in starting the war with heavy, sudden blows and in gaining rapid successes." Accordingly, "the task of the Wehrmacht is to destroy the Polish armed forces. For this reason a surprise attack is to be striven for and prepared."

Although the political preamble to *Fall Weiss* was phrased in pacific and defensive terms, Keitel's covering memorandum

bore ominous resemblance to the *Gruen* directive of May, 1938. For it informed the commanders-in-chief that Hitler had ordered that:

"1. Preparations must be made in such a way that the operation can be carried out at any time from and after September 1, 1939.

"2. The OKW is to draw up a precise time-table for *Fall Weiss* and to arrange by conferences the synchronized timing between the three branches of the Wehrmacht.

"3. The plans of the three branches and the timetable must be submitted to OKW by May 1, 1939."

On April 11th the entire directive was reissued. In addition to the three basic annexes on "Frontier Defence", "*Fall Weiss*" and "Danzig", it included a series of appendices and "special orders". These revealed that *Weiss* would probably not be preceded by a general, publicly announced mobilization, but more probably by the camouflaged "X-case". An eastern and a western "Zone of Operations" were delimited, in which Brauchitsch, as Commander-in-Chief of the Army, would have "executive power", which he was authorized to re-delegate to his Army commanders. Supporting Air Force and Waffen-SS units were also to be subordinated to Brauchitsch, while Army formations might be turned over to Goering for airborne operations.

The ensuing six weeks were chiefly occupied with the staff work to implement the general requirements of *Weiss*. On April 28th, Schniewind distributed to the principal naval commands a revised directive [14] for "Transport Exercise Stolpmuende" which also referred to *Weiss*, and informed the recipients that it envisaged conflict with Poland and that a "pertinent directive" would be forthcoming within a few weeks: "The measures immediately called for in such an event principally involve blockade operations before the Polish harbours, the blockading of Danzig Bay, and the usual security measures in the North Sea and the Baltic."

The Army's preparations were already much further advanced. By May 7th, a "Working Staff Rundstedt"—similar to the "Working Staff Leeb" set up in the summer of 1938 for *Gruen* *—had prepared an "Estimate of the Situation". [15] It was signed by Oberst Guenther Blumentritt, Chief of the Training Section (4) of the OKH General Staff in Berlin; the other two members were Manstein (then Commander of the 18th Infantry Division at Liegnitz) and Rundstedt himself, who was then in

* *Supra*, p. 210. In both cases Manstein and Blumentritt were the two staff officers.

retirement at Kassel, but who was soon ordered to Berlin to assume command of an Army group, with Manstein as his Chief of Staff, for the Polish campaign.

Blumentritt's estimate reveals that the disposition of forces and grand outlines of the Polish attack had already been determined. It was handwritten in two copies, of which one was retained by the Working Staff and the other sent to Heinrich von Stuelpnagel, the O. Qu. I of OKH.

Blumentritt drew up his plan on the assumption that the Poles would, if possible, defend western Poland, where the major industries were located, but that their over-all strategy would be determined by their judgment as to whether they could expect "speedy and certain" aid from other powers, or "count only on uncertain aid". In the former case, the Poles could be expected to "make a stand with the bulk of their forces *west* of the Vistula, offer stubborn resistance, and withdraw step by step behind the San–Vistula–Narew line". The German attacking forces would therefore be concentrated in the west and south to force a decision west of the Vistula. If, however, the Polish estimate of foreign aid were pessimistic, they would withdraw more rapidly to a stand east of the Vistula. In that event, the German Army should be split, and strong forces sent from East Prussia and Slovakia east of the Vistula, "in order to smash the bulk of the Polish Army, thus preventing any resistance behind the Vistula and in order to fight the decisive battle around Warsaw and not further east".

The strength of the Polish forces was estimated at "about fifty-five infantry divisions, twelve cavalry brigades and two motorized units". Accordingly, "if, like the Czechs in the autumn of 1938, they were to make the mistake of defending their entire border", there would be but one infantry division for every 18 kilometres of the Polish–German frontier. With such dispersion, Blumentritt concluded, the front "can easily be pierced by concentrated forces at several points". Wisdom, therefore, dictated that the Poles should hold the border only with screening forces and keep mobile concentrations in reserve.

The remainder of Blumentritt's memorandum sketched the composition and mission of Army Group South, to be commanded by Rundstedt; the Working Staff was actually a planning cadre for the staff of this Army group. Subordinate to Army Group South there were to be three armies—the Eighth in northern Silesia based on Breslau, the Tenth in the south-eastern tip of Silesia, and the Fourteenth in Moravia and Slovakia. The

Tenth, in the centre, was to be the strongest and the *Schwerpunkt* of the attack. It was to "push through in deep formation and advance, without worrying about its flanks, to Warsaw. In the vanguard will be the panzer and light divisions and behind, as support, the motorized infantry divisions; the whole will be supported by the Air Force and heavy artillery. The infantry divisions will then follow up as quickly as possible."

The Fourteenth Army, emerging from Moravia and Slovakia, would have the double mission of protecting the eastern flank of the Tenth, and advancing into Poland, east of the Vistula, to Przemysl: "Thus, although the Fourteenth will maintain contact with the Tenth, it will nevertheless dominate the area east of the Vistula by means of mobile units. . . . It will then also be in position to advance on Warsaw with the units east of the Vistula if no attack is expected from the east." The Eighth Army was to have a relatively minor role. Apparently the divisional strength of the armies had already been projected, for Blumentritt observed that it was "still too strong for its mission". The Eighth was simply to protect the north-western flank of the Tenth, and to advance through Lodz toward the Vistula when "the situation is cleared up".

Three days after the Blumentritt estimate, on May 10th, a new annex to the *Weiss* directive, dealing with economic warfare, was distributed by OKW. This declared that "the objective is to capture the Polish economic installations intact, so far as possible. They may be attacked only in case of immediate military necessity. The quick occupation of the industrial districts of Polish Upper Silesia and Teschen is important for the war economy. All sea-borne imports to Poland must be blocked by the Navy." If England entered the war, cutting off German imports from the Atlantic, the Navy should concentrate on protecting maritime trade in the Baltic and along the coasts of the North Sea. Funk, as Plenipotentiary for War Economy, would control economic warfare in co-operation with the Economic Staff of OKW, under Generalmajor Thomas. War with England would call for increased trade with Italy and the Balkans, and safeguarding of the vital Swedish iron-ore imports. On the economic offensive, "the most important instruments of the attack against the enemy economy are the Navy and Air Force. Their measures will be supplemented by sabotage warfare. . . . It may be the mission of the Army to extend our German living space by occupation of enemy territory of special importance to our economy."

The generality and superficiality of this economic directive is in striking and significant contrast to the sure, professional touch of the military plans. The officers' corps was still as narrow in outlook as it was skilled in its special trade; the Third Reich was not well organized for total war.

On May 16th, Raeder finally completed the initial naval directive for *Weiss*.[16] Admiral Albrecht (Group Commander East) was charged with both planning and execution of all naval action in the Baltic. Belligerent operations by the German Navy would begin prior to any formal declaration of war; consequently "a deviation from the pattern of a regular declaration of blockade and mine warning is expected". The hour for the commencement of belligerent action was fixed long before the day. Upon the insistence of the Navy and with the approval of OKW, it ("Y-hour") was fixed at three hours before sunrise. After fourteen hours had elapsed, German submarines in Danzig Bay were to sink Polish and neutral merchant ships without warning "in order to maintain the fiction of hits by mines".

The hardening of Hitler's attitude toward Poland in 1939 offers numerous striking parallels to what had happened a year earlier with respect to Czechoslovakia. In both cases Hitler began by manifesting a relatively calm intention to work toward a situation in which a combination of diplomatic and military pressures would enable him to "settle" matters on his own terms. In both cases the diplomatic offensive coincided with the preparation of a military directive which was phrased in terms of defence and precaution, but called for the completion of preparations by a certain date—October 1, 1938, in *Gruen* and September 1, 1939, in *Weiss*. In both cases an unexpected development abroad—the Czech call-up of reserves on May 21, 1938, in one case, Chamberlain's guarantee of March 31, 1939, in the other—either enraged Hitler or provided him with a "justification", so that his decision to force the issue at the scheduled time became fixed. And in both cases, he called a meeting of "high brass"—in 1938 the meeting of May 28th—to declare his will in the matter. In 1939 the meeting was held on May 23rd and, happily, the faithful Schmundt, promoted to *Oberstleutnant* after Munich, was on hand and took the minutes.[17]

The meeting was held in Hitler's study at the Reichschancellery in Berlin and, according to Schmundt's notes, there were present Keitel and Warlimont from OKW, Brauchitsch and Halder from the Army, Goering, Milch, Jeschonnek and Bodenschatz from the Air Force, Raeder and Schniewind from the

Navy, and three adjutants in addition to Schmundt.[18] At Nuremberg, Raeder pictured the occasion as an "academic lecture", and Brauchitsch labelled it as not a conference but a speech. It is clear from the minutes that Hitler did most of the talking, and Goering perhaps described it most accurately as "typical of the conferences which the Fuehrer used to hold when he had some particular purpose in mind which he wanted to achieve and wanted to give this aim the necessary emphasis".[19]

At the outset, Hitler methodically defined the purposes of the conference as:

"1. Analysis of the situation.
"2. Definition of the tasks of the Wehrmacht arising from that situation.
"3. Exposition of the consequences of the tasks.
"4. Ensuring the secrecy of all decisions and work resulting from the consequences. Secrecy is the first essential of success."

Schmundt's minutes set forth the exposition of these points in what he called "systematized form". We must examine Hitler's presentation, accordingly, through the lens of Schmundt's *précis*. Perhaps it is clouded or scratched, but there is no evidence of radical distortion. And, from the standpoint of historical analysis, this is one of the most remarkable and revealing of the Hitler military conferences—remarkable because so many of Hitler's intentions and predictions soon came to pass, and revealing because Hitler's internal uncertainty and confusion in the face of the ultimate in *Realpolitik* emerge so clearly. Although the war lay several months in the future, Hitler was no longer in full command of the situation he had created or in full control of himself and the power at his disposal. He was groping and, from this time on, his higher strategy was increasingly governed by jerky impulse rather than the continuity of sure planning.

Hitler began by stressing the enormous military, political and economic progress which Germany had made during the first six years of the Third Reich. This progress, however, had upset the "balance of power" which the other great powers had struck "without the participation of Germany". Consequently, all German demands were regarded as "encroachments". But Germany must press on despite this opposition:

"A mass of 80 million people has solved the ideological problems. So, too, must the economic problems be solved. No German can evade the creation of the necessary economic conditions for this. The solution of the problem demands courage. The principle, by which one evades solving the problem by adapting oneself to cir-

264

cumstances, is inadmissible. Circumstances must rather be adapted to aims. This is impossible without invasion of foreign states or attacks upon foreign property."

Hitler cautioned his listeners against being appeased by gifts of colonial territory. "This does not solve the food problem—blockade!" Whereas, and straight out of *Mein Kampf*, "if fate brings us into conflict with the west, the possession of extensive areas in the east will be advantageous". The hideous slave-labour practices of the war years were foreshadowed: "The population of non-German areas will ... be available as a source of labour."

Accordingly, since *Lebensraum* in eastern Europe was the prime objective, Poland was the logical target. Hitler now brought von Seeckt's thesis up to date:

"The Pole is no supplementary enemy. Poland will always be on the side of our adversaries. In spite of treaties of friendship, Poland has always had the secret intention of exploiting every opportunity to do us harm.

"Danzig is not the subject of the dispute at all. It is a question of expanding our living space in the east and of securing our food supplies, of the settlement of the Baltic problem. Food supplies can be expected only from thinly populated areas. Over and above the natural fertility, thoroughgoing German exploitation will enormously increase the surplus.

"There is no other possibility for Europe."

However, settlement of the Polish question could not be undertaken without regard to the western powers:

"The Polish problem is inseparable from conflict with the west.

"Poland's internal power of resistance to Bolshevism is doubtful. Thus Poland is of doubtful value as a barrier against Russia.

"It is questionable whether military success in the west can be achieved by a quick decision; questionable, too, is the attitude of Poland.

"The Polish government will not resist pressure from Russia. Poland sees danger in a German victory in the west and will attempt to rob us of the victory."

From all this, Hitler drew the categorical conclusion:

"There is, therefore, no question of sparing Poland, and we are left with the decision—

"*To attack Poland at the first suitable opportunity.*

"We cannot expect a repetition of the Czech affair. There will be war."

But when and under what circumstances? Here the presentation grew muddy and internally inconsistent. At first, Hitler seemed to say that there could be no war with Poland unless western non-intervention was assured.

> "Therefore, the Fuehrer must reserve the right to give the final order to attack. There must be no simultaneous conflict with the western powers (France and England)."

Immediately, however, he reversed his field:

> "If it is not certain that a German–Polish conflict will not lead to war in the west, then the fight must be primarily against England and France."

Then the two conflicting ideas were inextricably and hopelessly intermingled:

> "Fundamentally, therefore, conflict with Poland, beginning with an attack on Poland, will only be successful if the western powers keep out of it. If this is impossible, then it will be better to attack in the west and to settle Poland at the same time.
> "The isolation of Poland is a matter of skilful politics."

Almost immediately, however, there emerged an indication of how the Fuehrer hoped to solve the dilemma:

> "Economic relations with Russia are possible only if political relations have improved. A cautious trend is apparent in Press comment. It is not impossible that Russia will show herself to be disinterested in the destruction of Poland. Should Russia take steps to oppose us, our relations with Japan may become closer."

At first, it was not clear whether Hitler thought that Russian neutrality might sway England and France toward non-intervention in a German–Polish war, or whether he thought it would, by eliminating a two-front war, enable Germany to face war with the western powers. At all events, however, Hitler made it clear that he considered England, rather than France, the major threat to his plans:

> ". . . The Fuehrer doubts the possibility of a peaceful settlement with England. We must prepare ourselves for the conflict. England sees in our development the foundation of a hegemony which would weaken England. England is therefore our enemy, and the conflict with England will be a life-and-death struggle.
> "*What will this struggle be like?* England cannot deal with Germany and subjugate us with a few powerful blows. It is imperative for England that the war should be brought as near to the Ruhr

Basin as possible. French blood will not be spared (West Wall). The possession of the Ruhr Basin will determine the duration of our resistance."

To protect the Ruhr, German possession of the Low Countries would be vital. Having improved on Seeckt, Hitler now echoed Bethmann-Hollweg on "scraps of paper":

"The Dutch and Belgian air bases must be occupied by armed force. Declarations of neutrality must be ignored. If England and France intend the war between Germany and Poland to lead to a conflict, they will support Holland and Belgium in their neutrality and make them build fortifications, in order finally to force them into co-operation.

"Albeit under protest, Belgium and Holland will yield to pressure.

"Therefore, if England intends to intervene in the Polish war, we must occupy Holland with lightning speed. We must aim at securing a new defence line on Dutch soil up to the Zuider Zee."

As he went on, Hitler spoke less of Poland and centred his attention almost entirely on England. Certainly he was fully aware of the risks inherent in his proposed course of action: "The idea that we can get off cheaply is dangerous; there is no such possibility. We must burn our boats, and it is no longer a question of justice or injustice, but of life or death for 80 million human beings." He stacked up the odds favouring and opposing the English:

"*England* is the driving force against Germany. Her strength lies in the following.

"1. The British themselves are proud, courageous, tenacious, firm in resistance, and gifted as organizers. They know how to exploit every new development. They have the love of adventure and bravery of the Nordic race. Quality is lowered by dispersal. The German average is higher.

"2. World power in itself. It has been constant for 300 years. Extended by the acquisition of allies. This power is not merely something concrete, but must also be considered as a psychological force embracing the entire world. Add to this immeasurable wealth, with consequential financial credit.

"3. Geopolitical safety and protection by strong man-power and a courageous Air Force.

"*England's weakness.*

"If in World War I we had had two battleships and two cruisers more, and if the Battle of Jutland had begun in the morning, the British fleet would have been defeated and England brought to

her knees. It would have meant the end of the war. It was formerly not sufficient to defeat the fleet; landings had to be made in order to defeat England. England could provide her own food supplies. Today that is no longer possible.

"The moment England's food supply routes are cut, she is forced to capitulate. The import of food and oil depends on the fleet's protection.

"If the German Air Force attacks English territory, England will not be forced to capitulate in one day. But if the fleet is destroyed, immediate capitulation will be the result."

This talk of Jutland and of destroying the British fleet might have been more to the point had Hitler delayed his attack until 1944 or 1945, when the Z Plan would have approached completion. In 1939 it was nothing but wishful thinking. Hitler's celerity on the piano keys was, as usual, phenomenal, but he could no longer observe the tempo. He spoke hopefully of the results to be achieved by a surprise attack, but simultaneously recognized that its benefits could be nullified by weather, poor security or simple bad luck. In the end, he stated a basic strategy which predicted, with remarkable fidelity, the military events of 1939–40:

"1. An effort must be made to deal the enemy a significant or the final decisive blow. Considerations of right and wrong, or treaties, do not enter into the matter. This will only be possible if we are not involved in a war with England on account of Poland.

"2. In addition to the surprise attack, preparations for a long war must be made, while opportunities on the Continent for England are eliminated.

"The Army will have to hold positions essential to the Navy and Air Force. If Holland and Belgium are successfully occupied and held, and if France is also defeated, the fundamental conditions for a successful war against England will have been secured.

"England can then be blockaded from western France at close quarters by the Air Force, while the Navy, with its submarines can extend the range of the blockade."

Hitler next drew some lessons from the First World War. "With a more powerful Navy at the outbreak of war, or a wheeling movement by the Army toward the Channel ports, the end would have been different." In 1939, the Navy was not even a shadow of Tirpitz' High Seas Fleet. But the "wheeling movement toward the Channel ports" foreshadowed the 1940 alteration of the Schlieffen plan, and the armoured dash to Abbéville that split the Anglo-French forces and culminated in the Dunkirk evacuation. "A country cannot be brought to defeat by an

air force." This reflected the Luftwaffe's discarding of four-engined heavy bombers and Udet's concentration on medium bombers and tactical air strength. "The unrestricted use of all resources is essential." True, but owing to the dilettantism of the Nazi bigwigs and the narrow outlook of the officers' corps, efficient "total war" was never achieved, and not even approached until the advent to power of Albert Speer in 1943. "Once the Army, in co-operation with the Air Force and Navy, has taken the most important positions, industrial production will cease to flow into the bottomless pit of the Army's battles and can be diverted to benefit the Air Force and Navy." This great expectation went the way of all flesh with the invasion of Russia in 1941.

Hitler concluded by reading his audience a lecture on secrecy. This, he declared, could not be assured if high-level inter-service planning was committed to the three general staffs. "The Fuehrer has, therefore, decided to order the formation of a small planning staff at OKW." This may have been done, but no such staff appears to have played any important part in the planning or execution of *Weiss*. Nevertheless, three "working principles" of secrecy were laid down:

"1. No one must be admitted who is not concerned.

"2. No one may know more than it is necessary for him to know.

"3. When must the person concerned know, at latest? No one may know of a matter earlier than is necessary for him to know of it."

Schmundt's notes concluded with the following obscure passage:

"At the request of Feldmarschall Goering the Fuehrer decrees that:

"(a) The various services shall decide what construction is to be undertaken.

"(b) There shall be no alterations in the shipbuilding programme.

"(c) The armaments programmes are to be geared [abzustellen] to 1943 or 1944."

Why did Goering, if indeed he did, make these points? Milch denies that Goering was present, but Goering rejected the alibi.[20] Why did Goering invade Raeder's province and speak of ships? In fact, the Z Plan had already been abandoned. What was the meaning of "gearing" the armaments programme "to 1943 or 1944", with war just around the corner? Here the fog is impenetrable, be it Hitler's, Goering's or only Schmundt's.

Murky as the reasoning of the May 23rd monologue may have been, the plans and premises of immediate action were clear enough. They might be spelled out in summary as follows: (*a*) Danzig was a mere pretext for creating a state of tension with Poland: (*b*) the immediate purpose was to destroy Poland as a step in the acquisition of *Lebensraum* in eastern Europe; (*c*) the Poles would resist and there would be war, but Germany's newborn military power was ample to prevail; (*d*) it was to be hoped that the western powers would stand aside, but this was by no means certain; (*e*) there was hope that Russia would not oppose the dismemberment of Poland; (*f*) in the event that the western powers intervened, Germany must prepare for a long war; (*g*) again, in such an event, England would be the real enemy, and German possession of the North Sea and Channel coasts would be vital, both to protect the Ruhr and successfully to wage war against England; and (*h*) military preparations for these eventualities and for the destruction of Poland should speedily be brought to completion.

These preparations were, in fact, progressing rapidly. On the very day of the meeting in Hitler's study, Blumentritt distributed another planning memorandum from "Working Staff Rundstedt" to the three generals * acting as the chiefs of staff for the three incipient armies (Eighth, Tenth and Fourteenth) of Rundstedt's incipient Army group. Blumentritt informed them that he would prepare and distribute proposed orders of battle for the three armies, and that he would want the final orders of battle, as determined by the armies, not later than June 15th.

While the generals were pushing forward their military plans, the German diplomats were not far behind. On May 30th, as already noted,[21] the Foreign Office sent to Moscow the fateful instruction "to undertake definite negotiations with the Soviet Union". The discussions between the English and the Russians appeared to be bogging down. The Poles and Rumanians had welcomed British guarantees, but were not willing to accept similar protection from Russia. The Baltic States were too frightened even to accept British assurances. On May 31st, Estonia and Latvia signed non-aggression pacts with Germany. It was only too clear that a united front against German aggres-

* Generalmajor Felber, then Chief of Staff to Blaskowitz at Army Group 3, for the Eighth Army; Generalmajor von Mackensen, then Chief of Staff to List at Army Group 5, for the Fourteenth Army; Generalmajor Paulus, then Chief of Staff to Hoepner at the XVIth Army Corps, for the Tenth Army.

sion was unlikely to come to pass, in the face of Hitler's past triumphs and the menace of the Wehrmacht. The Wilhelmstrasse assiduously cultivated this panicky resignation; on July 8th a telegram of instructions was dispatched to all German legations, concerning the language to be used in discussing Poland, and reading as follows:

> "We do not want to surrender the hope that Poland will yet come to her senses for we are not looking for conflict but for the solution of the problem. We can hardly imagine that an intelligent Pole would wish to expose Poland to the lightning-like and annihilating German stroke of the fist, which would then have to be expected."

At about the same time the Soviet Ambassador to the United States, Constantine Oumansky, returning to Russia aboard the *Queen Mary*, was telling William L. Shirer [22] that "so far . . . the British and French have done nothing but stall in their negotiations with the Kremlin".

On the economic front, all armament exports to Poland had been stopped during May. On June 23rd, there was a plenary meeting of the Reich Defence Council, presided over by Goering, and attended by some thirty-five high civil and military officials—including Himmler, Frick, Funk and Todt, and Keitel, Raeder, Milch, Halder, Stumpff, Warlimont and Thomas—to discuss the man-power problems which war entailed.[23] The representative of the Ministry of Labour (Dr. Syrup) estimated a total employable population of 43·5 million, including 26·2 million men, of whom about 7 million would go to the Wehrmacht. Goering announced a basic policy of the Fuehrer that the Wehrmacht would take only about half of all those fit and liable for military service. Funk was "given the task of determining what work is to be given to prisoners of war, and to inmates of penitentiaries and concentration camps". Himmler announced that "greater use will be made of the concentration camps in wartime". Goering added that, during the war, hundreds of thousands of Czech workers "are to be employed under supervision in Germany, particularly in agriculture, and housed together in hutments". No one at the meeting could have failed to catch the whiff of slave labour and concentration camps.

The meeting had other facets. The tribulations of bureaucrats are the same the world over, and Frick (Minister of the Interior) was asked to report on "the saving of labour in the public administration". For all the myths about the efficiency

of dictatorship, the administrative organization of the Third Reich was wasteful and cumbersome. According to Frick: "Formerly there were in the Reich two main divisions—the civil service and the Wehrmacht. After the seizure of power the Party and the permanent organizations (Reich Food Estate, etc.) were added to these, with all their machinery from top to bottom. In this way the number of public posts and officials was increased many times over." So a committee was appointed to squeeze out the water.

From a military standpoint, the most significant report was that of Oberst Gercke, Chief of the Transport Section (5) of the OKH General Staff. "In the transportation sphere Germany is not, at the moment, ready for war." The fundamental difficulty was the sudden and secret nature of the troop concentrations required for surprise attacks, as envisaged under *Weiss*. The concentrations for the Sudetenland and Prague had been no real test, because "the troops were transported a long time beforehand near to the area of strategic concentration by camouflaged measures". But, confronted with "an unexpected and immediate military decision", the railways would not be in a position to bring up the necessary troops. Therefore, highways and canals would have to be intensively used to supplement the *Reichsbahn*. As matters worked out, the shortcomings of the German transport network, like those in aircraft reserves, proved a small handicap at the outset of the war, owing to its leisurely commencement in the west.

Late in July there were two large emergency meetings [24] called "in order to bring the West Wall, by August 25, 1939, at the latest, into the optimum condition of preparedness with the material that can be obtained by that time by an extreme effort". They were attended by some twenty officers and civilian officials of Army ordnance, and representatives of Krupp, the Bochumer Verein and other Ruhr steel plants. The West Wall was still short of shutters, turrets and machine-gun mounts. Every possibility of meeting the requirements by August 25th was fully canvassed, and certainly all present must have known or suspected that the military time-table called for something big, on or soon after that date.

What the Krupps knew, others knew. While Rundstedt and Bock were mapping their dispositions on the Polish frontier in accordance with *Weiss*, the Farben directors were carefully surveying the Polish chemical industries in anticipation of the benefits to be derived from conquest. On July 28, 1939, a com-

prehensive report was completed under direction of the Farben director Max Ilgner, entitled "The Most Important Chemical Plants in Poland". It set forth the structure and products of these plants, listed their owners and directors, and evaluated their adaptability to the German war economy. Farben had already started to cloak its foreign assets by fictitious transfers. On August 2nd, by government order, it started stock-piling the raw materials and components "necessary for the execution of the mobilization order".

The late spring and early summer thus witnessed the nearly final hardening of the plans for the conquest of Poland politically and economically as well as militarily. As for *Fall Weiss* itself, the Army's plans for the distribution and disposition of forces were practically complete by the middle of June. On the 15th of the month, Brauchitsch distributed the OKH deployment directive for the Army formations to be utilized against Poland.[25]

Brauchitsch's directive declared, with simplicity, that "the purpose of the operation is the destruction of the Polish armed forces. The political leadership demands that the war be opened with strong, surprise blows and lead to quick success." The plan was, therefore, "to prevent an orderly mobilization of the Polish Army by a surprise invasion of Polish territory and to shatter the bulk of the Polish Army, to be expected west of the Vistula–Narew line, by concentric attack from Silesia and Pomerania–East Prussia. . . . Army group and Army commands will make their preparations on the basis of surprising the enemy".

The grand design for the Polish campaign called for the creation of two Army groups—Army Group South, to which the Eighth, Tenth and Fourteenth Armies would be subordinated, and Army Group North, with the Third and Fourth Armies. Army Group South, the plans for which had already been drafted by Blumentritt, was to be built around "Working Staff Rundstedt", with Rundstedt as Commander-in-Chief and Manstein as Chief of Staff. Army Group North was to evolve from Army Group Command 1 at Berlin, and was therefore to be commanded by Bock, with Generalleutnant Hans von Salmuth as Chief of Staff.

The mission of Army Group South followed the outline which Blumentritt had drawn up early in May.[26] The headquarters staffs for the Eighth, Tenth and Fourteenth Armies were to be developed respectively by Army Group Commands 3, 4 and 5

and were to be commanded, accordingly, by Blaskowitz, Reichenau and List. Thus Reichenau was again entrusted, as he had been for *Gruen*, with the *Schwerpunkt* of the attack, and the mission of a *Blitzkrieg* push from Silesia direct to Warsaw.

Bock's Army Group North was to be based in Pomerania. The Third Army was to be commanded by Kuechler and formed from his Ist Corps headquarters in East Prussia. The Fourth Army, commanded by Kluge and formed from Army Group Command 6, was set up in Pomerania, separated from Kuechler by the narrow neck of the Polish Corridor. The primary mission of Kluge's army was to cut the Corridor and link Pomerania and East Prussia, isolating Danzig and Gdynia. Kuechler's main forces were also to attack due south, east of the Vistula, toward Warsaw. Danzig and Gdynia were to be "mopped up" later, though Danzig itself was to be declared German territory upon the outbreak of war and held by forces, smuggled in beforehand, which would be subordinated to Army Group North.

Other sections of deployment directive specified the head-quarters locations of and boundaries between the Army groups and armies, and described the supporting tasks of the Navy and Luftwaffe. The Navy was to blockade Danzig and Gdynia, and the Luftwaffe's far more important missions were to destroy the Polish Air Force and attack Polish railways, mobilization centres and arms depots. Rundstedt's Army group was to be supported by Loehr's Luftflotte 4, and Bock's by Kesselring's Luftflotte 1. Rundstedt and Bock were both ordered to submit to OKH, by July 20th, their orders to their armies implementing the deployment directive, a map showing the disposition of their forces, their operational agreements, with the supporting air forces, and, in Bock's case, his comparable operational agreements with the Navy (Naval Group Command East, under Albrecht).

Inasmuch as it was hoped that the western powers would not intervene, and there was no German intention to attack in the west, there was no operational plan for the western front corresponding to *Fall Weiss* in the east. The only plan was that the forces allocated to the western front would endeavour to hold any attack which might come from France or through the Low Countries. All German Army units in the west were to be subordinated to a third Army group, designated Army Group C, and developed from Army Group Command 2 at Frankfurt-am-Main. This was not, however, to be commanded by Witzleben, but by Leeb, who was thus recalled to active duty for the

second time since his retirement.* His Chief of Staff was von Sodenstern.

The plans for the western front called for three armies under Leeb's Army group. These were, just as under *Gruen*, the Seventh Army in the south along the Rhine, the First Army in the Rhineland, and the Fifth in the north. Liebmann was re-called to active duty to command the Fifth (the same post for which he had been assigned under *Gruen*). Witzleben took the First Army (by far the most important of the three), and Doll-mann stepped up from his IXth Corps to command the Seventh Army. Air defence in the west would be furnished by Felmy's Luftflotte 2 on the northern and Sperrle's Luftflotte 3 on the southern wings.

The over-all disposition of the German Army for the Polish adventure thus called for two Army groups and five armies for the attack, and one Army group and three armies screening the western frontiers. The concentration of forces against Poland was, however, much heavier than these figures reflect, for the armies committed against Poland were far stronger, both in numbers and quality. Of the eighteen peace-time corps head-quarters, all but four (V, VI, IX and XII), and of the total of twenty-three regular corps, seventeen, were assigned to *Weiss*.† Of the fifty-one regular peace-time divisions, Leeb was allowed barely a dozen (5, 6, 9, 15, 16, 25, 26, 33, 34, 35, 36 and two-thirds of 22) for the defence of the west. These were to be sup-plemented by about ten reserve and fifteen Landwehr divisions for static use in the West Wall and along the Belgian–Dutch frontier. The quality was poor, but Leeb was in a far stronger situation in 1939 than Adam had been in 1938. These precau-tions in the west left over fifty divisions, including twenty-seven regular infantry and all the armoured, motorized and mountain divisions, available to Rundstedt and Bock for *Weiss*.

Most of the corps were to be led by their regular peace-time commanders—Strauss (II), Haase (III), Schwedler (IV),

* The six peace-time Army group commands thus provided two of the three war-time Army groups and four of the five armies used for *Weiss*. The fifth army used for *Weiss* (the Third Army) was developed from Kuechler's Ist Corps in East Prus-sia. The *raison d'être* for "Working Staff Leeb" (under *Gruen*) and "Working Staff Rundstedt" (under *Weiss*) was, in each case, that an Army group headquarters had to be formed independently of any peace-time headquarters.

† Soon after the war began the three peace-time border commands Eifel, Saar-pfalz and Upper Rhine were redesignated as Corps XXIII, XXIV and XXV. In East Prussia, Generalleutnant Albert Wodrig organized an "irregular" corps from SA, home guard and other components which fought under Kuechler and was later "regularized" and designated Corps XXVI.

275

Ruoff (V), Foerster (VI), Schobert (VII), Busch (VIII), Emil Leeb (XI), Schroth (XII), Weichs (XIII), Wietersheim (XIV), Hoth (XV), Hoepner (XVI), Kienitz (XVII), and Beyer (XVIII).* The other corps commands were filled by recalling recently retired generals—Geyer (IX, replacing Dollmann, who moved up to command the Seventh Army), Ulex (X), von Kleist (XXII) and Ritter von Prager (XXVII)—or by the advancement of other active generals—Petzell (I, replacing Kuechler, who went up to the Third Army), Guderian (XIX), Falkenhorst (XXI), Wodrig (XXVI) and Hartmann (XXX). In general, the corps were distributed three to each army, but Reichenau's Tenth Army, which was to make the big push, was given no less than five corps, including the three regular corps for mobile and mechanized troops (XIV, XV and XVI).

As we have seen, the west was given no mechanized troops at all. Neither was Blaskowitz, whose weak Eighth Army had the limited role of guarding Reichenau's northern flank. Kluge's push across the Corridor was to be spearheaded by Guderian's new XIXth Corps, comprising one armoured and two motorized infantry divisions. Kuechler received very little armour at the outset, in the expectation that his push to the south could be strengthened by Kluge's armour after it had broken through the Polish Corridor. List's forces in Moravia and Slovakia were strong in mountain troops, but also included a panzer and a light division in Kleist's XXIInd Corps.

Following the promulgation of Brauchitsch's deployment directive of June 15th, the military preparations for the invasion were carried forward with utmost rapidity. Blaskowitz, for example, immediately circulated those portions pertinent to the mission of the Eighth Army, with the order that all preparations would have to be completed by August 20th. "All units have to maintain the initiative against the foe by quick action and ruthless attacks," Blaskowitz declared. A few days later, Keitel submitted to Hitler a "preliminary time-table" for the mobilization, which elicited from the Fuehrer the admonition that "in order not to disquiet the populace by calling up reserves on a larger scale than usual . . . employees or other private persons who make inquiry should be told that the men are being called up for the autumn manœuvres and for the training units to be formed for these manœuvres".

Late in June, difficulties developed between the Army and

* The subsequently regularized Corps XXIII, XXIV and XXV were under their peace-time commanders Raschick, Kuntze and Waeger.

Navy, because of the Army's anxiety that naval movements prior to the onslaught might give the show away and destroy the element of surprise. The Army was anxious, if possible, to capture intact the bridges across the Vistula at Danzig (the Dir-

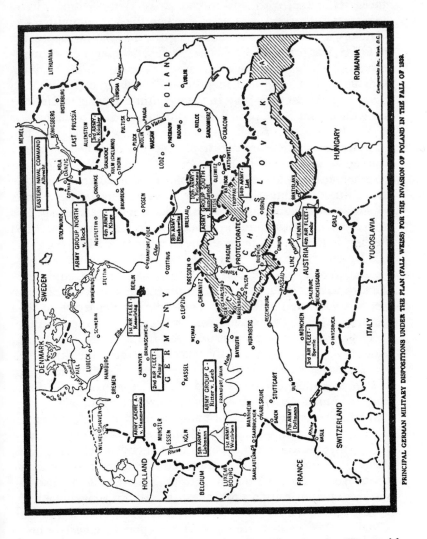

schau Bridge) and in the Corridor (at Graudenz). To avoid alarming the Poles and forestall their blowing up the bridges, the Navy agreed not to lay mines or molest shipping in Danzig Harbour until fifteen minutes before "Y-hour".

July and early August were devoted chiefly to refinements in

the basic plans and training of the newly mobilized units. Doenitz' submarines, too, held extensive training manœuvres in the Baltic, which Raeder attended. On July 24th, for example, OKW circulated a directive on supply and security measures in the Army operational areas. The seizure of hostages was authorized in order to quell hostile acts committed by civilians, and execution of the hostages, subject to the approval of OKH, was provided for. The next day, Schniewind informed the Foreign Office about the Navy's plans for blockading Gdynia and Danzig, and its proposed handling of Polish and neutral merchant shipping. In the meantime, Danzig was filling up with German troops and weapons smuggled in at night.

The Navy, of course, had to concern itself with the Atlantic as well as the Baltic. On August 5th, Schniewind issued a memorandum of instructions to Naval Group Command West "for additional measures in view of a possible expansion of the conflict". In addition to submarines, the pocket battleships *Graf Spee* and *Deutschland* would be sent to the Atlantic. For their refuelling, the supply ships *Altmark* and *Westerwald* would also put to sea; the former, indeed, was already bringing a cargo of Diesel oil from the United States, and "will be in the Atlantic with this cargo in time to meet the *Graf Spee*", which would, in turn, equip the *Altmark* with communications equipment and military personnel at their first rendezvous. The order for departure of the pocket battleships was tentatively scheduled for August 16th.

The high pitch of preparations for *Weiss*, as the middle of August approached, is vividly reflected in the "war diary" of the Ist Corps in East Prussia. General von Kuechler had left the corps to take over command of the Third Army; the new corps commander (Generalleutnant Petzell) arrived on August 1st, and the new staff was formally "activated" at Insterburg. The next day was spent by the staff "celebrating the twenty-fifth anniversary of the outbreak of the [first world] war". On August 3rd, manœuvres were planned for the intervening days up to August 27th. There were complaints about the insufficiency of motor transport for the corps staff "in view of the bad road conditions in Poland". Two days later, Petzell and his Chief of Staff went to Koenigsberg to report to Kuechler and receive a "first briefing on the tasks to be anticipated". On August 6th, they set out again "for reconnaissance of the terrain". Less than two weeks later, Petzell was again at Koenigsberg, but this time he received a "draft order for the moving of troops to advanced action stations", and the information that

"August 25th will be the initial Y-day". *Fall Weiss* was fully loaded, and the trigger was about to be pulled.

THE GENERALS AT THE *OBERSALZBERG*

The tension had been building up all summer, and reached a peak about August 10th. The customs officials of Nazi-dominated Danzig, and German officials on the Polish border, had been staging provocative incidents since the beginning of the month. On August 9th, Weizsaecker called in the Polish *Chargé d'Affaires*, Prince Lubomirski, and upbraided the Polish government for "threatening" Danzig. Goebbels turned his propaganda machine on full blast to inflame German opinion against the Poles.

At about the same time, it became clear that the Anglo-Russian negotiations were getting nowhere. Chamberlain had sent Sir William Strang, a career Foreign Office official, to Moscow. He was followed on August 10th by Admiral Drax and the French General Doumenc, who endeavoured to open military conversations. But, in view of Polish and Rumanian unwillingness to contemplate the transit of Russian troops, there was little basis for discussion. Several years later, Stalin told Churchill [27] that England's inability to put more than a handful of divisions in the field, and the consequent prospect that Russia would bear the brunt of the ground fighting, was a decisive obstacle to the success of the talks. The Anglo-Russian negotiations began to be overshadowed by reports that Russia and Germany were in the process of concluding a commercial treaty. The very day that Drax and Doumenc began their mission, Keitel, Admiral Canaris and other OKW officials flew to Salzburg to see Ribbentrop, and Canaris' diary for the day mentioned "hints about non-aggression pact with Russia".

Knowledge that such a pact might be in the offing was, nevertheless, confined to a very small circle. The Press had mentioned only commercial talks, and Hitler's denunciations of "Jewish Bolshevism" and references to the Ukraine as a promised land for *Lebensraum* hardly seemed a fit basis for a Russo-German *détente*. Up to the very end the Russian attitude was ambiguous, not to say duplicitous.

Accordingly, by about August 10th it had become openly apparent that (1) Hitler was about to press home by military power his demands against Poland, and was at least as determined as he had been eleven months earlier in the case of Czechoslovakia; (2) the Poles would resist; (3) England and France would,

in all probability, not repeat their 1938 tactics of appeasement, but would go to war in support of the Poles; (4) it was at least uncertain that Russia would intervene in the event of a European war precipitated by the Polish question; and (5) the prospects of such a war in the immediate future were very strong.

These prospects were not at all to the liking of Hermann Goering. Early in July a Swedish industrialist, Birger Dahlerus, had strongly impressed upon him the determination of the English to stand by their commitment to the Poles, and had suggested that Goering meet privately with a representative group of British businessmen, so that he might form his own firsthand impression. Such a meeting was in fact arranged, and took place on August 7th in Schleswig-Holstein, near the Danish border.[28] The discussion was amicable but inconclusive; Goering explained the claims against Poland but avowed his desire for peace, while the Englishmen insisted that their country would tolerate no more occupations by force. The desirability of a quadripartite conference, bringing in France and Italy, was discussed, but the idea was overtaken by events. Goering was impressed, but not sufficiently so that he could not make a public pronouncement two days later that German air defences were so strong that "the Ruhr will not be subjected to a single enemy bomb! If an enemy bomber reaches the Ruhr, my name is not Hermann Goering; you can call me Meier!"

While Goering was vainly seeking common ground with the English, and Ribbentrop was flirting with the Russians, what of Nazidom's Mediterranean ally? What of Il Duce and the Corporative State? On August 12th, Ciano went to the Obersalzberg for the week-end, and was treated to a long and (to him) alarming monologue by Hitler with interjections by Ribbentrop.[29] The Fuehrer was in high and confident fettle. The German fortifications in the west precluded any possibility of a French break-through. The operational range of the latest German bombers precluded any effective blockade of Germany by the British Navy. Furthermore, "in the event of a general war, after the destruction of Poland, which would not take long, Germany would be able to assemble hundreds of divisions along the West Wall. . . . The Fuehrer also thought the French would find it no easier to overrun the Italian fortifications than the West Wall." To this, however, Ciano reacted by showing "signs of extreme doubt".

Hitler then turned to the arguments in favour of an immediate settlement with Poland. That country was weak in anti-aircraft

and anti-tank defences, the western powers could not aid her, and she "could be struck to the ground by Germany in the shortest time". But, if time was allowed to pass, Poland could be bolstered by England and France and "German superiority would thereby be diminished". Furthermore, it was too late to draw back. Danzig was "a Nuremberg of the North" and must return to the Reich. Finally, Poland was an inevitable enemy, and her "quick liquidation" would be of great advantage to the Axis "for the unavoidable conflict with the western democracies". The Fuehrer dangled carrots before Ciano's nose:

"Generally speaking, the best thing to happen would be for the neutrals to be liquidated one after another. This process could be carried out more easily if on every occasion one partner of the Axis covered the other, while it was dealing with an uncertain neutral. Italy might well regard Yugoslavia as a neutral of this kind."

But Ciano was not to be so easily swayed. He "expressed the greatest surprise . . . over the unexpected seriousness of the position", and set forth at length the economic and military weakness of Italy's situation and the desirability of postponing any general war until 1942 or later. The western powers would certainly intervene in the Polish conflict. Hitler interrupted to predict that "the western democracies in the last resort would shrink from a general war", but Ciano blandly retorted that "he wished the Fuehrer were right but he did not think so". The Italian concluded by proposing a reassuring joint communiqué calling for an international conference to preserve the peace.

This was little to Hitler's taste: "for a solution of the Polish problem no time should be lost". After the middle of September, mud and fog in Poland would play havoc with German tanks and planes. There must be a settlement "by the end of August". The next Polish "provocation" would result in a German ultimatum, so "a move against Poland must be reckoned with any minute".

At the conclusion of the meeting, a telegram from Moscow was brought in, containing the momentous news that the Russians had "agreed to the dispatch of a political negotiator to Moscow". Thereupon, Ribbentrop advised Ciano that "the Russians were fully informed of Germany's intentions toward Poland", and Hitler added his opinion that Russia would never "pull the chestnuts out of the fire" for the democracies or interfere in favour of Poland, "whom she hated wholeheartedly".

The conversations were resumed the following day. Ciano

abandoned his request for a pacific communiqué, but would not commit Italy to any belligerent course of action. Hitler and Ribbentrop renewed their arguments of the previous day, and the Fuehrer reiterated that matters must be brought to an issue "at the latest by the end of August". Ciano replied that, if Hitler's estimate of Anglo-French reluctance to go to war was correct and Poland was indeed diplomatically isolated, "the Duce might not have to make any decision". He promised only to carry back full information to Mussolini, and the talks broke up on this non-committal note. It must, however, have been plain to Hitler and Ribbentrop that they could by no means count on Italian military support.

From the course of events during the spring and summer, and from the content of Hitler's arguments to Ciano, one may deduce, with reasonable assurance, Hitler's intentions and expectations as the time-table for *Weiss* approached its scheduled moment for fulfilment. Fortunately for history, his state of mind was even more clearly revealed immediately after Ciano's departure from the Obersalzberg. On Monday, August 14th, the German commanders-in-chief came to the mountain for an all-day conference with the Fuehrer. No official minutes of this meeting are available, but a very full account of it comprises the opening entry in General Halder's diary.* Outside of Halder himself there is no record of who was present, but in all probability the meeting comprised Brauchitsch, Goering and Raeder and probably the other two service chiefs of staff, Schniewind and Jeschonnek.[30]

Much of what Hitler told the commanders-in-chief was a repetition of what he had just said to Ciano. Once again he emphasized the necessity of taking risks. Once again he played upon the unreadiness for war of England and France: "The men of Munich will not take the risk." His estimate of Russian hostility toward Poland and unwillingness to "pull chestnuts out of the fire" was reiterated and amplified. He revealed that the German–Russian contacts had so far been "loose" and that the Russians were "distrustful". The questions of sending a German negotiator to Moscow, and whether he should be a "prominent figure", were still "under advisement". Hitler also informed his listeners that "Italy is not interested in a major con-

* Halder was proficient in Gabelsberger shorthand, and his diary contains a voluminous running account of what he heard and did as Chief of Staff from August 14, 1939, to his dismissal on September 24, 1942. On August 14th, Halder took notes while Hitler spoke, and then summarized them after the meeting was over.

flict", but predicted that "a victory for the democratic nations would be the end of Italy", as well as of Mussolini, whom he eulogized a "A Man!"

These observations, coupled with Hitler's expressed confidence that the smaller nations of Europe would stand aside, led him to view the situation in terms of only three other countries: England, France and Poland. And his analysis of the intentions and capabilities of these three countries was the core of his argument.

(1) In terms of the hazards, England preoccupied his mind. His conclusions were an extraordinary mixture of accurate detection of her immediate lack of striking power, and whistling in the dark about her ultimate potentialities. Britain, he opined, was suffering "the fate of rich countries". She could not possibly want a long war, because the cost of victory would far exceed its benefits. "Why should England fight? You don't let yourself get killed for an ally. Not even England has the money to fight a long war. Nothing can be had on credit." It would be months or even years before her naval building programme or recently introduced conscription of ground troops would show results. True, her Air Force was making progress. But, on the whole, her armament programme was "in the development stage, similar to our situation in 1934". Her uncertainty was manifested by failure to ratify formally the pact with Poland. Accordingly, she would look for a "line of retreat", and not take measures more drastic than recalling her ambassador and embargoing trade with Germany. Chiefly, the Fuehrer was "concerned lest England hamper the showdown by last-minute offers".

(2) Hitler had no fear of the French. They would not wage war on their own, but only if "pulled in after" England. Her age classes of conscripts were small, many troops were tied down in the colonies, and her armaments were run down. "France resembles a weak man trying to carry machine guns on his back." On the Continent, British support could not exceed "a few divisions". The combined Anglo-French forces could not breach the West Wall, and an attack through the Low Countries would require neutrality violations and promised no quick success. Therefore, for Poland, "no immediate relief would be provided by an Anglo-French action", and "all these factors argue for the likelihood of Britain and France refraining from entering the war, particularly since they are not under any compulsion".

(3) From all this it followed that "the last weeks have brought increasing conviction of Poland's isolation". Therefore "the

central problem is Poland. It must be carried off at all costs." The two prerequisites for action were *speed* and *determination*. As to the first, "Successes must be scored against Poland in the very near future. Within a week or two the world will have to be convinced that Poland is at the point of collapse." As to the second, "The other nations must be given proof that there will be a shooting war no matter what. . . . We must show determination to fight on all fronts. The build-up in the west must be completed to the last detail." To placate England, Hitler was dropping hints "that he will approach her with a new offer after disposing of the overriding Polish question". In conclusion, "The Fuehrer's attitude has registered in London. Paris, too, is no longer in any doubt as to his determination. The great drama is now approaching its climax."

After lunch, there was a discussion of purely military problems. With respect to the western front, there was some talk of "starting a drive to gain a better front line", and of occupying the northern corner of Holland and the Frisian Islands. These possibilities were left in abeyance "for lack of man-power". Attention was focused on "ensuring protection of our frontier with the least delay" and "investigating the possibility of creating new reserves or moving up existing ones". To this end, a decision was to be made within twenty-four hours on calling up the Landwehr divisions to bolster Leeb's defence forces. On the Polish frontier, study was again given to the surprise capture intact of the Dirschau and Graudenz bridges over the Vistula. For Dirschau, a *coup-de-main* by Himmler's SS troops in an armoured train was considered, and for Graudenz, paratroops and a raiding party in civilian clothes. Danzig was to be dealt with by the SA and smuggled forces. Another problem was whether or not to cancel the annual Nuremberg Party Rally; this, too, was to be decided by the next day.

The week following Hitler's meetings at the Obersalzberg with Ciano and the generals was like the eve of the typhoon—quiet, but foreboding. Winston Churchill, still a Cassandra, was touring the Maginot Line under the auspices of General Gamelin.[31] "What was remarkable about all I learned on my visit was the complete acceptance of the defensive which dominated my most responsible French hosts. . . . France no longer had the life-thrust to mount a great offensive. She would fight for her existence—*violà tout*."

At the Bendlerstrasse, a different atmosphere prevailed. The Nuremberg rally was secretly cancelled, and the generals busied

themselves with the calling up of reserves, marshalling the railroad system for a sudden deployment, the evacuation of Todt's workers and others from the fortified zone of the West Wall, moving OKH headquarters from Berlin to nearby Zossen by August 24th, and planning the capture of the Graudenz and Dirschau bridges. Another and even more sinister plot was brewing. By order from Keitel, Admiral Canaris' special operations unit turned over a large number of Polish uniforms to the SS. Under Heydrich's direction, these were to be used for a faked Polish attack on the German radio broadcasting station at Gleiwitz in Silesia near the Polish border.

It was the Navy, however, that first took up battle stations. On August 15th, the Naval War Diary reported that the *Graf Spee* and all the Atlantic submarines were ready to sail. The order for their departure was given on August 19th—a day of decisive developments. Between the 19th and the 21st, twenty-one submarines put out to positions north and north-west of the British Isles. The *Graf Spee* sailed on the 21st, to take up a waiting station off the Brazilian coast, and the *Deutschland* on the 24th for operations in the North Atlantic.[32]

The fact that the order inaugurating naval operations was given on August 19th is connected, by direct and convincing inference, to the suddenly favourable turn which the Russo-German negotiations took at the very same time.[33] On August 19th, Moscow made it known to Berlin that the proposal of a visit to Moscow by Ribbentrop would be favourably considered. By August 21st it had been arranged that Ribbentrop would fly to Moscow the next day, and that the pact would be signed on the 24th. According to Winston Churchill, Stalin had told the Politburo on the 19th that he intended to conclude the agreement, and the Tass Agency announced Ribbentrop's visit during the evening of the 21st.[34]

There is no doubt but that most of the leading Nazis were as astounded as the world in general. Ideologically, the pact was on both sides a reversal of field so magnificently preposterous as to beggar the imagination and out-Orwell Orwell. Diplomatically, Hitler and Ribbentrop had achieved a resounding *coup*, and Goebbels was quite equal to the occasion.[35] The *Angriff* on August 22nd boasted that: "The world stands before a towering fact: two peoples have placed themselves on the basis of a common foreign policy which, during a long and traditional friendship, produced a foundation for a common understanding."

Thus fortified from the direction least anticipated by others, Adolf Hitler summoned a great gathering of the German military leaders, to meet with him at the Obersalzberg at noon on August 22nd. They came by plane from Berlin, Silesia, the Rhineland, the northern marches and East Prussia—the three service commanders-in-chief and their chiefs of staff, the Army group and Army commanders and their chiefs of staff, and the equivalent Navy and Air Force leaders—Brauchitsch and Halder, Goering and Jeschonnek, Raeder and Schniewind, the *Feldherrn*, including Rundtsedt, Bock and Leeb, Kuechler, Kluge, Blaskowitz, Reichenau, Witzleben and List, many of the "bright young men" who were their *Chefs*, such as Manstein, Salmuth and Sodenstern, and Kesselring, Sperrle, Boehm and other generals of the air and admirals of the sea. Once again no list of this martial galaxy has come to light but, unlike the meeting of August 14th, several records of what Hitler said have survived. From the captured OKW files, an unsigned summary in two parts was retrieved, and widely publicized during the first Nuremberg trial.[36] Admiral Boehm, Chief of the High Seas Fleet, made another record, also put into evidence at Nuremberg.[37] Halder's diary contains a third account. These three versions correspond very closely both as to sequence and content, and are all certainly authentic. Still a fourth and more highly coloured version, from journalistic sources, was also published at Nuremberg;[38] this, too, is sufficiently like the others so that it cannot be dismissed as spurious, but its author is unknown and it bears the marks of exaggeration through hearsay repetition.

Hitler greeted his guests with the information that he had called them together "to give you a picture of the political situation, so that you may have insight into the individual elements on which I have based my decision to act and to strengthen your trust in my decision". The decision itself was "firmly made" and, therefore, after the exposition of its basis, "we will discuss military details".

The Fuehrer then made the rather surprising statement that, until the spring of 1939, it had been his intention to "turn against the west in a few years" and not move eastward until thereafter. However, the "preconditions" for this "theoretically more desirable" course of action had changed. It had proved impossible to establish "an acceptable relationship with Poland", and "increasingly plain" that "Poland would take advantage of any difficult situation to attack us in the back". Politicians

286

must be flexible. "It has, therefore, become necessary to dispose of the eastern problem before attacking the west." He then listed three reasons which favoured an immediate, rather than a delayed, solution; the Fuehrer was in one of his most ego-centric moods, and mighty proud of his fellow-dictators:

"It depends on me and my existence because of my political activities. Furthermore, the fact that probably no one will ever again have the confidence of the whole German people as I do. There will probably never again be a man in the future with more authority than I have. My existence is therefore a factor of great value, but I can be eliminated at any time by a criminal or an idiot.

"The second personal factor is the Duce. His existence is also justified. If something happens to him, Italy's loyalty to the alliance will no longer be certain. The basic attitude of the Italian Court is against the Duce. Above all, the Court sees in the expansion of the Empire a burden. The Duce is the man with the strongest nerves in Italy.

"The third factor favourable to us is Franco. We can ask only benevolent neutrality from Spain. But this depends on Franco's personality. He guarantees a certain uniformity and steadiness of the present system in Spain. We must take into account the fact that Spain does not as yet have a Fascist party of our internal unity."

The trinity of Hitler, Mussolini and Franco was an especially fortunate conjunction in contrast to the drabness on the other side: "There are no men of a calibre hard or heroic enough to carry through the decisions called for by the situation. . . . No personalities, no masters, no men of action."

Furthermore, Germany was the lean and hungry challenger, democracy the over-fed, self-indulgent title-holder. The German economy would collapse without geographical expansion. Therefore:

"For us it is easy to make decisions. We have nothing to lose; we can only gain. Our economic situation is such because of our restrictions that we cannot hold out more than a few years. Goering can confirm this. We have no other choice. We must act. Our opponents risk much and can gain only a little."

Other political factors favoured an immediate stroke. Italy, Japan and the Arab world were threatening British hegemony in the Mediterranean, the Far East and the Near East. England's 1918 victory had been a Pyrrhic one. The Empire was disintegrating, and the British economy tottering. Two of her allies of 1914, Russia and Italy, were now split away from her.

France was deteriorating. The Balkans were turbulent, and the Italian conquest of Albania had put Yugoslavia in jeopardy.

Personal, economic and political factors thus conspired to the same end. "All these fortunate circumstances may no longer prevail in two or three years. No one knows how long I shall live." And, therefore, "A clash which it might not be safe to put off for four or five years might as well come off now."

Finally, there were two psychological factors of great importance. "The relation to Poland has become unbearable." Poland had "changed her tone toward us" as a result of British support. "The initiative must not be allowed to pass to others." Therefore, the issue with Poland must not be resolved by "easy compromise" which would require "reconciliatory gestures". Arbitration by third parties was to be excluded. Otherwise, "there was danger of losing prestige" and of reviving "the language of Versailles".

In addition to preserving Germany's prestige and holding the initiative, it was necessary to "test the military". All of Hitler's previous triumphs had been achieved "through a bluff" by his own political leadership. "The Army must see actual battle before the big final showdown in the west." Since the likelihood of Anglo-French intervention was small, Poland offered a splendid opportunity to "test the Wehrmacht in a single, limited task". In substance, "What we want now is not a general showdown, but the disposition of specific issues: this is the proper procedure not only politically, but also from the military standpoint."

Of course, the decision to strike involved present risks, and possibly would lead to ultimate destruction. As to the immediate gamble, "Politicians do not receive directives from God the Father. You generals know this." However, he (the Fuehrer) had always been right up to now. In relying upon his own "iron nerves, iron resolution", he was following in the footsteps of Hannibal, Frederick the Great, and Hindenburg and Ludendorff before Tannenberg. His task would be much easier had it not been for the weakness and indiscretion of some highly placed Germans in 1938. Obviously referring to Beck and Adam, and in a way that must have given Halder and Witzleben a queasy moment, he declared:

"It has done much damage that many reluctant Germans said and wrote to Englishmen about the Czech question: 'The Fuehrer carried his point because you lost your nerve and capitulated too soon.' This explains the present propaganda war."

Following this admonition, Hitler launched into an analysis of the military weakness of England and France, repeating much of what he had said ten days earlier. Some of the additional detail, however, was noteworthy. He stressed England's lack of modern anti-aircraft artillery, and compared the strength of the Luftwaffe (390,000 men) to that of his opponents (England 130,000, France 72,000 and Poland 15,000 men). He also remarked, accurately enough, that the French soldier was "psychologically conditioned to a Maginot defence", and that it would be difficult indeed for the French to mount a costly attack against the West Wall. A blockade would be ineffective against Germany "because we have the resources of the entire Danube basin". An attack through the neutral countries was most improbable, and would take time. "England and France will not violate the neutrality of these countries." And this led him to the strategically sound verdict that "actually England cannot help Poland". The only way out of the dilemma of the English was for them to give in or face a long war. As to this, "A long war is an untempting prospect. It is nonsense to say that England wants a long war." The logic of the situation would thus force England to seek a way to renege on her Polish commitment, and Hitler thought that there already were signs of such a move, particularly in England's failure to take effective steps to strengthen Poland's armaments.

Then came the trump card. "The enemy had another hope, that Russia would become our enemy. . . . The enemy did not count on my power of resolution. Our enemies are little worms. I saw them at Munich." Litvinov's dismissal had had a "cannon-shot effect" on Hitler's appreciation of Russian intentions. He had at once commenced a cautious reversal of policy, initiated by unwonted personal courtesy to the Russian Ambassador at a reception. Meanwhile, the English and French had been unable to take a positive position on the matters of deepest concern to Russia. So, finally, he had proposed a non-aggression pact coupled with a settlement in the Baltic favourable to Russia. "Four days ago I took a special step, which brought it about that Russia answered yesterday that she is ready to sign. The personal contact with Stalin is established. The day after tomorrow Ribbentrop will conclude the treaty." And so—a deadly echo of Seeckt—"Now Poland is in the position in which I wanted her."

Hitler concluded with a pæan of triumph: "I have struck this weapon, the help of Russia, out of the hands of the western

powers. The possibility now exists to strike at the heart of Poland." The pact was the greatest political event of recent years. "We need not fear a blockade. The east will supply us with grain, cattle, coal, lead and zinc. . . . I am only afraid that, at the last moment, some *Schweinehund* will make a proposal for mediation. . . . Now that I have made the political preparations, the way is open for the soldier."

At about this point, the meeting was interrupted for lunch, at which the generals were joined by several Nazi notables, including Goebbels' deputy, Otto Dietrich. After the repast, Hitler turned to a statement of what he would expect from the military chiefs, and how the plan of action should be carried out. "The goal is the annihilation of the military power of Poland." The best way to prevent intervention from the west was to make it plain that such interference would not cause any flinching from the goal, "even if battles take place in the west. A quick decision in Poland is the best guarantee of a limited conflict."

Therefore, "We must all steel ourselves against humanitarian reasoning. We must make our hearts closed and hard." Getting down to tactical details, "Of paramount importance are the wedges that must be driven from the southeast toward the Vistula, and from the north to the Narew and Vistula." Success was assured if the nerves of the leaders did not give way: "Our technical superiority will break the nerves of the Poles."

As to the morality of launching the attack, "I shall give a propagandistic cause . . . never mind whether it be plausible or not." Morality had no proper place in the picture. "The victor is never called upon to vindicate his actions. The question is not one of the justice of our cause, but exclusively of achieving victory."

Reaching the military goal was "a precondition of the more limited political goal of rectification of frontiers". On this subject Hitler did not go into much detail. He spoke generally of "a new German frontier according to healthy principles", and the establishment of a "protectorate in the east". There was no need for the generals to be concerned about these questions, for "military operations need not be affected by regard for future frontiers".

Hitler concluded by announcing that the launching of the attacks would probably be scheduled for Saturday morning, August 26th. All in all, it had been an extremely effective presentation—one of Hitler's most powerful. Goering as the ranking officer acknowledged the speech on behalf of the Wehrmacht,

but there was no general discussion. The meeting broke up, and the commanders-in-chief and their *Chefs* returned to their individual posts to make final preparations for *der Tag*.

THE AGGRESSIVE DESIGN

Men confronted with grave and complicated issues rarely arrive at a decision on the basis of a single reason. To this principle Adolf Hitler was no exception, and it would be meretricious to attempt to say, in one breath, that "Hitler attacked Poland on September 1, 1939, because" of this or that one overriding purpose. Many factors, cumulative, conflicting and balancing, played a part in shaping his choice of a course of action. Some were highly personal, while others were drawn from his efforts to gauge objectively the play of circumstances beyond his power to control.

Furthermore, Hitler's state of mind and intentions, like those of all men, swam in the stream of time. So far from being immutable (although he loved to proclaim his "unalterable determination"), they were singularly shifting and flexible. Intense and singleminded in his broad purpose to aggrandize Germany, his methods were fluid in the extreme, until the time when disastrous reverses shattered his mental resilience. Whatever his other faults, he was no slave to Emerson's hobgoblin of false consistency. And it would be a serious mistake to picture Hitler as pursuing, regardless of other factors, a rigid time-table, constructed long in advance and calling for an attack on Poland on a certain date. Under other circumstances he might well have struck at another time or in a different direction.

The documents we have reviewed do, however, enable us to follow the course and sense the colour of Hitler's mental processes. They are historically remarkable because they are so uninhibited and so full that we can almost crawl into Hitler's mind and see with his eyes. For all their limitations and their ugliness, both were powerful instruments, and we will do well to linger here a moment longer and endeavour to marshal the salient and decisive factors so that they may strike our own minds in conjunction.

(1) Hitler's governing impulse and broad purpose was to arm Germany and use her might, on every propitious occasion, for aggrandizement. His intention in this respect was open and notorious. It was proclaimed in *Mein Kampf*, in Nazi literature, and repeated constantly, publicly and privately, by the Fuehrer and his close associates. Furthermore he was in a hurry, both

because he was an egomaniac who feared his own death by illness or assassination, and because the nature of Nazism and the tempo of the rearmament programme required recurring triumphs. By the spring of 1939, the succession of rearmament, the Rhineland, *Anschluss*, the Sudetenland, and Prague, coupled with Hitler's avowed intention to settle the problem of *Lebensraum* within a few years, had made it clear that new aggressive moves were a certainty.

(2) Nevertheless, there is no evidence that Hitler had previously settled on any specific programme to follow the Austrian and Czech ventures. On the contrary, it appears that the consummation of *Anschluss* and *Gruen*, as outlined on November 5, 1937, had emptied his first bag of tricks, and left him surveying the horizon for the next conquest. In *Mein Kampf* and elsewhere, Hitler had both coveted the rich eastern lands and clamoured for a "settlement" in the west. At the Obersalzberg on August 22nd, he spoke of the theoretical desirability of first striking westward as opposed to the practical necessity of first crushing Poland. Apparently his intentions had been wavering between the two alternatives.

(3) After 1938, the governing factor in Hitler's calculations was England. He had no fear of any Continental power. Churchill and Hitler both shrewdly diagonised the defensive mood and debilitated state of French arms, and were far closer to the truth than Beck and other military men who exalted the French Army as the strongest in Europe.

(4) The key to an understanding of Hitler's behaviour after 1938 is that he was never able to make up his own mind how to cope with the English. He belittled their striking power and scoffed at them as sons of the idle rich, yet respected their ingenuity and prowess, and feared their resourcefulness and staying power in a long war. On November 5, 1937, he coupled them with the French as "hated enemies", but at other times, with unquestionable if transient sincerity, he expressed his desire to live at peace with them. He would concoct elaborate and preposterous deals which he thought would please them and then, when crossed, threaten their utter destruction.

Underneath this confusion and indecision, it appears that Hitler was working toward an outcome whereby he would leave their Empire to the British, and they would leave Europe to him. To achieve this he pursued a tactic of building up his strength on and dominion over the Continent, partly to avert the threat of a naval blockade, but primarily to discourage Britain and

convince them of the hopelessness of interference. In a very real sense, the Polish war and every major military action Hitler took after 1938 were regarded by him as moves in the chess game with England. If the match could be won without costly hostilities, so much the better; if war was necessary, he hoped to postpone it until Germany's naval strength and economic self-sufficiency were improved. But inasmuch as Continental conquest was his principal weapon, it was an essential part of his tactic that war with England had to be risked. To borrow a phrase from today's diplomatic vocabulary, he wished to "negotiate from strength". We need not ponder whether, if successful, he would have stuck to such a bargain with England, for it never became other than an academic question.

(5) Despite Hitler's expressions of preference on August 22nd for "turning against the west in a few years", the logic of events pushed him eastwards again. The success of the Czech venture left Poland half surrounded and helpless. British intervention in the event of an attack on France or the Low Countries was certain, whereas (so Hitler believed) eastern Europe might be left in the lurch, as Czechoslovakia had been.

(6) This almost automatic continued eastward gravitation manifested itself immediately after Munich in the military plans for the occupation of Memel and Danzig and the diplomatic approaches to the Poles for Danzig and an extra-territorial transport route across the Corridor to East Prussia. In its origin, this was a limited programme which Hitler hoped to achieve without war. Memel was easily accomplished, but Danzig and the Corridor road foundered on the rock of Polish opposition, soon supported by the Anglo-French guarantee.

(7) These unwelcome developments had a decisive effect on the Fuehrer's mind and mood. His personal appetite for speedy and uninterrupted triumphs, his lingering resentment of western interference at Munich, and his inability to suffer opposition where he felt possessed of the power to dispose found expression in his rationale that the time was ripe for a showdown on the Polish question. In what proportions emotional rationalization was mixed with objective analysis may well be debated, but the ingredients of the compound are unmistakable.

(8) Thus Hitler reached the decision to attack Poland in 1939. It was scheduled for late August or early September because this allowed sufficient time for military preparations and harvesting, but was early enough to enable a decision to be reached before the mud and fog of late autumn would set in.

Since it was to be a showdown *vi et armis,* Danzig and the Corridor road were forgotten, and *Lebensraum* took over.

(9) Polish territory was desired not so much for its own sake as to cement Germany's economic grip on eastern Europe and strengthen Germany against a possible naval blockade. It was in this sense that Hitler regarded the Polish campaign as a move in the struggle with England. Nevertheless, *immediate territorial aggrandizement was not the primary objective. Rather, it was to dispose of the Polish issue unilaterally.* This is what he had failed to accomplish with the Czech issue, and this explains his deliberate and intemperate rejection of all attempts at mediation and all efforts on the part of the Poles to reopen discussion. "I am only afraid that . . . some *Schweinehund* will make a proposal for mediation." Only in this way could he establish his unchallenged overlordship of central and eastern Europe. Only in this way could he maintain the initiative and safeguard his prestige, a vital attribute of the master race, but insufferable in others.

(10) Hitler wanted a showdown, and a military triumph over Poland, but he did not want a general European war in 1939. He made every effort to isolate Poland and restrict the war to Polish soil. His activities in this regard were concentrated on Russia and England. The French, he was sure, would follow England's lead, and other countries did not concern him.

(11) As to Russia, Hitler followed to the letter the strategy laid down by von Seeckt in 1922, and made a deal with the Kremlin for the partition of Poland. Would he have attacked in 1939 had this strategy failed and had Moscow either remained inscrutable or openly joined the western powers? It has been forcefully argued that Hitler did not regard the Russo-German pact as a *sine qua non,* and would have moved even in the teeth of an Anglo-French-Russian alliance.[39] On the other hand, the coincidence of the sailings of the submarines and pocket battleships with the favourable turn in the Moscow negotiations bears witness to the importance which Hitler had consistently proclaimed of avoiding a two-front war (Poland alone he did not regard as true "front"). It may be doubted that Hitler pondered this question much, as he appears to have been completely confident, after the Litvinov dismissal, that Russia would not step in, and the real question in his mind was whether a pact with Stalin was necessary to assure Russia's neutrality.

(12) Toward England, Hitler adopted a policy of "unalterable determination" to settle the Polish question on his own terms and without brooking any interference. By this means he

hoped to "call her bluff". The policy failed, and it was the logical and inevitable result that Hitler was left facing war with England and France, a result which he did not at all desire at that time. But as between facing this unwanted outcome or backing down and postponing the showdown, his choice was clear—*he must have the showdown*. He was confident, and rightly, that England and France could do nothing to help Poland and little to harm Germany in a short war. So he would have his military triumph over Poland, confront the western powers with a *fait accompli*, and then make pacific gestures and otherwise endeavour to discourage them from continuing an undertaking which would by then look highly unpromising and at best bloody, costly and long-drawn-out.

So ran Hitler's thinking in the summer of 1939. It carried him far, and it might have carried him even farther and to less transient conquest but for the overreaching blunders into which his demon subsequently led him. We may not pause to speculate on the academic question whether, from his standpoint, another course of action in 1939 would have been "better". We have peered into Hitler's mind; what were, then, the thoughts of his generals? Why was the officers' corps so easily persuaded to lead the Wehrmacht into war with Poland when, less than a year before, so many of its leaders had opposed the Czech venture?

When asked this question at Nuremberg, Halder laid decisive emphasis on Witzleben's transfer from Berlin, and the impossibility of using his successor, Haase, for the role in a military revolt that Witzleben would have filled.[40] This was accurate enough as a detail, but Halder grossly overstated its importance in the entire picture. In fact, there is no evidence of any determined efforts by the generals, individually or in concert, to prevent the consummation of *Weiss*. And the reasons for this lie far deeper than the military assignments of Witzleben and Haase. The facts are that, almost to a man, they welcomed the pact with Stalin and, in large majority, shared Hitler's desire for the conquest of Polish territory which they considered rightfully German. Even less than Hitler did they want a general European war, but in 1939 they believed they could hold the French on the western front, while in 1938 they had been certain that this would be impossible and that a military disaster was inevitable.

(1) We will deal with this last point first, since it is crucial. Just before the Obersalzberg meeting of August 14th, Halder made and entered in his diary a long estimate of the probable

situation on the western front in the event of Anglo-French intervention. It revealed that the total strength of the French Army at the outbreak of war would be 106 divisions (almost exactly equal, as we have seen,[41] to the German Army strength in divisions). Of these, fifteen would remain on the Italian frontier, and forty-one (of which all but eight mobile divisions were fortress brigades and second-line troops) would be in or behind the Maginot Line, facing the Rhine and the West Wall, between Switzerland and Belgium. These forty-one would be opposed by thirty-one German divisions under Leeb (seven in Liebmann's Fifth Army, thirteen in Witzleben's First, six in Dollmann's Seventh, and five directly under Leeb's Army group).

Deducting from her total strength the fifty-six divisions in the Maginot Line and opposite Italy, France would have forty-seven divisions "immediately available for the offensive". Perhaps twenty additional divisions could be taken from the reserves "if France feels sure we are not going to attack her". Halder's estimate centred around the contingency that "if the French feel sure that large German forces are being committed in the east, they may decide to take the offensive". The possibility of an attack directly from France into Germany between Switzerland and Belgium—across the Rhine or against the West Wall—was so remote that Halder did not consider it. The only cause for concern was an attack through the Low Countries. From the German standpoint, the danger of such an offensive lay almost entirely *in its timing*. The Polish campaign was not expected to require more than a few weeks, after which large numbers of front-line troops could be released to reinforce the west. Could the French move quickly enough to strike a dangerous blow before Poland was cleaned up?

This raised the theoretical possibility of a fast French march through Belgium, without Belgian consent, but Halder thought it "more than doubtful that it will occur, because France's decisions in all likelihood are contingent on Germany's initiative, and France must at least observe the form of diplomatic talks with Belgium". French operations through Holland would encounter even greater delays and obstacles.

> "For operations through Holland with troops of any substantial strength, the French would first have to cross Belgium. Considering the time required for mobilization and covering the distance, such a French force need not be expected at the German frontier before the third week after mobilization day. Advance motorized elements of course could reach the line much earlier.

However, in view of what we know about French operational doctrine and the political difficulties which would first have to be overcome, such a thrust would be unlikely. Discounting the possibility of any serious Dutch opposition to the French, we would have to be prepared to meet a major attack at the German–Belgian–Dutch border as of the beginning of the third week after mobilization day. In the event that Belgium should permit movement on Belgian railways, this date would have to be considerably advanced."

Should the French embark on such an offensive, Halder assumed that it would probably come in three stages: (*a*) five or six divisions would occupy Luxembourg within three days, but their "mission will not be a local offensive against German territory, but merely the securing of Luxembourg as a French base of operations"; (*b*) seven to nine mobile divisions would drive across Belgium and reach the German frontier at Aachen on the fifth day "to occupy the Belgian–Dutch operations base, and nothing else", so "an offensive with long-range objectives need not be expected of this group"; and (*c*) a concentration of twenty-two to thirty English and French divisions, with very strong artillery and fifty to sixty tank battalions, "could launch a major offensive across the Belgian–Dutch–German border on about M + 14 day" (the beginning of the third week after mobilization day).

To oppose the Allied forces in Luxembourg, Germany would have two regular divisions (the 16th and 26th), which, in Halder's opinion, "will just about do it". But the German forces available to hold the mobile force at Aachen on the fifth day would be "decidedly inadequate". To meet the all-out offensive on M + 14, however, Liebmann's Fifth Army would have twenty-two to twenty-six divisions, and more could be brought up from the newly mobilized "waves". Therefore, "the trouble does not lie so much in man-power as in the deficiencies with respect to artillery and anti-tank guns. The maximum that could be taken out of the western front is . . . a round total of 300 pieces, not counting divisional artillery. They are confronted with 1,600 pieces on the French side, on top of which we must bear in mind that French divisional artillery is stronger than the artillery of German divisions. Accordingly, the defensive battle at the Dutch–Belgian border calls for transfer of medium artillery from the east and shifting the defence line to a water (tank) obstacle, i.e., the Meuse River."

In short, there were risks, but they were not insuperable, and

Halder was ready with proposals for "forestalling the temporary crisis which might develop in the west". Field fortifications were to be constructed along the Dutch border, ten or twelve reserve divisions were to be immediately activated "under camouflage", and anti-aircraft artillery brought from the east "as soon as the enemy air force is eliminated in the eastern theatre".

Halder's estimate was the work of a cautious military craftsman, prepared for all eventualities, but it is clear that he regarded the whole problem as virtually academic. In summing up, he announced his conclusion that:

> "France is not very likely to take any steps in anticipation of our own moves, but rather may be expected to react to our measures, move by move. Accordingly, an early French mobilization, which would materially affect the time-table of our preparedness measures, is improbable; nor is there any reason to expect a march through Belgium 'against Belgian wishes'."

There is every reason to conclude that Halder's cool and unworried gauge of the western front was shared by the officers' corps as a whole.* He was not only Chief of the General Staff; he was a conservative and competent tactician whose views can be regarded as both representative and authoritative. A year earlier, he had not shrunk from planning Hitler's overthrow in order to avert what he then regarded as certain disaster. In 1939, however, he viewed the immediate military prospects in the west with equanimity, and we may safely assume that the same was true of his brother generals.

(2) This is not to say that Halder or any other officers relished the prospect of a general European war or a long one. We must not, however, misunderstand or over-estimate the significance of this reluctance. Since the end of the war, many of the generals have sought to convey the impression that Hitler somehow hoodwinked them into war, and that there was a great gulf between Hitler's secret intentions and what he told them at the Obersalzberg. In fact, there was no such gulf, inasmuch as Hitler himself did not want a general war, and was pulling all the diplomatic stops he could reach in an effort to localize the engagement in Poland. Furthermore, there is no credible evidence of secret or undisclosed intentions in Hitler's mind; on the contrary, he spoke to the generals with great frankness.

---

* See, however, the contrary view expressed in Westphal, *The German Army in the West* (London, 1951), at pp. 69–74. Westphal's analysis, based on a considerable understatement of German strength and a gross over-estimate of the French forces available for an immediate offensive, is unconvincing.

There is not a single point in the analysis of Hitler's attitude, which we have just made, that he did not repeatedly and forcefully impress on the generals.

To be sure, there were differences among the military leaders in the weight which they attached to the risk of an unwanted war with the west. To Raeder, facing the Royal Navy without even the nucleus of a High Seas Fleet, and relying strongly on Hitler's intention to avoid or at least postpone hostilities with England, the hazards no doubt seemed graver than they did to, say, Guderian or Reichenau. Certainly all the generals were thoroughly alive to the danger; in 1938, Beck, Adam and Halder had based their opposition primarily on their political judgment as opposed to Hitler's. In 1939 none of the leading generals chose to stake his professional reputation on an estimate contrary to Hitler's.

Unquestionably, the fact that Hitler had struck nearer the truth on the earlier occasion, and the consequences of his success, may well have left the generals with less stomach for opposing him in 1939. So, too, the departure of Beck and Adam, the transfer of Witzleben and other such individual details, would have made such opposition more difficult and dangerous. But the truly significant circumstance is that there was substantially *no* opposition, even latent, to the consummation of *Weiss*. The greatly improved security on the western front—in terms of both man-power and the increased strength of the West Wall—was, as we have seen, largely responsible for their changed attitude. But there were other major determinants in the east, which we will now examine.

(3) Fundamental was the fact that, whereas the conquest of Czechoslovakia was welcomed by the generals for strategic reasons, the recovery of the Pomeranian and Silesian lands transferred to Poland under the Versailles Treaty touched much deeper chords. At Nuremberg, Blomberg and Blaskowitz declared under oath: [42]

"From 1919, and particularly from 1924, three critical territorial questions occupied attention in Germany. These were the questions of the Polish Corridor, the Ruhr and Memel.

"I myself, as well as the whole group of German staff officers, believed that these three questions, outstanding among which was the question of the Polish Corridor, would have to be settled someday, if necessary by force of arms. About ninety per cent of the German people were of the same mind as the officers on the Polish question. A war to wipe out the desecration involved in the

creation of the Polish Corridor and to lessen the threat to separated East Prussia surrounded by Poland and Lithuania was regarded as a sacred duty though a sad necessity. This was one of the chief reasons behind the partially secret rearmament which began about ten years before Hitler came to power and was accentuated under Nazi rule."

These statements of Blomberg and Blaskowitz were disputed by other generals at Nuremberg. It is doubtful that they would be today, now that the Oder–Neisse line has, as was inevitable, become a critical issue in European *grosse Politik*. In any event, the substantial accuracy of the two generals' diagnosis is unassailable. Unlike Czechoslovakia, none of which had been part of the modern German Empire, the Polish Corridor was a creation of the hated Versailles *Diktat*. Some of the Junker officers had been born there, and many of the older officers had been there on manœuvres before the First World War. The elimination of the Corridor and, indeed, the destruction of Poland, was a basic aim of Seeckt, mentor of the officers' corps in the post-war years, under whom all the senior generals of the Second World War had served.

Of course, all of these generals would have welcomed a favourable solution of the Polish question without actual war, if diplomatic pressure or military threats would do the trick. But if these failed, a settlement must nevertheless be had, in Blomberg's words, "*if necessary* by force of arms". Generaloberst Reinhardt, also testifying at Nuremberg, decried risking a "world war on two or three fronts", but agreed that "the question of the Polish Corridor was one of the most essential points of the Versailles Treaty. This question had to be solved soon."[43] Or, as Blaskowitz put it, "we felt that, if political negotiations came to naught, the Polish question would unavoidably lead to war, not only with Poland herself, but also with the western powers."

(4) This deep desire to regain the lost eastern lands was reinforced and brought to a high pitch by Hitler's last-minute *coup*— the pact with Stalin. Once again, this fitted in perfectly with the teachings of Seeckt. Many of the generals had trained in Russia during the twenties and early thirties. All of them recalled the two-front war which Germany had been unable to survive in 1914–18. Blomberg, Brauchitsch, Manstein, Halder and many other leading generals were disappointed that Hitler broke off their previous contacts with the Red Army, and disapproved his violent harangues against Russia.

So it is little wonder that Hitler's announcement to the generals at the Obersalzberg on August 22nd that the pact was about to be concluded brought pleased smiles to the faces of his audience. At Nuremberg, Kesselring described their reactions:[44]

"It was a tremendous relief to me and to the others. Otherwise we could not have dismissed the possibility of an extension of the war towards the east. Now that Russia was going to hold herself aloof, the Luftwaffe at least . . . had a superiority which guaranteed a rapid and decisive success, and which over and above this, in my opinion, would possibly prevent expansion of the war."

Rundstedt's version was even more optimistic: very possibly there would be no war at all, even with Poland: [45]

"This treaty made us, the old soldiers, very happy and satisfied us very much. Good relations with Russia were considered very important within the Reich's sphere.

"Official delegations of officers from Russia and from Germany visited one another.[46] This pact with Russia meant a very big threat to Poland, and we now believed that Poland would not dare to make war. We left the Berghof feeling that now the war that was going to take place would be a flower war, the same as it had been in 1938 in the Sudetenland."

These remarks of Rundstedt may also serve to illuminate another question much mooted since the end of the war: whether the military leaders quitted the Obersalzberg on August 22nd expecting a war. It may be that Rundstedt and others really believed that the Russo-German pact would prove too much for the spirit of Poland and the determination of the western powers, and that Hitler could bring off another triumph by threat alone. Raeder, who had ample cause for wishful thinking, took much the same line.[47] Certainly, however, there was little on the horizon to suggest that the Poles would give in under any circumstances, and Hitler himself had declared on May 23rd (in Raeder's hearing) that [48] "we cannot expect a repetition of the Czech affair. There will be war."

The audience at the Obersalzberg on August 22nd was remarkably homogeneous, for reasons we have already examined, but they were, nevertheless, individuals of a certain attainment in military affairs, accustomed to command and the confrontation of difficult issues. We may safely assume that their estimates of the probable outcome of *Weiss* differed. The principal imponderable—the reaction of England and France—was beyond the control of Hitler and generals alike. "Politicians do not receive directives from God the Father." In all probability

most of the generals shared Hitler's opinion that Poland would fight, as well as his hope that England might confine herself to face-saving gestures, or make peace after a *fait accompli*. Others may have been more of Blaskowitz' frame of mind:

> "When in the middle of June I received an order from OKH to prepare myself for an attack on Poland, I knew that this war was even closer to the realm of possibility. This conclusion was only strengthened by the Fuehrer's speech on August 22, 1939, on the Obersalzberg when it clearly seemed to be an actuality."

But the surmises of individual generals and admirals as to what England and France might or might not do are not the true issue. It is, rather, *what course of action the military leaders embraced, and for what reasons*. On the question of moral responsibility for war, we will have a few words to say in conclusion. But the record of act and intent needs no further elaboration. Hitler and the officers' corps alike were bent upon recovering the territory lost to Poland in 1919. Hitler and the officers' corps alike welcomed the opportunity to accomplish this which rearmament, the Austro-Czech annexations and the Russo-German pact afforded. Hitler and many of the officers were eager to destroy Poland by means of a "fourth partition", along the lines laid down by Seeckt. Hitler and the military leaders embarked upon a course of action to achieve these ends by military power, under circumstances carrying the grave threat of a European conflagration, which in fact ensued. Nowhere in the officers' corps was voice raised or finger lifted in opposition.

CHAPTER VIII

ACHTUNG! FORWARD MARCH!

ON AUGUST 23, 1939 (the day after the generals' gathering at the Obersalzberg), there was a meeting of the principal staff officers in Berlin at OKW. The day for the attack (Y-day) was set for Saturday, August 26th, at 04·15 or 04·30 in the morning (X-hour). This schedule was to be regarded as definitive; Halder recorded in his diary: "There will be no more orders re Y-day and X-hour. *Everything is to roll automatically.*"

The next few days, accordingly, were spent in last-minute military preparations. On the 23rd, the OKH assumed control of the puppet army of Slovakia, from where part of List's Fourth Army was to debouch into southern Poland. Plans for the capture of the Graudenz and Dirschau bridges over the Vistula were refined, with special emphasis on the necessity for camouflage to avoid compromising the security of the master plan. The hinge of the German forces facing Poland, between Bock's northern and Rundstedt's southern army groups, was weak, and Halder noted the risk of a Polish attack into German territory at Schneidemuehl, which would not be dangerous but would be "inconvenient politically, question of prestige".

On the 24th, all Army furloughs were frozen. It was laid down that ammunition was to be used sparingly and artillery drills avoided in the west, where a tactic of "playing dead" was to prevail. Intelligence of French, British and Polish military preparations occupied much attention in Halder's office. A foretaste of developing friction between OKW and OKH was to be detected in Halder's diary note that OKW, and Jodl especially (returning to duty there), "will not interfere in the conduct of operations".

On August 25th, however, there was a last-minute crisis of hesitancy. At noon, Halder received a telephone call from OKW that the "decision may have to be postponed". An hour and a half later, Halder was informed by OKW that a "postponement must go into effect" because of "Henderson" (British Ambassador to Germany). Orders cancelling the scheduled attack were hastily dispatched to the field commands, and

arrived just in the nick of time. In East Prussia, for example, Petzel's Ist Corps received the news by telephone at thirty-seven minutes after nine o'clock in the evening; the corps' war diary reveals that "by sending out numerous officers it was possible to stop the troops at the last moment", and apparently without arousing Polish suspicions. In the south, the motorized troops of Kleist's corps were stopped only by landing a staff officer in a Fieseler Storch (liaison) airplane on the frontier. Elsewhere, one or two small "special operations" were carried out because the orders did not arrive soon enough. There was some shooting by special sabotage units in Reichenau's sector, and demolition of tunnels at the Jablonka Pass on the Polish–Slovak border. Inasmuch as there had been provocative incidents along the Polish border for some days, the Poles seem not to have realized that a full-scale attack had been mounted and then called off at the last moment.

The reasons for this extraordinary military "balk" lay in the diplomatic arena. The last phase in the discussions between Germany and the western powers had opened on August 15th. Since April, in accordance with Hitler's deliberate tactics, there had been substantially no diplomatic contact between Berlin and Warsaw. Realizing that an explosion was imminent, England and France directed their Ambassadors in Berlin to initiate discussions, and on August 15th first Coulondre and then Henderson appeared at the Wilhelmstrasse and were received by Weizsaecker.

Both of these diplomatic gentlemen found Weizsaecker in a cold and unyielding mood. As Henderson reported to his government, Weizsaecker "seemed very confident, and professed to believe that Russian assistance to the Poles would not only be entirely negligible, but that the U.S.S.R. would even in the end join in sharing the Polish spoils. Nor did my insistence on the inevitability of British intervention move him." Coulondre fared no better. Both of them were lectured by Weizsaecker on the stupidity of their guarantee to the Poles, which had encouraged them to "run amuck" and pursue an "unbridled suicidal policy", including "suppressive, coercive and expulsive" measures against the German minority groups in Poland. Henderson retorted that the Polish government "had shown extreme prudence hitherto", and this led to acrimonious wrangling. Both Coulondre and Henderson came away deeply concerned over "the seriousness and acuteness of the situation"

Hard on the heels of these gloomy reports from Henderson and Coulondre came the news of the German-Soviet pact of August 23rd. The British government reacted immediately by mobilizing coastal and anti-aircraft defence forces, calling up reservists and requisitioning merchant vessels for conversion to armed cruisers. The same day Chamberlain dispatched a personal letter to Hitler, explaining that these precautionary measures were necessitated by "military movements which have been reported from Germany" and in order to make manifest Britain's determination to honour her obligation to Poland. He urged Hitler to stay his hand pending discussions with the Poles "to avoid a catastrophe that will involve Europe in war". Hitler answered promptly in the vein of Weizsaecker to Henderson. England's guarantee to Poland had unloosed "a wave of appalling terrorism" against Germans in Poland. The questions of Danzig and the Corridor "must and shall be solved". Germany wanted England's friendship, but would be obliged to settle the issue with Poland, irrespective of Anglo-French intentions.

While Hitler and Weizsaecker were thus proclaiming the wickedness of the Poles, the latter was bringing to a climax the German campaign of deliberate provocation and incitement to violence in Danzig. Six weeks earlier, Weizsaecker had advised the Wehrmacht to conceal temporarily the artillery which had been smuggled into Danzig: [1] ". . . it will be advisable to wait a while longer before displaying the guns in public . . . the Poles will certainly commit a new blunder and they can then be answered by a public appearance of the batteries."

By the middle of August, the moment for maximum pressure had arrived, and Weizsaecker sent a Foreign Office official, Veesenmayer, to Danzig to bring things to the boiling point. On August 19th, Veesenmayer reported to Weizsaecker the progress of a dispute involving Polish customs guards, together with his recommendations: [2]

> "Poland is willing to withdraw about twelve of the customs guards concerned. . . .
>
> "Gauleiter Forster [Nazi gauleiter of Danzig] intends to extend claims . . . to about 50 Polish customs guards and their immediate withdrawal. Should the Poles yield again, it is intended to increase the claims further, in order to make accord impossible."

These proposals Weizsaecker approved, with the caution that "responsibility for failure to come to an agreement and the consequences rest with Poland". On August 22nd, Veesenmayer

submitted a more comprehensive programme, which called for: [3]

"1. Long-drawn negotiations on the question of customs guards will end in a complete deadlock. Poles to be blamed for it.

"2. Complete removal of all Polish customs guards and abolition of the customs-frontier to East Prussia will follow.

"3. The Poles will react, one way or the other.

"4. We shall retaliate with the arrest of numerous Poles in the Danzig area and seize numerous hidden Polish stocks of arms. The discovery of these hidden arms is assured.

"5. If the Poles do not sufficiently react to this, then finally the Westerplatte [a Polish munitions depot in Danzig Harbour] shall be attacked."

All except point four of Veesenmayer's programme were duly approved by his superiors. On August 23rd, another provocative step was taken when Gauleiter Forster was appointed "head of state" of the Free City of Danzig, a position not authorized by the international statute under which Danzig was constituted. All this, of course, was part of an elaborate programme to provoke the Poles into counter-action, so that they could be depicted as "running amuck." By such mendacious means, Hitler and the Wilhelmstrasse hoped to drive a wedge between Poland and the western Allies, and thus localize the war.

During the last few days before the date scheduled for the attack, Berlin was bent chiefly on exploiting the Soviet pact and trumped-up charges of Polish "madness" primarily to undermine the Anglo-French guarantee, and secondarily to win over Mussolini to full support of Germany. Neither objective was achieved. On August 23rd, the Reich Finance Minister, Schwerin von Krosigk, conferred with Ciano in Rome. Ciano acknowledged that the Soviet pact was a "great diplomatic success", but was in no wise moved from the reserved attitude he had expressed at the Obersalzberg on August 12th and 13th, and reiterated his view that a general European war should be avoided for at least the next three years. And then, two days later, Britain formalized the guarantee to Poland by the conclusion of a formal treaty of mutual assistance, signed in London on August 25th.

The news of the Anglo-Polish treaty reached Hitler about midday, and was the immediate cause of the first warning to the Wehrmacht that the next morning's attack might be called off. Henderson was summoned to the Chancellery, where Hitler

reiterated his charges against the Poles and his determination to "solve" the problem. On this occasion, however, the Fuehrer pulled a new card from his sleeve and made an extraordinary offer to "guarantee" the British Empire and enter into an accord for mutual assistance and the limitation of armaments. Later the Italian Ambassador, Attolico, appeared and confirmed Mussolini's decision that Italy could not join in the war unless Germany would undertake to provide large quantities of raw materials to meet Italian deficiencies. Soon thereafter, the orders cancelling the attack were sent out. As expressed in a naval document, the reasons were [4] "Close alliance pact England–Poland of August 25 and information from Duce that he would stand by his word, but would be forced to ask for large supplies of raw materials".

These were the events that required German officer-couriers all along the border to jump into their cars on Friday evening, August 25th, and scurry about to head off the scheduled troop movements across the border. But the cancellation did not signify uncertainty of basic intention; Hitler simply wanted a few more days to bulldoze the British and cajole Mussolini. The Duce's raw-materials demands arrived the next morning, and proved exorbitant, including large quantities of aviation petrol and tubes for anti-aircraft guns. Hitler resigned himself to Italian non-participation, and had to be content with Mussolini's undertaking to maintain an appearance of incipient belligerency to draw off French strength to the Italo-French frontier.

Having done the best he could with Italy, Hitler settled back to observe the effect of his "offer" to Britain. To allow time for British reflection, *Weiss* was re-scheduled for August 31st or September 1st. In the meantime, he was deluged with pleas for peace from Daladier, President Roosevelt and the Pope, none of which had any effect on the Fuehrer, whose mind was focused on England. On August 27th, late in the afternoon, Hitler called many Nazi notables—including Himmler, Heydrich, Goebbels, Bormann and Karl Wolff—to the Chancellery to outline the situation and justify his pact with Stalin, which had met with a far less favourable reception within the Party than the Wehrmacht. Through Oster of Canaris' OKW intelligence service, Halder received an account of the gathering, thus reflected in his diary:

"Situation is very grave. Determined to have eastern question settled one way or another. Minimum demands: return of Danzig,

settling of Corridor question. Maximum demands: depending on military situation. If minimum demands not satisfied, then war. Brutal! He will himself be in the front line. Position taken by Duce serves our best interests. The war will be tough, we may even fail, but 'as long as I am alive there will be no talk of capitulation'. Soviet pact widely misunderstood in Party. A pact with Satan to cast out the Devil—economic situation. Applause on proper cues, but thin. Personal impression of Fuehrer: worn, haggard, creaking voice, preoccupied. Keeps himself completely surrounded now by his SS advisers."

By the next day, however, Hitler had recovered his poise. Brauchitsch conferred with him during the afternoon, and found the Fuehrer "very calm and clear". *Weiss* was definitely set for September 1st, subject to further postponements contingent upon developments. Hitler was hopeful that England was softening, and would agree to the transfer to Germany of Danzig and one or several "corridors across the Corridor", and a plebiscite in other areas. Everything hung on what news Henderson might bring back from London.

Henderson reached Berlin a few hours later, and visited Hitler at ten-thirty on the evening of August 28th. The British reply was conciliatory in tone, but yielded nothing on fulfilment of the Polish guarantee. In essence, the note declared that the issue between Germany and Poland should be settled by diplomatic discussions between them, and the solution secured by international guarantee. Henderson also indicated orally that the minorities problem might be alleviated by "an exchange of populations".

The proposal to resettle minorities seems to have attracted Hitler, who characterized it as "not a bad idea at all". Henderson, however, detected that this favourable reaction assumed that there would also be annexations of Polish territory. As for the insistence on international guarantees, this merely excited Hitler's sarcasm: "That is an idea to my liking; from now on I shall act only on an international basis. Send in international troops, including Russians." Perspicacious as ever, Hitler did not fail to exploit the fact that his pact with Stalin must bring Russia into any attempted international solution of the Polish issue, whereas the western powers at Munich had left Russia out in the cold, and the Polish–Baltic–Balkan fear of Russian participation had been the rock on which Anglo-French efforts to achieve an *entente* with Russia had foundered.

The next evening (August 29th), Hitler handed his reply to Henderson. It demanded the return to Germany of Danzig and the Corridor, guarantees for the benefit of German minorities, Soviet participation in any international settlement, and the arrival in Berlin of a Polish plenipotentiary by the next day. Henderson remarked that this last demand "sounded like an ultimatum", but transmitted Hitler's memoir to London for study. At the same time, Hitler informed Brauchitsch that "we strike either on 1 or 2 Sept." If the attack was not launched by then it would be "all off", presumably because the season was growing late.

But there was no intention to call matters off. Henderson brought the British reply suggesting "normal contact" with Warsaw, to Ribbentrop, at midnight on August 30th. Ribbentrop thereupon, with most insulting demeanour, read out a list of German demands against Poland. He declined to give Henderson the text, observing that August 30th had expired without the arrival of a Polish emissary. Henderson informed London, and then routed out the Polish Ambassador [Lipski] in the early hours of morning and "advised the establishment of direct Polish–German contact". After obtaining instructions from Warsaw, at about noon on August 31st Lipski requested an audience with Ribbentrop to present "the Polish government's favourable attitude to any proposal for direct negotiations". This took six hours to arrange, while Weizsaecker raised the question whether Lipski could speak as a plenipotentiary. When Lipski finally saw Ribbentrop that evening, the same objection was raised. Ribbentrop complained that "he had thought [Lipski] would come as a fully empowered delegate", and agreed only to inform Hitler of the Polish government's declaration.

All this was merely shadow-boxing. Hitler had given the final order for the "jump-off" early in the morning of August 31st, and at about four-thirty in the morning on September 1st, German troops crossed the Polish border at all points of attack. *Weiss* was under way.

The diplomatic window-dressing for the invasion of Poland was furnished by an official communiqué broadcast by the German radio during the evening of August 31st, and Hitler's speech to the Reichstag the following morning. The communiqué rehearsed the discussions of the last few days, laying the blame for their failure on the Poles, for neglecting to send a plenipotentiary within the appointed time. It then set forth

sixteen "practical proposals" for a peaceful settlement, including all the demands which Hitler and Ribbentrop had voiced in their talks with Henderson.

Hitler's speech in the Reichstag, delivered after hostilities had already been under way for nearly six hours, was one of his weaker efforts. The faked attack on the Gleiwitz radio station, arranged by the SS with the aid of Polish uniforms furnished by the Wehrmacht, was exploited by Hitler's charge that "last night for the first time regular soldiers of the Polish Army fired shots on our territory. Since 5.45 A.M. we have been returning their fire." *Weiss* was, after all, a strictly defensive undertaking! There was plenty of egodrama in Hitler's worst vein. The shade of Frederick the Great was invoked, as the Fuehrer proclaimed that "once again I have put on the tunic which was to me the holiest and most beloved of garments. I shall take it off only after victory—or I shall not live to see the end."

The spuriousness of the "practical proposals" in the German communiqué, already sufficiently apparent, was underscored by the Reichstag's "statute" of September 1st annexing Danzig to the Reich. These were not proposals but unilateral pronouncements. German law was extended to Danzig, Forster was given full civil power, and Frick (Reich Minister of the Interior) was vested with authority "for matters connected with the reunion of Danzig with the German Reich".

As far as the broader military consequence of the invasion of Poland was concerned, the next move was up to the western powers. Little more than forty-eight hours elapsed until the die was cast. Hitler's strategy of intransigent determination failed to shake the Anglo-French *entente*. During the afternoon of September 1st, Henderson conveyed to the Wilhelmstrasse a demand that Germany suspend all aggressive action and withdraw from Poland; otherwise "His Majesty's Government in the United Kingdom will without hesitation fulfil their obligations to Poland". No reply was made, and early on the morning of September 3rd, Britain sent a final ultimatum, to expire at 11.00 A.M. that day. Shortly after that hour, Chamberlain proclaimed a state of war with Germany, and the French followed suit later that day. A last-minute effort by Mussolini, under French stimulus, to arrange an armistice and a negotiated peace came to nothing.

And thus, at about noon on Sunday, September 3rd, 1939, World War II began.

German troops invaded Poland on September 1st, but in a logistical sense the campaign began on August 26th, according to the original schedule. August 26th was the planned "mobilization day" (M-day), and it was so labelled in Halder's diary, where each succeeding day was given the appropriate "plus" according to conventional military lingo, so that September 1st was actually "M + 6".

For the economic mobilization, August 26th was the day of "X-case", or camouflaged mobilization.[5] Generalmajor Thomas, of the OKW economic staff, unsuccessfully pleaded for a total mobilization, but was overridden by Keitel, no doubt on Hitler's orders, who decided "that a war with Poland did not necessitate a general mobilization, and any other form of mobilization was out of the question for political reasons". Thus the civilian economy was left in many respects untouched. Amazingly enough, as General Thomas' memoirs reveal,[6] and as is confirmed by many other sources, the half-way character of the economic mobilization persisted to a considerable degree for nearly four years, and was not finally turned to total mobilization until 1943, after the advent of Albert Speer as Reich Minister for Armaments.

For the Wehrmacht, however, there were no such half-way measures. On August 25th, five additional Air Force groups were ordered to the east. The mobilization of reserves was put on a war footing. The railways were placed on military schedule, with maximum traffic load planned for August 27th.

August 26th was also, for the Army, the day on which most of the war-time commands were formally activated. The active commanders and the retired officers recalled for field duty took command of their corps or other units in the field, and the home commands were taken over by other retired generals or those who had been rejected for field duty. Brauchitsch and Halder were deluged with personnel problems.

Despite the profound convulsions which had gripped the officers' corps during the preceding two years, nearly all of the retired generals rallied to the trumpet of Mars and requested active duty. Only Beck and Adam held aloof. Blomberg's application was quietly rejected. Fritsch, still wounded to the quick, was allowed to go off to war with his regiment in East Prussia as a supernumerary honorary *Chef*. Joachim von Stuelpnagel was called up as Chief of the Home Army (*Ersatzheer*),

but was relieved on August 31st as a result of pressure by Goering, and replaced by Fromm. Kress von Kressenstein, too, was relieved within a short time after reporting for duty as the substitute *Wehrkreis* commander in Munich.

But the other retired generals, including most of those "purged" on February 4, 1938, were welcomed back into the fold. Rundstedt, the elder Leeb, Liebmann, Kleist, Geyer, Ulex and Ritter von Prager held field commands at Army group, Army or corps level. The replacement commanders for the *Wehrkreise* included Hammerstein, who thus made a surprising and belated re-entry on the active-duty roster, as well as such other relics of the past as von Vollard Bockelberg, Feige, Oskar von Hindenburg, Falkenhausen, Otto von Stuelpnagel, von Steppuhn, Friedrich von Cochenhausen and two of Goering's three old mentors, Halm and Wachenfeld (the latter replacing Kress von Kressenstein), who were restored to Army rank as *Generale*. The third, Kaupisch, was given command of a special formation of border troops and armour in Pomerania, supporting Guderian's XIXth Corps. Other old-timers such as Gruen (Inspector of Artillery), Lutz, von Pogrell, Niebelschutz, Zwengauer and the von Roques brothers were called up for secondary command or staff assignments.

For the Army General Staff, the six days from August 20th to September 1st were feverish and full. Halder's diary shows him to have been at his desk or in the field from early morning to late evening. On the 29th, Brauchitsch and Halder flew to Rundstedt's headquarters at Neisse to review the operational plans of Army Group South. The next day they were in Pomerania conferring with Bock and Kluge. On the 31st, after final orders for the attack had been issued, they visited Frankfurt-am-Main for a full-dress conference on the western defences with Leeb, Dollmann, Witzleben and Liebmann. Leeb, who had taken formal command of the Army group only five days earlier, reported that his forces were "ready for defence". Most of his divisions were by now in position, and Leeb insisted that there be "no decrease in total of 34 divisions as at present".

After his return to Berlin on the eve of the attack, Halder reviewed the Army's over-all investment of man-power with Oberst Eduard Wagner, Chief of Staff to Generalmajor Eugen Mueller, the newly appointed *Generalquartiermeister* of the General Staff, in charge of supplies for the field Army. Halder and Wagner calculated the Army's total strength in the field at about 2,500,000 men, of whom 1,000,000 were in the west

and 1,500,000 in the east. Against Poland, the breakdown was tabulated as follows:

Third Army (Kuechler)	320,000
Fourth Army (Kluge)	230,000
Army Group North Reserve	80,000
Total Army Group North (Bock)	630,000
Eighth Army (Blaskowitz)	180,000
Tenth Army (Reichenau)	300,000
Fourteenth Army (List)	210,000
Army Group South Reserve	196,000
Total Army Group South (Rundstedt)	886,000
Grand Total	1,516,000

Halder's strength figure for the Third Army is surprisingly high, particularly in comparison to the Tenth Army, where the *Schwerpunkt* of attack was fixed, and the possibility of error in his tabulation cannot be excluded. It is probable that border guards, SA units, or other irregular formations in East Prussia were included in and swelled Kuechler's total. Likewise, Rundstedt's Army group was probably stronger in comparison to Bock's than these figures indicate. An earlier tabulation by Halder (in his report to Goering on August 22nd, just before the Fuehrer's conference at the Obersalzberg) put the strength of Bock's Army group at seventeen divisions and a cavalry brigade, and that of Rundstedt's at thirty-five divisions. Allowing for thirty-four divisions on the western front (Leeb's count on August 31st), there were at the outbreak of war over fifty-two divisions deployed against Poland,* eighty-six divisions de-

---

* Churchill (*The Gathering Storm*, p. 442) puts the figure at fifty-six divisions, which, if all border troops, cavalry and fortress brigades, SS units, and other special formations are included, may be an only slightly generous estimate. General J. F. C. Fuller (*The Second World War*, p. 50) states that forty-five German divisions were used, but the documentary evidence makes it clear that he is on the low side by at least seven divisions. Inaccuracy in this area is prevalent even among the direct participants. A memorandum prepared at Nuremberg in November, 1945, signed by Brauchitsch, Manstein, Halder, Warlimont and Westphal, declared that "forty-one infantry and fourteen motorized divisions advanced against Poland. On the western border of Germany five infantry and one armoured division remained. That meant that no reserves remained for the . . . Army". Almost every statement herein is inaccurate. No armour was left in the west, and not even by adding all panzer (six), light (four) and motorized infantry (three) divisions can one reach the fifteen motorized divisions postulated. Not five but thirty-four or thirty-five infantry divisions manned the west front, and there was an earmarked reserve to meet the contingency of a French attack through Belgium.

ployed on both fronts, and about twenty more (all second-line troops) forming in or available to move up from the interior of Germany.

The ground troops on the eastern front were supported by 1,500 to 2,000 aircraft under Kesselring in the north and Loehr in the south. According to Asher Lee's estimates,[7] these included about 700 medium bombers, 400 fighters, 150 Stukas (dive-bombers) and 600 reconnaissance, transport and other miscellaneous types. The medium bombers were already obsolescent (none of the new Junkers 88s were used), but the fighters were mainly the new and highly serviceable Messerschmitt 109s.

And what of the opposing Polish forces? The Polish Army was only slightly inferior in numbers to the 1,500,000 men under Bock and Rundstedt. Halder's diary gives an estimated Polish strength of thirty-three infantry divisions and fifteen cavalry brigades; Churchill speaks of thirty divisions and twelve brigades, and General Fuller of thirty infantry and ten reserve divisions and twenty-two brigades. But the precise numerical strength of the Polish ground forces need concern us now as little as it did Brauchitsch in 1939, because of its woeful deficiencies in tanks and heavy artillery, and the impotence of its cavalry against modern mechanized troops. In the air, the Poles were even weaker. They could put up less than a thousand combat planes, and this outnumbered force was fatally handicapped by poor communications and inadequate anti-aircraft protection. Courage and dash could not make up for lack of the sinews of modern warfare; the Poles never had a chance.

The Wehrmacht took the field under the governance of Hitler's "Directive No. 1 for the Conduct of the War", issued on August 31st. So far as Poland was concerned, this was little more than a confirmation of *Weiss*. The first two paragraphs stated: [8]

"1. After all political possibilities have been exhausted to eliminate by peaceful means a situation on the eastern frontier intolerable to Germany, I have decided on a solution by force.

"2. The attack on Poland is to be executed according to the plans made for 'Case White', adopting those changes in the Army which have taken place following the troop concentrations which have meanwhile been almost completed. Assignments and operational objective remain unchanged.

"Day of Attack: September 1, 1939.

"Time of Attack: 0445 hours.

"The operations Gdynia–Danzig Bay and Dirschau Bridge will start at the same time."

There remained, before Y-hour, only the faked Polish attack on the southern Silesian border for which Canaris had been called upon to supply Polish uniforms. The execution of this delectable task, under the ægis of Himmler and Heydrich, was committed to Heinrich Mueller (Chief of the Gestapo) and an SS official named Naujocks.* At about eight o'clock in the evening of August 31st, Germans in Polish uniforms appeared on the border and fired some shots; about a dozen prisoners of the Gestapo (furnished by Mueller under the cover-name "canned goods") were left dead on the ground for verisimilitude. Another group under Naujocks "captured" the German radio station at Gleiwitz, and a Polish-speaking German broadcast a short speech announcing a Polish attack on Germany. Although Hitler utilized this ugly little affair in his Reichstag speech the next day, it seems to have had little propaganda value at the time,† and to have been of serious consequence only to the unfortunate "canned goods" from the Gestapo prisons.

The day of attack was signalized not only by Hitler's speech to the Reichstag and the "laws" for the annexation of Danzig but also by a public Fuehrer proclamation to the Wehrmacht. Therein, Hitler sought to incite the troops by reference to "bloody terror" against Germans in Poland and "frontier violations". The troops were exhorted to fight "as representatives of National Socialist Greater Germany". Brauchitsch supported Hitler's appeal with a proclamation to the people of Danzig, hailing the Free City's return to the Reich. He announced the delegation of military executive power in Danzig to Kuechler, and the designation of Gauleiter Forster as head of the civil administration. "Long live the Fuehrer!"

By mid-morning on September 1st, when Hitler appeared in the Reichstag, the Germans were already several kilometres deep in Polish territory along most of the front, and German planes were busily bombing Polish airfields and railways. In the Corridor and along the Upper Silesian border the onslaught

* Nuremberg Document 2751-PS. The "incident" was known to Keitel, Halder and Heinrich von Stuelpnagel, and is mentioned in Halder's diary entry for August 17, 1939.

† The Gleiwitz incident was, however, reported by the foreign press from Berlin, as were other outbreaks near Kreuzburg and Ratibor, in the same general vicinity. See the *New York Times*, September 1, 1939.

315

came with the first glimmerings of dawn in a rush of tanks and motorized infantry; elsewhere foot-soldiers pushed forward more in the manner of earlier wars. The day broke clear in the south, but Bock's northern front was foggy and his forces attacked initially without benefit of air support.

The invasion of Poland has been commonly depicted as a smooth, perfectly co-ordinated and rapidly moving *Blitzkrieg* without substantial flaws of execution. Certainly, it so appeared to the world at large and to the bewildered, reeling Poles. After the first few days, the Poles lost control of their own movements, German battle discipline improved rapidly, and the impression of irresistible *Macht* was confirmed by the total disaster that speedily overtook Polish arms.

But in fact the German Army, well trained as it was, lacked battle experience, and the baptism of fire, as with all virgin armies, brought nervousness, confusion, delays and unnecessary casualties. Had the Wehrmacht been opposed by battle-hardened troops with modern arms, things would have gone hard with the Germans. Guderian has described some of the misadventures of his corps in the opening days of the campaign —artillery firing into the fog and bracketing the advancing German tanks, attacks stalled and troops waiting idly at critical moments for lack of orders or determined leadership, failures to transmit orders between higher units, bridges built and immediately dismantled because of conflicting orders, "fear of the dark" and narrowly averted panic, and other boners.

But the Poles were quite unable to exploit these flaws in the attack. Within little more than forty-eight hours they had lost their air cover. The Polish airfields were poorly protected and their planes insufficiently dispersed on the ground. The Luftwaffe descended on them from the moment of attack, and destroyed large numbers of aircraft on the ground, burning the installations and causing many casualties to flying personnel and ground crews. By the end of the first day, the Luftwaffe claimed "air domination over Polish territory", and on the second day it announced "unlimited control" over all of Poland, so that German planes could thereafter be devoted entirely to other missions, such as tactical support of the Army and the bombing of communications, supplies and factories.

Apart from the losses thus inflicted, the Luftwaffe attacks and the armoured thrusts combined to throw the entire Polish command structure into confusion and reduced the Army to individual, unco-ordinated groups, battling valiantly but futilely

with small arms—even the swords and lances of the horse cavalry brigades—against tanks, other armoured vehicles and modern artillery. The Germans needed to do little more than send their armour on ahead, move the infantry and supporting

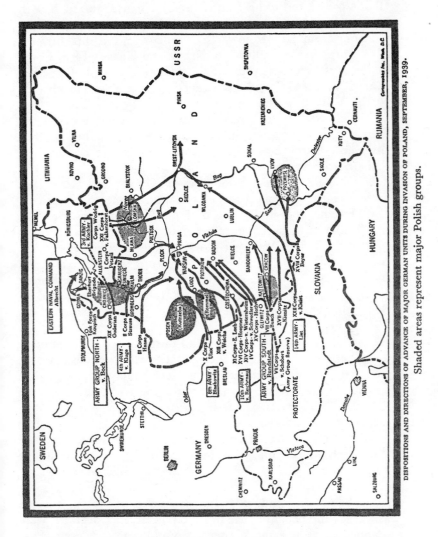

DISPOSITIONS AND DIRECTIONS OF ADVANCE OF MAJOR GERMAN UNITS DURING INVASION OF POLAND, SEPTEMBER, 1939.

Shaded areas represent major Polish groups.

artillery in behind, and keep going as hard and fast as they could.

While the overall pattern of attack on the ground was for the five German armies to converge on Warsaw from the north, west and south, and cut off the Polish escape route to the east,

Kluge's Fourth Army in Pomerania had the critical preliminary mission of cutting the Corridor and linking with Kuechler in East Prussia. For this task Kluge deployed Kaupisch's battle group (including the new 10th Panzer Division) on the northern (Baltic coast) end of his front, Guderian's mechanized XIXth Corps to make the main strike across the narrow neck of the Corridor from Konitz toward Graudenz and Kulm, Strauss' IInd Corps to the south of Guderian, and Haase's IIIrd Corps at the southern end around Schneidemuehl. While Guderian "raced" across to Graudenz, Strauss and Haase were to advance to the Vistula in the vicinity of Bromberg and Thorn, and Kaupisch was to go across the extreme northern tip of the Corridor to Danzig, cutting off Gdynia and linking up with the German troops that had been smuggled into Danzig (the "Eberhard Brigade").

It was to expedite the junction of Kluge's and Kuechler's forces that the special operations to capture intact the Graudenz and Dirschau bridges had been planned. These, however, did not "come off", partly because of the fog that hampered air operations; the bridges were blown. Otherwise, however, good progress was made, despite the errors of execution recounted by Guderian. On the first day, his troops captured Konitz (Chojnice) and crossed the Brahe at Hammermuehle,* and on September 2nd his panzer reconnaissance battalion reached the Vistula near Schwetz (Swiecie) and cut the Corridor. In the meanwhile, Strauss and Haase had bitten deep, and Kaupisch and Eberhard had effected their junction. In the Baltic, where Admiral Albrecht commanded the German naval forces, Polish submarines and destroyers were scattering and seeking escape, and the old German battleship *Schleswig-Holstein* had moved into Danzig Bay and was shelling Polish installations, while German troops emerged from the holds of freighters and assisted the Eberhard Brigade. Within a few hours, Polish resistance had been reduced to hold-out strongpoints at Westerplatte, Gdynia and the Hela Peninsula.

On September 2nd, in order to accentuate the *fait accompli* aspect for the benefit of the western powers, special efforts were planned to reduce the Westerplatte and capture Posen (Poznan). The next day, however, England and France declared

---

* It was symbolic of the *Polonia irredenta* attitude of the officers' corps that Guderian, on the very first day of the campaign, overran the little village of Gross Klonia, which had been the property of his great-grandfather, and where his father was born. Guderian himself was born in Kulm on the Vistula.

war, and these projects were abandoned. Nevertheless, the Poles in the Corridor were nearly finished. Their forces were practically encircled, and antediluvian, though valiant, cavalry charges against Guderian's tanks by the Pomorska Brigade merely bloodied the ground. By the evening of September 4th, the battle of the Corridor had ended.

Accordingly, on September 5th there was a general re-grouping of Kluge's army. The 10th Panzer Division had already been detached from Kaupisch and sent into East Prussia to reinforce Kuechler. Now Guderian's XIXth Corps was likewise transferred to the Third Army, and commenced the crossing of the Vistula into East Prussia. Strauss and Haase swung to the south-east, and pushed down the Vistula toward Warsaw, Strauss on the northern bank and Haase on the southern. Kaupisch's troops, the Eberhard Brigade, the Navy and the Air Force were left to complete the reduction of the Westerplatte, Gdynia and Hela, where the Poles held out obstinately for many days.

These redispositions gave Guderian a pleasant breathing spell. On September 5th, he was honoured by a visit from Hitler, and escorted the Fuehrer on a drive up and down the neck of the Corridor, inspecting the carnage which, as the panzer general was at pains to point out, was the work of German tanks rather than Stukas. Inter-service jealousies thrive as well in execution as in preparation. But the achievements of Guderian's armour were undeniable. Several Polish infantry divisions, a cavalry brigade and thousands of pieces of artillery had been swept off the boards, and the roads of the Corridor were littered with the debris of battle.

For the next three days, Guderian had little to do but hunt the stag while his troops crossed the Vistula and East Prussia over to the left flank of Kuechler's Third Army. He set up his corps headquarters at Schloss Finckenstein, which Napoleon had used for the same purpose. Not until the evening of September 8th was he called to Bock's Army group headquarters (now at Allenstein in East Prussia) to receive new orders.

Bock had it in mind that Guderian's tanks should strike from East Prussia (Arys) to Lomsha and then turn westerly toward Warsaw. By this time, however, Hoepner's armour under Reichenau was already hammering at Warsaw from the southwest, and Guderian had other ideas. After discussion with Bock and his Chief of Staff (Salmuth), it was agreed that

Guderian would instead attack to the south-east, and make for Brest-Litovsk in order to cut off the probable Polish retreat from Warsaw to the east.

Guderian's views were sound. In fact, while another ten days of hard fighting remained, Poland's destruction was already assured, one week after the outbreak of war. Except for occasional adventurers who got short shrift, the sky was clear of Polish planes. During the morning of September 5th, Brauchitsch and Bock had concluded that the Poles were "practically beaten". The Polish government had evacuated Warsaw during the night of September 6th and moved to Lublin. On September 7th, Halder was already preoccupied with the transfer of troops to the western front and plans for the occupational administration in Poland.

In the south, List had taken Cracow on September 6th and Sandomierz on the 8th. Reichenau's armoured onslaught had captured Kielce and Piotrokow, and on September 8th the 4th Panzer Division (of Hoepner's XVIth Corps) reached the outskirts of Warsaw.* Only Blaskowitz and Kuechler had encountered real obstacles. Posen and Lodz were still in Polish hands, and the Polish forces around Posen, reinforced by troops falling back from the Corridor, were offering Blaskowitz tough opposition. South of East Prussia, the Poles had fortified the Narew River line, and Kuechler's XXIst Corps (under Falkenhorst) had been stopped at Lomza, although his right wing made better progress and had reached Pultusk.

With Hoepner at the gates of Warsaw, the Corridor conquered, Polish planes driven from the sky and a complete German victory assured, the "second phase" of the Polish campaign began on September 9th and ended on September 17th. The only question was how fast the Germans could overrun the remainder of Poland, cut off any retreat of substantial Polish forces to the east and south-east, and force the capitulation of the remaining isolated large Polish groups between Posen and Warsaw and on the Narew line south of East Prussia. The "grand encirclement" was to be accomplished through a southward strike of Bock's left wing (Guderian's XIXth Corps) aimed at Brest-Litovsk, where a junction was to be effected with List's right wing (Kleist's XXIInd Corps) coming up

* Gen. J. F. C. Fuller (*The Second World War*, p. 53) credits "Gen. Guderian's tanks" with the capture of Kielce and Piotrokow and the first approach to Warsaw. In fact, as we have seen, Guderian was hundreds of miles to the north-east in East Prussia, and never came near these cities.

from Slovakia. The reduction of the major Polish forces west of Warsaw (in the area bounded by Warsaw–Thorn–Posen–Lodz–Radom) was the task of Kluge, Blaskowitz and Reichenau.

For Guderian, newly launched into battle from East Prussia, the Narew River, which had stalled Falkenhorst, was the major obstacle. Elements of the 10th Panzer Division were already across when Guderian arrived at the front on the morning of September 9th, but stubborn Polish resistance at Lomza, confusion with respect to the location of bridges to be built by the engineers, and the consequent necessity of ferrying tanks over the river, delayed his advance. It was the 11th before his troops were well across and Lomza was evacuated. On the 14th, advanced armoured elements pierced the outer fortifications of Brest-Litovsk, and Guderian brought up his corps with all speed to exploit the opportunity. The citadel, however, held out gallantly, and attacks on the 15th and 16th were repelled. On the 17th, however, the citadel capitulated, and Guderian's advanced patrols (of the 3rd Panzer Division, commanded by Geyr von Schweppenburg) met those of List's Fourteenth Army at Wlodawa, about fifty miles south of Brest-Litovsk.

On this day, as Guderian observed,[9] "the campaign came to a definite conclusion". Poland was cut in twain, roughly along the Bug River. Warsaw was encircled, as was Lvov, and to the west the main Polish armies were pocketed. The Polish government had fled from Lublin to Krzemieniec in Volhynia on the 10th, and to the Rumanian border (Zaleszczyki and Kuty) on the 15th and 16th. The Luftwaffe was hammering at Lvov, Lublin and other hold-out points, and Polish soldiers were streaming across the border into Rumania. And finally, just as Brest-Litovsk fell and the circle was completed, the Russians marched into Poland, ending even the desperate chance of a last stand in the east.

There were, to be sure, violent and bloody death-throes. On September 9th, the Polish forces between Posen and Warsaw, under General Kutrzeba, had launched a violent counter-attack against Reichenau's left flank and Blaskowitz's small Eighth Army. Blaskowitz had to make a temporary retreat, much to Hitler's disgust, and parts of Kluge's and Reichenau's army had to be diverted to cope with the situation. Fierce but one-sided fighting raged there until September 19th, when Kutrzeba's group disintegrated. In the meantime, Gdynia had finally capitulated. On the 20th, Brauchitsch issued an

order of the day to his troops announcing the conclusion of operations against Poland. The *Blitzkrieg* was over.

By this time, German troops were streaming back from Poland, and the western front could be strongly reinforced. The American newspaper correspondent William Shirer drove from Berlin to Danzig on September 18th, and reported [10] that throughout Pomerania and the Corridor the roads were "full of motorized columns of German troops returning from Poland". He found Gdynia in German hands, though to the north of the city isolated groups of Poles still held out against the combined assaults of infantry, tanks, artillery, Stukas and the guns of the *Schleswig-Holstein*, anchored in Danzig Bay. On September 20th, Hitler, who had been frustrated in his desire to make a victory speech in Warsaw, made it in the Danzig Guild Hall instead. He entered escorted by Keitel, Himmler and others, and obviously inflamed by both victory and anger against England. As Shirer put it, "We had expected Hitler to offer peace to the west and announce what the future of Poland would be. He did neither, merely remarking that Poland would never be re-created on the Versailles model and that he had no war aims against Britain and France, but would fight them if they continued the war."

While Hitler was fretting at the gates of Warsaw and holding forth in Danzig, the Russian armies were spreading over eastern Poland. Guderian was farthest to the east, and his troops made the first contact with the advancing Russian forces east of Brest-Litovsk. The temporary military demarcation line obliged the Germans to withdraw behind the Bug, which left the fortifications of Brest-Litovsk, as well as Bialystok and Lvov, to the Russians. Guderian, for example, was instructed to evacuate Brest-Litovsk by September 22nd. He had been fighting hard, and this schedule did not even give him enough time to evacuate his wounded and repair his damaged tanks. However, when the Russian commander (Brigadier General Krivoschein) arrived on September 22nd, he and Guderian hit it off well, assisted by their mutual knowledge of French, and Guderian was able to make satisfactory local arrangements, signalized by a parade and exchange of flags. He made a comfortable withdrawal, departed for a rest in East Prussia, and his divisions returned to Germany for rest and refitting, preparatory to their transfer to the Western Front.

The *Blitzkrieg* was indeed over, but Brauchitsch's proclamation of the end of the campaign was a trifle premature: Warsaw

and Modlin (twenty-odd miles north-west of Warsaw on the Vistula) were still holding out, as well as the Hela Peninsula, north of Danzig. On the evening of September 15th, Jodl had telephoned Halder to declare that "we must now come to a decision as to what to do about the Polish capital" and ask for an "appraisal of the ground situation". Halder had replied (as recorded in his diary) that Warsaw was about to be completely encircled, and that he was "against an attack into the city", which "must be starved into capitulation" because "we are in no hurry and don't need the forces now outside Warsaw anywhere else".*

However, this was not Hitler's view. On September 12th, in Hitler's private railway carriage, Admiral Canaris had protested to Keitel, Ribbentrop and Jodl against the proposal to reduce Warsaw by aerial bombardment, which he knew was under advisement. Keitel replied that this had been agreed upon by Hitler and Goering, and that nothing could be done to change the decision.[11] According to Halder's later recollection, Hitler wanted to capture Warsaw before the expected Russian entry into Poland.[12] As matters worked out, however, the Russians came in on the 17th, before a final decision was reached on the Warsaw issue. In the meantime, leaflets were dropped urging surrender, and a combined air-ground attack, which had been scheduled for the 17th, was cancelled by Hitler's order on the 16th, presumably because he knew that the Russians were about to move.

On the 17th and 18th, there were radio discussions between the Warsaw Poles and the Germans concerning the sending of a *parlementaire* to arrange for evacuation of the diplomatic corps. However, these came to nothing, and Brauchitsch ordered a heavy artillery barrage, and special efforts to destroy power-stations and water-works. The infantry was to attack on the eastern side of the city if opportunity offered, but there was to be "no battle for the centre of the city if avoidable". On the 20th it was decided to continue this "softening up" for eight days, and then unloose an air attack.

Thus began the first of the numerous and terrible batterings which the unhappy city was fated to suffer. The sustained shelling—broken only by a short truce to let out diplomats and other neutrals—worked heavy destruction and loss of life. On the

* In his postwar pamphlet *Hitler als Feldherr* (Munich, 1949), however, Halder states (at pp. 26–27) that another reason he wanted to forgo an attack was so that heavy artillery could be shifted to the west.

24th, Manstein (Rundstedt's Chief of Staff) reported to OKH that masses of refugees were streaming westward out of the city toward the German lines. On orders to shoot, they were driven back because, as Halder recorded, "if the refugees were allowed to leave, it would be impossible to starve out the city. Moreover, the city's garrison would be enabled to take full advantage of the opportunities for street fighting, with all its incalculable complications."

At this time Reichenau's armoured forces and his Army headquarters were sent away to prepare for their transfer to the western front, and the reduction of Warsaw was entrusted to Blaskowitz' Eighth Army west of the Vistula surrounding Warsaw itself, and the Ist Corps (under Petzel) from Kuechler's Third Army, surrounding the suburb of Praga on the east bank of the Vistula. On September 25th, Hilter, Brauchitsch and Halder visited Blaskowitz' headquarters at Grodzisk to review his plan of attack. A heavy artillery bombardment was to open the following morning, behind which Weichs' XIIIth Corps, which was already inside the outer fortifications on the southwestern side of the city, would launch an infantry attack. The following day, the 27th, Emil Leeb's XIth Corps (transferred to Blaskowitz from Reichenau) would move against the outer forts on the north-western side.

On the 26th, the attack was launched according to plan, and that evening an emissary from the Polish general (by name Rommel) commanding the Warsaw garrison requested a twenty-four-hour armistice. The Germans refused to consider the request without a simultaneous promise of surrender, and orders were given to continue the attack on the 27th, with close support from the Luftwaffe. But the stricken city could endure no more. On the morning of the 27th, General Kutrzeba, representing General Rommel, met with Blaskowitz at the Skoda Airplane Factory in Rakow, just outside Warsaw. Within an hour an agreement for the "unconditional surrender" of Warsaw was signed, and on October 5th, after evacuation of the garrison, Hitler entered the city and reviewed a triumphal march-past.

The fortress of Modlin surrendered the following day. Lvov, caught between the Germans and Russians, had been overrun several days before; the Russians proclaimed themselves its "liberators", much to the disgust of the Germans. On the tiny Hela Peninsula the Poles held out a few days longer, but on October 2nd this last futile, valiant spark was extinguished.

Fall Weiss had run its full course. The Poland of Versailles and Pilsudski was dead, and the Poles were about to find that the horrors of their twentieth-century enslavement beggared the worst memories of imperial oppression. Crushed once more between the German and Russian millstones, Poland's fate indeed fulfilled Seeckt's prophecy, but after a pattern that Seeckt himself would hardly have relished. It was symbolic of the passing of the old regime, therefore, that as Pilsudski's beloved Warsaw crumbled into rubble, Seeckt's protégé and successor, von Fritsch, found a not unwelcome soldier's death in the outskirts of the stricken city.

THE DEATH OF GENERALOBERST FREIHERR VON FRITSCH

From February, 1939, until August, Fritsch had been living quietly in his new home in Berlin-Zehlendorff. It was a lonely life; as war approached, his brother officers were increasingly preoccupied with plans and manœuvres, and none of them could expect his career to be furthered by being known as an intimate of the man whom the Fuehrer had broken. He was separated from his regiment, and sank into a bored, restless and bitter desuetude, relieved only slightly by riding and correspondence with his mother and an old family friend living near Kassel, the Baronin Margot von Schutzbar-Milchling. One of these letters, the authenticity of which has not been unquestionably established, has for that reason, and because of its contents, aroused much controversy. It is dated December 11, 1938, at Achterberg, slightly before Fritsch's removal from there to Berlin, and reads as follows: *

"Achterberg, 11 Dec. 38.

"My dear Baroness:
"Many thanks for your two letters. I am very sorry to hear your father's health is causing you worry. It is always terrible to see someone suffering without being able to assist. But perhaps the weather has helped a little in the meantime. For the last two days the sky has been clear here and we had frost yesterday until noon.

* The letter is reproduced in part as Document 1947-PS in *Nazi Conspiracy and Aggression*. It was quoted in salient part by Mr. Justice Jackson in his opening statement before the International Military Tribunal at Nuremberg. However, the prosecution was unable to produce the original letter, and it was never admitted into evidence. Counsel for the General Staff and High Command (Dr. Hans Laternser) strongly contested its authenticity, and produced an affidavit (No. 180, dated July 4, 1946) from the Baronin stating that she had never received such a letter from Fritsch.
The Baronin had turned over her letters from Fritsch to American military

"On the whole I am feeling quite well and every day I go riding alone for several hours. This is the best medicine for quieting the nerves and getting some peace. I have also had quite a number of visitors. It is really peculiar that so many people should look to the future with increasing fears, in spite of the Fuehrer's indisputable successes during the past years. Herr von Wiegand's letter interested me very much and I am returning it herewith. Unfortunately, I am afraid he is right when he speaks of the profound hate which is directed to us by a large part of the world.

"Soon after the war I came to the conclusion that we should have to be victorious in three battles, if Germany were to become powerful again:

"1. The battle against the working class—Hitler has won this.
"2. Against the Catholic Church, perhaps better expressed against Ultramontanism, and
"3. Against the Jews.

"We are in the midst of these battles and the one against the Jews is the most difficult. I hope everyone realizes the intricacies of this campaign.

"I hope that your reconciliation with the Meissner family has been a complete one and I regret that I was the cause of this estrangement. It was necessary though that I made it quite clear that I was not willing to tolerate persons who gossiped about me.

"My removal to Berlin will probably take place in the second half of January. The house Albertinenstrasse 16 is to be ready by then. In many respects I would much rather stay here for what shall I do in Berlin? I shall rarely be able to see people who are still in life, i.e., those who are still able to follow their trades or professions. The demands of their professional activities spare them no time to occupy themselves with those who have fallen by the wayside.

"The only thing open to me, therefore, is that I swell the ranks of the grumblers by one more.

"At Christmas I shall go to Kassel for a short while. I wish you from all my heart, my dear Baroness, that your father's health will improve sufficiently so that you will have no cause to worry over the Christmas days. I am always glad when these days are over.

authorities soon after the end of the war. A translation of the letter in question was delivered by the Office of Strategic Services in Paris to representatives of the American prosecution in July, 1945. Some weeks later, when its contents were noticed at Nuremberg, efforts were made to obtain the original, but the search was unsuccessful.

It seems most improbable that anyone would have been motivated to forge such a letter, and the factual details recited therein conform to what is known of Fritsch's circumstances at the time. For these reasons, I believe the letter to be genuine (apart from possible errors in translation), but this conclusions rests on inference rather than legal proof.

It is not only the worst and darkest time of the year, but since the war I have experienced a series of unhappy events during this period. But that does not mean you need worry about me. I hope that we shall soon be able to meet again though I hardly believe it a possibility before my removal to Berlin. Then I hope I shall be able to show you around the new house. I myself am anxious to know what it will look like. Grosskreutz was there again recently to discuss the wallpaper and curtain question. I sent my housekeeper Frl. Kunau there at the same time. She knows much better than I do what I have in the way of curtains etc. Unfortunately she has a habit of bringing her knowledge to the fore in a terrible gush of words. But it is often the case that things of an indifferent nature, with which we have to deal, are discussed very volubly by some persons. However, I shall close for today before I give you the impression that I belong to this latter category of people.

"With the very best wishes for your father and with hearty greetings, I remain, your truly devoted,

"(signed): FRITSCH."

If genuine, the contents of the letter are hardly surprising, except perhaps the vehemence of the remarks about the Jews. On the other hand, the officers' corps was notably arrogant and exclusive in its attitude toward the Jews. It uniformly supported authoritarian economic organization, as best suited to the needs of a strong military nation, and distrusted the growing power of labour. As for the anti-"Ultramontane" sentiments, Fritsch and his mother's family were pillars of the Evangelical Church in Germany.*

Accurate or not as a representation of Fritsch's political ideology, the letter gives a good picture of his circumstances and feeling of isolation and frustration. Still in full command of his formidable military faculties, and genuinely impressed by the enormous successes which Hitler had won for Germany, he chafed at his enforced idleness and brooded over the dastardly injustice by which the Fuehrer had relegated him to the ranks of "those who have fallen by the wayside". Yet his pride foreclosed any effort to resume an active role. On June 30, 1939, he wrote to the Baronin that he had been so mistreated by Hitler's failure to punish those guilty of the frame-up, that he could not return to duty in peace or war.

It must have been this mood of mingled bitterness and restlessness that dictated Fritsch's extraordinary behaviour after

* Fritsch's mother was a Bodelschwingh, and the Rev. Dr. Friedrich von Bodelschwingh was Reichsbishop until forced to resign as the result of Nazi pressures.

Brauchitsch told him, in the middle of August, that war was inevitable.[13] As a disciple of Seeckt, and despite his hatred of Hitler, Fritsch must have heartily approved the reconquest of the Corridor and Silesia. To such a man in such a state of mind, the opportunity to break out of the boredom of retirement and take to the field was irresistible. And if he had no Army group or army to command, he was nevertheless the *Chef* of Artillery Regiment 12, and listed as such in the official Army register. So Fritsch quietly left Berlin soon after his talk with Brauchitsch, and on August 24th he joined his regiment, which was already drawn up on the southern border of East Prussia, ready to strike south into Poland.

Of course, the *Chef* of a regiment was a purely honorary designation, with no power or responsibility of command. Artillery Regiment 12, like all others, had its own regular *Kommandeur*, an *Oberst*. Furthermore, it was a military absurdity for a *Generaloberst* and one-time Commander-in-Chief of the Army to be stationed at the regimental level. It had never been intended that a *Chef* would actually go into battle with his regiment; indeed, there were only three other *Chefs*—the nonagenarian Mackensen, Hitler's old-time supporter von Epp, who was over seventy and had not been on active duty since 1923, and Rundstedt, who was recalled in fitting capacity as an Army group commander.*

Nevertheless, Fritsch was within his technical military rights in acting as he did. Except for regimental *Chefs*, regular German officers who have been relieved from active duty were listed either as *ausser Dienst* (a.D.—out of service) if no longer fit for duty, or *zur Verfuegung* (z.V.—available for duty) if fit and available for recall. But regimental *Chefs*, although honorary, were listed as if on active duty, much as American Generals of the Army are considered to be on the active list until death, even if they have no assignment. So Fritsch was able to treat his active status as *Chef* literally instead of figuratively, and proceed to his "station". No doubt Hitler could have put his foot down, but either he did not know that Fritsch had gone to the front or he decided not to interfere.

Artillery Regiment 12 was a component of the 12th Infantry Division, with peace-time station in Pomerania (Wehrkreis II). During the summer of 1939, however, it was transferred to East Prussia, and under the dispositions for *Weiss* was assigned

* Blomberg had been designated *Chef* of Infantry Regiment 73, but lost the honour when stricken from the Army list.

to Kuechler's Third Army.* When the attack was launched, Fritsch marched into Poland with his regiment but, according to his biographer, he in no way presumed on his rank and did not interfere in the handling of the regiment. Within a week the regiment was approaching Warsaw from the north. Fritsch's presence at the front had become known, and a garbled news dispatch reported that Fritsch was leading the drive from the north.[14]

Soon thereafter Fritsch's regiment gained the outskirts of Praga (the suburb of Warsaw on the eastern side of the Vistula) and, when the final attack on the city was launched, joined in the artillery bombardment. On the morning of September 22nd, Fritsch went forward with a *Stosstrupp* (combat patrol), which penetrated close to the outlying houses of Praga. Fritsch had made an appointment to visit Kuechler's Army headquarters later in the day and, in order to keep his engagement, he started to make his way back to the German lines, accompanied by Oberleutnant Rosenhagen. While passing through a field, they were caught by Polish machine-gun fire, and forced to take cover in a ditch. Soon a bullet struck Fritsch in the thigh, severing the main artery. He bled profusely, and died within a few moments. The body was recovered with some difficulty. There was a military ceremony at Kuechler's headquarters the following day, and the coffin was then sent to Berlin for a state funeral.

Sensational rumours immediately began to surround the circumstances of Fritsch's death. Even before the funeral, a dispatch from Warsaw quoted German prisoners as charging that he had been assassinated by the Gestapo.[15] Others have asserted that Fritsch never went with the patrol at all, and was shot by SS men while observing the fire of one of the regimental batteries.[16] For these stories there seems to be not the slightest foundation. Fritsch was already a ruined man, and Hitler and Himmler would have had little to gain and much to risk by his murder. At Nuremberg Kuechler denied the truth of the rumoured assassination, and no other officer who was in the vicinity has ever lent credence to the charges. Were they true, the generals surely had every reason and opportunity to expose the facts at Nuremberg.

More plausible is the inference that Fritsch deliberately "bared his breast" and sought death on the battlefield. Had he been so minded, surely there were many opportunities

* Apparently it was part of Petzel's Ist Corps.

earlier in the campaign; by September 22nd it was virtually over. Nor was it in character for him to make an appointment with Kuechler and seek death before he could keep it. His letters from the front to his mother and his adjutant were devoid of hints of impending self-destruction. That life held little value for him, and that he quite unnecessarily risked it, is clear enough, but there seems to be no sufficient basis to mark Fritsch down as a suicide.

Curiously enough, Adolf Hitler had also been near Praga when Fritsch was struck down. He did not attend the funeral, however, and took no notice of Fritsch's death other than to send a wreath, which Goering laid on the coffin. Goering, of course, carried the field-marshal's baton which he had been given by Hitler at the time of Fritsch's entrapment, and the bleak irony of the occasion was heightened by the weather, which was rainy, dark and cold. Brauchitsch, who had clung to the mantle of command that Fritsch's misfortunes laid on the former's shoulders, read a stereotyped military eulogy. From the "old Army", Mackensen and others were on hand, but there were a number of mourners—Keitel, Milch, Goebbels, Hess, Frick and Funk—whose presence must have made the dead *Generaloberst* writhe in his grave.

After the ceremony, the coffin was taken to the *Invalides-Friedhof*. Mackensen read a prayer over the grave, and the remains were laid to rest under a stone bearing the name and date and the three stars of a *Generaloberst*. It was a hollow and bitter ceremony for a man whose life had come to a hollow and bitter end.

SITZKRIEG IN THE WEST: THE ATHENIA

The German invasion of Poland, followed by the British and French declarations of war against Germany, sent a wave of horrified anticipation over the world. Recollections of the slaughter of World War I had been kept alive and apprehensions sharpened by numerous books, articles and motion pictures depicting the terrors of modern warfare. Events in China, Ethiopia and Spain, especially the bombings of Canton, Guernica and Barcelona, furnished ample basis for these fears, and Hitler was not slow to exploit them at the time of Munich.

And so, when World War II turned from nightmare into reality, there was almost universal expectation of a rain of death from the air with great cities crumbling into fiery ruin, of *Lusitanias* by the score, and of countless other disasters un-

imaginable. The air-raid sirens wailed in London immediately after Chamberlain's broadcast announcing that England was at war. Before the war was a day old, the *Athenia* went down in the North Atlantic. with the loss of over a hundred lives.

But then, everywhere except in Poland, a strange quiet settled over western Europe. There was war, but there was very little fighting. There were black-outs but no bombs—only leaflets and occasional alerts. People began to talk about the "phony war"—the *Sitzkrieg*. Apprehension gave way to bewilderment and then to a feeling almost of irritation. Had everyone been hoodwinked? Did the Allies really mean business? Where was the Luftwaffe?

Such questions were on all lips. In retrospect, the answers are clear enough. The French Army did not think itself strong enough to strike, and gathered itself together, almost resignedly, for a defensive war. The French were especially fearful of the Luftwaffe, and discouraged any notion of sending the Royal Air Force against Germany, lest retaliation be provoked. The British were determined enough but, except at sea, their strength was latent rather than present, and there was no immediate way to bring their naval might to bear other than by instituting a blockade. On the German side, Hitler and other generals alike wanted to postpone the showdown with the western powers, and hoped that a speedy victory in Poland might induce them to back down and accept a new "settlement". On neither side, therefore, was there any desire for an immediate, large-scale engagement.

German military policy in the west was embodied in Hitler's "Directive No. 1 for the Conduct of the War", issued on August 31st,[17] which stated:

> "In the *west* it is essential that England and France are unequivocally held responsible for opening the hostilities. Minor frontier violations are to be counteracted locally, for the time being.
> "The neutrality of Holland, Belgium, Luxembourg * and Switzerland, which we guaranteed, is to be observed most scrupulously. Germany's western frontier will not be crossed *on land* at any place without my express authorization.
> "At *sea* the same applies to all acts of war or acts to be interpreted as such.†

* [Handwritten notation on copy for Navy]: and Denmark.

† [Handwritten notation on copy for Navy]: Accordingly, the forces in the Atlantic Ocean are to remain at action stations.

331

"For the time being, the defensive measures of the *Air Force* are to be absolutely limited to the defence against enemy air attacks at the Reich frontiers, whereby the frontiers of the neutral countries are to be respected, as long as possible, in repelling individual planes and small units. Only if the commitment of major French and British attack formations across neutral countries against the German territory causes an imminent threat to the western air defences, is defensive action over this neutral territory also permitted.

"The OKW must be informed immediately about any violation of the neutrality of third countries by the western enemy, which is especially important."

The ensuing portion of the directive covered the possibility that the western powers might intervene:

"*If England and France start hostilities against Germany*, it will be the task of the branches of the armed forces operating in the west to ensure that such conditions prevail which are conducive to a victorious conclusion of the operations against Poland, at the same time economizing the available forces as much as possible. Within the scope of this task, the forces of the enemy and his war industries are to be incapacitated as much as possible. In every individual case I shall reserve to myself the right of ordering attacks. The *Army* will hold the West Wall and will make preparations to prevent its encirclement in the north—by the western powers invading Belgian or Dutch territory. If French forces should enter Luxembourg, the frontier bridges may be blown up. The *Navy* will conduct the war against merchant shipping with its main effort directed against England. To increase its effect, it can be expected that danger zones will be declared. The High Command of the Navy will report in what sea areas and to what extent danger zones are considered expedient. The text of a public announcement is to be prepared in co-operation with the Foreign Office, and is to be submitted to me for approval via the OKW.

"The Baltic is to be secured against an enemy intrusion. The decision whether the entrances to the Baltic may be mined for this purpose will be made by the C.-in-C. Navy.

"The main task of the Air Force will be to prevent the commitment of the French and British Air Forces against the German Army and the German living space. For the war against England, preparations are to be made for Air Force operations to disrupt the British seaborne supplies, their armament industry, and troop transports to France. Favourable opportunities for an effective attack on concentrations of British naval units, especially on battleships and aircraft carriers, are to be exploited.

"Attacks on London will await my decision. The attacks on

the British homeland are to be prepared by considering that an incomplete success with partial forces is to be avoided by all means."

When the British and French declarations of war turned the contingency into actuality, German military operations were confined within the limits of this directive. Halder's diary entry for September 3rd reveals that Leeb was directed not to open hostilities, but to "return fire". The Navy might attack "enemy commerce and naval forces" and the Air Force was "authorized to attack naval forces, but not the homeland [Britain]".

The western air, in fact, was almost entirely peaceful. The British on September 4th attempted a small-scale air raid on naval installations at Wilhelmshaven and Brunsbuettel (at the entrance to the Kiel Canal), but it was both ineffective and costly, and thereafter the R.A.F. limited itself to leaflet "attacks" which proved equally fruitless. The Luftwaffe, in line with the governing directive, was utterly quiescent. Goering suggested a surprise raid against the British fleet at Scapa Flow, but Hitler put his foot down.[18] Indeed, it was not until September 10th that Sperrle's Air Fleet 3, facing France, was authorized to cross the frontier for aerial combat and reconnaissance flights, and even then it was laid down that "close liaison with Air Fleet 3 is essential, since unleashing of an air war must be avoided at this time".

On the ground things were but little livelier. On the Rhine front between Basle and Karlsruhe, there was a sort of informal truce. French and German troops on either side of the river moved about and built fortifications, in plain sight and easy gunshot of each other, quite unmolested. Opposite the Rhineland, between the Rhine and the Moselle, a few French patrols moved forward cautiously a few miles in the Saarbruecken area, but made no effort to penetrate even the outermost defences of the West Wall. Throughout September the western Press made much of these insignificant advances, but they amounted to nothing. They are not even mentioned in Halder's diary or Churchill's memoirs; indeed, the latter contents himself with the simple statement [19] that "the French armies made no attack upon Germany".

To be sure, there was little to recommend a French offensive, much as popular opinion held otherwise at the time. It would have taken at best two weeks until the French could have mounted one, and by then Poland's fate was plain and German reinforcements for the west were becoming available. France's

temporary numerical superiority rapidly disappeared, and England could do nothing to tip the scales. The entire initial British Expeditionary Force comprised only four divisions, and even this small force was not fully deployed until mid-October. Had France been strong in tanks and planes and of good spirit something might have been done, but her weapons were obsolete and her troops enervated—a far cry from the "strongest army in Europe" of popular imagination.

All this the German generals well knew and, as Halder's diary shows,[20] the prospect of a French offensive caused them scant concern. Immediately after the Anglo-French declaration of war, Leeb ordered the evacuation of children and invalids from Karlsruhe, and the Organisation Todt moved several thousand tons of industrial machinery out of Saarbruecken. But Leeb's main preoccupation was the remote chance of an attack through the Low Countries, and immediately plans were made to call up more reserve divisions to reinforce the Belgian and Dutch frontiers. Furthermore, it soon appeared that there would be too many divisions and too long a front from Luxembourg to the North Sea for efficient command by Liebmann's Fifth Army, and it was decided to establish another Army headquarters along the Lower Rhine. For its commander, Otto Hasse and Falkenhausen were considered, but the former was rejected as too old (he was seventy), and the choice fell on Hammerstein, who assumed command of a cadre for the headquarters * on September 10th. Since the army was in process of formation, it was administratively subordinated to the Fifth Army, but operationally Hammerstein reported directly to Leeb.

Hammerstein's unexpected emergence as an Army commander-in-chief was short-lived. On the very day that he took command, the OKH laid plans to shift Bock's Army group and Kluge's and List's Army headquarters to the west as soon as the progress of the Polish campaign should permit, and to use Kluge's Fourth Army headquarters to replace Hammerstein's. By September 20th substantial reinforcements were moving in along the northern end of the front, and reports of German "concentrations" near Aachen caused the Belgians and Dutch to open the dykes for defensive flooding. Early in October Bock's Army group and several Army headquarters moved from Poland to the west, and there was a general reorganization of the German command structure in the west, in

* The cadre was designated Armee-Abteilung A.

the course of which Hammerstein was relieved of his command and once more relegated to the inactive list.*

And so, as the Polish campaign ended, the military initiative on the western front fell to the Germans. The Allies had been able to accomplish nothing other than mobilization, and the transfer of four British divisions to France, where they were deployed along the Belgian frontier near Lille. The western front remained inactive, and to all appearances the "phony war" continued for another six months. In fact, however, Hitler, as early as September 25th, brought up the proposal of an autumn western offensive. After he realized that his peace overtures of early October had fallen on deaf ears, it was simply a question of how soon the blow would fall.

In the meantime, the sea had witnessed much more action and sudden death than the land or the air. For the time being there were no more *Athenias*, but merchantment and men-o'-war went to the bottom from the earliest days of the war. Nevertheless, on the German side, political considerations dictated a considerable measure of restraint for many weeks. In fact, the fluctuations of German naval policy reflected with considerable fidelity the development of Hitler's overall strategy in the early stages of the war.

Of the three service chiefs, Raeder seems to have been the most disturbed by the failure of Hitler's efforts to isolate Poland. On September 3rd, he committed to the naval archives a doleful memorandum "for the record", which opened with the observation: "Today, the war against England and France broke out, the war which, according to the Fuehrer's previous assertions, we had no need to expect before about 1944." The memorandum went on to tabulate Germany's naval strength in 1944 if the Z Plan had been carried out, and concluded that "especially with the co-operation of Japan and Italy, who would have held down a section of the British fleet, the prospect of defeating the British fleet and cutting off supplies, in other words of settling the British question conclusively, would have been good". Unhappily, no such favourable prospects were present in 1939:

"As far as the Navy is concerned, obviously it is in no way adequately equipped for the great struggle with Great Britain in the

* Leibmann was relieved at about the same time. Neither he nor Hammerstein was given any further assignment. Gisevius (*To the Bitter End*, p. 431) declares Hammerstein had planned to arrest Hitler "when the Fuehrer made a visit to the western front", but that Hitler relieved him before the plan could be carried out. See also *Offiziere gegen Hitler*, by Fabian von Schlabrendorff, p. 33, and *Germany's Underground*, by Allen W. Dulles, p. 53.

autumn of 1939. It is true that, in the short period since 1935, the date of the Fleet Treaty, it has built up a well-trained, suitably organized submarine arm, of which at the moment about twenty-six boats are capable of operations in the Atlantic; the submarine arm is still much too weak, however, to have any decisive effect on the war. The surface forces, moreover, are so inferior in number and strength to those of the British fleet that, even at full strength, they can do no more than show that they know how to die gallantly and thus are willing to create the foundations for later reconstruction."

Accordingly, at the outset Raeder was more than glad to pursue a policy of limited warfare. The submarines and the two pocket battleships (*Graf Spee* and *Deutschland*) were to concentrate on British warships and merchantmen. As to the latter, the Hague Rules against attack without warning were to be carefully followed. Passenger vessels were to be spared; the sinking of the *Athenia* was due to an error of identification, and was most unwelcome to the German naval leadership.

The British, however, did not know this, and the loss of the *Athenia* had an immediate effect on their naval tactics. As Churchill relates,[21] despite the proven merits of the convoy system for the protection of merchant shipping against submarines, "our weakness in escort vessels . . . forced the Admiralty to devise a policy of evasive routing on the oceans, unless and until the enemy adopted unrestricted U-boat warfare, and to confine convoys in the first instance to the east coast of Britain. But the sinking of the *Athenia* upset these plans, and we adopted convoy in the North Atlantic forthwith." This decision was reinforced when three British merchantmen were sunk off the Spanish coast on the 5th and 6th of September.*

The scope of the German naval offensive, however, was even further confined as the result of a conference between Hitler and Raeder on September 7th. Both were still hopeful of a settlement at the conclusion of the Polish campaign. They both remarked the "hesitant conduct of British warfare" and the "impartial attitude of the neutral countries", including the United States. Raeder further expressed the view that "France fails to see any war aim, and is therefore trying to stay out of the war", and from all this he concluded that "an attack should not be forced and our strength should be saved for the time being". Hitler and Raeder agreed on a policy to "exercise

* Eleven British ships of 64,595 gross tons were sunk by submarines during the first week of the war. This was about half the weekly tonnage sunk at the peak of the U-boat campaign in April, 1917. Churchill, *op. cit. supra*, p. 436.

restraint until the political situation in the west has become clearer", to be embodied in the following specific measures: (a) no offensive action to be taken against the French; (b) passenger ships, even in convoy, to be spared; (c) part of the submarines to be recalled from operations; and (d) the *Graf Spee* and *Deutschland* to return to their waiting stations and undertake no actions.

These new restrictions, together with the increasing effectiveness of the convoy system (which was put into actual operation on September 8th), caused an immediate reduction in British maritime losses.* The downward trend was interrupted on September 18th by the torpedoing of the aircraft carrier *Courageous* in the English Channel. Nevertheless, Mr. Churchill (then First Lord of the Admiralty) felt that he had a "good tale to tell" when he addressed Parliament on September 26th: "One must not dwell upon those reassuring figures too much, for war is full of unpleasant surprises. But certainly I am entitled to say that so far as they go these figures need not cause any undue despondency or alarm."

For sure, unpleasant surprises in plenty were in store for the sceptred isle. The Wehrmacht's sweep through Poland produced none of the diplomatic repercussions for which Hitler and the Wehrmacht leaders had hoped. Soon the German admirals were kicking against the pricks, and complaining volubly about the "great difficulties for U-boats" arising from existing restrictions. On September 21st, the submarines were ordered to attack all vessels sailing in the English Channel without lights.[22] Two days later, Raeder prevailed upon Hitler to lift the restrictions against attacks on French shipping, and to let loose the *Graf Spee* and the *Deutschland*.[23] Hitler also agreed to permit the U-boats to attack enemy merchantmen without warning, but this permission was withdrawn early in October, just before the Fuehrer's "peace offer" of October 6th. However, after Chamberlain's rejection of a settlement, attack without warning was again authorized, and the exemption for enemy passenger vessels was likewise eliminated. Two days earlier, the submarine arm had scored its most notable single exploit of the entire war when the *U-47*, commanded by Oberleutnant Gunther Prien, slipped through the defences of Scapa

---

* During the third week of the war only three merchant ships were lost to submarines, and during the fourth week only one. During the entire month of September, the British lost twenty-nine merchant ships (twenty-six to submarines, two to mines, and one to a surface raider), totalling 152,040 gross tons.

Flow and sank the battleship *Royal Oak*,[24] a feat for which Doenitz vicariously won his promotion from *Kommodore* to *Kommandierender Admiral* of submarines, and Prien the Knight's Cross of the Iron Cross. This triumph was exploited to the full by Raeder in persuading the Fuehrer to give the Navy greater leeway for offensive action.

The victorious conclusion of the Polish campaign was thus marked as well by naval successes. But this period was also signalized by the extraordinary embarrassment of the *Athenia* incident. When the disaster occurred during the evening of September 3rd, Raeder and Doenitz were as ignorant of its true cause as anyone else. The German Propaganda Ministry, after checking with OKM, denied German responsibility and declared that no U-boats were in the vicinity of the sinking.[25] Weizsaecker, a former naval officer, received similar assurances and then called in the United States Chargé d'Affaires (Alexander Kirk) and vehemently denied that any German naval unit could have participated in the sinking.[26] On September 16th, at Ribbentrop's instigation, Raeder received the United States Naval Attaché, and declared that "he had now received reports from all submarines, as a result of which it has been definitely ascertained that the steamer *Athenia* was not sunk by a German submarine", and stressed the "courteous and chivalrous behaviour" and "marvellous discipline" of the submarine commanders.[27]

There seems to be no reason to doubt the sincerity of these protestations of innocence, but Raeder misstated the facts to the Naval Attaché in one important respect: the U-boats which were at sea on September 3rd had not all returned by September 16th. And on September 27th the *U-30*, commanded by Oberleutnant Lemp, pulled in to Wilhelmshaven and was met by Doenitz, who later related: [28]

> "I met the captain, Oberleutnant Lemp, on the lockside at Wilhelmshaven, as the boat was entering harbour, and he asked permission to speak to me in private. I noticed immediately that he was looking very unhappy and he told me at once that he thought he was responsible for the sinking of the *Athenia* in the North Channel area. In accordance with my previous instructions he had been keeping a sharp look-out for possible armed merchant cruisers in the approaches to the British Isles, and had torpedoed a ship he afterwards identified as the *Athenia* from wireless broadcasts, under the impression that she was an armed merchant cruiser on patrol. I had never specified in my instructions any particular type of ship as armed merchant cruiser nor mentioned

any names of ships. I dispatched Lemp at once by air to report to the SKL at Berlin; in the meantime, I ordered complete secrecy as a provisional measure. Later the same day or early on the following day, I received a verbal order from Kapitaen zur See Fricke that—

"1. *The affair was to be kept a total secret.*

"2. *The OKM considered* that a court-martial was not necessary as they were satisfied that the captain had acted in good faith.

"3. *Political explanations would be handled by the* OKM."

It had taken the OKM less than a day to solve this moral and tactical dilemma. There had been no more *Athenias*, Lemp's mistake, for an inexperienced commander on the first day of war, was understandable, and a frank confession of error might, in the long run, have done the German cause more good than harm. Furthermore, if the truth should come out from other sources (a wounded crew member of the *U-30*, sworn to secrecy by Lemp, had been disembarked at Reykjavik on September 19th),[29] the credibility of all future German communiqués would be seriously prejudiced. However, twenty-eight Americans had gone down with the *Athenia*, and American opinion was uppermost in the German mind, as Weizsaecker's and Raeder's interviews with the Chargé d'Affaires and the Naval Attaché demonstrated. As Raeder's Chief of Staff (Schulte-Moenting) put it at Nuremberg:[30]

". . . we thought that any discrepancies which might arise and lead to political ill-humour in America were to be avoided as much as possible. Stirring up this case once more would have greatly aroused public feeling. I remember, for instance, the *Lusitania* case during the First World War. To have stirred up this case again after a few weeks and to arouse public opinion, and then to force entry into the war, would have made little sense."

And so the decision was reached, in complete agreement between Hitler and the OKM, to hush the matter up. Raeder issued the three-point order, as described by Doenitz. Schulte-Moenting swore the crew of the *U-30* to secrecy. On the orders of Doenitz and his chief of operations (Godt), the log of the *U-30* and Doenitz' war diary were both altered or falsified so as to exclude any mention of the *Athenia*.[31]

But the affair was not allowed to rest at mere suppression of the truth. On October 23rd, the *Voelkischer Beobachter* came out

with a sensational article charging that Churchill had sunk the *Athenia* by causing an infernal machine to be placed aboard her.[32] According to the then Chief of the German Press Section of the Propaganda Ministry (Hans Fritzsche), this was done at Hitler's orders, and after continued assurances by OKM that no U-boat had been near the scene of the disaster.[33] At the time this article appeared, at least five senior officers of the Navy (Raeder, Doenitz, Fricke, Godt and Schulte-Moenting) knew it to be utterly mendacious. Raeder admitted that he had "misgivings about it", but he did nothing because, as explained by Schulte-Moenting, "he valued the interests of the state more than a newspaper article. The interests of the state required that in any event all complications with the United States were to be avoided." [34]

The sinking of the *Athenia* was soon overshadowed by a welter of far greater catastrophes, and the true cause remained an enigma until the truth was unearthed at Nuremberg.* The conduct of the German admirals, if far from laudable, was understandable, and can hardly be labelled criminal. But it was weak—weak in the way that the generals and admirals so often were in the face of the pressures exerted by the Third Reich, of which they had become an integral part—a "pillar" in Reichenau's words.[35] And this weakness was soon to lead them into dark matters beside which the *Athenia* affair was the merest peccadillo, important only as a suggestive forerunner. Already in Poland the shadow of mass death and slavery lay across the land, and the generals had been made privy to Himmler's black programme.

THE FOURTH PARTITION OF POLAND, 1939

The speedy conquest of Poland was accomplished by the Wehrmacht at amazingly low cost in terms of men and matériel. However, it was achieved only at the price of a bargain with Soviet Russia—a price which the red legions were on hand to exact. It had been fixed in Moscow on August 23rd simultaneously with the signing of the non-aggression pact. By a secret protocol the "spheres of influence of both parties" had been delimited after "strictly confidential conversations"

In essence, the protocol of August 23rd marked out the Baltic countries and Poland as available for conquest by Russia and Germany and drew a tentative line of partition. "In the event

* Lemp was subsequently drowned in the sinking of the *U-110* on May 9, 1941.

of a territorial and political rearrangement in the areas belonging to the Polish state," it recited "the spheres of influence of Germany and the U.S.S.R. shall be bounded approximately by the line of the rivers Narew, Vistula and San." The future of the Polish state, if any, was wholly subsidiary to German and Russian interests; on this subject, the protocol stated:

> "The question of whether the interests of both parties make desirable the maintenance of an independent Polish state and how such a state should be bounded can only be definitely determined in the course of further political developments. In any event, both governments will resolve this question by means of a friendly agreement."

In the Baltic, the bargain was simply that Finland, Estonia and Latvia fell to the Russians and Lithuania to the Germans, with the single qualification that both parties recognized "the interest of Lithuania in the Vilna area". In addition, Russian "interest" and German "disinterestedness" in Bessarabia were recognized. Finally, the protocol stated that its existence and terms were to be kept strictly secret.

When the Russians started moving into Poland on September 17th, the Germans were already far beyond the Narew–Vistula–San line, and orders were promptly given to the German troops to halt on the line Bialystok–Brest-Litovsk–Wlodzimierz–Lvov–Skole. At the same time, however, the OKH made strong representations to OKW against abiding by the line laid down in the protocol, which would have required that the German Army pull back all the way from the Bug at Brest-Litovsk to the Vistula at Warsaw, and German evacuation of the entire province of Lublin.

Such an outcome was little to the liking of the German generals, and Brauchitsch remonstrated vigorously. Russo-German friction became especially sharp at Lvov, where the citadel was still in Polish hands; both sides wanted the credit for its capture. Nevertheless, on September 20th Hitler told the generals that the Narew–Vistula–San was "final", and that the Russians would be recognized as the "liberators of Lvov". The Fuehrer's thoughts were already turning westward, and he admonished Brauchitsch "that we must not lose another man east of this line". Halder angrily noted in his diary that it was "a day of disgrace for German political leadership".

During the next forty-eight hours detailed time-tables were drawn up for the German withdrawal and the Russian advance. The Russians were to start moving into the territory evacuated

by the Germans on September 23rd, and half a day's march separation was to be maintained all the way. However, to avert sabotage and banditry, all important military targets such as aerodromes, railway stations and large cities were to be handed over directly to the Russians. The schedule called for the Russians to reach the Vistula at Warsaw on October 3rd, and for the withdrawal of all German troops behind the line to be completed by October 4th.

In the meantime, however, discussions had been proceeding on the diplomatic front that led to a different outcome. These negotiations revealed an extraordinary situation in which the German Foreign Office was actually exhorting the Russians to invade and occupy Poland up to the Narew–Vistula–San line, while the Russians albeit for very different reasons, shared the German Army's dislike for this course of action.[36]

As early as September 3rd, Ribbentrop wired the German Ambassador in Moscow (von der Schulenburg) that the Polish Army would be defeated "in a few weeks", and that Germany would keep the area within its agreed "sphere of interest" under military occupation. Ribbentrop instructed Schulenburg to urge the Russians to move in "at the proper time" and occupy the area allocated to them. In reply, Schulenburg dispatched a note from Molotov expressing the view that "this time has not yet come" because "through excessive haste we might injure our cause and promote unity among our opponents".

Again on September 9th and 15th Schulenburg, on Ribbentrop's instructions, pressed the Russians to take military action and occupy their allotted share of Poland. Still Molotov temporized. At first he explained that the rapid German advance had taken Moscow by surprise, and that military preparations for the Russian move were not yet complete. Later he declared that Russia could not formulate an adequate political justification for the invasion until Warsaw had fallen. Finally, at two o'clock in the morning on September 17th, Stalin summoned Schulenburg and "declared that the Red Army would cross the border this morning at six o'clock. . . . Soviet planes would begin today to bomb the district east of Lemberg [Lvov]".

Clearly, the Kremlin wanted Germany, in the eyes of the world, to bear the blame for the destruction of Poland, and itself to appear on the scene only at the last moment as a "protector" of the Ukrainians and White Russians of eastern

342

Poland. But Stalin had still other doubts about the wisdom of displaying a grasping attitude. On September 18th, Schulenburg reported a conversation in which

". . . Stalin said, somewhat suddenly, that on the Soviet side there were certain doubts as to whether the German High Command at the appropriate time would stand by the Moscow agreement and would withdraw to the line that had been agreed upon (Pissa–Narew–Vistula–San). I replied with emphasis that of course Germany was firmly determined to fulfil the terms of the Moscow agreements precisely. . . . Stalin replied that he had no doubt at all of the good faith of the German government. His concern was based on the well-known fact that all military men are loath to give up occupied territories. At this point the German Military Attaché here, Lieutenant General Koestring, interjected that the German armed forces would do just as the Fuehrer ordered."

Two days later, Molotov advised Schulenburg that the Soviet government had concluded that it would be unwise "to permit the existence of a residual Poland", and that the Russian inclination was to partition Poland along the Narew–Vistula–San line, as previously agreed upon. Ribbentrop replied that the Soviet decision "coincides in general with the view of the Reich government". On September 25th, however, Stalin's caution and love of bargaining reasserted themselves. Thus the German generals found support in an unexpected quarter for their opposition to a German withdrawal to the agreed line. Stalin and Molotov called Schulenburg again and, as the Ambassador thereafter reported:

"Stalin stated the following: In the final settlement of the Polish question anything that in the future might create friction between Germany and the Soviet Union must be avoided. From this point of view he considered it wrong to leave an independent Polish rump state. He proposed the following: From the territory to the east of the demarcation line, all the Province of Lublin and that portion of the Province of Warsaw which extends to the Bug should be added to our share. In return, we should waive our claim to Lithuania."

And so it was decided. Ribbentrop paid a second visit to Moscow on September 27th, and the following day Stalin's proposal was embodied in a "German-Soviet Boundary and Friendship Treaty" and a second "Secret Supplementary Protocol" to the non-aggression pact.

The barter of Lithuania for Lublin enabled the Germans to retain their line on the Bug. Lvov and Bialystok, however,

passed into Russian hands. Poland disappeared from the political map. The 1939 demarcation line was destined to endure little over a year and a half, but the stage was set, on both sides of the line, for a ruthless and bloody occupation, compared to which the regimes of the eighteenth-century despots appear almost beneficent. For in 1939, the aim on both sides was to obliterate Polish culture, and pull up the very roots of Polish national individuality.

HIMMLER'S HOUSECLEANING: "MISSIONS MUST BE KNOWN TO THE ARMY"

For Heinrich Himmler, the outbreak of war was the dawn of a new era of opportunity. Now, at last, the fearful architecture of the "SS state", the foundations of which he had been quietly laying for several years, began to take shape. Hitler was increasingly preoccupied with military affairs, and soon allowed the internal management of the Reich to slip into the hands of Himmler and Goebbels and, later, Martin Bormann. As the chances of peace dwindled, Ribbentrop's importance declined correspondingly. The generals were at the front. An internal power vacuum developed into which Himmler was able to step almost unopposed.

Poland had long been marked out by Himmler as an area ideally suited for the practical application of SS ideology. The structure and hierarchy of the German occupational regime in Poland concerned him chiefly in that it should allow free play for the "programme" which he had in mind. His few Waffen SS regiments, distributed among the armies, had already fought their way into Poland as part of the Wehrmacht, and his police units followed hard on the heels of the front-line troops.

Curiously, in view of the meticulously developed military plans for *Weiss*, little advance planning seems to have been made for the German occupational administration in Poland. No doubt this is partly to be explained by uncertainty as to whether the campaign would be pushed to a total conquest, whether a rump Poland would be tolerated, whether a face-saving deal would be made with England and France, where the new Russian border would be drawn, and other such contingencies. Likewise, the future division of occupational authority between the Wehrmacht and the civil authorities had not been worked out in advance. A very fluid situation rapidly developed, in which Himmler's ambitions were greatly aided by the desire of both Hitler and the generals to concen-

trate their forces and their own energies on the western front as soon as possible.

During September and October, however, the OKH did devote considerable attention to the problems of occupational administration in Poland. Within the General Staff, these matters were the direct concern of Generalmajor Eugen Mueller and his Chief of Staff, Oberst Eduard Wagner, who were charged (under Halder) with General Staff planning in the fields of military administration and supply. Brauchitsch, Halder and Wagner discussed the shape of things to come in Poland as early as September 5th to 7th, and settled on the retired General der Artillerie von Vollard Bockelberg to head the military occupational administration in northern Poland. On September 10th, these plans were elaborated; additional occupational staffs were to be set up in Danzig–West Prussia (under General der Artillerie Heitz), Cracow and Lodz. It was proposed to transfer Hammerstein and Liebmann to Poland to relieve Kluge and List for transfer to the western front. All of these were to be subordinated to a supreme occupational head-quarters (High Command East, called *Oberost*), to be formed by Rundstedt's Army Group South. Hans Frank * was to be attached to *Oberost* as Chief of Civil Administration.

These tentative plans were substantially modified, however, when the civil administration of German-occupied Poland was determined early in October. By a Hitler decree of October 8th, large portions of western Poland were annexed to the Reich. The Corridor and the Posen–Lodz region were divided into the Reich Districts (*Gaue*) of West Prussia and Wartheland. The Kattowice area was attached to Silesia. The remainder of German-occupied Poland, including Warsaw, Cracow and Lublin Province, was denominated (by another decree dated October 12th) the Government-General and administered from Cracow substantially as a colony of the Reich. Hans Frank was appointed Governor-General, and Seyss-Inquart Deputy Governor-General; Frank was also relieved of his sub-ordination to *Oberost* and made responsible directly to Hitler.

The military administration followed the same general pattern. Wehrkreis I was enlarged by adding the region north of Warsaw, and Wehrkreis VIII absorbed the Kattowice area. The Corridor (including Danzig) and the Wartheland were each constituted as new *Wehrkreise*, numbered XX and XXI

---

* Frank had been Reichsminister without Portfolio since 1934, and was Leader of the National Socialist Lawyers' Association.

respectively. A Military Commander (*Militaerbefehlshaber*) was appointed to command the troops in the Government-General. The troops in the Government-General and the two new *Wehrkreise* were brought under the over-all command of *Oberost*.

Oberost was officially established on October 3rd under Rundstedt, but within a few weeks he was called to take command of an Army group on the western front and replaced by Blaskowitz. Hammerstein and Liebmann were retired instead of being transferred to Poland, and Heitz was given command of a corps.* Bockelberg took command of the enlarged Wehrkreis I, and Petzel and Max Bock † of Wehrkreise XX and XXI respectively. Ulex was relieved as Commander of the Xth Corps, and became the Military Commander in the Government-General.

The resultant division of authority between the military and civil administrations was further complicated by the virtual autonomy of Himmler's police forces and special SS units (*Einsatzgruppen*). The mission of the SS and police in Poland was by no means confined to customary security tasks in occupied territory. It was, on the contrary, a far-reaching programme for the total extermination of Polish Jews and the destruction of Polish culture. The programme was secret in the sense that Himmler did not publish it broadcast, but in the nature of things it could not remain a secret where there were eyes to see and ears to hear, and of this Himmler was well aware.

To be sure, it should not be thought that the Wehrmacht's conquest and occupation of Poland was carried out with any remarkable degree of humanitarianism. All hostile acts by the civilian population were ruthlessly dealt with by summary court-martial and firing-squads; early in September Shirer heard eye-witness accounts [37] of the execution of "men, women and boys". Stories were soon circulating [38] of "the way villages were surrounded and set on fire, because of civilian snipers, while the population inside shrieked frantically". Some of Goering's young Nazi pilots played unnecessary havoc in the countryside.[39] Refugees from the Bolshevik invasion and from besieged Warsaw were ruthlessly driven back with rifle-fire.[40] After territory had been occupied, "pacification" of the in-

---

* The VIIIth Corps, replacing Busch, who was moved up to command the newly formed Sixteenth Army on the western front.

† To be distinguished from Fedor von Bock, the then *Generaloberst*.

habitants was frequently (and ineffectually) promoted by the shooting of hostages.*

All this was hardly sweetness and light, but there was something to be said on the other side. The conduct of the Poles was not above reproach. There is no evidence that the Luftwaffe pilots were given orders to attack non-military objectives in Poland—rather the contrary. Snipers and *franc-tireurs* must be dealt with, and the laws of war allowed the occupying forces considerable, if by no means unlimited, freedom of action to ensure the security of their troops and the preservation of order behind the lines. There is nothing to suggest that the Wehrmacht or its generals were interested in the wholesale slaughter of Poles, but rather that they were simply bent on the rapid conquest of a country and a people that they held in low esteem and to whose fate they were indifferent.

Ruthless this attitude may have been, but it was far removed from the theretofore incredible campaign of mass extermination that Himmler and Heydrich were preparing to launch. Since the end of the war the generals have customarily advanced the ill-matched defences that they knew nothing of these foul designs, at least until much later, and that they did all that could be done to block their execution. The inconsistency betrays the flimsiness of these excuses, and the contemporary documentation that has since come to light shows conclusively that the leaders of the officers' corps knew of these "genocidal" plans (although that word had not yet been coined) from the very outset, and that their efforts in opposition are flattered by the adjective "half-hearted".

During the early days of the campaign, a group of SS artillery soldiers attached to Kuechler's army herded a number of Polish Jews into a synagogue and massacred them with revolver fire. The SS troops were court-martialled but given only a one-year prison sentence, which Kuechler, in a display of decency which he did not often repeat later in the war, set aside as too lenient. Himmler defended the action as a mere "excess of zeal", and the culprits never received their just deserts. The incident was reported to OKH, and is recorded in Halder's diary for September 10th. Soon the episode was common knowledge among the well-informed in Berlin.[41]

* German military directives for the Polish campaign authorized the taking o civilian hostages to ensure order, and their shooting, in the event of hostile acts, but only with the permission of a division commander or officer of equivalent rank See *Trials of War Criminals before the Nuremberg Military Tribunals*, Vol. XI, p. 797.

The furore thus aroused may well have helped to convince Himmler that mass slaughter could not be carried out unknown to the Army, and that the tacit approval or, at least, acquiescence of the Army must be obtained. At all events, on September 19th, Reinhard Heydrich paid a call on Oberst Wagner (Chief of Staff to the *Generalquartiermeister* of OKH) and laid the cards on the table. Wagner promptly reported back to Halder, who noted in his diary:

"Heydrich (Wagner):

"(*a*) Missions must be known to the Army. Liaison officers Himmler/Ob.d.H.*

"(*b*) Housecleaning: Jews, intelligentsia, clergy, nobility.

"(*c*) Army insists that 'house-cleaning' be deferred until Army has withdrawn and the country has been turned over to civil administration. Early December."

The stark meaning is plain enough even in Halder's cryptic shorthand. The SS programme—euphemistically dubbed "house-cleaning"—was the elimination of the Jews and the "upper classes" from Polish life. To ensure its accomplishment, this terrible *mission must be known to the Army*. And the Army's reply to Himmler, so far from being one of outrage or even opposition, was a shameful (and, as it soon proved, futile) effort at back-turning. So far had the demoralization of the military leadership already progressed, and a long and ugly road lay ahead.

The next day, Brauchitsch and Halder discussed the organizational basis of the occupation and some of the problems raised by the proposed house-cleaning. Halder's diary reveals that there was to be full interchange of information between Hitler, Himmler and Brauchitsch, and between the local police chiefs and military commanders in Poland. A "large-scale resettlement" was already in prospect; former German territory was to be "cleared of all those who moved in after 1918. For every German moving into these territories, two people will be expelled to Poland". Furthermore, a plan for the reconstitution of the ghetto existed "in broad outline" though "details are not yet settled". There was also to be a "central agency for the house-cleaning". A note of caution—tactical rather than moral—was sounded:

"Nothing must occur which would afford foreign countries an opportunity to launch any sort of atrocity propaganda based on such incidents. Catholic clergy! Impractical at this time."

* *Oberbefehlshaber des Heeres*, i.e. Brauchitsch.

348

On September 21st, many details of the "ghetto plan" were embodied in a long directive by Heydrich, a copy of which was sent to OKH.[42] From this, the Army leaders learned that "the first prerequisite for the ultimate goal is the concentration of rural Jews in the large cities". All Jewish communities "under five hundred heads" were to be dissolved, and their members "transferred to the nearest concentration centres". There, "general reasons of security will probably bring about orders forbidding Jews to enter certain sections of the city, and that ... they cannot for instance leave the ghetto, they cannot go out after a designated evening hour, etc."

If these projects were, to put it mildly, unsavoury, those of Hans Frank were little better. On October 3rd, the day that *Oberost* was activated under Rundstedt, Frank (at that time Rundstedt's subordinate) conferred with Army staff officers in Posen, and outlined his concept of the occupational mission: [43]

> ". . . Poland can only be administered by utilizing the country through ruthless exploitation, removal of all supplies, raw materials, machines, factory installations, etc., which are important for the German war economy, availability of all workers for work within Germany, reduction of the entire Polish economy to absolute minimum necessary for bare existence of the population, closing of all educational institutions, especially technical schools and colleges, in order to prevent the growth of a new Polish intelligentsia. Poland shall be treated as a colony; the Poles shall be the slaves of the Greater German World Empire."

If, after all this, the Army leaders still questioned whether these delectable designs were serious, their doubts were dispelled two weeks later. On October 18th, Wagner reported to Halder the results of a conference with Hitler, wherein the Fuehrer laid down, as recorded in Halder's diary, that:

> "We have no intention of rebuilding Poland. . . . Assembly area for future German operations.*
>
> "Poland is to have its own administration. It is not to be turned into a model state by German standards. Polish intelligentsia must be prevented from establishing itself as a new governing class. Low standard of living must be conserved. Cheap slaves. All undesirable elements must be thrown out of German territory.
>
> "The administration in Poland will have complete authority except on military matters.
>
> "Only one supreme authority: Governor-General.
>
> "Total disorganization must be created! . . .

* Perhaps the first indication that Hitler envisaged the probability of an eventual attack against Russia.

"The Reich will give the Governor-General the means to carry out this devilish plan."

Himmler and Frank lost no time in putting the "devilish plan" into execution. Inevitably, news of the state of affairs in Poland rapidly spread through Germany, as officers and men, civilian officials, and others returned with shocking stories. On Christmas Day, 1939, von Hassell recorded in his diary: [44]

"Gogo Nostitz,* very depressed, told about absolutely shameless actions in Poland, particularly by the SS. Conditions there as regards sanitation defined description, especially in the Jewish district and in the resettlement areas. The shooting of hundreds of innocent Jews was the order of the day. Furthermore, an increasingly insolent attitude was adopted by the SS toward the Army, which they did not salute but jeered at and undermined.

"Blaskowitz † had written a memorandum describing all this quite frankly. It also contained a sentence to the effect that, judging from the conduct of the SS in Poland, it was to be feared they might later turn upon their own people in the same way. Blaskowitz, as a matter of fact, had executive power only in case of a 'revolt'. Otherwise he had nothing to say outside the military sphere. Frank was carrying on like a megalomaniacal pasha. . . . Perhaps we may hope that the behaviour of the SS will be the quickest way to enlighten the Army."

But "enlightenment" was not what the Army needed. Himmler and Heydrich had already seen to that: *missions must be known to the Army*. The officers' corps had been exposed, ever since the SS murdered Schleicher and Bredow in June, 1934, to a sequence of vivid, illustrated lectures on the nature and trend of affairs in the Third Reich, and by the end of 1939 the educational process had little more to offer.

What the officers' corps needed and lacked were the leadership and moral discipline to protect the German name and their own tradition against the degradation with which the Third Reich had threatened both ever since its birth. Instead, for reasons which we have traced, the generals chose to become, themselves, a pillar of the Third Reich. Now the terrible consequences of that choice lay before them.

Ever since the turn of the century the officers' corps had been taught to honour von Schlieffen's motto: "Be more than you seem to be." By the end of 1939, history had inverted the maxim, and the officers' corps seemed to be far more than it really was.

* A German diplomat and ormer Consul in Geneva.
† Blaskowitz had been in command of *Oberost* since October 23rd.

CHAPTER IX

THE RESPONSIBILITY OF THE OFFICERS' CORPS

To THOSE who have read the foregoing narrative, this may seem a strange point at which to bring it to a close. Why begin a description of the war if its events are to be traced only through the first months? Why should the last chapter have been included in this volume at all?

Nevertheless, the breaking-off point is, from an historical standpoint, logically chosen. The conquest of Poland was the war that Hitler and the generals planned. We have seen that war through to its military conclusion and to the realization of its immediate objectives. We have followed the simultaneous play of *Realpolitik* between Germany and Russia, and how Hitler delivered up the Baltic countries and Bessarabia as the price of Soviet co-operation. We have observed the opening of Himmler's campaign to turn the superstitions of Nazi ideology into stark realities.

Had Hitler and the generals had their way, the war would have ended, if temporarily, in October, 1939. The determination of the English and French to stop the German march of conquest confronted the leaders of the Third Reich with the challenge of a general European war, and with military and political problems which they had hoped to avoid by "localizing" the Polish question. For the solution of these problems, neither the Bendlerstrasse nor the Wilhelmstrasse had developed any plans. Now they had to be drawn under the pressure of a major war, and from the German point of view the Second World War may be said to have begun not in September but in October, after Hitler's "peace offensive" failed.

From the standpoint of moral judgment, too, it may be useful to pause at this point. What share of blame—what degree of responsibility—do the leaders of the officers' corps bear for *bringing on the war*? During its later course the Wehrmacht became a vehicle, an accessory and, all too often, a principal in the commission of crimes and the perpetration of atrocities that beggar description. Many of the most eminent names in recent

German military history were tarnished beyond all possibility of apologetic polishing.

These things cannot and should not be excluded from an over-all judgment on the role of the officers' corps in the Second World War. Nevertheless, and for the purposes of this volume, they came later. In this account we have been concerned with the part the military caste played in the birth and development of the Third Reich, and in the deliberately planned conquests of Austria, Czechoslovakia and Poland. These were the ideals and deeds that brought on the war. The record of the officers' corps during these years has been spread before us. By what standards should it be judged, and what should the judgment be?

This book is a historical study and not a legal treatise. The responsibility under international law of a number of German military leaders was tried at Nuremberg, and of their Japanese opposite numbers at Tokyo. This is not the place to review the numerous legal issues—the trial of vanquished by victors, the nature of international criminal jurisdiction, and the validity of the concept of "crimes against peace", to mention only three—that arose in those proceedings.

At the bar of history the issues are far broader. How does the record of the officers' corps measure up to its own standards of conduct? How enlightened were those standards? What are the political and moral responsibilities of military men? What were the responsibilities of the German officers, in the light of the exalted niche they had come to occupy in the German social and political scheme of things? More particularly, how culpable were the leaders of the officers' corps for the fastening of a ruthless tyranny upon the German people, and for bringing the Second World War upon the world? More generally, how will history remember them in terms of human qualities—courage and cowardice, integrity and corruptibility, wisdom and folly?

I have tried to write the narrative and lay out the facts, probabilities and improbabilities, so that the reader can judge for himself, and it is not my intention to conclude with a brief for the prosecution or the defence. Nevertheless, any author approaches such an undertaking with certain preconceptions, and conceives again in the course of its completion. Rather than attempt a futile and meretricious suppression, I have tried to make these conceptions manifest, for what they are worth. And now, in conclusion, I do not presume to pronounce

judgment on the record, but only to suggest a few guiding lines of thought for those who may be tempted to don wig and robe.

To understand is not necessarily to forgive, but understanding is the foundation of a just appraisal. Simple justice no less than charity requires that the officers' corps be judged for what it actually was, and not for what it is sometimes, but erroneously, imagined to have been. Despite the enormous prestige which the military profession enjoyed in Germany, the generals were not all-powerful and, partly as a result of their own blunders, their power decreased as Hitler's grew. The Reichswehr, small as it was, was far more dominant in the affairs of the Weimar Republic than was the Wehrmacht in those of the Third Reich. The idea that Hitler was a puppet who danced on strings pulled by the generals is utterly groundless; neither is the reverse the truth, although, in the later stages of the war, it approached the truth.

Neither is there the slightest warrant for picturing the generals as a coldly efficient coterie bent on world conquest. Cold they were, but their outlook was too archaic for efficiency, and their goal was not world conquest but the re-establishment of German military supremacy in Europe. With the exception of Seeckt they pursued this goal, not boldly and imaginatively, but with a narrow, cautious and often stodgy professionalism. It was precisely because Hitler brought boldness and imagination to the military leadership that the generals became his willing collaborators and, eventually, his followers.

Furthermore, it is futile to test the officers' corps by standards and values to which their leaders were almost totally oblivious. The generals were the product of imperial times and, almost to a man, they faithfully reflected the narrow, caste-conscious authoritarianism in which they had been trained. To "blame" such men, as individuals, for failing to risk their careers to preserve democracy in Germany is too much like cursing the crow for not singing sweetly. To expect German generals to "renounce war as an instrument of national policy" is to blind one's eyes to the hard facts of life.

But all this is merely a setting for the problem, not its solution. If nonconformity did not flourish under the Kaiser, neither did concentration camps. If the Jew was not highly regarded in imperial society, neither was he hounded and preyed upon, subjected to disgusting indignities or officially labelled as subhuman. Neither the Kaiser nor the politicians of imperial times dealt with their opponents by massacre, as

353

did Hitler in the Roehm purge. Least of all were generals and their wives murdered in their homes. All of these things and many more happened in the early years of the Third Reich, when the officers' corps was still powerful. It is one thing to understand that the generals were ill-equipped to become leaders in the movement for world order under the rule of law. It is quite another to forgive their becoming a pillar of the Reich.

But what duty did the officers' corps owe, and to whom? Even field-marshals are soldiers in the service of the state; is it for them to affect or check its course, even if depraved or suicidal? Were they not bound to follow Hitler, no less by their oath of allegiance than by the duty of obedience that every soldier owes? So many of them said during the years since the war, and even much earlier: "Brauchitsch hitches his collar a notch higher and says 'I am a soldier; it is my duty to obey,' " wrote von Hassell.[1]

On this question much ink has been and will be spilled. A passage in one of General MacArthur's speeches, which attracted unfavourable editorial comment,[2] touches the heart of the problem:

> "I find in existence a new and heretofore unknown and dangerous concept that the members of our armed forces owe primary allegiance or loyalty to those who temporarily exercise the authority of the Executive Branch of Government rather than to the country and its Constitution which they are sworn to defend. No proposition could be more dangerous."

This paragraph might easily have been written by Seeckt. In so far as it speaks, literally, in terms of *allegiance*, which, of course, American officers owe to the Constitution (as Seeckt and his fellows owed it to the Weimar Republic), the sentiment is unexceptionable. But the setting of MacArthur's observation—a strongly worded attack on the policies of the administration—raised by clear implication the idea that an officer's duty of *obedience* to "those who temporarily exercise the authority of the Executive Branch" (by which he can only mean the President, who is the Constitutional Commander-in-Chief, just as were the German Presidents in Seeckt's time) is qualified by an overriding obligation to defend the Constitution.

Seeckt, too, conceived that he was under such a transcendent responsibility, though not to the Weimar Constitution. "Reichswehr will never shoot at Reichswehr," he had declared in

1920, as he flatly refused Noske's demand for military aid against the Kapp insurrection.[3] "The Reichswehr . . . will stick to *me*," he coolly informed Ebert at the time of Hitler's "Beer-Hall *Putsch*".[4] This conception of the Army's unanswerability to the politicians of the moment was general throughout the officers' corps, and survived Seeckt. "We soldiers mistrusted all parties. . . . We all considered ourselves the trustees of the unity of Germany," declared Manstein at Nuremberg.[5]

Seeckt and his colleagues have been much criticized for their unwillingness to give true fealty and full obedience to the political leaders of the Weimar Republic, and General MacArthur was relieved of his command on the ground that he, too, had refused fully to subordinate himself to the President. How, then, is there any basis for criticizing the German generals of the Third Reich? Did they not likewise owe full obedience to Adolf Hitler, who had been appointed Chancellor by Hindenburg, confirmed in office by popular election and acclaimed in Hindenburg's political testament? Is it the duty of generals to obey to the letter the orders of a democratic government, but to confound, undermine and destroy an authoritarian regime? *

The apparent dilemma is not superficial. It is a cardinal tenet of republicanism that the military are servants of the state, not an autonomous caste. Nor can we find any solution in the verbalism that generals may urge their views only on "purely military" matters. The adjective "military" has long since lost its purity, as Clausewitz cogently demonstrated. It is quite impossible for generals to analyse military problems without the analysis carrying a direct impact on political and diplomatic issues of the times.

Nevertheless, there is a profound and, I believe, sound public attitude that military leaders should enter these controversies as expert technical advisers, and not as advocates with a political stake in the decision. To this extent, Seeckt was on sure ground in excluding the Reichswehr from affinity with political parties. The spectacle of a military establishment in which generals take to the hustings, or covertly contrive to interject themselves (beyond their own ballot-box) in the political process, is not an appealing one to any believer in democratic government.

* Yes, according to R. H. S. Crossman: "A democracy can only be preserved by the soldier's studied refusal to play politics under a dictatorship, freedom can only be restored if the soldier leads the revolt." See his book review of Paget's *Manstein*, in *The New Statesman and Nation* for October 13, 1951.

To this extent at least the military are under an obligation of political restraint to which the ordinary citizen is not subject. But the dilemma which we have posed arises only out of efforts to push this principle of political neutrality to much more distant limits. Are military men absolutely bound to follow the orders of *whatever* political regime holds sway, even though it be patently a bloody tyranny, bent on conquest? Are they mere janitors of the military machine, with no responsibility for the use to which it is put? Are they, in short, political eunuchs, deprived of the capacity of moral judgment on their own behalf?

If so, then surely history will acquit Brauchitsch and Rundstedt, and even Keitel, and must condemn Beck and Witzleben and the other officers who attempted Hitler's murder and the overthrow of Nazism in 1944. Russian and Polish officers who oppose the designs of their Communist masters, whether by conspiracy or escape, must equally answer to the charge of unmilitary insubordination. What shall be their defence?

There come times in the affairs of nations when their very foundations are tested by a powerful challenge to basic tenets or governmental habits. These times we call "revolutionary", and the era of the Third Reich was truly revolutionary. The Third Reich was dedicated to the overthrow of many such tenets, among them those of government responsive to the popular will, justice under the rule of law, the equality of races, nationalities and sects before the law, and the dignity of the individual man.

These concepts touch the root of the governmental process and the social organism, and the issues they raise are commonly regarded as "revolutionary" in character by democrats and authoritarians of all hues. Is it either the privilege or the obligation of generals to stand aside from their solution, or to act by always putting their services at the disposal of the *de facto* regime, whatever its nature? In the answer to this question, I believe, lies the resolution of the dilemma we have posed.

In the case of the German generals, however, the question is not a naked abstraction, but is overlaid and coloured by the established traditions of the officers' corps and the trust which the German people reposed in the generals. This trust was not only a fact—it was publicly proclaimed by the leaders of the officers' corps on all occasions. For Groener, the Army was "the rock upon which the state is built". In 1919, he had described it as "a centre for the physical and moral education of German youth". As late as 1937, Beck wrote that the Ger-

man people "place a confidence in the Wehrmacht which hardly knows limits. . . . To them the Wehrmacht is both people and state." [6] In his testament, Hindenburg wrote of the Reichswehr as "the guardian of the state" and "the pattern of state conduct". And Stresemann, no soldier but a good nationalist, exalted "that old National Army on which we all depended. In this institution I have always seen the embodiment of the old Prussian idea of the state." [7]

The trust was confidently extended and proudly acknowledged. It was not a trust to determine evanescent political issues, but to preserve the "old Prussian virtues" and safeguard the state. It was unpartisan, but nevertheless a political and social trust in the deepest sense. As we have seen, the struggle to govern the training of German youth was the core of the issue between Fritsch and Himmler. The depth of the trust, even among intellectual and aristocratic civilians, was pathetically reflected in the hopes—at first confident, later agonized and despairing—that were reposed in the generals by von Hassell, Goerdeler, Gisevius, Schacht and other organizers of the clandestine anti-Hitler groups that spun their shadowy and futile plots during the later years of the Third Reich. "On the Reichswehr . . . on its attitude, feeling and inclination, depended primarily the fate of Germany and therewith of Europe, according to my opinion," writes the historian Meinecke. [8]

Did the generals of the Hitler era live up to their own standards and discharge the trust? However one may assess the blame, the record of failure can hardly be gainsaid. By the end of 1938, there was precious little "Prussian cleanliness and simplicity" (Beck's phrase) left in the Third Reich. The scales of justice were sadly warped. The religion—Catholic or Protestant—which was a traditional ingredient of the military ethos was being deliberately and effectively discredited by the government. The battle for the mind of German youth was being lost. The honour of Schleicher and Fritsch was unredeemed. The power of the generals had declined immeasurably, and their control of strategic and even tactical military matters was gravely threatened. The emperors had always listened to them; now Hitler lectured them. The generals were convinced that Germany was not yet ready for war, but they no longer governed its timing. Their traditions were being flouted, and they were increasingly impotent to discharge their trust.

How had it all come about? Primarily, as we have seen, it was the wide area of agreement on objectives between Hitler and the generals that brought them together. Having become a pillar of the Third Reich, they were disinclined to bring the edifice crashing down about their own ears. In the struggle for mastery of the house they were repeatedly outwitted, and the efforts of a few to re-establish their power were constantly set at naught by the individual ambitions of others.

The *esprit de corps* and unity inherited from the days of Moltke and Schlieffen had atrophied. And, as Hossbach put it, the officers' corps lacked any "Fuehrer-personality" to revitalize its leadership.[9] Hammerstein, Blomberg, Fritsch, Beck, Rundstedt, Brauchitsch and their colleagues, individually and collectively, failed to manifest the capacity for aggressive and enlightened leadership that might have repulsed the onslaught of Nazism and safeguarded the integrity of the corps.

At bottom, the failure of the generals was due to the same political and social archaism that had characterized them during the First World War. The officers' corps was simply incapable of making the passage from century to century. They were in but not of modern times, and thus insensitive to many of the most important forces that played about their heads. Even today, this blindness is reflected in ways that would be amusing had not the consequences been so tragic. Manstein, proclaiming his dislike for the Nazis, explains through his apologist [10] that "they were Bavarian, and Prussians do not think much of Bavarians. They were led by an Austrian corporal with, for all he knew, a bit of Czech or God knows what, about him." Men so provincial and caste-ridden were unlikely to grasp the dynamics of the twentieth-century western world, or hit upon ways and means of checking the versatile, terrible genius of Hitler, even had they so desired.

"History will indict the highest leaders of the Wehrmacht with blood-guilt if they do not act in accordance with expert and statesmanlike knowledge and assurance. Their duty of soldierly obedience finds its limit when their knowledge, conscience and responsibility forbid the execution of an order." So wrote Beck [11] in July, 1938, as he reflected bitterly on the course events were taking, and on his ability to stir his brother generals to counteraction. Perhaps the foregoing narrative will assist the reader, the juror of history, to return a just verdict.

A NOTE ON GERMAN RANKS

THE RANK system of modern European armies and navies developed during the eighteenth and nineteenth centuries. The terminology is eclectic: "lieutenant" and "colonel" are French in origin, "captain" is Italian and "admiral" is Arabic. By the end of the nineteenth century, a high degree of uniformity had been achieved among the various nations.

Discrepancies persist, however, particularly at the upper and lower extremes of the rank ladder. Likewise, changes still occur. During the recent war, the American Navy revived the rank of commodore, and all our services added the topmost "five-star" rank to match the European field-marshals. In 1936 when promoted by Hitler, the Commander-in-Chief of the German Navy (Raeder) revived and assumed the rank of *"generaladmiral"*, last used in the eighteenth-century Dutch Navy. After the First World War, the British brigadier general ceased to be a general and was reduced to a mere "brigadier"—a sort of supercolonel. But the British have two classes of commodores, and the sleeve stripes of the upper class are indistinguishable from those of a rear-admiral. The Royal Air Force added a whole new set of ranks to military vocabulary, whereas the German and American Air Forces adhered to the Army terminology.

Most of the German ranks can be translated accurately by their English equivalents, but to avoid confusion and preserve atmosphere it has seemed best to stick to the original German in the text of this book. For example, although the Germans have a rank equivalent to that of our brigadier-general, they have no rank by that name. It is unsatisfactory to translate *Generalleutnant* either as "major-general" (the equivalent rank) or "lieutenant-general" (the terminological equivalent). Accordingly, the original German word is used throughout.

By and large, the German officer ranks follow the orthodox pattern common to the military in all countries. The Army rank of captain is *Hauptmann*, except in the cavalry, where it is *Rittmeister*. The Army rank equivalent to our lieutenant-general (*General*) is always given with the bearer's branch of service—*General der Infanterie, General der Artillerie*, etc., as the case might be. In practice, this was merely a convention, as officers of this rank ordinarily commanded a corps or, at least, a division, or held a high staff position involving general, rather than special responsibilities. The revival of the naval rank of

Generaladmiral had a special history, as explained in the narrative.*
An entire new set of titles was established for the ranks in the SS.

From time to time, either on retirement or to meet some special situation, Army generals were given a sort of brevet rank, in which case their titles of rank were preceded with the word *charakterisiert* (literally "in the character of", and commonly abbreviated as *char.*). Thus von Kleist was promoted from *Oberst* to *Char. Generalmajor* on January 1, 1932, when he was jumped over several senior *Obersten* and given command of a cavalry division. Beck and Adam were both given the *charakterisiert* rank of *Generaloberst* when they were retired at the end of 1938. These officers wore the insignia of their *charakterisiert* rank, but remained junior on the rank list, regardless of date, to those who held the equivalent rank without the prefix.

When officers were relieved of active duty, they were either declared ineligible for further duty, in which case they were listed as *ausser Dienst* (out of duty, abbreviated *a.D.*), or, if subject to recall, as *zur Verfuegung* (at disposal, abbreviated *z.V.*).

In the Reichswehr of the Weimar Republic, there were usually only three officers above the rank of *Generalleutnant*. The *Chef der Heeresleitung* always held the rank of *General* or, toward the end of his tenure, *Generaloberst*; the commanders-in-chief of the two *Gruppen-kommandos* also held the rank of *General*. The *Wehrkreis* commanders were *Generalleutnante*, or, sometimes, *Generalmajore*, as were a few senior staff officers. When the Army expanded under Hitler, and the *Wehrkreis* troops became the equivalent of a corps rather than a division, the *Wehrkreis* commanders customarily held the rank of *General*, and several of the *Gruppenkommando* (later *Heeresgruppe*, or Army group) chiefs, to wit Rundstedt, Bock and List, were promoted to *Generaloberst*. After the retirement of Hindenburg in 1919, and until after the fall of France in 1940, the only active field-marshals were Blomberg in the Army and Goering in the Luftwaffe; in 1939 Raeder was appointed to the equivalent naval rank of *Grossadmiral*.

There was a hierarchy of Army titles for command as well as rank. In the Reichswehr, the commanders of regiments and *Wehrkreis* divisions alike bore the command designation *Kommandeur*, while the commands of the two *Gruppenkommandos* carried the title *Oberbefehls-haber* (literally, "over-command-holder"). Later on the regimental commander was a *Kommandeur*, the divisional commander a *Divisions-kommandeur*, the *Wehrkreis* corps commander a *Kommandierender General* and the *Heeresgruppe* commander an *Oberbefehlshaber*.

* *Supra*, pp. 119–121.

COMPARATIVE TABLE OF RANKS

German Army and Air Force	Army	SS
Generalfeldmarschall	Field Marshal	Reichsfuehrer SS (RFSS)
Generaloberst	General	Oberstgruppenfuehrer (Obstgruf.)
General (der Inf. etc.)	Lt. General	Obergruppenfuehrer (Ogruf.)
Generalleutnant	Major General	Gruppenfuehrer (Gruf.)
Generalmajor	Brig. General	Brigadefuehrer (Brif.)
—	—	Oberfuehrer (Oberf.)
Oberst	Colonel	Standartenfuehrer (Staf.)
Oberstleutnant	Lt. Colonel	Obersturmbannfuehrer (Ostubaf.)
Major	Major	Sturmbannfuehrer (Stubaf.)
Hauptmann ⎱ Rittmeister ⎰	Captain	Hauptsturmfuehrer
Oberleutnant	Lieutenant	Obersturmfuehrer
Leutnant	Second Lieutenant	Untersturmfuehrer

German Navy	Navy
Grossadmiral	Admiral of the Fleet
Generaladmiral	—
Admiral	Admiral
Vizeadmiral	Vice-Admiral
Konteradmiral	Rear Admiral
Kommodore	Commodore
Kapitaen zur See	Captain
Fregattenkapitaen	Commander
Korvettenkapitaen	Lt. Commander
Kapitaenleutnant	Lieutenant
Oberleutnant zur See	Sub-Lieutenant
Leutnant zur See	Midshipman

APOCRYPHA OF THE BLOMBERG–FRITSCH CRISIS

THE BLOMBERG–FRITSCH crisis, as we have seen, was full of intrigue, and many of the events of that period remained jealously guarded secrets. The war broke out a year and a half later, cutting off other countries from such touch as they had theretofore retained with internal German affairs. The inevitable result was a flood of rumours about the crisis. Some of these gained considerable currency as the result of the publication of articles and books during the war, when the authors were unable to verify the facts and had little but rumour on which to rely. Even the well-informed Mr. Milton Shulman, in his post-war *Defeat in the West*, was sadly misled (presumably by Fritsch's honorary designation as *Chef* of Artillery Regiment 12) in declaring * that Fritsch was "reduced to the rank of a colonel".

Two of these war-time works in particular,† which seem to be based in part on the same source or sources, merit comment. According to these accounts, Fritsch seized upon Blomberg's *mésalliance* as the occasion for a showdown with Hitler on various policy issues, including Spain, religious worship in the Wehrmacht, the role of the Luftwaffe and the programme to "liquidate" Austria–Czechoslovakia. With this end in view, Fritsch is said to have called, on January 29, 1938, a meeting of all the *Gruppenkommando* and *Wehrkreis* commanders to secure their support for his *démarche*. From this supposed conclave of generals there developed a sharp division of opinion, with Reichenau, List, Kleist and Bock siding with Hitler, and Rundstedt, Leeb and Kress von Kressenstein backing Fritsch.‡ Fritsch's dismissal is declared to have resulted from his having presented Hitler with a virtual ultimatum after this meeting.

After analysis and several attempts at verification, I am convinced that this tale is completely without basis in fact. Not one of the surviving generals who would have participated in such a meeting has

* *Defeat in the West*, by Milton Shulman (1948), p. 30. Shulman also charges (p. 29) that Fritsch "collaborated with Himmler in producing a police dossier" on Blomberg's bride. I know of no basis for such a suggestion, which is in conflict with all the known facts.

† *The Self-Betrayed*, by Curt Riess (Putnam's, 1942) and *Hitler's Generals*, written under the pseudonym of W. E. Hart (Doubleday, Doran, 1944).

‡ These are the names on which both accounts agree. Riess mentions several other generals on each side of the alleged fence.

supported the account. Adam, Sodenstern (then Kluge's Chief of Staff at Wehrkreis VI, Muenster), Kress von Kressenstein and Hossbach all dismissed it, under questioning, as a fabrication. Nor is the story in character; if Fritsch had been disposed to go to such lengths before his dismissal, he certainly would not have behaved with such lack of *élan* when he realized that he was the object of a conspiracy.

Hart's and Riess' versions contain several errors common to both, which again suggest a single and misinformed source. Both refer to the "old" Kress von Kressenstein, who was in fact one of the more junior *Wehrkreis* commanders (he was not yet fifty-seven). The mistake is understandable, as military Kress von Kressensteins are very numerous, and an uncle (Fritz) of the one in question (Franz) had in fact been a *Gruppenkommando* commander during the twenties, and was still living in retirement. Hart has Kressenstein resigning by means of a brusque letter to Hitler; Riess goes him one better, and declares that Kressenstein left Germany and retired to Zurich. Under questioning, Kressenstein denied all these details, and in fact he was twice (though very briefly) recalled to duty, and continued to reside near Munich, where I questioned him in 1949.

Numerous other errors of fact in both books do not warrant the space for correction here. For example, Hart (but not Riess) sets forth the apocryphal story of Fritsch's assassination by the SS during the Polish campaign. Riess (but not Hart) declares that Rundstedt was dismissed "for a few weeks" at the same time as Leeb, Kleist, Kressenstein and the others. Continuing to later times, Riess tells us that Beck resigned as Chief of Staff *after* the Munich crisis, that Blaskowitz "vanished into obscurity" after the Polish campaign (in fact, he was one of very few senior pre-war generals who still held an active command at the end of the war in 1945), and that General "Hans" von Wietersheim (correct name Gustav) was Chief of Operations of the Army General Staff until the end of 1941 (in fact Wietersheim gave way to Manstein in this capacity in 1936, and never again held a staff position; he commanded the 29th Division from 1936 to 1938 and the XIVth Corps from its establishment in 1938 until his dismissal in 1942 at the time of Stalingrad).

GENERALOBERST WILHELM ADAM AND HIS MEMOIRS

W$_{ILHELM}$ A$_{DAM}$, a Bavarian and a Protestant, was born at Anspach on September 15, 1877. He became an officer in the Bavarian Army, served throughout the First World War, and was taken into the Reichswehr with the rank of *Major*. He was promoted to *Oberstleutnant* in 1922 and to *Oberst* in 1927.

During his post-war career, Adam acquired an enviable reputation both as a General Staff officer and as a specialist in mountain warfare. By 1930, he was a newly promoted *Generalmajor* and Chief of Staff to General der Infanterie Otto Hasse, the Commander-in-Chief of Gruppenkommando 1, at Berlin. He was in high favour with Hammerstein, and later that year, when the latter was appointed *Chef der Heeresleitung*, Adam was designated his successor as *Chef des Truppenamtes* (the equivalent of Chief of the Army General Staff), and was promoted to *Generalleutnant* on December 1, 1931. The remainder of Adam's military career is set forth in the narrative.

After his retirement from active duty at the end of 1938, Adam returned to his native Bavaria, and at the end of the war was living quietly in Garmisch-Partenkirchen, with his wife and infant grandson. While preparing the case for the prosecution in one of the Nuremberg trials, I learned of Adam's whereabouts, and arranged for him to come to Nuremberg.

Generaloberst Adam arrived on January 15, 1948; much of the information that he gave me is embodied in the narrative. Although somewhat enfeebled and with failing eyesight, he was in full possession of his remarkable faculties. His account was given with precise dates, which he explained on the basis of his memory, the phenomenal retentiveness of which he freely acknowledged, and his habit of preserving notes of important events and meetings.

In the course of the interview, the General revealed that the well-known writer Sigrid Schultz, upon "discovering" him in Garmisch after the war, had suggested that he write his memoirs. This he had done, to the tune of some seven hundred pages, but he did not wish to have them published until after his death. He declared that he wanted the memoirs to reflect the way things looked to him without taking account of the evidence at the Nuremberg trials.

No doubt Adam could have been required to produce the memoirs in response to court order. However, while it seemed certain that they might be of historical value, it did not appear likely that they

would contain information necessary to the Nuremberg criminal proceedings, over and above the background information which he had already furnished to both the prosecution and the defence.* Accordingly, it seemed ungracious to repay courtesy and co-operation with coercion, and no such action was taken or attempted.

In February, 1949, after the conclusion of the last Nuremberg trial involving members of the Wehrmacht, I visited the General at his home in Garmisch. In the course of a friendly and informative conversation, the memoirs were displayed, and the table of contents read aloud, from which it was apparent that Adam's bluntness (abundantly demonstrated at his meetings with Hitler) had not deserted him ; among others, Brauchitsch and Halder were sharply dealt with because of their failure to oppose Hitler determinedly. The memoirs were written in a somewhat informal manner, suitable for distribution among friends, and Adam thought they would require editing prior to general publication.

The General expressed considerable interest in the possibility of editing and translating the memoirs for publication in English, but was unable to come to an immediate decision, as he wished to consult with Frau Adam, and with his close friend, the Abbot of the famous Benedictine abbey at nearby Ettal. As I took my leave to enjoy some winter sports, my host, then in his seventy-second year, remarked wistfully that he had not been skiing "for nearly five years".

I returned to Germany for the last time early in April, and learned that Generaloberst Adam had died during the night of April 8th, 1949. Shortly thereafter, I visited the Abbot of Ettal, Dr. Angelus Kupfer, who informed me that he and the General had discussed publication of the memoirs, but that the latter had died without coming to a decision, and had left the matter in the hands of Frau Adam.

Subsequent correspondence with Dr. Kupfer, and a friend's visit to Frau Adam, have elicited information that she has been advised not to permit publication of the memoirs. One may surmise that Adam's critical comments on persons, some of whom are still alive, are a reason for her reluctance.

From a historical standpoint, it is regrettable that the memoirs have remained unavailable. From a political standpoint, it is disheartening that the present atmosphere in Germany is such as to give rise to the understandable caution which apparently accounts for their unavailability.

* Several affidavits by Adam were offered in evidence by defence counsel at the first Nuremberg trial.

CHART A : Organization of the Reichswehr (1920–1935)

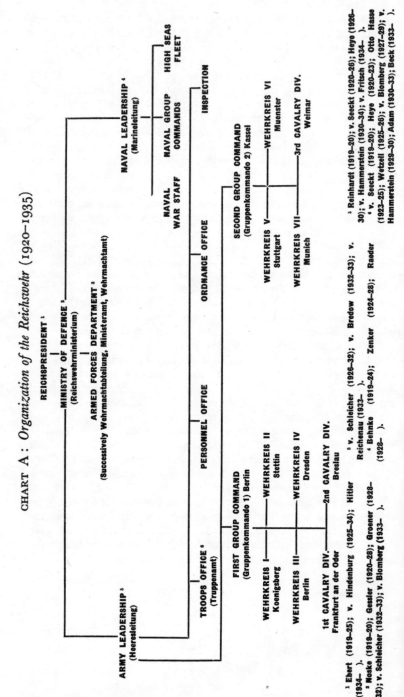

REICHSPRESIDENT [1]

MINISTRY OF DEFENCE [2]
(Reichswehrministerium)

ARMED FORCES DEPARTMENT [3]
(Successively Wehrmachtabteilung, Ministeramt, Wehrmachtamt)

ARMY LEADERSHIP [5]
(Heeresleitung)

NAVAL LEADERSHIP [4]
(Marineleitung)

TROOPS OFFICE [6]
(Truppenamt)

PERSONNEL OFFICE

ORDNANCE OFFICE

NAVAL WAR STAFF

NAVAL GROUP COMMANDS

HIGH SEAS FLEET

INSPECTION

FIRST GROUP COMMAND
(Gruppenkommando 1) Berlin

SECOND GROUP COMMAND
(Gruppenkommando 2) Kassel

WEHRKREIS I — Koenigsberg
WEHRKREIS II — Stettin
WEHRKREIS III — Berlin
WEHRKREIS IV — Dresden
1st CAVALRY DIV. — Frankfurt an der Oder
2nd CAVALRY DIV. — Breslau

WEHRKREIS V — Stuttgart
WEHRKREIS VI — Muenster
WEHRKREIS VII — Munich
3rd CAVALRY DIV. — Weimar

[1] Ebert (1919–25); v. Hindenburg (1925–34); Hitler (1934–).

[2] Noske (1919–20); Gessler (1920–28); Groener (1928–32); v. Schleicher (1932–33); v. Blomberg (1933–).

[3] v. Schleicher (1926–32); v. Bredow (1932–33); v. Reichenau (1933–).

[4] Behnke (1919–24); Zenker (1924–28); Raeder (1928–).

[5] Reinhardt (1919–20); v. Seeckt (1920–26); Heye (1926–30); v. Hammerstein (1930–34); v. Fritsch (1934–).

[6] v. Seeckt (1919–20); Heye (1920–23); Otto Hasse (1923–25); Wetzell (1925–26); v. Blomberg (1927–29); v. Hammerstein (1929–30); Adam (1930–33); Beck (1933–).

CHART B1 : *Organization of the Wehrmacht* (1935–February, 1938)

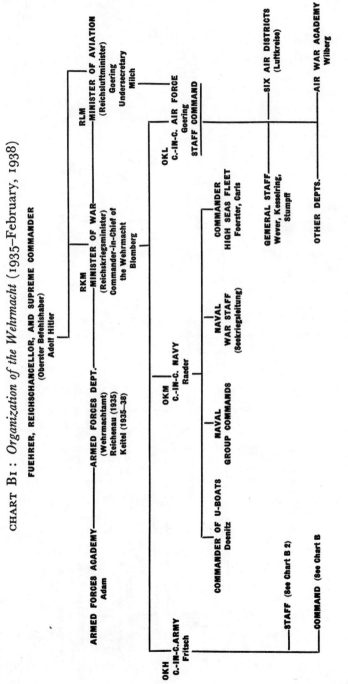

FUEHRER, REICHSCHANCELLOR, AND SUPREME COMMANDER
(Oberster Befehlshaber)
Adolf Hitler

RKM — MINISTER OF WAR
(Reichskriegsminister)
Commander-in-Chief of the Wehrmacht
Blomberg

RLM — MINISTER OF AVIATION
(Reichsluftminister)
Goering
Undersecretary
Milch

ARMED FORCES DEPT. (Wehrmachtamt)
Reichenau (1935)
Keitel (1935–38)

ARMED FORCES ACADEMY
Adam

OKH C.-IN-C. ARMY
Fritsch

STAFF (See Chart B 2)
COMMAND (See Chart B)

OKM C.-IN-C. NAVY
Raeder

COMMANDER OF U-BOATS
Doenitz

NAVAL GROUP COMMANDS

NAVAL WAR STAFF
(Seekriegsleitung)

COMMANDER HIGH SEAS FLEET
Foerster, Carls

OKL C.-IN-C. AIR FORCE
Goering
STAFF COMMAND

GENERAL STAFF
Wever, Kesselring, Stumpff

SIX AIR DISTRICTS
(Luftkreise)

OTHER DEPTS.

AIR WAR ACADEMY
Wilberg

CHART B2 : *Organization of OKH* (1935–February, 1938)

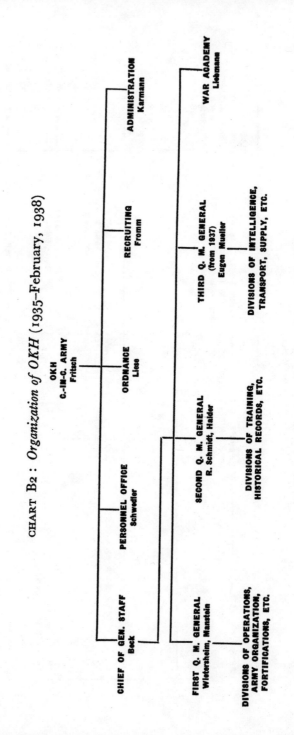

CHART B3 : *Organization of the German Field Army* (1935–February, 1938)

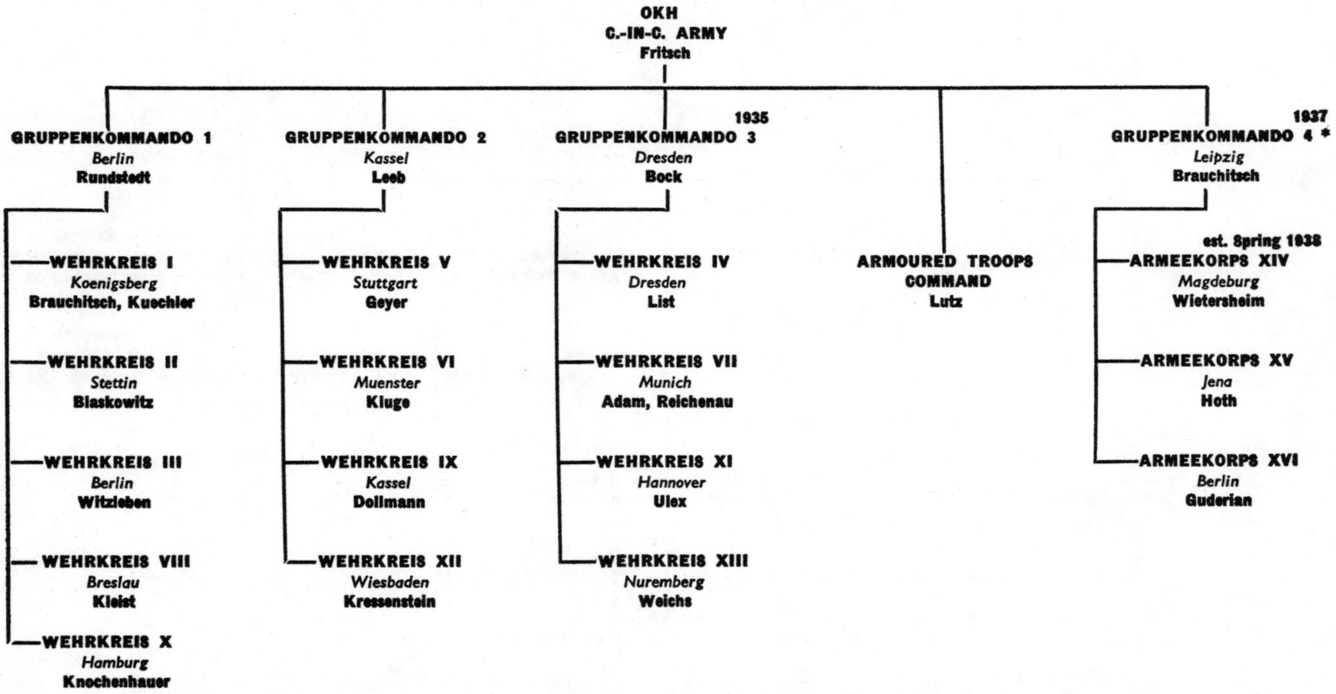

OKH
C.-IN-C. ARMY
Fritsch

GRUPPENKOMMANDO 1
Berlin
Rundstedt

- **WEHRKREIS I**
  Koenigsberg
  Brauchitsch, Kuechler
- **WEHRKREIS II**
  Stettin
  Blaskowitz
- **WEHRKREIS III**
  Berlin
  Witzleben
- **WEHRKREIS VIII**
  Breslau
  Kleist
- **WEHRKREIS X**
  Hamburg
  Knochenhauer

GRUPPENKOMMANDO 2
Kassel
Leeb

- **WEHRKREIS V**
  Stuttgart
  Geyer
- **WEHRKREIS VI**
  Muenster
  Kluge
- **WEHRKREIS IX**
  Kassel
  Dollmann
- **WEHRKREIS XII**
  Wiesbaden
  Kressenstein

1935

GRUPPENKOMMANDO 3
Dresden
Beck

- **WEHRKREIS IV**
  Dresden
  List
- **WEHRKREIS VII**
  Munich
  Adam, Reichenau
- **WEHRKREIS XI**
  Hannover
  Ulex
- **WEHRKREIS XIII**
  Nuremberg
  Weichs

ARMOURED TROOPS COMMAND
Lutz

1937

GRUPPENKOMMANDO 4 *
Leipzig
Brauchitsch

- est. Spring 1938
  ARMEEKORPS XIV
  Magdeburg
  Wietersheim
- **ARMEEKORPS XV**
  Jena
  Hoth
- **ARMEEKORPS XVI**
  Berlin
  Guderian

* When Gruppenkommando 4 was established in 1937, there were subordinated to it the Armoured Troops Command (later renamed Armeekorps XVI), four divisions (2, 13, 20 and 29) which were being motorized, a "light" brigade and other miscellaneous supporting units.

369

CHART C1 : *Organization of the Wehrmacht* (February, 1938–September, 1939)

FUEHRER, REICHSCHANCELLOR, AND SUPREME COMMANDER
Adolf Hitler

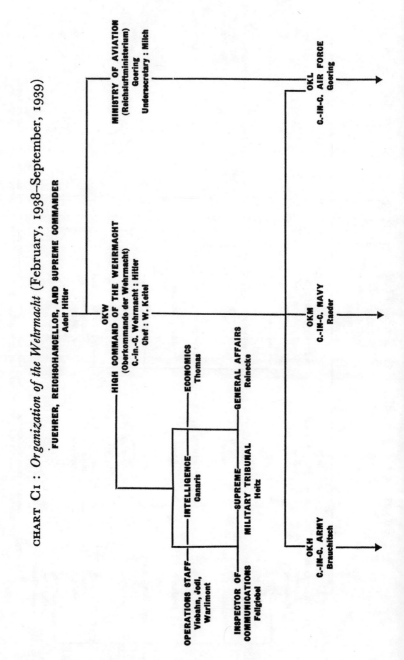

OKW
HIGH COMMAND OF THE WEHRMACHT
(Oberkommando der Wehrmacht)
C.-IN.-C. Wehrmacht : Hitler
Chef : W. Keitel

MINISTRY OF AVIATION
(Reichsluftministerium)
Goering
Undersecretary : Milch

OPERATIONS STAFF
Viebahn, Jodl, Wartimont

INTELLIGENCE
Canaris

ECONOMICS
Thomas

INSPECTOR OF
COMMUNICATIONS
Fellgiebel

SUPREME
MILITARY TRIBUNAL
Heitz

GENERAL AFFAIRS
Reinecke

OKH
C.-IN.-C. ARMY
Brauchitsch

OKM
C.-IN.-C. NAVY
Raeder

OKL
C.-IN.-C. AIR FORCE
Goering

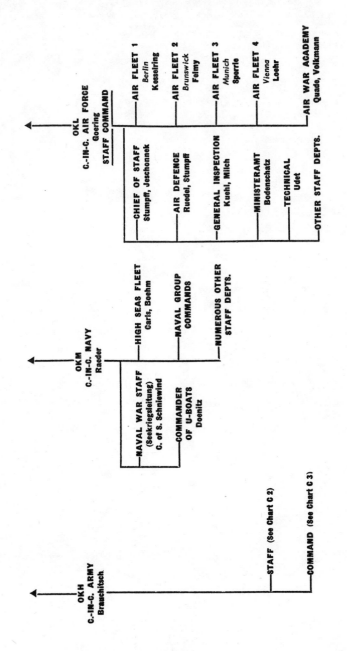

OKH
C.-IN-C. ARMY
Brauchitsch

STAFF (See Chart C 2)

COMMAND (See Chart C 3)

OKM
C.-IN-C. NAVY
Raeder

NAVAL WAR STAFF
(Seekriegsleitung)
C. of S. Schniewind

COMMANDER
OF U-BOATS
Doenitz

HIGH SEAS FLEET
Carls, Boehm

NAVAL GROUP
COMMANDS

NUMEROUS OTHER
STAFF DEPTS.

OKL
C.-IN-C. AIR FORCE
Goering
STAFF COMMAND

CHIEF OF STAFF
Stumpff, Jeschonnek

AIR DEFENCE
Ruedel, Stumpff

GENERAL INSPECTION
Kuehl, Milch

MINISTERAMT
Bodenschatz

TECHNICAL
Udet

OTHER STAFF DEPTS.

AIR FLEET 1
Berlin
Kesselring

AIR FLEET 2
Brunswick
Felmy

AIR FLEET 3
Munich
Sperrle

AIR FLEET 4
Vienna
Loehr

AIR WAR ACADEMY
Quade, Volkmann

CHART C2 : *Organization of OKH* (February, 1938–September, 1939)

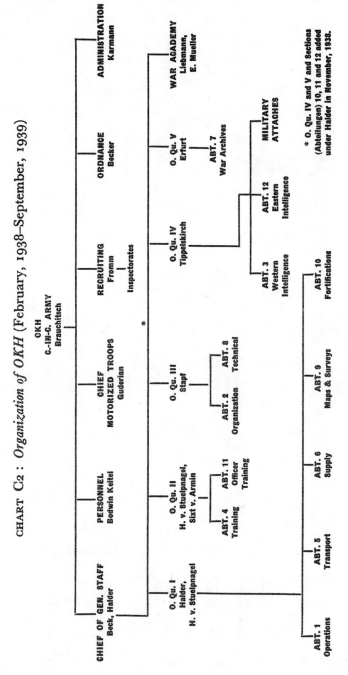

OKH
C.-IN-C. ARMY
Brauchitsch

CHIEF OF GEN. STAFF
Beck, Halder

PERSONNEL
Bodwin Keitel

CHIEF
MOTORIZED TROOPS
Guderian

RECRUITING
Fromm
Inspectorates

ORDNANCE
Becker

ADMINISTRATION
Karmann

O. Qu. I
Halder,
H. v. Stuelpnagel

O. Qu. II
H. v. Stuelpnagel,
Sixt v. Armin

O. Qu. III
Stapf

O. Qu. IV
Tippelskirch

O. Qu. V
Erfurt

WAR ACADEMY
Liebmann,
E. Mueller

ABT. 4
Training

ABT. 11
Officer
Training

ABT. 2
Organization

ABT. 8
Technical

ABT. 3
Western
Intelligence

ABT. 12
Eastern
Intelligence

MILITARY
ATTACHES

ABT. 7
War Archives

ABT. 1
Operations

ABT. 5
Transport

ABT. 6
Supply

ABT. 9
Maps & Surveys

ABT. 10
Fortifications

* O. Qu. IV and V and Sections
(Abteilungen) 10, 11 and 12 added
under Halder in November, 1938.

373

CHART C3 : *Organization of the Field Army* (1938–1939) *

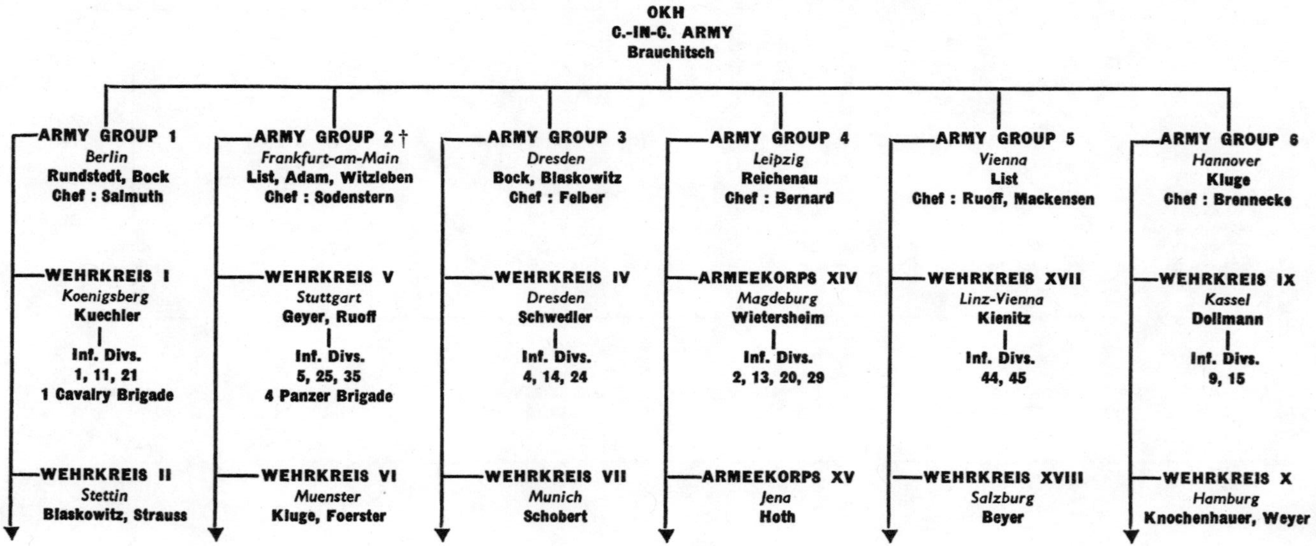

OKH
C.-IN-C. ARMY
Brauchitsch

ARMY GROUP 1
Berlin
Rundstedt, Bock
Chef : Salmuth

WEHRKREIS I
Koenigsberg
Kuechler
Inf. Divs.
1, 11, 21
1 Cavalry Brigade

WEHRKREIS II
Stettin
Blaskowitz, Strauss

ARMY GROUP 2 †
Frankfurt-am-Main
List, Adam, Witzleben
Chef : Sodenstern

WEHRKREIS V
Stuttgart
Geyer, Ruoff
Inf. Divs.
5, 25, 35
4 Panzer Brigade

WEHRKREIS VI
Muenster
Kluge, Foerster

ARMY GROUP 3
Dresden
Bock, Blaskowitz
Chef : Felber

WEHRKREIS IV
Dresden
Schwedler
Inf. Divs.
4, 14, 24

WEHRKREIS VII
Munich
Schobert

ARMY GROUP 4
Leipzig
Reichenau
Chef : Bernard

ARMEEKORPS XIV
Magdeburg
Wietersheim
Inf. Divs.
2, 13, 20, 29

ARMEEKORPS XV
Jena
Hoth

ARMY GROUP 5
Vienna
List
Chef : Ruoff, Mackensen

WEHRKREIS XVII
Linz-Vienna
Kienitz
Inf. Divs.
44, 45

WEHRKREIS XVIII
Salzburg
Beyer

ARMY GROUP 6
Hannover
Kluge
Chef : Brennecke

WEHRKREIS IX
Kassel
Dollmann
Inf. Div.
9, 15

WEHRKREIS X
Hamburg
Knochenhauer, Weyer

374

WEHRKREIS X
Hamburg
Knochenhauer, Weyer
Inf. Divs.
22, 30

WEHRKREIS XI
Hannover
Ulex, E. Leeb
Inf. Divs.
19, 31

WEHRKREIS XVIII
Salzburg
Beyer
Mountain Divs.
2, 3
2 Panzer Div.
4 Light Div.

ARMEEKORPS XV
Jena
Hoth
Light Div.
1, 2, 3

ARMEEKORPS XVI
Berlin
Guderian, Hoepner
Panzer Divs.
1, 3, 4, 5

WEHRKREIS VII
Munich
Schobert
Inf. Divs.
7, 27
1 Mountain Div.

WEHRKREIS XIII
Nuremberg
Weichs
Inf. Divs.
10, 17, 46

WEHRKREIS VI
Muenster
Kluge, Foerster
Inf. Divs.
6, 16, 26
6 Panzerbrigade

WEHRKREIS XII
Wiesbaden
Schroth
Inf. Divs.
33, 34, 36

BORDER COMMAND SAARPFALZ
Kaiserslautern
Kuntze

WEHRKREIS II
Stettin
Blaskowitz, Strauss
Inf. Divs.
12, 32

WEHRKREIS III
Berlin
Witzleben, Haase
Inf. Divs.
3, 23

WEHRKREIS VIII
Breslau
Busch
Inf. Divs.
8, 18, 28

* In 1939, prior to the outbreak of war, some 20 additional divisions were formed within the various Wehrkreise.

† Army Group 2 moved from Kassel to Frankfurt am Main in July, 1938.

SELECTED GERMAN RANK LISTS, 1924–1939

The figure in parentheses gives the seniority within the group promoted on the same date. It should be borne in mind that the date of rank does not always represent the original date of promotion, as dates of rank were sometimes predated or postdated when it was desired to increase or decrease the seniority of officers.

LIST No. 1

April 1, 1924

THE TWENTY-FIVE SENIOR GENERALS AND TWENTY-FIVE SELECTED COLONELS AND LIEUTENANT-COLONELS

As of April 1, 1924, there were 25 *Generalmajore*, 106 *Obersten*, and 190 *Oberst-leutnante*. The *Obersten* and *Oberstleutnante* listed are those mentioned in the narrative.

Name	Rank	Seniority	Assignment
1. v. Seeckt	General	1.10.20(1)	C.-inC. Army
2. v. Berendt	,,	1.9.21	Gruppenkommando 1
3. v. Moehl	,,	1.1.23	,, 2
4. Reinhardt	General-leutnant	16.6.20(2)	Wehrkreis V
5. v. Poseck	,,	1.10.20(2)	Inspector, Cavalry
6. v. Lossberg	,,	1.10.20(3)	Wehrkreis VI
7. v. Horn	,,	1.10.20(4)	Wehrkreis III
8. Bleidorn	,,	1.7.21(2)	Inspector, Artillery
9. Mueller	,,	1.7.21(4)	Wehrkreis IV
10. Hasse, Ernst	,,	1.4.22(1)	2nd Cavalry Div.
11. Heye	,,	1.4.22(2)	Wehrkreis I
12. Hasse, Paul	,,	1.1.23	3rd Cavalry Div.
13. v. Tschischwtiz	,,	1.2.23	Wehrkreis II
14. v. Taysen	,,	1.7.23	Inspector, Infantry
15. Kress v. Kressenstein, Fritz	,,	1.10.23	Wehrkreis VII
16. Felsch	,,	1.11.23	Infantry Leader, Wkr. IV
17. v. Ledebur	,,	1.3.24	,, ,, Wkr. II
18. Ritter v. Danner	General-major	1.7.21(8)	Commandant, Munich
19. Wurtzbacher	,,	1.7.21(11)	Chief of Ordnance
20. Kraehe	,,	1.7.22	Infantry Leader, Wkr. V
21. Edelbuettel	,,	1.4.22(1)	,, ,, Wkr. III
22. v. Jagow	,,	1.1.23(2)	1st Cavalry Div.
23. v. Pawelsz	,,	1.2.23(1)	Chief of Staff, GK 1
24. Woellwarth	,,	1.2.23(2)	,, ,, GK 2
25. Hasse, Otto	,,	1.2.23(3)	Chief, Truppenamt

v. Stuelpnagel, Edwin	Oberst	1.1.22(1)	4th Infantry Reg.
Hierl, Konstantin	,,	1.4.22(4)	Staff of GK. 1
Ritter v. Prager	,,	1.7.22(1)	in Army General Staff
Frhr. Seutter v. Loetzen	,,	1.2.23(11)	Chief of Staff, Wkr. IV

376

Name	Rank	Seniority	Assignment
v. Rundstedt	Oberst	1.2.23(12)	Chief of Staff, Wkr. II
v. Vollard Bockelberg	,,	1.2.23(14)	with 2nd Artillery Reg.
v. Falkenhausen	,,	1.4.24(3)	Chief of Staff, Wkr. VI
Ritter v. Leeb	Oberst-leutnant	1.10.20(116)	,, ,, , Wkr. VII
v. Blomberg	,,	1.10.20(137)	,, ,, , Wkr. V
Frhr. v. Gienanth	,,	1.10.20(138)	13th Cavalry Reg.
v. Bock	,,	1.10.20(140)	with 4th Infantry Reg.
Frhr. v. Hammerstein-Equord, Curt	,,	1.10.20(141)	Chief of Staff, Wkr. III
v. Stuelpnagel, Otto	,,	1.4.21(1)	Staff of Wkr. VI
Halm	,,	1.6.21(10)	in Truppenamt
Wachenfeld	,,	1.6.21(11)	with 5th Artillery Reg.
v. Stuelpnagel, Joachim	,,	1.6.21(13)	in Truppenamt
Liebmann	,,	1.6.21(17)	with 1st Infantry Reg.
v. dem Bussche-Ippenburg	,,	1.6.21(18)	in Truppenamt
v. Schleicher	,,	1.6.21(20)	in Army General Staff
Adam	,,	15.11.22(2a)	with 20th Infantry Reg.
Kaupisch	,,	15.11.22(4a)	with 7th Artillery Reg.
Frhr. v. Fritsch	,,	15.11.22(5)	Chief of Staff, Wkr. I
List	,,	15.11.22(6a)	with 19th Infantry Reg.
Beck	,,	15.11.22(10)	Staff of Wkr. VI
Lutz	,,	1.2.23(8)	Army Ordnance Staff

LIST No. 2

May 1, 1932
THE FIFTY SENIOR OFFICERS OF THE ARMY

Name	Rank	Seniority	Assignment
1. Frhr. v. Hammerstein-Equord, Curt	General	1.3.29	C.-in-C. Army
2. Hasse, Otto	,,	1.4.29	Gruppenkommando 1
3. Frhr. Seutter v. Loetzen	,,	1.12.31	,, 2
4. v. Rundstedt	General-leutnant	1.3.29	Wehrkreis III
5. v. Vollard Bockelberg	,,	1.4.29	Chief of Ordnance
6. v. Blomberg	,,	1.10.29(3)	Wehrkreis I
7. Ritter v. Leeb	,,	1.12.29	,, VII
8. Fleck	,,	1.3.30	,, VI
9. Frhr. v. Gienanth	,,	1.2.31(1)	,, IV
10. v. Bock	,,	1.2.31(2)	,, II
11. Wachenfeld	,,	1.4.31	Chief of Staff, GK 1
12. Liebmann	,,	1.10.31(1)	Wehrkreis V
13. Frhr. v. d. Bussche-Ippenburg	,,	1.10.31(2)	Chief of Army Personnel
14. v. Schleicher	,,	1.10.31(3)	Chief, Ministeramt RWM
15. Adam	,,	1.12.31	Chief, Truppenamt
16. Ritter v. Mittelberger	,,	1.1.32	Inspector, Army Schools
17. Kaupisch	,,	1.3.32	Artillery Leader, Wkr. V
18. Frhr. v. Fritsch	General-major	1.11.30(3)	1st Cavalry Div.
19. List	,,	1.11.30(5)	Commander, Infantry School
20. Boehm-Tettelbach	,,	1.11.30(6)	Chief , Army Admin.
21. Beck	,,	1.2.31(5)	Artillery Leader, Wkr. IV
22. v. Roques, Karl(?)	,,	1.2.31(8)	Infantry Leader, Wkr. VI
23. Lutz	,,	1.4.31(1)	Inspector, Mobile Troops
24. Bonin	,,	1.4.31(5)	,, , Communications
25. v. Roques, Franz(?)	,,	1.5.31	Infantry Leader, Wkr. I
26. v. Boetticher	,,	1.10.31(1)	Commander, Artillery School
27. Knochenhauer	,,	1.10.31(2)	3rd Cavalry Div.
28. Schoenheinz	,,	1.10.31(3)	Section Chief in Truppenamt
29. Muff	,,	1.10.31(4)	Infantry Leader, Wkr. V
30. Kuehlenthal	,,	1.10.31(6)	Chief of Staff, GK 2
31. Feige	,,	1.10.31(7)	Chief Operations Sec., Truppenamt
32. v. Brauchitsch	,,	1.10.31(8)	Inspector, Artillery
33. Karlewski	,,	1.10.31(9)	Section Chief, Ordnance
34. Neumann-Neurode	,,	1.11.31	Infantry Leader, Wkr. II
35. Frhr. v. Hammerstein-Equord, Gunther	,,	1.12.31(1)	Inspector, Infantry

Name	Rank	Seniority	Assignment
36. v. Witzendorf	General-major	1.12.31(2)	Commandant, Berlin
37. Curtze	,,	1.2.32(2)	Artillery Leader, Wkr. VII
38. Bitthorn	,,	1.2.32(4)	Section Chief, Army Admin.
39. Starke	,,	1.3.32	Artillery Leader, Wkr. I
40. Haenicke	,,	1.4.32(1)	2nd Infantry Reg.
41. Frhr. v. Hirschberg	,,	1.4.32(2)	Inspector, Cavalry
42. Roese	,,	1.4.32(3)	4th Infantry Reg.
43. v. Waldow	,,	1.4.32(4)	Inf. Leader, Wkr. III
44. v. Kleist	,, Char.	1.1.32	2nd Cavalry Div.
45. v. Selle	Oberst	1.4.29(8)	Art. Leader, Wkr. VI
46. Hopff	,,	1.10.29(8)	Inspector, Engineers
47. Dollmann	,,	1.10.29(10a)	6th Artillery Reg.
48. Wilberg	,,	1.10.29(13)	Commandant, Breslau
49. Braemer	,,	1.10.29(14)	,, , Insterburg
50. Blaskowitz	,,	1.10.29(15)	14th Infantry Reg.

LIST No. 3

October 16, 1935
THE FIFTY SENIOR OFFICERS OF THE ARMY

Name	Rank	Seniority	Assignment
1. v. Blomberg	General-oberst	30.8.33	Minister of War and C.-in-C. Wehrmacht
2. Frhr. v. Fritsch	General	1.9.32	C.-in-C. Army
3. v. Rundstedt	,,	1.10.32	Army Group 1
4. Ritter v. Leeb	,,	1.1.34	,, ,, 2
5. v. Bock	,,	1.3.35	,, ,, 3
6. Liebmann	,,	1.4.35(1)	War Academy
7. Adam	,,	1.4.35(2)	Armed Forces Academy
8. List	,,	1.10.35(1)	Wehrkreis IV
9. Beck	,,	1.10.35(2)	Chief of General Staff
10. Lutz	General-leutnant	1.2.33(2)	Commander, Armoured Forces
11. v. Boetticher	,,	1.10.33(1)	Military Attaché, Washington
12. Knochenhauer	,,	1.10.33(2)	Wehrkreis X
13. Kuehlenthal	,,	1.10.33(4)	Military Attaché, Paris
14. v. Brauchitsch	,,	1.10.33(6)	Wehrkreis I
15. Dollmann	,,	1.10.33(9)	,, IX
16. v. Kleist	,,	1.10.33(10)	,, VIII
17. Blaskowitz	,,	1.12.33(1)	,, II
18. Geyer	,,	1.1.34	,, V
19. Schindler	,,	1.2.34(1)	Inspector of Recruiting, Hamburg
20. Gruen	,,	1.2.34(2)	Inspector, Artillery
21. v. Kluge	,,	1.4.34	Wehrkreis VI
22. Heitz	,,	1.10.34(1)	Commandant, Koenigsberg
23. Frhr. v. Dalwigk zu Lichtenfels	,,	1.10.34(2)	Cavalry School
24. Prof. Dr. Becker	,,	1.10.34(3)	in Army Ordnance
25. Brandt	,,	1.12.34(1)	15th Div.
26. v. Witzleben	,,	1.12.34(2)	Wehrkreis III
27. Frhr. v. Weichs	,,	1.4.35(1)	1st Panzer Div.
28. Frhr. Kress von Kressenstein, Franz	,,	1.4.35(2)	14th Div.
29. Schwandner	,,	1.5.35	20th Div.
30. v. Pogrell	,,	1.6.35(1)	Inspector, Cavalry
31. Gercke	,,	1.6.35(2)	2nd Div.
32. Frhr. v. Wilmowsky	,,	1.8.35(1)	1st Cavalry Div.
33. Tscherning	,,	1.8.35(2)	Inspector of Recruiting, Munich
34. Ulex	,,	1.8.35(3)	12th Div.
35. Heinemann	,,	1.9.35(1)	Artillery School
36. v. Boehm-Bezing	,,	1.9.35(2)	2nd Cavalry Div.
37. v. Niebelschuetz	,,	1.10.35(1)	11th Div.
38. Fessmann	,,	1.10.35(2)	3rd Panzer Div.

Name	Rank	Seniority	Assignment
39. v. Reichenau	General-leutnant	1.10.35(3)	Wehrkreis VII
40. Muff	,, Char.	1.10.32	Military Attaché, Vienna
41. Schaumburg	,, ,,	20.4.35	Commandant, Berlin
42. v. Gimborn	,, ,,	20.4.35	Inspector, Eastern Fortifications
43. Doehla	,, ,,	1.9.35	Commandant, Munich
44. Sachs	,, ,,	1.10.35	Communications School
45. Luedke	General-major	1.2.34	9th Div.
46. Liese	,,	1.3.34	Chief of Ordnance
47. Fischer	,,	1.4.34(1)	Military Attaché, Rome
48. v. Kuechler	,,	1.4.34(2)	Inspector, Army Schools
49. Praetorius	,,	1.4.34(3)	Inspector of Recruiting, Dresden
50. v. Gossler	,,	1.4.34(4)	19th Div.

LIST No. 4

January 1, 1938

THE FIFTY SENIOR OFFICERS OF THE ARMY JUST BEFORE THE REORGANIZATION
CONSEQUENT UPON THE BLOMBERG–FRITSCH CRISIS AND THE *ANSCHLUSS*

Name	Rank	Seniority	Assignment
1. v. Blomberg	General-feld-marschall	20.4.36	Minister of War and C.-in-C. Wehrmacht
2. Frhr. v. Fritsch	General-oberst	20.4.36	C.-in-C. Army
3. v. Rundstedt	General	1.10.32	Army Group 1
4. Ritter v. Leeb	,,	1.1.34	,, ,, 2
5. v. Bock	,,	1.3.35	,, ,, 3
6. Liebmann	,,	1.4.35(1)	War Academy
7. Adam	,,	1.4.35(2)	Armed Forces Academy
8. List	,,	1.10.35(1)	Wehrkreis IV
9. Beck	,,	1.10.35(2)	Chief of General Staff
10. v. Brauchitsch	,,	1.10.35(3)	Army Group 4
11. Lutz	,,	1.11.35	Commander, Armoured Forces
12. Knochenhauer	,,	1.1.36	Wehrkreis X
13. Dollmann	,,	1.4.36	,, IX
14. v. Kleist	,,	1.8.36(1)	,, VIII
15. Blaskowitz	,,	1.8.36(2)	,, II
16. Geyer	,,	1.8.36(3)	,, V
17. v. Kluge	,,	1.8.36(5)	,, VI
18. Prof. Dr. Becker	,,	1.10.36(1)	in Army Ordnance
19. v. Witzleben	,,	1.10.36(2)	Wehrkreis III
20. Frhr. v. Weichs	,,	1.10.36(3)	,, XIII
21. Frhr. Kress v. Kressenstein, Franz	,,	1.10.36(4)	,, XII
22. v. Pogrell	,,	1.10.36(5)	Inspector, Cavalry
23. Ulex	,,	1.10.36(6)	Wehrkreis XI
24. v. Reichenau	,,	1.10.36(7)	,, VII
25. Heitz	,,	1.4.37(1)	President, Military Court
26. Liese	,,	1.4.37(2)	Chief of Ordnance
27. v. Kuechler	,,	1.4.37(3)	Wehrkreis I
28. Keitel, Wilhelm	,,	1.8.37	Armed Forces Dept., RKM
29. v. Boetticher	General-leutnant	1.10.33(1)	Military Attaché, Washington
30. Kuehlenthal	,,	1.10.33(4)	Military Attaché, Paris
31. Frhr. von Dalwigk zu Lichtenfels	,,	1.10.34(2)	Attached to Wehrkreis III
32. Schwandner	,,	1.5.35	20th Div.
33. Erfurth	,,	1.6.35(3)	in Army General Staff
34. Frhr. v. Wilmowsky	,,	1.8.35(1)	Inspector of Recruiting, Potsdam
35. v. Niebelschuetz	,,	1.10.35(1)	Inspector, Army Schools
36. Luedke	,,	1.11.35(1)	Attached to Wehrkreis X

Name	Rank	Seniority	Assignment
37. Fischer	General-leutnant	1.12.35(1)	at disposal, C.-in-C. Army
38. v. Gossler	,,	1.1.36(1)	19th Div.
39. Waeger	,,	1.3.36(1)	10th Div.
40. Wodrig	,,	1.3.36(2)	21st Div.
41. Osswald	,,	1.4.36(1)	9th Div.
42. v. Wietersheim	,,	1.4.36(2)	29th Div.
43. Kuehne	,,	1.4.36(3)	26th Div.
44. Schroth	,,	1.4.36(4)	1st Div.
45. Raschick	,,	1.8.36(1)	4th Div.
46. Kuntze	,,	1.8.36(2)	6th Div.
47. Halder	,,	1.8.36(3)	O. Qu. II, General Staff
48. Hahn	,,	1.8.36(4)	5th Div.
49. Muff	,,	1.8.36(5)	Military Attaché, Vienna
50. Hoth	,,	1.10.36(1)	18th Div.

LIST No. 5

September 1, 1939

THE FIFTY SENIOR OFFICERS OF THE ARMY ON THE OUTBREAK OF WAR

Name	Rank	Seniority	Assignment
1. v. Brauchitsch	General-oberst	4.2.38	C.-in-C. Army
2. v. Bock	,,	1.3.38(2)	Army Group 1
3. Keitel, Wilhelm	,,	1.11.38	Chief, Wehrmacht High Command
4. List	,,	1.4.39	Army Group 5
5. Blaskowitz	General	1.12.35(1)	,, 3
6. v. Kluge	,,	1.12.35(2)	,, 6
7. v. Witzleben	,,	1.3.36	,, 2
8. Dollmann	,,	1.4.36(2)	Wehrkreis IX
9. Prof. Dr. Becker	,,	1.10.36(1)	Chief of Ordnance
10. Frhr. v. Weichs	,,	1.10.36(3)	Wehrkreis XIII
11. v. Reichenau	,,	1.10.36(7)	Army Group 4
12. Heitz	,,	1.4.37(1)	President, Military Court
13. v. Kuechler	,,	1.4.37(3)	Wehrkreis I
14. v. Wietersheim	,,	1.2.38(2)	XIV Corps
15. Schroth	,,	1.2.38(3)	Wehrkreis XII
16. Kuntze	,,	1.2.38(4)	Border Troops, Saarpfalz
17. Halder	,,	1.2.38(5)	Chief of General Staff
18. v. Schwedler	,,	1.2.38(6)	Wehrkreis IV
19. Ritter v. Schobert	,,	1.2.38(7)	,, VII
20. Busch	,,	1.2.38(8)	,, VIII
21. Kienitz	,,	1.4.38(1)	,, XVII
22. Foerster	,,	1.4.38(2)	,, VI
23. Beyer *	,,	1.4.38(3)	,, XVIII
24. Waeger	,,	1.11.38(1)	Border Troops, Upper Rhine
25. Guderian	,,	1.11.38(1a)	Chief of Mobile Troops
26. Hoth	,,	1.11.38(2)	XV Corps
27. Strauss	,,	1.11.38(3)	Wehrkreis II
28. Haase	,,	1.11.38(4)	,, III
29. Raschick	,,	1.4.39(1)	Border Troops, Eifel
30. Karmann	,,	1.4.39(2)	Chief of Administration
31. Leeb, Emil	,,	1.4.39(3)	Wehrkreis XI
32. Friderici	,,	1.4.39(4)	Wehrmacht Plenipotentiary, Bohemia and Moravia
33. v. Stuelpnagel, Heinrich	,,	1.4.39(5)	O. Qu. I, General Staff
34. Fromm	,,	1.4.39(6)	Chief of Recruiting and Training
35. Hoepner	,,	1.4.39(7)	XVI Corps
36. Ruoff	,,	1.5.39	Wehrkreis V
37. Muff	,, Char. 25.3.38 †		Attached to Wehrkreis XI
38. v. Boetticher	General-leutnant	1.10.33(1)	Military Attaché, Washington

384

Name	Rank	Seniority	Assignment
39. Frhr. von Dalwigk zu Lichtenfels	General- leutnant	1.10.34(2)	Attached to Wehrkreis III
40. Schwandner	,,	1.5.35	Attached to Wehrkreis VII
41. Erfurth	,,	1.6.35(3)	O. Qu. V, General Staff
42. Frhr. v. Wilmowsky	,,	1.8.35(1)	Inspector of Recruiting, Potsdam
43. Luedke	,,	1.11.35(1)	Attached to Wehrkreis X
44. Wodrig	,,	1.3.36(2)	,, ,, I
45. Osswald	,,	1.4.36(1)	,, ,, V
46. Glokke	,,	1.10.36(4)	,, ,, VI
47. Dr. v. Rabenau	,,	1.1.37(2)	Chief of Army Archives
48. Otto	,,	1.1.37(3)	13th Div.
49. Koch	,,	1.4.37(2)	8th Div.
50. Schaller-Kalide	,,	1.4.37(4)	Attached to Wehrkreis XVIII

* Assimilated from the Austrian Army.

† Muff and the senior *Generalleutnante,* as their assignments show, were no longer in the running for principal command or staff assignments, and were of less importance in the scheme of things than younger *Generalleutnante* and *Generalmajore* such as Falkenhorst, Geyr v. Schweppenburg, Vietinghoff, Manstein, Rudolf Schmidt, Reinhardt, Salmuth, Felber, von Arnim, Sodenstern, Sixt von Armin, Model and Dietl, and even *Obersten,* such as Paulus, Jodl and Blumentritt.

LIST No. 6

COMPARATIVE TABLE SHOWING RELATIVE SENIORITY IN 1924 AND 1932 OF THE FORTY SENIOR OFFICERS OF 1938 AND 1939 *

Apr. 1, 1924		May 1, 1932		Jan. 1, 1938		Sept. 1, 1939	
106. Rundstedt	Obst.	4. Rundstedt	Genlt.	1. *Blomberg*	FM	1. Brauchitsch	Genobst.
164. v. Leeb	Obstlt.	6. Blomberg	,,	2. *Fritsch*	Genobst.	2. Bock	,,
178. Blomberg	,,	7. v. Leeb	,,	3. *Rundstedt*	Gen.	3. Keitel, W.	,,
181. Bock	,,	10. Bock	,,	4. *v. Leeb*	,,	4. List	,,
206. Erfurth †	,,	12. Liebmann	,,	5. *Bock*	,,	5. Blaskowitz	Gen.
207. Liebmann	,,	15. Adam	Genmaj.	6. *Liebmann*	,,	6. Kluge	,,
251. Adam	,,	18. Fritsch	,,	7. *Adam*	,,	7. Witzleben	,,
256. Fritsch	,,	19. List	,,	8. List	,,	8. Dollmann	,,
258. List	,,	21. Beck	,,	9. *Beck*	,,	9. Becker	,,
267. Beck	,,	23. Lutz	,,	10. Brauchitsch	,,	10. Weichs	,,
277. Lutz	,,	26. Boetticher	,,	11. *Lutz*	,,	11. Reichenau	,,
348. Knochenhauer	Maj.	27. Knochenhauer	,,	12. *Knochenhauer*	,,	12. Heitz	,,
351. Muff	,,	29. Muff	,,	13. Dollmann	,,	13. Kuechler	,,
371. Kuehlenthal	,,	30. Kuehlenthal	,,	14. *Kleist*	,,	14. Wietersheim	,,
373. Brauchitsch	,,	32. Brauchitsch	,,	15. Blaskowitz	,,	15. Schroth	,,
380. Kleist	,,	44. Kleist	,,	16. *Geyer*	,,	16. Kuntze	,,
390. Boetticher	,,	47. Dollmann	Obst.	17. Kluge	,,	17. Halder	,,
488. Lichtenfels	,,	50. Blaskowitz	,,	18. Becker	,,	18. Schwedler	,,
497. Dollmann	,,	54. Geyer	,,	19. Witzle bn	,,	19. Schobert	,,
499. Becker	,,	58. Kluge	,,	20. Weichs	,,	20. Busch	,,
505. Blaskowitz	,,	61. Heitz	,,	21. *Kressenstein*	,,	21. Kienitz	,,
532. Geyer	,,	65. Lichtenfels	,,	22. *Pogrell*	,,	22. Foerster	,,
534. Weichs	,,	67. Becker	,,	23. *Ulex*	,,	23. Waeger ‡	,,
535. Kressenstein	,,	76. Weichs	,,	24. Reichenau	,,	24. Guderian	,,
540. Kluge	,,	77. Kressenstein	,,	25. Heitz	,,	25. Hoth	,,
542. Schwandner	,,	80. Schwandner	,,	26. *Liese*	,,	26. Strauss	,,
559. Heitz	,,	83. Pogrell	,,	27. Kuechler	,,	27. Haase	,,
577. Pogrell	,,	85. Wilmowsky	,,	28. Keitel, W.	,,	28. Raschick	,,
581. Wilmowsky	,,	87. Ulex	,,	29. Boetticher	Genlt.	29. Karmann	,,
592. Ulex	,,	94. Niebelschuetz	,,	30. *Kuehlenthal*	,,	30. Leeb, E.	,,
625. Niebelschuetz	,,	99. Luedke	,,	31. Lichtenfels	,,	31. Friderici	,,
635. Luedke	,,	100. Liese	,,	32. Schwandner	,,	32. Stuelpnagel, H.	,,
636. Liese	,,	101. Witzleben	,,	33. Erfurth †	,,	33. Fromm	,,
639. Witzleben	,,	102. Fischer	,,	34. Wilmowsky	,,	34. Hoepner	,,

640. Fischer	,,	104. Kuechler	,,	35. *Niebelschuetz*	,,	35. Kuon	,,
642. Kuechler	,,	107. Gossler	,,	36. Luedke	,,	36. Muff char.	Gen.
646. Gossler	,,	109. Keitel, W.	,,	37. *Fischer*	,,	37. Boetticher	Genlt.
648. Keitel, W.	,,	111. Waeger	,,	38. *Gossler*	,,	38. Lichtenfels	,,
650. Waeger	,,	113. Wodrig	,,	39. Waeger	,,	39. Schwandner	,,
653. Wodrig	,,	117. Schroth	,,	40. Wodrig	,,	40. Erfurth †	,,
660. Schroth	,,	118. Raschick	,,	42. Wietersheim	,,	41. Wilmowsky	,,
661. Raschick	,,	119. Kuntze	,,	44. Schroth	,,	42. Luedke	,,
662. Kuntze	,,	121. Halder	,,	45. Raschick	,,	43. Wodrig	,,
667. Halder	,,	124. Hoth	,,	46. Kuntze	,,		
671. Hoth	,,	125. Karmann	,,	47. Halder	,,		
672. Karmann	,,	127. Schwedler	,,	49. Muff	,,		
677. Schwedler	,,	129. Foerster	,,	50. Hoth	,,		
696. Schobert	,,	130. Reichenau	,,	51. Karmann	,,		
697. Strauss	,,	136. Schobert	,,	52. Schwedler	,,		
735. Haase	Hpt.	137. Strauss	,,	54. Foerster	,,		
737. Leeb, E.	,,	149. Kienitz	,,	57. Schobert	,,		
752. Wietersheim	,,	159. Haase	Obstlt.	58. Strauss	,,		
835. Foerster	,,	162. Leeb, E.	,,	62. Kienitz	,,		
836. Reichenau	,,	172. Wietersheim	,,	65. Haase	,,		
848. Ruoff	,,	176. Busch	,,	66. Leeb, E.	,,		
892. Kienitz	,,	177. Friderici	,,	70. Busch	,,		
932. Busch	,,	179. Stuelpnagel, H.	,,	71. Friderici	,,		
933. Friderici	,,	198. Hoepner	,,	72. Stuelpnagel, H.	,,		
935. Stuelpnagel, H.	,,	235. Ruoff	,,	87. Fromm	,,		
973. Hoepner	,,	250. Guderian	,,	94. Hoepner	,,		
1070. Guderian	,,	273. Fromm	,,	113. Ruoff	Genmaj.		
1100. Fromm	,,			119. Guderian	,,		

* The table is based upon the forty senior officers as of January 1, 1938 and September 1, 1939. Of the forty seniors of January 1, 1938, nineteen (listed in italics) had retired or (Knochenhauer) died by September 1, 1939, and three more (Wilmowsky, Luedke, and Wodrig) had dropped just below the line on the later date. Accordingly, twenty-two officers were newly numbered among the top forty on January 1, 1939, and there are sixty-two officers in all in the table.

The columns for 1924 and 1932 show the relative seniority of the sixty-two officers in those years. The numbers at the left of the names give the position of each officer in the Army rank list on each of the dates in question. The general stability in the comparative positions clearly shows the operation of the principle of promotion according to length of service. On the other hand, a few will be noted who lost ground (e.g. Boetticher and Lichtenfels) and others who were promoted over the heads of many of their contemporaries (e.g. Keitel, Reichenau, Guderian, and Fromm).

† Erfurth retired in 1931, but returned to the active list in 1935. This is why the column for 1932 comprises only sixty-one officers.

‡ Between Foerster and Waeger, one officer (Beyer), taken over from the Austrian Army after the *Anschluss* in 1938, has been omitted.

September 1, 1939

THE PRINCIPAL RETIRED GENERALS OF THE GERMAN ARMY AVAILABLE
FOR DUTY AT THE OUTBREAK OF WORLD WAR II

v. BLOMBERG—Generalfeldmarschall—20.4.36—stricken from Army list in 1938 and never recalled to duty.

HEYE—Generaloberst—1.1.30—not recalled.

Frhr. v. HAMMERSTEIN-EQUORD, Curt—Generaloberst—31.1.34—recalled in August, 1939, as a deputy *Wehrkreis* commander and later (September 10, 1939) as Commander-in-Chief of an Army headquarters on the western front, but returned to inactive status in October.

Frhr. v. FRITSCH—Generaloberst—20.4.36—went to the front as *Chef* of Artillery Regiment 12; killed in action near Warsaw on September 22, 1939.

v. RUNDSTEDT—Generaloberst—1.3.38(1)—recalled in August, 1939, as Commander-in-Chief, Army Group South.

RITTER v. LEEB—Generaloberst—1.3.38(3)—recalled in August, 1939, as Commander-in-Chief, Army Group C.

BECK—*char.* Generaloberst—1.11.38—not recalled.

ADAM—*char.* Generaloberst—1.1.39—not recalled.

HASSE, Otto—General—1.4.29—not recalled.

SEUTTER v. LOETZEN—General—1.12.31—not recalled.

v. VOLLARD BOCKELBERG—General—1.10.33—recalled in October, 1939, as Deputy Commander of Wehrkreis I.

LIEBMANN—General—1.4.35(1)—recalled in August, 1939, as Commander-in-Chief of the Fifth Army, but returned to inactive status in October.

LUTZ—General—1.11.35—recalled for minor assignments.

v. KLEIST—General—1.8.36(1)—recalled in August, 1939, as Commanding General of the XXIInd Corps.

GEYER—General—1.8.36(3)—recalled in August, 1939, as Commanding General of the IXth Corps.

GRUEN—General—1.8.36(4)—recalled as Inspector of Artillery.

KRESS v. KRESSENTSTEIN, Franz—General—1.10.36(4)—recalled in August as Deputy Commander of Wehrkreis VII, but immediately relieved and returned to inactive status.

v. POGRELL—General—1.10.36(5)—recalled in September, 1939, for minor assignments.

ULEX—General—1.10.36(6)—recalled in August, 1939, as Commanding General of the Xth Corps.

LIESE—General—1.4.37(2)—recalled for minor assignments.

v. GOSSLER—General—1.2.38(1)—?

RITTER v. PRAGER—*char.* General—1.2.31—recalled to duty in autumn, 1939, as Commanding General of the XXVIIth Corps.

SCHNIEWINDT—*char.* General—1.10.31—recalled to duty in autumn, 1939, as a deputy *Wehrkreis* commander.

v. STUELPNAGEL, Joachim—*char.* General—1.1.32—recalled to duty in August 1939, as Commander of the replacement (home) Army, but relieved almost immediately and returned to inactive status.

Frhr. v. GIENANTH—*char.* General—1.10.33—recalled to duty in 1939 or 1940 as Commander of German troops in the Gouvernement General (occupied Poland).

v. FALKENHAUSEN—retired as Generalleutnant in 1930. Headed German military mission to China, 1934–1938, with rank of *char.* General der Infanterie; recalled in 1939 as Deputy Commander of Wehrkreis IV; appointed Military Commander in occupied Belgium and northern France on May 22, 1940, and promoted to General der Infanterie, September 1, 1940.

FEIGE, v. NIEBELSCHUETZ, the brothers v. ROQUES, STEPRUHN—all Generalleutnante—all recalled as deputy *Wehrkreis* commanders or in other minor assignments.

Former Reichswehr officers, who had transferred to the Luftwaffe and thereafter retired, but who returned to service on the outbreak of war:

HALM—Generalleutnant in Reichswehr—1.2.31(4)—retired shortly thereafter; taken into Luftwaffe as General der Flieger; retired from Luftwaffe February, 1938; taken back into the Army in September, 1939, with rank of General der Infanterie and as Deputy Commander of Wehrkreis VIII.

WACHENFELD—Generalleutnant in Reichswehr—1.4.31—retired in 1932 or early 1933; taken into Luftwaffe as General der Flieger; retired from Luftwaffe February, 1938; appointed Deputy Commander of Wehrkreis VII in August, 1939 and given the rank of General der Artillerie on April 17, 1940.

KAUPISCH—Generalleutnant in Reichswehr—1.3.32—retired in 1932 or early 1933; taken into Luftwaffe as General der Flieger; retired from Luftwaffe in February, 1938; taken back into the Army in August, 1939, with rank of General; commanded a task force during invasion of Poland, and later Commander in occupied Denmark.

v. STUELPNAGEL, Otto—Generalmajor in Reichswehr—1.2.29(10)—retired shortly thereafter; taken into Luftwaffe and attained rank of General der Flieger; retired from Luftwaffe; returned to active duty in 1939 as Deputy Commander of Wehrkreis XVII; given Army rank of General and later Commander in occupied France.

v. COCHENHAUSEN, Friedrich—Generalmajor in Reichswehr—1.3.30(2)—retired shortly thereafter; taken into Luftwaffe and attained rank of *char.* General der Flieger; retired from Luftwaffe; returned to active duty in 1939 as Deputy Commander of Wehrkreis XIII; given Army rank of General—1.12.40(1).

KARLEWSKI—Generalmajor in Reichswehr—1.10.31(9)—retired shortly thereafter; taken into Luftwaffe and attained rank of Generalleutnant; retired from Luftwaffe in February, 1938; returned to active duty during war in minor assignments.

WILBERG—Oberst in Reichswehr—1.10.29(13)—taken into Luftwaffe and attained rank of Generalleutnant; retired as *char.* General der Flieger in March, 1938; killed in a flying accident, November 20, 1941.

VOLKMANN—Oberstleutnant in Reichswehr—1.10.32(22)—taken into Luftwaffe and attained rank of General der Flieger after commanding Condor Legion in Spain (November 1, 1937–November 1, 1938); returned to Army with rank of General—1.1.39(1); commanded 94th Infantry Division; killed in an automobile accident, August 21, 1940.

LIST No. 8

November 1, 1938

RANK LIST OF ADMIRALS IN THE GERMAN NAVY

Name	Rank	Seniority	Assignment
1. Raeder	General-admiral	20.4.36	(C.-in-C. Navy; promoted to Grossadmiral 1.4.39)
2. Albrecht	Admiral	1.12.35(2)	(Eastern Naval Command)
3. Saalwaechter	,,	1.6.37(1)	(Northern Naval Station)
4. Carls	,,	1.6.37(2)	(Eastern Naval Station)
5. Witzell	,,	1.11.37	(Naval Ordnance)
6. Boehm	,,	1.4.38(2)	(High Seas Fleet)
7. Goetting	Vize-admiral	1.10.37(2)	(Naval Inspection)
8. v. Nordeck	,,	1.10.37(3)	
9. Stobwasser	,,	1.10.37(4)	
10. Witthoeft-Emden	,,	1.11.37(1)	(Naval Attaché, Washington)
11. Guse	,,	1.11.37(2)	(Naval Inspection)
12. Canaris	,,	1.4.38(1)	(Chief, Wehrmacht Intelligence)
13. Schuster	,,	1.4.38(2)	(Naval Training)
14. v. Fischel	,,	1.4.38(3)	(Naval Administration)
15. Densch	,,	1.4.38(4)	(Reconnaissance)
16. Wolf	Konter-admiral	1.6.36	
17. Marschall	,,	1.10.36(2)	(Armoured Ships)
18. Rother	,,	1.1.37	
19. Memis	,,	1.4.37(1)	
20. v. Schrader	,,	1.4.37(2)	
21. Moutz	,,	1.10.37(1)	
22. Gratzmann	,,	1.10.37(2)	
23. Luetjens	,,	1.10.37(3)	
24. Schniewind	,,	1.10.37(4)	(Chief, Naval Staff)
25. Patzig	,,	1.11.37	
26. Hormel	,,	1.4.38(1)	
27. Kamien	,,	1.4.38(2)	
28. Schmundt	,,	1.4.38(3)	
29. Fanger	,,	1.10.38(1)	
30. Fuchs	,,	1.10.38(2)	
31. v. Seebach	,,	1.10.38(3)	
32. Wehr	,, char.	16.4.38	
Doenitz	Kapitaen zur See	1.10.35(2)	(Commander, Submarines)
Fricke, Kurt	,,	1.1.37(3)	
Langsdorff	,,	1.1.37(6)	(Commander, Graf Spee)
Krancke, Kurt	,,	1.4.37(2)	

LIST No. 9

Summer of 1939

RANK LIST OF LUFTWAFFE SENIOR OFFICERS *

Name	Rank	Seniority	Assignment
Goering, Hermann	General-feld-marschall	4.2.38	C.-in-C. Luftwaffe
Milch, Erhard	General-oberst	31.10.38	Inspector-General
Kesselring, Albert	General der Flieger	1.6.37	1st Air Fleet
Ruedel, Guenther	General der Flak-artillerie	1.10.37	Air Defence
Sperrle, Hugo	General der Flieger	1.11.37	3rd Air Fleet
Felmy, Helmuth	,,	1.2.38(1)	2nd Air Fleet
Stumpff	,,	1938	Air Defence
Schweickhard, Karl	,,	1.6.38	Military Science, Air Min.
Christiansen, Friedrich	,,	1.1.39(3)	National Socialist Air Corps
Klepke, Waldemar	,,	1.1.39(?)	Reconnaissance
v. Witzendorff, Bodo	,,	1.2.39	At Air Ministry
Kuehl, Bernhard	,,	1.4.39	Training, Air Min.
Loehr, Alexander †	,,	1.4.39	4th Air Fleet
Hirschauer, Friedrich	,,	1.8.39(1)	Air District XVII
Keller, Alfred	,,	1939	Air Commander, East Prussia
Grauert, Ullrich	,,	1939	1st Air Corps
Weise, Hubert	General-leutnant	Apr. 1938	1st Anti-Aircraft Corps
Udet, Ernst	,,	1939	Aircraft Production
Ritter v. Greim, Robert	,,	1939	Chief of Personnel
Wolff, Ludwig	,,	1939	Air District XI
Geissler, Hans	,,	1939	Coastal Command
Loerzer, Bruno	,,	1939	IInd Air Corps
v. Richthofen, Wolfram	General-major	1938	VIIth Air Corps
Student, Kurt	,,	1938	Paratroops
Bodenschatz, Karl	,,	1938	Ministeramt, Air Min.
Jeschonnek, Hans	,,	1939	Chief of Staff
Pflugbeil, Kurt	,,	1939	Inspector, Bombers

* No rank list of the Luftwaffe prior to the outbreak of war has been available to me. The above list is constructed from several sources and is incomplete and possibly inaccurate in a few details.

† Taken over from the Austrian Air Force.

NOTES

The page references given below refer to the editions listed in the Bibliography (see page 398). Where both an American and a British edition are listed, the page references apply to the edition marked with an asterisk.

CHAPTER ONE

1. *The History of Militarism*, by Alfred Vagts (1937), p. 215.
2. *My Memoirs*, by Grand-Admiral von Tirpitz (1919), Vol. I, p. 120.
3. *My Memoirs*, Vol. I, p. 140.
4. "The What and Why of German Militarism," from the *Frankfurter Zeitung* for August 23, 1924, reprinted in English translation in *The Living Age*, November 1, 1924, p. 244.

CHAPTER TWO

1. In a speech on January 18, 1927. See *Gustav Stresemann*, by Eric Sutton (1940), Vol. III, pp. 299–300.
2. *Inside Germany*, by Albert C. Grzesinski (1939), pp. 90–91.
3. Valuable new evidence on the decisive role of Seeckt is contained in his personal files, now available to scholars at the National Archives in Washington.
4. See *Aus Seinem Leben (1918–36)*, by General der Artillerie Friedrich von Rabenau (Leipzig, 1940), based on papers left by Seeckt.
5. In John W. Wheeler-Bennett's excellent study of Hindenburg, *Wooden Titan* (1936).
6. A good account of Seeckt's activities at that time, utilizing fresh material from the Seeckt papers on deposit in Washington, is Miss Alma Luckau's "Kapp Putsch—Success or Failure", printed in the *Journal of Central European Affairs* for January, 1948.
7. Wehrkreis VII, with headquarters in Munich.
8. Testifying before a Munich jury in February, 1924.
9. See George W. Hallgarten, "General Hans von Seeckt and Russia", printed in the *Journal of Modern History* (March, 1949).
10. Gesellschaft zur Foerderung Gewerblicher Unternehmungen.

11. Reproduced in Rabenau's *Aus Seinem Leben*, pp. 558–61.
12. In his *Wooden Titan*, at pp. 297–299 (1936).
13. In his unpublished manuscript (now in the custody of the Adjutant General, United States Army), von Blomberg makes the same charge.

CHAPTER THREE

1. See Gordon Craig's excellent monograph on this period entitled "Reichswehr and National Socialism; The Policy of Wilhelm Groener (1928–1932)", in the *Political Science Quarterly* for June, 1948.
2. *The German Catastrophe*, by Friedrich Meinecke (published in German in 1946 and in English translation by Sidney B. Fay in 1950), pp. 44–45. Meinecke was a good friend of and in frequent contact with Bruening and Groener, and, at a later time, Beck.
3. The above analysis of Hammerstein is based upon the author's personal discussions with the late Generaloberst Wilhelm Adam (who succeeded Hammerstein as *Chef des Truppenamtes* and served under him in that capacity from October, 1930, to October, 1933), and Generaloberst Franz Halder (Chief of the General Staff from 1938 to 1942). See also the sketch of Hammerstein in *Es Geschah in Deutschland*, by Schwerin Krosigk (Tuebingen, 1951).
4. Reichenau came naturally by both his violent nationalism and his political proclivities. His father, an ambassador in imperial times, had been a well-known pan-Germanist, as a leader of the *Alldeutsche Verband* and founder of the *Verein fuer der Deutschtum im Ausland*.
5. *Wooden Titan*, by J. W. Wheeler-Bennett (1936), pp. 445–46.
6. Hans B. Gisevius, *To the Bitter End* (1947), p. 173.
7. Gisevius, *loc. cit. supra*.
8. See p. 42, *supra*.

CHAPTER FOUR

1. Quoted from a memorandum written by Grossadmiral Eric Raeder shortly after the end of the Second World War, printed in Vol. VIII, *Nazi Conspiracy and Aggression*, Statement VII.

2. See *Ein General Kaempft gegen den Krieg*, by Wolfgang Foerster (Munich, 1949), at p. 22.

3. The figures are taken from the official German Army rank lists and Berthold Jacob, *Das neue deutsche Heer und seine Fuehrer* (1936), pp. 44–45.

4. See pp. 51–54.

5. In his article "The Army of the Future" in the *Revue de Genève*, reprinted in translation in *The Living Age* for November, 1929, pp. 288–294.

6. *Supra*, p. 53.

7. See Raeder's statement at Moscow in the fall of 1945, *Nazi Conspiracy and Aggression*, Vol. VIII, p. 734.

8. See p. 35.

9. *Zwischen Wehrmacht und Hitler*, by Friedrich Hossbach (Wolfenbuettel and Hanover, 1949).

10. See Appendix One.

11. *Ein General Kaempft gegen den Krieg*, by Wolfgang Foerster, at p. 17.

12. *Zwischen Wehrmacht und Hitler*, by Friedrich Hossbach, at p. 9.

13. *Idem*, at p. 107.

14. Hossbach, *op. cit. supra*, pp. 173–83.

15. *Das neue deutsche Heer und seine Fuehrer*, by Berthold Jacob (1936), at pp. 25–26.

16. *The German Catastrophe*, by Friedrich Meinecke (1950), at p. 97.

17. *The Revolution of Nihilism*, by Hermann Rauschning (1939), at pp. 158–59.

18. *To the Bitter End*, by Hans B. Gisevius (1947), at p. 179.

19. This statement was prepared by Blomberg at Nuremberg in November, 1945, but because of its length and primarily historical importance, was never offered in evidence at the trials.

20. In an article entitled "The Reichswehr over Europe," published that month in *Harper's Magazine*.

CHAPTER FIVE

1. *Account Settled*, by Hjalmar Schacht (1949 ed.), p. 90.

2. See the *New York Times* for May 3, 1936 (p. 38), and May 4, 1936 (p. 13).

3. *Account Settled*, pp. 281–82.

4. The extract is quoted from Goering's speech at the Preussenhaus in Ber-lin on December 17, 1936. See Nuremberg Document N1-051, printed in *Trials of War Criminals before the Nuremberg Military Tribunals*, Vol. XII, pp. 460–65.

5. *Account Settled*, p. 199.

6. See his book, *Zwischen Wehrmacht und Hitler*, especially pp. 15–17, and 29–31.

7. Well described in Eugen Kogon's well-known book, *Der SS Staat*.

8. Taken from a statement distributed throughout the armed forces in the spring of 1941, and reproduced in *Nazi Conspiracy and Aggression*, Vol. VII, pp. 172–73.

9. See Appendix One, "Note on German Military Ranks".

10. These meetings are chronicled in the diary kept by Jodl during the period of his service under Keitel in the *Wehrmachtamt*.

11. An account of the Condor Legion's activities, signed by Sperrle, was published in 1939 in a special edition of the German military periodical *Die Wehrmacht*.

12. See Document 3474-PS, reproduced in Vol. VI, *Nazi Conspiracy and Aggression*, pp. 199–200.

13. There is a surprising dearth of precise and reliable literature dealing with the Spanish Civil War. Summary chapters are to be found in *Politics, Economics and Men of Modern Spain, 1808–1946*, by A. Ramos Oliveira (Gollancz, London, 1946), *A Short History of International Affairs, 1920–1939*, by G. M. Gathorne-Hardy (Oxford Press, 1942), and *The Between War World*, by J. Hampden Jackson (Gollancz, London, 1947).

14. Document C-175, reproduced in Vol. VI, *Nazi Conspiracy and Aggression*, pp. 1006–11.

15. Document 386-PS, reproduced in Vol. III, *Nazi Conspiracy and Aggression*, pp. 295–305.

16. *Zwischen Wehrmacht und Hitler*, pp. 138–39.

17. In his Nuremberg affidavit of November, 1945.

18. Hossbach, *op. cit. supra*, at pp. 134–35.

19. April 19, 1938. Document L-211, reproduced in part in Vol. VII, *Nazi Conspiracy and Aggression*, pp. 1043–45.

20. Jodl's diary is the source of most of the available information on this subject.

21. See *Schuld und Verhaengnis*, by Hermann Foertsch (Stuttgart, 1951), p. 101.

22. See Anne O'Hare McCormick and Otto Tolischus in the *New York Times*, February 7, 1938, pp. 1 and 14.

23. Hossbach, *op. cit. supra*, p. 203.

CHAPTER SIX

1. *Trials of the Major War Criminals,* Vol. XX, p. 568.
2. *Id.,* Vol. XX, p. 604.
3. *Id.,* Vol. XXI, p. 23.
4. Mimeographed transcript of testimony before Commissioners of the International Military Tribunal, p. 2594.
5. *Supra,* p. 141.
6. *Supra,* pp. 141–42.
7. *Supra,* p. 141.
8. *Erinnerungen eines Soldaten,* by Heinz Guderian (Heidelberg, 1951), p. 46.
9. *Trial of the Major War Criminals,* Vol. XV, p. 355.
10. *Supra,* p. 141.
11. Guderian, *op. cit. supra,* p. 42.
12. *Trial of the Major War Criminals,* Vol. XX, pp. 568–69.
13. *Supra,* p. 146.
14. These memoranda are described *in extenso* in Foerster's book on Beck, pp. 81–119.
15. *The von Hassell Diaries,* Doubleday (1947), p. 347. See *supra,* pp. 5–10.
16. *To the Bitter End,* pp. 279–83.
17. For the source of this portion of the narrative, see Appendix III on Generaloberst Wilhelm Adam and his memoirs.
18. *Trial of the Major War Criminals,* Vol. XV, p. 361.
19. *To the Bitter End,* p. 319.
20. *Rommel the Desert Fox,* by Desmond Young (1950), p. 42.

CHAPTER SEVEN

1. See E. H. Carr, *German-Soviet Relations Between the Two World Wars, 1919–1939* (1951), p. 128.
2. *Stellenbesetzung des Heeres* 1938.
3. *Trial of the Major War Criminals,* Vol. XV, p. 351.
4. *The German Air Force,* by Asher Lee (London, 1946), p. 15.
5. *Trial of the Major War Criminals,* Vol. IX, pp. 202–6.
6. *Trial of the Major War Criminals,* Vol. IX, pp. 60–61.
7. *Nazi Conspiracy and Aggression,* Vol. VI, Document C-23.
8. See Churchill, *The Gathering Storm,* pp. 424 and 689; Martienssen, *Hitler and His Admirals,* pp. 14–18.
9. *Supra,* p. 129.
10. *Supra,* pp. 251–52.
11. See Nuremberg Documents C-137 and NOKW-2883.
12. Nuremberg Document R-100.
13. Nuremberg Document C-120.
14. Nuremberg Document NOKW-2657.
15. Nuremberg Document NOKW-2584.
16. Nuremberg Document C-126.
17. Nuremberg Document L-79.
18. At Nuremberg, Milch denied that Goering was present, but Goering himself testified that he well remembered the occasion and that Milch was mistaken. *Trial of the Major War Criminals,* Vol. IX, pp. 48 and 308.
19. *Trial of the Major War Criminals,* Vol. IX, p. 309; Vol. XIV, p. 179; Vol. XX, pp. 570–71.
20. *Supra,* p. 264, footnote 18.
21. *Supra,* p. 238.
22. *Berlin Diary,* by William L. Shirer, p. 169.
23. Nuremberg Document 3787-PS.
24. Nuremberg Document NIK-13136.
25. Nuremberg Document L-142, also designated NOKW-229.
26. *Supra,* pp. 261–62.
27. Churchill, *The Gathering Storm* (1948), p. 391.
28. See *Trial of the Major War Criminals,* Vol. IX, pp. 457–74, and Frischauer, *The Rise and Fall of Hermann Goering* (1951), pp. 164–66. The names of the British industrialists—none well known—are given by Frischauer.
29. Nuremberg Document TC-77.
30. This is according to Halder's personal recollection. The date and general tenor of the meeting are confirmed by *The Von Hassell Diaries* (Doubleday, 1947), pp. 60–61.
31. *The Gathering Storm,* pp. 382–84.
32. See Martienssen, *Hitler and His Admirals* (1949), pp. 18–19.
33. See the excellent analysis in F. H. Hinsley, *Hitler's Strategy* (1951), pp. 1–27.
34. *The Gathering Storm* (1948), pp. 392–94.
35. See William L. Shirer, *Berlin Diary* (1940), p. 182.
36. Nuremberg Documents 798-PS and 1014-PS.
37. Nuremberg Document Raeder No. 27.
38. Nuremberg Document L-3.
39. See Hinsley's *Hitler's Strategy,* pp. 15–27.
40. *Nazi Conspiracy and Aggression,* Supplement, B, p. 1561.
41. *Supra,* pp. 246–47.
42. Nuremberg Documents 3704-PS and 3706-PS. The language used is Blomberg's, subsequently subscribed to by Blaskowitz. The last sentence quoted is Blomberg's only.
43. I. M. T. Commission Hearings, Transcript p. 1631.
44. *Trial of the Major War Criminals,* Vol. IX, p. 182.

45. I. M. T. Commission Hearings, Transcript pp. 1351–52.
46. Presumably Rundstedt is speaking of pre-Hitler times.
47. *Trial of the Major War Criminals*, Vol. XIV, p. 48.
48. *Supra*, p. 265.

CHAPTER EIGHT

1. Nuremberg Document NG-2029.
2. Nuremberg Document NG-2172.
3. Nuremberg Document NG-3615.
4. Nuremberg Document C-170.
5. *Supra*, pp. 257–58.
6. Nuremberg Document 2353-PS.
7. *The German Air Force*, pp. 41–42.
8. Nuremberg Document C-126G. The balance of the directive was concerned with the west. See *infra*, pp. 331–32.
9. *Erinnerungen eines Soldaten*, p. 72.
10. *Berlin Diary*, by William L. Shirer, p. 212.
11. *Trial of the Major War Criminals*, Vol. II, pp. 446–47.
12. *Hitler als Feldherr*, p. 27.
13. See *Der Fritsch-Prozess 1938*, by Graf Kielmansegg, pp. 140–50.
14. See the United Press dispatch datelined Berlin, September 7, printed in the *New York Times* the following day.
15. See the *New York Times*, September 26, 1939.
16. *Hitler's Generals*, by W. E. Hart, pp. 35–37.
17. Nuremberg Document C-126. For the portion dealing with Poland, see *supra*, pp. 314–15.
18. *Nazi Conspiracy and Aggression*, Supplement B, p. 1119.
19. *The Gathering Storm*, p. 422.
20. *Supra*, pp. 295–97.
21. *The Gathering Storm*, p. 424.
22. Nuremberg Document C-191.
23. The orders to the two pocket battleships were sent out on September 26th.
24. See the account from the log of the *U-47* in Martienssen, *Hitler and His Admirals*, pp. 28–36.
25. *Trial of the Major War Criminals*, Vol. XVII, p. 191.
26. *Id.*, p. 277.

27. Nuremberg Document D-804.
28. Nuremberg Document D-638.
29. Nuremberg Document D-654.
30. *Trial of the Major War Criminals*, Vol. XIV, p. 325.
31. *Trial of the Major War Criminals*, Vol. XIII, pp. 390–91 and 529–31; Nuremberg Documents D-659 and D-662.
32. Nuremberg Document 3260-PS.
33. *Trial of the Major War Criminals*, Vol. XVII, pp. 191, 234–35.
34. *Id.*, pp. 216, 327–28.
35. *Supra*, p. 114.
36. *Nazi-Soviet Relations 1939–1941*, published by the U.S. Department of State (1948), pp. 78–109.
37. *Berlin Diary*, by William L. Shirer, p. 206.
38. *The von Hassell Diaries*, p. 75.
39. Shirer, *op. cit. supra*, p. 229.
40. *The von Hassell Diaries*, p. 90, and the *Halder Diary*, entry for September, 24, 1939.
41. *The von Hassell Diaries*, p. 79.
42. Nuremberg Document 3363-PS.
43. Nuremberg Document EC-344 (17).
44. *The von Hassell Diaries*, p. 100.

CHAPTER NINE

1. *The von Hassell Diaries*, p. 6, entry for September 29, 1938.
2. See the editorials in the *Washington Post*, March 25 and 28, 1952.
3. *Supra*, p. 43.
5. John W. Wheeler-Bennett, *Wooden Titan*, p. 290.
5. Hearings before the Commission of the International Military Tribunal, Transcript p. 3632.
6. See the excellent article, "The German Army and Hitler", in *The Times Literary Supplement* for June 9, 1950.
7. *Gustav Stresemann*, by Eric Sutton, Vol. III, 299–300 (1940).
8. *The German Catastrophe*, p. 46.
9. *Zwischen Wehrmacht und Hitler*, p. 173.
10. *Manstein, His Campaigns and His Trial*, by R. T. Paget, p. 4.
11. Hossbach, *op. cit. supra*, p. 203.

SOURCES, ACKNOWLEDGMENTS AND BIBLIOGRAPHY

THIS BOOK is based primarily on information acquired and impressions formed during the period of my service as a U.S. Army intelligence officer in Europe (May, 1943–May, 1945) and as prosecution counsel at the Nuremberg war crimes trials (June, 1945–August, 1949). The basic narrative and point of view are derived from captured documents, interrogations and conversations far too numerous to catalogue or separately identify.

To round out and fill in the account of these times and arrive at a historical cross-section of logical outline, I have relied upon secondary sources, most of which are listed in the Bibliography appended hereto. As is to be expected from the scope of my personal contact with these events, there is less original material in the first two than in the subsequent chapters. To provide the necessary pre-Hitler background, I have relied especially upon the writings of Craig, Hallgarten, Luckau, Gen. J. H. Morgan, Rabenau, Rosinski, Vagts, and Wheeler-Bennett.

The most extensive single source of primary documentation is, without question, the records of the Nuremberg trials. The complete record of testimony at the first Nuremberg trial, and reproductions of all documents introduced before the International Military Tribunal, are available in the forty-two volume *Trial of the Major War Criminals*, published at Nuremberg (1947–49). Additional documents, affidavits and interrogatories collected for that trial are printed in the series *Nazi Conspiracy and Aggression*, published by the U.S. Government Printing Office. Furthermore, there is additional testimony given before Commissioners of the International Military Tribunal which was, unhappily, omitted from the forty-two-volume record, and is available only in mimeographed form. Finally, selections from the testimony offered and documents submitted during the twelve subsequent Nuremberg trials are to be found in the fifteen-volume series *Trials of War Criminals before the Nuremberg Military Tribunals* (U.S. Government Printing Office, 1949–52).

For additional diplomatic material, I have had recourse to *Nazi–Soviet Relations, 1939–1941*, and other publications of the U.S. Department of State. Winston Churchill's *The Second World War—The Gathering Storm* is, of course, a mine of information and documentation for any student of this period. Data concerning the ranks, promotions and assignments of German military personnel are based chiefly upon the official *Rangliste* of the German Army and Navy,

the order of battle books prepared by the American and British intelligence services during the war, and other military publications.

Invaluable information for the period January, 1937, to September, 1938, is contained in the diary kept by Oberst (later Generaloberst) Alfred Jodl. In the closing pages, I have also drawn upon the diary of General (later Generaloberst) Franz Halder, which contains a running account (beginning August 14, 1939) of his activities and observations as Chief of the General Staff. Both diaries were introduced into evidence at Nuremberg, and both are deserving of complete publication, as they are historical sources of the first importance. The memoirs of von Blomberg (unpublished manuscript in the custody of the Adjutant General, United States Army) are of secondary value.

The years since 1947 have witnessed the publication in Germany of a large number of books by or about former German generals and other officials. Some of them have been translated and published in England, and a few in the United States. Their quality and reliability are variable, but they are a useful supplementary source of information for the circumspect reader. Among the more important works in this category are those by Wolfgang Foerster (on Beck), Gisevius, Guderian, Halder, Heusinger, Hossbach, Kielmansegg (on Fritsch), Schacht, and Westphal. The posthumously published diary of Ambassador von Hassell is an especially valuable document.

Much as I have relied upon publications of various descriptions, however, this book is far more the product of experience and observation than of research. And at the head of what would, if complete, be a very long list of acknowledgments, stand my two close friends, colleagues in the intelligence service, and co-workers at Nuremberg, Peter Calvocoressi and Walter Rapp, with whom these experiences were shared.

In the preparation of the text, my wife has contributed greatly to the organization and presentation of the material, and has laboured mightily as researcher, stenographer, bibliographer, and indexer, despite many other cares and the churlish preoccupation of the part-time author. I am deeply grateful for the assistance in translation of Hannah and Rolf Wartenberg, John W. Mosenthal, Jan Witlox, Fred Kaufman, David Blair, and Hedy Clark, and to my secretary, Zelda Golden, who typed the greater part of the manuscript. Professor Franz Neumann, of Columbia University, generously gave his time to read the manuscript, and made many valuable suggestions. The Office of the Chief of Military History (through Major Leonard O. Friesz), the War Crimes Branch of the Judge Advocate General's Department (through Colonel J. Hamilton Young and Mr. Edward Lyons), and the Adjutant General's Office (through Mr. Philip P. Brower) were of great assistance in answering questions and making available to me rank lists and other military publications. To the Wiener Library in London and to my former colleagues at Nuremberg, Benjamin Ferencz and Dr. Robert M. W. Kempner, I am in-

debted for procuring numerous European publications. Last but by no means least, I want to express my grateful remembrance of the education I received during the war in German military matters from my friends in the British intelligence services, especially Jim Rose, Peter Calvocoressi, Bill Marchant, Terry Leathem, Allen Pryce-Jones, Asher Lee, and Harry Hinsley.

BIBLIOGRAPHY

BLASKOWITZ, GENERALOBERST JOHANNES: *Die Einnahme von Warschau*, in *Illustrirte Zeitung*, 7 March, 1940.

BLOOD-RYAN, H. W.: *The Great German Conspiracy*. Lindsay Drummond, 1943.

CALVOCORESSI, PETER: *Nuremberg and the Consequences*. Chatto and Windus, 1947.

CARR, EDWARD H.: *German–Soviet Relations Between the Two World Wars, 1919–1939*. *Johns Hopkins Press, Baltimore, 1951. Oxford University Press, London, 1952.

CARRIAS, COL. EUGÈNE: *La Pensée Militaire Allemande*. Presses Universitaires de France, Paris, 1948.

CHURCHILL, WINSTON: *The Second World War—The Gathering Storm*. *Houghton Mifflin Company, Boston, 1948. Cassell and Co., London, 1948.

VON CLAUSEWITZ, KARL: *On War*. Infantry Journal Press, 1950.

CRAIG, GORDON A.: "Reichswehr and National Socialism: The Policy of Wilhelm Groener, 1928–32", *Political Science Quarterly*, Vol. LXIII, No. 2, June, 1948; "Portrait of a Political General: Edwin von Manteuffel and the Constitutional Conflict in Prussia", *Political Science Quarterly*, Vol. LXVI, No. 1, March, 1951.

DE MENDELSSOHN, PETER: *Nuremberg Documents*. Allen and Unwin, 1946.

DE WEERD, H. A.: *Great Soldiers of the Two World Wars*. Robert Hale, 1943.

DULLES, ALLAN WELSH: *Germany's Underground*. Macmillan, 1947.

EARLE, EDWARD MEAD, editor: *Makers of Modern Strategy*. Oxford University Press, 1948.

EBELING, DR. H.: *The Political Role of the German General Staff between 1918 and 1938*. New Europe Publishing Co., London, 1945.

FOERSTER, WOLFGANG: *Ein General kaempft gegen den Krieg*. Muenchener Dom-Verlag, Munich, 1949.

FOERTSCH, HERMANN: *Schuld und Verhaengnis*. Deutsche Verlags-Anstalt, Stuttgart, 1951.

FRIED, HANS ERNEST: *The Guilt of the German Army*. The Macmillan Company, New York, 1943.

FRISCHAUER, WILLI: *The Rise and Fall of Hermann Goering*. *Houghton Mifflin Company, Boston, 1951. Odhams Press, London, 1951. (English title: *Goering*.)

FULLER, MAJOR-GENERAL, J. F. C.: *The Second World War*. Eyre and Spottiswoode, 1948.
GISEVIUS, HANS B.: *To the Bitter End*. *Houghton Mifflin Company, Boston, 1947. Jonathan Cape, London, 1948.
GOERLITZ, WALTER: *Der Deutsche Generalstab*. Verlag der Frankfurter Hefte, Frankfurt-am-Main, 1950.
GRZESINSKI, ALBERT C.: *Inside Germany*. E. P. Dutton & Co., Inc., New York, 1939.
GUDERIAN, HEINZ: *Erinnerungen eines Soldaten*. Bei Kurt Vowinckel/ Heidelberg, 1951. English translation, *Panzer Leader*. Michael Joseph, 1952.
HALDER, FRANZ: *Hitler als Feldherr*. Muenchener Dom-Verlag, Munich, 1949. English translation, *Hitler as War Lord*. Putnam, 1950.
HALLGARTEN, GEORGE W. F.: "General Hans von Seeckt and Russia 1920–22". *Journal of Modern History*, Vol. XXI, No. 1, March, 1949.
HARSCH, JOSEPH C.: *The Pattern of Conquest*. Heinemann, 1942.
HART, B. H. LIDDELL: *The German Generals Talk*. *William Morrow & Co., New York, 1948. Cassell and Co., London, 1948. (English title: *The Other Side of the Hill*.)
HART, W. E.: *Hitler's Generals*. *Doubleday, Doran & Co., Inc., New York, 1944. Cresset Press, London, 1944.
VON HASSELL, AMBASSADOR ULRICH: *The von Hassell Diaries*. *Doubleday & Company, Inc., New York, 1947. Hamish Hamilton, London, 1948.
HEUSINGER, ADOLF: *Befehl im Widerstreit*. Rainer Wunderlich Verlag, Tuebingen and Stuttgart, 1950.
HINSLEY, F. H.: *Hitler's Strategy*. Cambridge University Press, 1951.
HOSSBACH, FRIEDRICH: *Zwischen Wehrmacht und Hitler*. Wolfenbuttler Verlagsanstalt G.m.b.H., Wolfenbuttel and Hannover, 1949.
JACKSON, J. HAMPDEN: *The Between-War World*. Gollancz, 1947.
JACOB, BERTHOLD: *Das neue deutsche Heer und Seine Fuehrer*. Editions du Carrefour, Paris, 1936.
KIELMANSEGG, GRAF: *Der Fritschprozess 1938*. Hoffmann and Compe Verlag, Hamburg, 1949.
KLOTZ, DR. HELMUT, editor: *The Berlin Diaries May 30, 1932– January 3, 1933*. 2 vols. Jarrolds, 1934–5.
LAVERGNE, BERNARD: *La crise Européenne ou la grande défaite des démocraties. L'Année Politique—française et étrangère*, November, 1838.
LEE, W/CDR. ASHER: *The German Air Force*. Duckworth, 1946.
LEHMANN-RUSSBUELDT, OTTO: *Germany's Air Force*. Allen and Unwin, 1935.
LEMKIN, RAPHAËL: *Axis Rule in Occupied Europe*. Carnegie Endowment for International Peace, Division of International Law, 1944.
LUCKAU, ALMA: "*Kapp Putsch*—Success or Failure", *Journal of Central European Affairs*, Vol. 7, No. 4, January, 1948.

MARTIENSSEN, ANTHONY K.: *Hitler and His Admirals.* *E. P. Dutton & Co., Inc., New York, 1949. Secker and Warburg, London, 1948.

MEINECKE, FRIEDRICH: *The German Catastrophe.* *Harvard University Press, 1950. Oxford University Press, 1950.

MORGAN, BRIGADIER-GENERAL J. H.: *Assize of Arms.* Methuen & Co., 1945.

NEUMANN, FRANZ: *Behemoth.* Gollancz, 1942.

OBERKOMMANDO DER WEHRMACHT: bi-monthly periodical *Die Wehrmacht*, 1935–1939 (up to February 1, 1938, published by the Reichskriegsministerium).

OLIVEIRA, A. RAMOS: *Politics, Economics and Men of Modern Spain, 1808–1946.* Gollancz, 1946.

PAGET, R. T.: *Manstein, His Campaigns and His Trial.* Collins, 1951.

VON RABENAU, GEN. DR. FRIEDRICH: *von Seeckt Aus Seinem Leben 1918–1936.* v. Hase and Koehler Verlag/Leipzig, 1940.

RAUSCHNING, HERMANN: *The Revolution of Nihilism.* Alliance Book Corporation, Longmans, Green & Co., 1939.

RAUSCHNING, HERMANN: *The Voice of Destruction.* *G. P. Putnam's Sons, 1940. Butterworth, 1939. (English title: *Hitler Speaks.*)

RIESS, CURT: *The Self-Betrayed.* Long, 1944.

ROSINSKI, HERBERT: *The German Army* (2 eds.). Hogarth Press, London, 1939. Infantry Journal Press, Washington, 1944.

SCHACHT, DR. HJALMAR: *Account Settled.* Weidenfeld & Nicolson, 1949.

SCHEIDEMANN, PHILIP: *The Making of New Germany.* Hodder and Stoughton, 1929.

SCHMIDT, DR. PAUL: *Hitler's Interpreter.* Heinemann, 1951.

SHIRER, WILLIAM L.: *Berlin Diary.* *Alfred H. Knopf, New York, 1941. Hamish Hamilton, London, 1941.

SHOTWELL, JAMES T.: *What Germany Forgot.* Macmillan, 1940.

SHULMAN, MILTON: *Defeat in the West.* Secker and Warburg, 1949.

SPERRLE, GENERAL DER FLIEGER HUGO: *We are Fighting in Spain*, in a special issue (1939) of *Die Wehrmacht.*

SUTTON, ERIC, editor: *Gustav Stresemann: His Diaries, Letters and Papers.* 3 vols. Macmillan, 1935–1940.

VON TIRPITZ, GRAND ADMIRAL: *My Memoirs* (Vols. I and II). *Dodd, Mead and Company, New York, 1919. Hurst and Blackett, 1919.

VAGTS, ALFRED: *The History of Militarism.* *W. W. Norton & Company, Inc., New York, 1937. Allen and Unwin, London, 1938.

VON WEIZSAECKER, ERNST: *Memoirs.* Gollancz, 1951.

WESTPHAL, SIEGFRIED: *Herr in Fesseln.* Athenæum-Verlag, Bonn, 1950. English translation, *The German Army in the West.* Cassell & Co., London, 1951.

WHEELER-BENNETT, JOHN W.: *Munich: Prologue to Tragedy.* Macmillan, 1948.

WHEELER-BENNETT, JOHN W.: *Wooden Titan.* *William Morrow & Co., New York, 1936. Macmillan & Co., London, 1936. (English title: *Hindenburg: The Wooden Titan.*)

YOUNG, BRIGADIER DESMOND: *Rommel, The Desert Fox.* *Harper & Brothers, New York, 1950. Collins, London, 1950.

INDEX

QUADRANGLE PAPERBACKS

American History

Frederick Lewis Allen. *The Lords of Creation.* (QP35)
Lewis Atherton. *Main Street on the Middle Border.* (QP36)
Thomas A. Bailey. *Woodrow Wilson and the Lost Peace.* (QP1)
Thomas A. Bailey. *Woodrow Wilson and the Great Betrayal.* (QP2)
Charles A. Beard. *The Idea of National Interest.* (QP27)
Carl L. Becker. *Everyman His Own Historian.* (QP33)
Ray A. Billington. *The Protestant Crusade.* (QP12)
Allan G. Bogue. *From Prairie to Corn Belt.* (QP50)
Kenneth E. Boulding. *The Organizational Revolution.* (QP43)
David M. Chalmers. *Hooded Americanism.* (QP51)
John Chamberlain. *Farewell to Reform.* (QP19)
Alice Hamilton Cromie. *A Tour Guide to the Civil War.*
Robert D. Cross. *The Emergence of Liberal Catholicism in America.* (QP44)
Richard M. Dalfiume. *American Politics Since 1945.* (NYTimes Book, QP57)
Chester McArthur Destler. *American Radicalism, 1865-1901.* (QP30)
Robert A. Divine. *American Foreign Policy Since 1945.* (NYTimes Book, QP58)
Robert A. Divine. *The Illusion of Neutrality.* (QP45)
Elisha P. Douglass. *Rebels and Democrats.* (QP26)
Herman Finer. *Road to Reaction.* (QP5)
Felix Frankfurter. *The Commerce Clause.* (QP16)
Lloyd C. Gardner. *A Different Frontier.* (QP32)
Edwin Scott Gaustad. *The Great Awakening in New England.* (QP46)
Ray Ginger. *Altgeld's America.* (QP21)
Gerald N. Grob. *Workers and Utopia.* (QP61)
Louis Hartz. *Economic Policy and Democratic Thought.* (QP52)
William B. Hesseltine. *Lincoln's Plan of Reconstruction.* (QP41)
Granville Hicks. *The Great Tradition.* (QP62)
Dwight W. Hoover. *Understanding Negro History.* (QP49)
Stanley P. Hirshson. *Farewell to the Bloody Shirt.* (QP53)
Frederic C. Howe. *The Confessions of a Reformer.* (QP39)
Louis Joughin and Edmund M. Morgan. *The Legacy of Sacco and Vanzetti.* (QP7)
William Loren Katz. *Teachers' Guide to American Negro History.* (QP210)
Edward Chase Kirkland. *Dream and Thought in the Business Community, 1860-1900.* (QP11)
Edward Chase Kirkland. *Industry Comes of Age.* (QP42)
Adrienne Koch. *The Philosophy of Thomas Jefferson.* (QP17)
Gabriel Kolko. *The Triumph of Conservatism.* (QP40)
Walter LaFeber. *John Quincy Adams and American Continental Empire.* (QP23)
David E. Lilienthal. *TVA: Democracy on the March.* (QP28)
Arthur S. Link. *Wilson the Diplomatist.* (QP18)
Huey P. Long. *Every Man a King.* (QP8)
Gene M. Lyons. *America: Purpose and Power.* (QP24)
Jackson Turner Main. *The Antifederalists.* (QP14)
Ernest R. May. *The World War and American Isolation, 1914-1917.* (QP29)
Henry F. May. *The End of American Innocence.* (QP9)
George E. Mowry. *The California Progressives.* (QP6)
William L. O'Neill. *American Society Since 1945.* (NYTimes Book, QP59)
Frank L. Owsley. *Plain Folk of the Old South.* (QP22)
David Graham Phillips. *The Treason of the Senate.* (QP20)
Julius W. Pratt. *Expansionists of 1898.* (QP15)
Moses Rischin. *The American Gospel of Success.* (QP54)
John P. Roche. *The Quest for the Dream.* (QP47)
David A. Shannon. *The Socialist Party of America.* (QP38)
Andrew Sinclair. *The Available Man.* (QP60)
John Spargo. *The Bitter Cry of the Children.* (QP55)
Richard W. Van Alstyne. *The Rising American Empire.* (QP25)
Willard M. Wallace. *Appeal to Arms.* (QP10)
Norman Ware. *The Industrial Worker, 1840-1860.* (QP13)
Albert K. Weinberg. *Manifest Destiny.* (QP3)
Bernard A. Weisberger. *They Gathered at the River.* (QP37)
Robert H. Wiebe. *Businessmen and Reform.* (QP56)
Bell I. Wiley. *The Plain People of the Confederacy.* (QP4)
William Appleman Williams. *The Contours of American History.* (QP34)
William Appleman Williams. *The Great Evasion.* (QP48)
Esmond Wright. *Causes and Consequences of the American Revolution.* (QP31)

European History

William Sheridan Allen. *The Nazi Seizure of Power*. (QP302)
W. O. Henderson. *The Industrial Revolution in Europe*. (QP303)
Raul Hilberg. *The Destruction of the European Jews*. (QP301)
Telford Taylor. *Sword and Swastika*. (QP304)

Philosophy

F. H. Bradley. *The Presuppositions of Critical History*. (QP108)
William Earle. *Objectivity*. (QP109)
James M. Edie, James P. Scanlan, Mary-Barbara Zeldin, George L. Kline. *Russian Philosophy*.
    (3 vols, QP111, 112, 113)
James M. Edie. *An Invitation to Phenomenology*. (QP103)
James M. Edie. *Phenomenology in America*. (QP105)
Manfred S. Frings. *Heidegger and the Quest for Truth*. (QP107)
Moltke S. Gram. *Kant: Disputed Questions*. (QP104)
Lionel Rubinoff. *Faith and Reason*. (QP106)
Paul Tibbetts. *Perception*. (QP110)
Pierre Thévenaz. *What Is Phenomenology?* (QP101)

Social Science

George and Eunice Grier. *Equality and Beyond*. (QP204)
Charles O. Lerche, Jr. *Last Chance in Europe*. (QP207)
David Mitrany. *A Working Peace System*. (QP205)
Martin Oppenheimer and George Lakey. *A Manual for Direct Action*. (QP202)
Fred Powledge. *To Change a Child*. (QP209)
Lee Rainwater. *And the Poor Get Children*. (QP208)
Clarence Senior. *The Puerto Ricans*. (QP201)
Arthur L. Stinchcombe. *Rebellion in a High School*. (QP211)